terra australis 51

Terra Australis reports the results of archaeological and related research within the south and east of Asia, though mainly Australia, New Guinea and Island Melanesia — lands that remained terra australis incognita to generations of prehistorians. Its subject is the settlement of the diverse environments in this isolated quarter of the globe by peoples who have maintained their discrete and traditional ways of life into the recent recorded or remembered past and at times into the observable present.

List of volumes in Terra Australis

terra australis 51

Archaeologies of Island Melanesia

Current approaches to landscapes, exchange and practice

Edited by Mathieu Leclerc and James Flexner

Australian
National
University

PRESS

ANU
PRESS

Published by ANU Press
The Australian National University
Acton ACT 2601, Australia
Email: anupress@anu.edu.au

Available to download for free at press.anu.edu.au

A catalogue record for this book is available from the National Library of Australia

ISBN (print): 9781760463021
ISBN (online): 9781760463038

WorldCat (print): 1110722299
WorldCat (online): 1110722285

DOI: 10.22459/TA51.2019

Cover design and layout by ANU Press. Cover photograph by Tim Thomas on Tetepare, Solomon Islands, looking across Blanche Channel to New Georgia in the distance.

Contents

Contributors   215

List of figures

List of tables

1

Complexities and diversity in archaeologies of Island Melanesia

James Flexner and Mathieu Leclerc

It has been over 20 years since Spriggs' (1997) synthesis *The Island Melanesians* was published. In the ensuing two decades, a massive and accelerating amount of archaeological fieldwork, analysis, and publication has taken place in the region (see Kirch 2017:55–183 for a recently updated synthesis). There have since been a number of synthetic works highlighting the archaeology of specific archipelagos in Island Melanesia, including Vanuatu (Bedford 2006; Bedford and Spriggs 2014), the Solomon Islands (Walter and Sheppard 2017) and Fiji (Burley 2013; Clark and Anderson 2009). There have also been periodic volumes covering the archaeology of the Lapita Cultural Complex, which is a phenomenon primarily located in Island Melanesia, though also in the neighbouring Polynesian archipelagos of Tonga and to a lesser extent Samoa (e.g. Bedford et al. 2007; Sand and Bedford 2010; Sand et al. 2015). As more sites are discovered, the notion of what Lapita is, where it is located and how to interpret possibly related findings remains a matter of vibrant debate.

This book is not intended as a new synthesis of Melanesian archaeology in the true sense. Rather, the book features a series of case studies highlighting the great diversity of contemporary approaches to archaeologies of Island Melanesia from a thematic perspective. The field is transforming rapidly in response to a variety of forces both inside and outside the discipline of archaeology. One of the more significant developments in 21st-century Melanesian archaeology is the emergence of a sense of 'salvage' archaeology, in which large-scale fieldwork is carried out to document sites ahead of economic development projects (Richards et al. 2016; Sand et al. this volume). We imagine this kind of research will become increasingly prominent in coming years.

In introducing this collection of essays, we focus on two significant themes that are immediately apparent to anyone who has worked in Melanesia: the great *diversity* of environmental and cultural processes that have shaped, and continue to shape, human life in the region; and the *complexity* of Melanesian societies, which is itself a highly diverse phenomenon.

At the outset, we should offer a caveat similar to the one that Kirch (2017:4) gives in a much broader-ranging synthesis of Pacific archaeology. When we refer to Island Melanesia, we are referring to a *geographic* region comprising the islands in the contemporary nation-states of Papua New Guinea, the Solomon Islands, Vanuatu, Fiji and the French colony of New Caledonia. This grouping makes sense because of the history of research in the Pacific, but it certainly does not reflect the complex culture histories of Melanesian people. The boundary with neighbouring Polynesia is problematic considering the long history of interaction and connections between the regions. Dumont d'Urville's tripartite division of the Pacific into Polynesia, Melanesia and Micronesia has remained influential in the ways that scholars understand the Pacific (Clark 2003) and how the inhabitants construct their identities.[1] Dumont d'Urville created divisions that are still used heuristically, but it is well understood that the boundaries are in some ways inappropriate, particularly for the racialised division of Melanesia.

Thus, while Melanesia can be used to distinguish an area of sea and islands, it does not bear any relationship to the histories of the people who live in those islands. This is in contrast to Polynesia, which has been argued to represent a 'phyletic unit' composed of cultures with a traceable shared ancestry (Kirch and Green 2001). Roger Green (1991) long ago noted that Melanesia might be better conceived of in terms of *Near Oceania*, those islands that were colonised initially during the Pleistocene, and *Remote Oceania*, those islands first settled by Lapita-age populations beginning around 3000 years ago. Further, Dumont d'Urville's boundaries have always been permeable, and perhaps the clearest evidence for this is the presence of Polynesian Outliers, islands with Polynesian languages and cultural traits that are located within the geographic boundaries of Melanesia and Micronesia (Feinberg and Scaglion 2012).

Diversity in Island Melanesia

Melanesia is arguably the most linguistically diverse region of the world. From the Papuan languages of the New Guinea highlands and interiors of some high islands in the Solomon Islands (Reesink et al. 2009), to the immense number of Austronesian languages present in the small population of Vanuatu (Crowley 2000; François 2012), the level of diversity in the region is simply astonishing. This linguistic diversity is a reflection of the complex history of settlement in the region reaching back to the Pleistocene, though there is not necessarily a simple relationship between languages and populations (Posth et al. 2018).

Environmentally, Melanesia is also highly diverse. Island size varies from New Guinea, the world's second-largest island with an interior massif featuring many peaks that reach over 4000 m in height, to tiny atolls a few kilometres in surface area and no more than a few metres high at their highest point. Often the biogeographic variability of Melanesian islands is represented within small groups of neighbours. For example, the south of Vanuatu features two older, dormant volcanic high islands, Erromango and Aneityum; a still-active volcanic island, Tanna; a nearby coral atoll, Aniwa; and a *makatea*-type island of raised limestone, Futuna (Flexner et al. 2018). Islands also vary in terms of the sizes and productivity of fringing coral reefs and mangrove swamps, both of which were an essential resource for islanders, particularly as a source of fish and shellfish (see Oertle and Szabó this volume). On larger islands, it might be several days' walk from the interior to the sea. Islanders often adapted to this kind of ecological variability by developing complex exchange networks to redistribute surpluses and deficits not only of food but also other essentials such as oven stones, raw materials, finished tools and valuables (see Bayliss-Smith et al. this volume).

Cultural diversity, of course, goes hand in hand with this linguistic and biogeographical diversity. Histories of Melanesian islands are both variable, and often follow radically different trajectories from many Old World–focused archaeological models. For example, Papua New Guinea's highlands produced one of the earliest inventions of agriculture in the world (Golson et al. 2017). The concept of the 'Neolithic revolution' expected to accompany such an invention does not apply readily to this case, however (Denham this volume). Melanesian ritual practices took on a variety of forms, some involving monumental stone constructions, some not (Bedford this volume). Melanesians had a remarkable diversity of ways of treating the dead and mediating

---

1   There are numerous examples of grassroots events associated with Melanesian culture, such as the Melanesian Arts and Cultural Festival, the Melanesian Regional Championships (Athletics), Wansol Melanesian Music Festival, etc.

relationships with ancestors (Valentin et al. 2011; Valentin and Sand this volume). Social organisation was likewise remarkably diverse, and it is here that we turn to the concept of complexity for understanding Melanesia.

Melanesian complexities

In what has now become a classic work in cultural anthropology, Sahlins (1963) defined a concept of 'big man' societies that he saw as typical of Melanesian social complexity, in contrast to the hereditary titles passed down through Polynesian chiefdoms. This work has been challenged on various fronts, including suggestions that the big man phenomenon was associated specifically with Papuan, as opposed to Austronesian-speaking groups (Scaglion 1996). More critically, the big man societies recorded ethnohistorically were often a reflection of the dramatic demographic and cultural shifts resulting from European colonialism (Sand et al. 2003; Spriggs 2008).

Much of the scholarship on social complexity in Oceania focuses on chiefs and chiefdoms (e.g. Earle and Spriggs 2015; Kirch 1984). Most contemporary Melanesian languages use some version of *jif* (chief) to describe individuals who hold positions of power and authority. However, the kinds of power, and how it is asserted, contested and defended, are highly variable. The evolution of chiefly systems in the Solomon Islands, for example, involved complex processes of niche construction and entanglement as people adapted to relationships of both exchange and warfare (Sheppard this volume; Thomas this volume).

Complex exchange systems evolved hand in hand with the chiefly systems, as Melanesian chiefs often relied on generosity to solidify their authority through gifts and feasting. Prestigious objects for use in exchange systems were produced through technologically sophisticated and meaning-laden processes (Gaffney this volume). Remains of feasts are found in a variety of scales and materials, from faunal remains to microscopic residues found on the inside of pots (Leclerc et al. this volume). In the period of European contacts, these systems further evolved to include settlers such as missionaries (Flexner 2016; Flexner et al. this volume).

The structure of this book

The themes of diversity and complexity permeate the chapters in this volume in a number of ways. The book is separated into three main thematic sections ('Landscapes and complexities'; 'Exchange and contacts'; 'Practices'), sandwiched between smaller contextual sections. The volume opens with a historical overview covering the history of archaeological research in Island Melanesia. The chapters in 'Landscapes and complexities' examine the ways that different processes shaped social complexity and landscape transformation. 'Exchange and contacts' focuses on systems of exchange and cross-cultural interactions. 'Practices' includes in-depth examinations of different forms of practice that were essential to Melanesian ways of life. Finally, we leave the last word to our colleague Edson Willie of the Vanuatu Cultural Centre, who offers the perspective of an indigenous Melanesian archaeologist.

Acknowledgements

Funding for this publication was granted by ANU Press and the ANU Pacific Institute.

References

Bedford, S. 2006. *Pieces of the Vanuatu puzzle: Archaeology of the north, south, and centre.* Terra Australis 23. Canberra: ANU E Press. doi.org/10.22459/pvp.02.2007.

Bedford, S, C Sand and SP Connaughton. 2007. *Oceanic explorations: Lapita and western Pacific settlement.* Canberra: ANU E Press.

Bedford, S and M Spriggs. 2014. 'The archaeology of Vanuatu: 3,000 years of history across islands of ash and coral'. In *The Oxford handbook of prehistoric Oceania*, edited by E Cochrane and T Hunt. Oxford: Oxford University Press. doi.org/10.1093/oxfordhb/9780199925070.013.015.

Burley, DV. 2013. 'Fijian polygenesis and the Melanesian/Polynesian divide'. *Current Anthropology* 54 (4):436–462. doi.org/10.1086/671195.

Clark, G. 2003. 'Dumont d'Urville's Oceania'. *Journal of Pacific History* 38 (2):155–161. doi.org/10.1080/0022334032000120503.

Clark, G and A Anderson. 2009. *The early prehistory of Fiji.* Terra Australis 31. Canberra: ANU E Press. doi.org/10.22459/TA31.12.2009.

Crowley, T. 2000. 'The language situation in Vanuatu'. *Current Issues in Language Planning* 1:47–132. doi.org/10.1080/14664200008668005.

Earle, TK and M Spriggs. 2015. 'Political economy in prehistory: A Marxist approach to Pacific sequences'. *Current Anthropology* 56 (4):515–544. doi.org/10.1086/682284.

Feinberg, R and R Scaglion. 2012. *Polynesian Outliers: The state of the art.* Pittsburgh: University of Pittsburgh Press.

Flexner, JL. 2016. *An archaeology of early Christianity in Vanuatu: Kastom and religious change on Tanna and Erromango, 1839–1920.* Terra Australis 44. Canberra: ANU Press. doi.org/10.22459/TA44.12.2016.

Flexner, JL, S Bedford, F Valentin, R Shing, T Kuautonga and W Zinger. 2018. 'Preliminary results of the South Vanuatu archaeological survey: Cultural landscapes, excavation and radiocarbon dating'. *Asian Perspectives* 57 (2):244–266. doi.org/10.1353/asi.2018.0016.

François, A. 2012. 'The dynamics of linguistic diversity: egalitarian multilingualism and power imbalance among northern Vanuatu languages'. *International Journal of the Sociology of Language* 214:85–110. doi.org/10.1515/ijsl-2012-0022.

Golson, J, T Denham, P Hughes, P Swadling and J Muke. 2017. *Ten thousand years of cultivation at Kuk Swamp in the Highlands of Papua New Guinea.* Terra Australis 46. Canberra: ANU Press. doi.org/10.22459/TA46.07.2017.

Green, RC. 1991. 'Near and Remote Oceania: Disestablishing "Melanesia" in culture history'. In *Man and a half: Essays in Pacific anthropology and ethnobiology in honour of Ralph Bulmer*, edited by A Pawley, 481–592. Auckland: The Polynesian Society.

Kirch, PV. 1984. *The evolution of the Polynesian chiefdoms.* Cambridge: Cambridge University Press.

Kirch, PV. 2017. *On the road of the winds: An archaeological history of the Pacific Islands before European contact.* Second ed. Berkeley: University of California Press.

Kirch, PV and RC Green. 2001. *Hawaiki, ancestral Polynesia: An essay in historical anthropology.* Cambridge: Cambridge University Press. doi.org/10.1017/CBO9780511613678.

Posth, C, K Nägele, H Colleran, F Valentin, S Bedford, KW Kami, R Shing, H Buckley, R Kinaston, M Walworth, G Clark, C Reepmeyer, JL Flexner, T Maric, J Moser, J Gresky, L Kiko, KJ Robson, K Auckland, SJ Oppenheimer, AVJ Hill, AJ Mentzer, J Zech, F Petchey, P Roberts, C Jeong, RD Gray, J Krause and A Powell. 2018. 'Language continuity despite population replacement in Remote Oceania'. *Nature: Ecology & Evolution* 2:731–740. doi.org/10.1038/s41559-018-0498-2.

Reesink, G, R Singer and M Dunn. 2009. 'Explaining the linguistic diversity of Sahul using population models'. *PLoS Biology* 7 (11):e1000241. doi.org/10.1371/journal.pbio.1000241.

Richards, T, B David, K Aplin and IJ McNiven. 2016. *Archaeological research at Caution Bay, Papua New Guinea: Cultural, linguistic and environmental setting.* Caution Bay Studies in Archaeology 1. Oxford: Archaeopress.

Sahlins, M. 1963. 'Poor man, rich man, big-man, chief: Political types in Melanesia and Polynesia'. *Comparative Studies in Society and History* 5 (3):285–303. doi.org/10.1017/S0010417500001729.

Sand, C, J Bolé and A Ouetcho. 2003. 'Prehistory and its perception in a Melanesian Archipelago: The New Caledonia example'. *Antiquity* 77 (297):505–519. doi.org/10.1017/S0003598X00092565.

Sand, C and S Bedford. 2010. *Lapita: Ancêtres Océaniens/Lapita: Oceanic ancestors.* Paris: Musée de Quai Branly and Somogy Éditions d'Art.

Sand, C, S Chiu and N Hogg. 2015. *The Lapita cultural complex in time and space: Expansion routes, chronologies and typologies.* Nouméa: Institut d'archaeologie de la Novelle-Caledonie et du Pacific.

Scaglion, R. 1996. 'Chiefly models in Papua New Guinea'. *The Contemporary Pacific* 8:1–31.

Spriggs, M. 1997. *The Island Melanesians.* Oxford: Blackwell.

Spriggs, M. 2008. 'Ethnographic parallels and the denial of history'. *World Archaeology* 40 (4):538–552. doi.org/10.1080/00438240802453161.

Valentin, F, M Spriggs, S Bedford and H Buckley. 2011. 'Vanuatu mortuary practices over three millennia: Lapita to the early European Contact period'. *Journal of Pacific Archaeology* 2 (2):49–65.

Walter, R and P Sheppard. 2017. *Archaeology of the Solomon Islands.* Honolulu: University of Hawai'i Press.

Historical perspective

2

Towards a history of Melanesian archaeological practices

Matthew Spriggs

> To be ignorant of what occurred before you were born is to remain always a child. For what is the worth of human life, unless it is woven into the life of our ancestors by the study of history.
>
> —Cicero, *Orator*, 120

There are obvious advantages to understanding the history of our discipline, as it is the intellectual baggage we all bring to the trowel's edge, whether we know it or not, and whether we have absorbed it consciously or unconsciously from our teachers and peers. This was brought home to me when reading the *Kulturkreis* archaeologist/ethnologist Robert Heine-Geldern's account of Austronesian migrations into the Pacific, written nearly 90 years ago (Heine-Geldern 1932). There seemed little difference to me, including the use of the word Austronesian, between his general outline of migration and interaction and what one can find today in a general work such as Peter Bellwood's latest survey (2017). There has been nearly a century of Pacific archaeology since Heine-Geldern wrote, with a particular acceleration in research over the last 50 years or so, and yet the basic narrative arguably remains the same. This can only be either because he precociously got the story right or, alternatively, because his schema was so influential in organising knowledge as archaeology developed in the region that we have never managed to question its basic direction.

We clearly need more of what David Clarke (1973) called in another archaeological context 'critical self-consciousness' to examine whether the bases of our explanations are in fact grounded in unthinking and outmoded ways of thought, perhaps colonialist, imperialist and/or racialised. As George Santayana (1905:284) put it in an oft-quoted but ironically otherwise depressingly racist passage: 'those who cannot remember the past are condemned to repeat it'. Critical self-consciousness of our intellectual past, however, goes beyond just understanding the background to the master narratives of the discipline in the Pacific. We cannot understand the old excavation and survey reports that we all build on in our work without knowing what techniques and practices were available at the time to be deployed in constructing the details of prehistory that we take for granted today, and what sort of lag there was between the availability and the take-up of particular analytical techniques. This can give us an idea of how networked or isolated Pacific archaeology has been during its history with regards to global developments in the field. This in turn reflects back on our larger-scale grand narratives, by asking what building blocks were used to construct them; what tools and materials could be deployed at particular times in developing the Pacific archaeologist's theoretical superstructure?

This paper will not delve into the history of the wider theoretical frameworks that we use to organise our data, the subject being too vast to cover here, but it will illustrate the point made above about the availability of particular scientific practices and techniques. It will provide a few select case studies concerning when particular techniques were first available, when they were first deployed in Pacific archaeology more generally and when in the archaeology of the Melanesian region in particular. Certain kinds of evidence-based discussions were not possible until particular technical advances in practice in archaeological science were deployed; some questions simply could not be asked.

Radiocarbon dating is the obvious place to start the discussion, and then the lead is given by the three themes for the volume identified by the editors. I will draw illustrations from each of these in turn, before using this history to evaluate the networked or isolated status of archaeology in our region at particular times. The themes lend themselves to the examination of particular facets of our discipline. The first, 'Landscapes and complexities', requires an engagement with settlement patterns and landscape archaeology. The second, 'Exchange and contacts', relies on characterisation and provenance studies of such artefacts as stone adzes, pottery and obsidian flakes. I will use this as my primary 'case study' and cover the topic in most detail. The final theme, 'Practices', involves such topics as manufacturing sequences, environmental reconstruction and funerary (bio)archaeology. Has there been a slow unfolding of knowledge or were there particular, perhaps serendipitous, moments that have shaped the course of archaeological investigation?

The radiocarbon revolution

One such defining moment was surely the invention of radiocarbon dating by Willard Libby and colleagues in the late 1940s, becoming potentially available to archaeologists throughout the world around 1949–50. It was very quickly deployed by Pacific archaeologists, with Bishop Museum archaeologist Kenneth Emory getting the first date back from a Polynesian archaeological site in 1950, the Kuli'ou'ou rock shelter on O'ahu, Hawaii. It was published originally on 21 September 1951 in the second date list from Libby's laboratory at the University of Chicago, along with two Australian archaeological samples collected by Edmund Gill from Victorian middens (Libby 1951). Melanesia was not far behind with Edward Winslow Gifford publishing multiple dates from two significant Fijian sites he had excavated in 1947 and judiciously kept the charcoal from (Gifford 1952, 1955, as anticipated in his earlier monograph [1951:203]), and then from his 1952 New Caledonia excavations, including at the site of Lapita (Crane 1956; Gifford and Shutler 1956:89–92). In this case we can see very little lag between the invention of the technique and its Pacific and Melanesian deployment.[1]

---

1   It is also worth noting that the first radiocarbon laboratory in the Pacific region was established in 1951 and later became known as the Rafter Laboratory at Lower Hutt, New Zealand, named in honour of its founder, Athol Rafter. It is currently the world's oldest continuously operating radiocarbon laboratory (www.gns.cri.nz/Home/Services/Laboratories–Facilities/Rafter–Radiocarbon–Laboratory/About–Us/The–History–of–Rafter). The second such laboratory was established at the Museum (later Institute) of Applied Science in Melbourne and opened officially in 1961 after a long set-up period beginning in 1954 and with advice from Athol Rafter, but it had continual equipment problems and closed in 1970 (Rae 2018). A dating facility was also established at the University of New South Wales in the early 1960s but only produced one date list before closing (Green et al. 1965). The third was that set up at The Australian National University in 1965 by Henry Polach, who had transferred from Rafter's New Zealand Laboratory (Mulvaney 1993:22).

It must be recalled that prior to the development of radiocarbon dating, Pacific chronologies relied upon oral traditions and genealogical dating; there simply were no other methods beyond putative links of pottery styles in the Pacific to those in other parts of the world (invariably wrong in hindsight), or the superficial resemblance of particular artefact types to supposed 'Palaeolithic' tools and thus suggestive of a deep antiquity (Kirch 2017). An interesting history could be written, although this is not the place to present it, of the increasingly long vistas opened up by the development of a 'deep time' history that radiocarbon dating allowed in the very largely unglaciated Pacific; in Europe it was the geological record of past glaciations that had created a framework for a Pleistocene prehistory from the late 19th century onwards (Daniel 1975). In our part of the world the general belief, albeit with some notable early exceptions,[2] was that prehistory had been, if not necessarily nasty and brutish, certainly short. We started with a thousand-year history in Hawaii; with the Fijian radiocarbon dates it became 2000 years for Melanesia, and in New Caledonia by 1956 it was approaching 3000 years (Gifford and Shutler 1956). The first dates from New Guinea in the 1960s pushed Pacific chronology back to over 10 000 years (Bulmer 1964a),[3] reaching 26 000 BP (uncalibrated) by 1970 (White et al. 1970). The first Pleistocene date in Island Melanesia was obtained in 1981 by Jim Specht with a date from Misisil on New Britain in the Bismarck Archipelago (Specht et al. 1981, 1983). It was from 1993 that a reliable means of calibrating radiocarbon dates back into the Pleistocene was established (Stuiver and Reimer 1993), ultimately to allow extension back to the limits of the method in 2009 (Reimer et al. 2009).

The radiocarbon barrier at about 40 000 years (now extended by calibration a few thousand years earlier (Summerhayes et al. 2010)) was first breached in New Guinea by the discovery of waisted axes in stratigraphic position on the Huon Terraces in 1986 by Les Groube and his students, dated using thermoluminescence to 60 000–40 000 years (Groube et al. 1986); Uranium series dating later confirming the age of the marine terrace on which this deposit sits to be 61 000–52 000 years old (Chappell et al. 1994). For comparison, in Australia the barrier was breached only in 1990 at the site now known as Madjedbebe, initially using thermoluminescence but later the more developed optically stimulated luminescence (OSL), most recently on single sand grains (Clarkson et al. 2017; Roberts et al. 1990, 1993).

The results of the 1984–85 Lapita Homeland Project (Allen and Gosden 1991) pushed Island Melanesian occupation back towards 40 000 years on New Ireland in the Bismarcks, with later results providing potentially even older dates for New Britain using OSL (Torrence et al. 2004). A project developing directly out of the Lapita Homeland Project pushed the dates on Buka Island in the neighbouring Solomons back to 28 000 BP (uncalibrated) (Wickler and Spriggs 1988). And there the Pleistocene frontier in Melanesia has remained, with no dates earlier than c. 3000 BP from anywhere in Remote Oceania to date, despite concentrated efforts during the 1990s and early 2000s in Vanuatu to look for earlier settlement there (Bedford and Spriggs 2008). The Pleistocene frontier that we are confident of today between Near and Remote Oceania was thus only firmly established in the early years of the 21st century.

The point is that to evaluate statements made about the archaeology of the Pacific at any particular date, we need to know what chronological models and constraints those writing them were living under at the time. They simply did not know what we know now.

---

2   Fritz Sarasin went to New Caledonia in search of Palaeolithic 'river drift man' in 1911–12, without success (Sarasin 2009 [1929]). Alphonse Riesenfeld posed the question in the 1950s of whether there was a Pleistocene history in Melanesia (Riesenfeld 1952). Neither intervention had any significant influence on subsequent archaeological practice, however.

3   Recall that in Australia a terminal Pleistocene prehistory had only been securely established in 1962 (Mulvaney 2011:113).

Landscapes and complexities: Settlement patterns and landscape archaeology in the Pacific

Roger Green is generally credited with introducing a settlement pattern approach to the Pacific, derived from his Harvard background in the 1950s, where he was taught by Gordon Willey who was a major American pioneer in such studies (Willey 1953). Green's Harvard classmate, Kwang-Chih Chang was later to write a standard text, *Settlement Patterns in Archaeology* (1972; see also Chang 1958). In a perceptive paper that deserves a wider audience Phillips and Campbell (2004) survey the field in New Zealand, but with further reference to the Pacific, providing a history which covers the range of approaches from the original settlement pattern approach to what is now called landscape archaeology. They refer to the claim of Parsons (1972:134) that the Pacific regional 'school' of settlement archaeology, led by Green, was the first anywhere outside the United States. But they also note some earlier applications of somewhat similar methods by scholars such as HD Skinner, and the British contribution via figures such as Cyril Fox (1923) and OGS Crawford (1953) that was part of the intellectual baggage brought to New Zealand by Golson in 1954 as 'field archaeology' (Golson 1957b; Golson and Green 1959; see also Golson 1986). They also recognise the novel developments of the approach by others in New Zealand, including Les Groube in particular (partially published in Groube 1965).

Green was also very influential in Hawaii, where he was based at the Bishop Museum from 1966 to 1970, helping to initiate large-scale settlement pattern surveys, particularly of the various dryland field systems at Lapakahi on Hawai'i Island, and irrigated and dryland systems at Makaha in O'ahu and at Halawa Valley on Moloka'i (Kirch 1985:18–19).

Aerial photography has long been a staple technique of Pacific geographers. Its first explicitly archaeological applications were called for by Blake-Palmer (1947) in New Zealand, citing the pioneering work in Britain by OGS Crawford (1928) and others. Blake-Palmer called for an archaeologist to be attached to the New Zealand Survey Department so that the many Maori sites visible on aerial photographs could be placed on maps. Golson (1957b) also noted the value of aerial photography in surveys. Its first sustained use in Melanesia in examining prehistoric settlement patterns was by the geographer John Parry in Fiji. Covering particularly deltaic and swampy areas he was able to identify fortified settlements and also agricultural features. This research was published in a series of papers between 1977 and 1997 (see Parry 1977, 1997 for examples and references). Similar work was carried out in New Caledonia on the irrigated taro terraces and other agricultural systems there (Roux 1990, reporting on early 1980s work).

Landscapes (and seascapes) have also been foci in Melanesia more recently, seen by Phillips and Campbell as deriving mainly from British post-processual approaches: they note particularly Ballard (1994) and Gosden and Pavlides (1994). Such an influence was clearly there but they miss the strong influence from human and cultural geography associated with scholars such as Brookfield and Hart (1971) and Bonnemaison (1974, 1979). The former influenced several generations of New Guinea archaeologists at The Australian National University (ANU) and elsewhere, and the latter was a particular influence on those working in Vanuatu (for instance Spriggs 1985, 1987 [orig. 1981]).

Most recently, the deployment of aerial laser scanning or LiDAR (light detection and ranging) imagery in the Pacific and elsewhere, literally 'seeing' beneath the trees to pick out even subtle human alterations in the landscape, has opened up interpretive vistas almost impossible to imagine even a few years ago. The technology particularly took off in the remote sensing literature at the very end of the 20th century and archaeological applications began to appear in the first decade of the current one (Barnes 2003; Bewley 2003; Bewley et al. 2005; Devereux et al. 2005). Spectacular results have come particularly from tropical regions (Chase et al. 2012 for Mesoamerica, and Evans et al. 2014 for the Angkor Wat complex in Cambodia). First use in Pacific archaeology appears to have been in Hawaii in 2011 (Ladefoged et al. 2011; McCoy et al. 2011), American Samoa in 2015 (Quintus et al. 2015) and Tonga in 2016 (Freeland et al. 2016). Entire cultural landscapes are being revealed, previously 'lost' under heavy vegetation or otherwise scarcely visible to the naked eye in cleared cattle paddocks—such as recently investigated on the island of Efate in central Vanuatu (Bedford et al. 2018). The latter research revealed the unsuspected extent of dryland intensified agricultural systems and a hitherto undescribed site type of large circular earthworks whose function is at present unknown.

Previous achievements in settlement pattern and landscape archaeology in the Pacific have been rather overshadowed by the LiDAR revolution. The earlier shift in attention, however, from single sites to sites within a natural and cultural landscape, and to the investigation of settlement hierarchies and other features of settlement patterns, were what created the frameworks for understanding newly deployed techniques. The open landscapes of parts of Fiji which allowed Parry to use extensive aerial photographic coverage in many ways prefigured current LiDAR developments. Without such wide-scale coverage of settlements within their cultural and agricultural landscapes, issues of prehistoric demography and agricultural intensification could not be seriously addressed. Already the Efate and Vanuatu LiDAR data can be used to suggest much higher population densities at European contact than previously demonstrable (Bedford et al. 2018). The tragedy of catastrophic population declines due to introduced Western diseases is thus more starkly brought into focus.

Exchange and contacts: The history of characterisation and provenance studies

Characterisation is the act of discriminating between artefacts derived from different sources, whereas provenance hazards at least a guess as to where the sources might be. A precocious chemical analysis of jade artefacts was published in 1865 in Paris by Damour, from an explicitly archaeological science perspective (Damour 1865). It seems to have been very largely overlooked by historians of archaeology—the only archaeological reference in English to this work I can find is in W Campbell Smith's work on 'Jade axes from sites in the British Isles' (Smith 1963:151–152). Damour's work is particularly notable as the chemical analyses included a nephrite axe from New Zealand, and the study included further axes claimed to be from the Marquesas, as well as an obsidian artefact from Easter Island.[4]

Thin sections of pottery from Peru, and from Santorini in the Greek Mediterranean, of Greek and of Mexican obsidian were being undertaken in the 1880s and 1890s (references from Cann et al. 1969; Matson 1969). Petrology was to become a staple of provenance studies of British Neolithic axes from the 1930s onwards (Grimes 1979), and of North American pottery from at least the 1930s (Keiller et al. 1941; Kidder and Shepard 1936).

In the late 1940s Gifford had tried to secure the services of Anna O Shepard (unsuccessfully) to thin section pottery from his Fijian excavations.[5] He got some interest from his geologist colleague Howel Williams, but the work was completed by GH Curtis, also of University of California, Berkeley, who later would conduct the petrological analysis of Gifford's New Caledonian pottery as well (in Gifford 1951; Gifford and Shutler 1956). Reba W Benedict,

---

4   Some of Damour's work was known to GHF Ulrich, the first Professor of Geology at Otago University, New Zealand, but the reference he cites in a table provided to his colleague FB Chapman is to Damour's analysis of a Chinese jade object (Chapman 1891: 539).

5   Information from letters archived in the Bancroft Library, University of California, Berkeley.

a geology student supervised by Curtis, carried out petrological analysis of Yapese pottery from Gifford's last expedition of 1956. The Yap monograph was published posthumously in 1959 (Gifford and Gifford 1959), and perhaps because of this Benedict's work rates only the merest mention (Gifford and Gifford 1959:184–185).

The early Melanesian characterisation work was later to inspire geologist Bill Dickinson in starting his 40-plus-year association with Pacific archaeological pottery analysis (summarised in Dickinson 2006). Dickinson recounted how he was engaged in geological research in Fiji in 1965, while his graduate anthropologist wife Peggy decided to study a modern pottery-making community there (Dickinson and Sykes 1965). He was introduced to Helen and Lawrence Birks, then digging at the Sigatoka Dune site, who were trying to find a way to establish if the Lapita pottery discovered there was local or exotic. They naturally asked if there were applicable geological techniques for doing so. Knowing from his wife's study that local potters added mineral temper to the clay constituents of the pottery they were making, Dickinson concluded that petrological analysis was the answer to their question. He was later able to establish a local source for the pottery (Dickinson 1971).

Richard Shutler Jr, the graduate student who had accompanied Gifford to New Caledonia in 1952, was serendipitously visiting the Bishop Museum in Honolulu when Dickinson dropped in on his way home from Fiji. Dickinson later reported that upon meeting him and hearing of his expertise, Shutler exclaimed 'where have you been all my life?' They immediately embarked upon a collaborative project on Pacific pottery characterisation through thin section analysis that continued until Shutler's death in 2007.[6]

The initial summary publication of Dickinson's ceramic studies was in Yawata and Sinoto's edited volume from the 11th Pacific Science Congress held in Japan in 1966 (Dickinson and Shutler 1968), soon followed by his published specialist report in Green and Davidson's first volume on *The Archaeology of Western Samoa* (Dickinson 1969:271–273).[7] This was some years after Curtis' pioneering work on the petrology of New Caledonian pottery, suggesting a significant time lag. But it must be noted that apart from PhD theses, there had been no monographic treatments of the archaeology of Pacific pottery-using areas in that interval, apart from Gifford's own already-mentioned 1959 monograph, Alex Spoehr's work on *Marianas Prehistory* (1957) and Douglas Osborne's *The Archaeology of the Palau Islands* (1966). Spoehr did not include any petrological analysis, while Osborne had thin sections of pottery made and analysed by Dale Kramer of the University of Washington Geology Department, but made very little of them in the absence of detailed knowledge of regional geology. In this, Dickinson had the clear advantage and from the start was able to establish distinct temper regions within the broader Pacific (Dickinson and Shutler 1968).

As Gifford's Fiji monograph (1951), containing Curtis' petrological report, was the first to report substantive excavations in any area of the Pacific where pottery was in use, it can hardly be said of that that it represented a significant time lag after common use in the United States and elsewhere of petrographic analysis of ceramics.

Others, independently however, had also embarked upon petrographic analysis of Pacific ceramics in the 1960s, notably the pioneer archaeological scientist Con Key in Jack Golson's unit within the Anthropology and Sociology Department at ANU in Canberra. Hired for a five-year

---

6   The sources for the history of Bill Dickinson's involvement in pottery studies in the Pacific are from personal communications over a long period of time, particularly over dinner in San Francisco in April 2015, just a few months before his death on fieldwork in Tonga in July of that year, backed up by the account in the Preface to Dickinson's summary monograph (2006:vii).

7   Burley and Weisler (2016:83) note that the first of Dickinson's generally unpublished specialist reports, numbering 322 at his death, was dated 1966 and 'characterizes the temper of a Lapita sherd from Efate, Vanuatu'. His first published Fiji summary report is dated as submitted in 1968 (Dickinson 1971).

fellowship in 1965, having been trained in geology in Holland and South Africa, Key initiated a number of innovative characterisation studies of both pottery and obsidian in his position as Research Fellow in Environmental Archaeology. The lack of a job after his fellowship finished meant he was lost to archaeology, going to work for the Western Australia Department of Main Roads; he died soon afterwards (Jack Golson, pers. comm. November 2017).

Key's petrological reports were at first appended to various PhD theses coming out of what became in May 1969 the Department of Prehistory in the Research School of Pacific Studies at ANU, led by Jack Golson. These started with a 1966 report for Jens Poulsen who was working on Tongan Lapita sites (later published in Poulsen 1987) and was followed by a 1967 report for J Peter White who was researching in the Eastern Highlands of Papua New Guinea (PNG, published in White 1972). Key carried out independent studies of ethnographic and some prehistoric pottery in the Massim area of PNG, establishing there had been exchange between the Collingwood Bay area and the Trobriands (Key 1968a). His other major work was on the sourcing of New Guinea obsidians using spectrographic analysis of trace elements (Key 1968b, 1969), showing that obsidian from the Lapita sites on Watom Island could be sourced to the Talasea area of West New Britain some 270 km away. This was the first archaeologically oriented study of Melanesian obsidians; they did not feature at all in Cann et al.'s (1969) world survey.

Spectrographic methods had first been developed near the beginning of the 19th century, but optical spectroscopy had been first applied to archaeological materials such as metals and faience beads in the 1950s (Britton and Richards 1969). The first publication on trace elements detected using optical spectroscopy for characterising obsidians was in 1964, starting a major study of Anatolian and other obsidian exchange in the Eastern Mediterranean and Middle East (Cann and Renfrew 1964). Roger Green and colleagues in New Zealand were quick on the uptake (Green et al. 1967), with Key's work being a further development of the technique.

Green had initially become interested in obsidian for its potential as a tool for dating, and as a visiting Fulbright Scholar had issued an appeal in the December 1958 issue of the *New Zealand Archaeological Association Newsletter* for samples (Scarlett 1958:3). He had read of the use of refractive index as a means of characterising obsidian (Boyer and Robinson 1955) and heard of the development of hydration dating from American researchers, who were later to publish their results (Clark 1961; Friedman et al. 1960). Working with Auckland geologist RN Brothers (an early collaborator of Jack Golson in Auckland in the mid-1950s), Green used general appearance and refractive index measurements in an attempt to characterise sources in New Zealand, as had earlier been applied with some success in the Southwest of the United States and in Japan (Green 1962).[8] Working also with Wal Ambrose at Auckland, Green was quick to publish the first New Zealand obsidian hydration results (Ambrose and Green 1962). There was clearly no time lag in that particular application from its successful development and publication to a Pacific application. In 1964 Green published a further report on New Zealand obsidian sources and the dating of their use (Green 1964), and Green and colleagues' 1967 sourcing paper using emission spectroscopy was again, as we have seen, published within three years of the earliest published work anywhere on obsidian sourcing using this technique (Green et al. 1967).

Ambrose and Green teamed up again in 1972, using emission spectrography in the first paper to establish inter-archipelago movement of materials during the Lapita period, in this case obsidians from Talasea being transported some 2000 km to the outer eastern islands of the

---

8   And also in New Zealand: the earliest specifically petrological interest in archaeological obsidians in the Pacific seems to be that of Prof. DS Coombs of Otago University (see also footnote 11, below). Golson (1957a:285) refers to him reporting on a unique obsidian piece from Pounawea, South Island, New Zealand, that it had a refractive index and chemical constituents different from Mayor Island obsidian. This predates Green's New Zealand involvement in the subject.

Solomons (Ambrose and Green 1972). Before this date it was scarcely possible to discuss Lapita exchange, although Key's work had shown the way; subsequently it has become a major topic of Lapita studies.

Ambrose had relocated to ANU in 1963, lured by Jack Golson's earlier move there from Auckland in 1961, and as a research officer had been a colleague of Key's. Ambrose's obsidian interests continued, and he soon became the major archaeological specialist on obsidian characterisation in the Pacific. Summerhayes et al. (1998, updated in Summerhayes 2009) provide a useful history of the successive techniques used to refine the sourcing of Pacific, mainly Melanesian, obsidians: X-ray fluorescence (XRF) was applied in 1974, neutron activation analysis (NAA) in 1976, but was quickly succeeded by proton-induced gamma emission analysis (PIGME) that same year (a technique developed only in 1972), to be combined with proton-induced X-ray emission analysis (PIXE) by 1979 as PIXE-PIGME, and finally with laser ablation inductively coupled plasma mass spectrometry (LA-ICP-MS) taking over as the technique of choice around 2008.

Other techniques have been used intermittently as well since the 1990s (Summerhayes 2009:110), most significantly portable XRF (pXRF). This technique allows the researcher to come to where the samples are, rather than the other way around, is non-destructive, relatively inexpensive and requires little specialised training to use, in contrast to many of the other available techniques. The aim of all this technique shifting has been to allow rapid characterisation of multiple samples and an ever more refined differentiation of subsamples within general source areas, while also being mindful of cost, of what equipment was available in any particular institution and of being able to gain the interest of those who were in charge of the equipment. Ambrose's name appears as one of the authors on papers on almost every new development in the field to the present.

Petrography of ceramics has been mentioned as having been a long-standing technique in Pacific archaeology, and thin section analysis of Pacific stone resources similarly did not lag far behind its use elsewhere. Histories of the use of petrology in the United Kingdom such as that by Grimes (1979) usually begin with reference to HH Thomas' (1923) study of the source of the Stonehenge bluestones, identified as coming from the Preseli Mountains of Wales. Thomas was the petrographer of the United Kingdom Geological Survey from 1911 to his untimely death in 1935 (Harker 1935). His earliest involvement with the sourcing of axes was reported in a paper on the Graig Lwyd axe quarry in 1919 (Warren 1919, 1921) and he continued to advise on axe petrology until his death (Keiller et al. 1941). His immediate successor as Geological Survey petrographer was James Phemister who also gets an honourable mention for his petrographic work on British stone axes in the 'First Report of the South-Western Group of Museums and Art Galleries on the Petrological Identification of Stone Axes', covering the period 1936 to 1941 (Keiller et al. 1941, and references therein).

In a discussion of seemingly exotic basaltic stone adzes found on the coast of New South Wales, Australia, and on Norfolk Island, WW Thorpe (1929), the ethnologist at the Australian Museum in Sydney, sought out the petrologist T Hodge Smith to examine thin sections of the specimens and a comparator from Great Barrier Island in New Zealand. Smith was unable to suggest a clear source for these adzes, noting only that 'similar basalts are very widely distributed in the Pacific regions' (quoted in Thorpe 1929:126).

In an 1891 paper, 'On the working of greenstone or nephrite by the Maoris', that does not otherwise include any scientific analysis of nephrite artefacts, there is appended a table provided by the Foundation Geology Professor at Otago University, GHF Ulrich (Chapman 1891:539), already referred to (see footnote 4). In addition to Damour's analysis of a Chinese jade, the table also included chemical analyses of New Zealand nephrites by Scheerer and Melchior and Meyer, but no sources are given.

However, the earliest published petrology on New Zealand nephrite artefacts aimed at understanding provenance was published in 1935, based on an oral presentation of 1932 (Turner 1935).[9] FJ Turner, a geologist at Otago University appointed in 1926, was inspired to undertake the study of 120 artefacts by ethnologist HD Skinner. Skinner maintained strong academic links with British archaeologists and would have heard of the work of Thomas in this field. At the time of publication of Turner's research, it was in fact the largest-scale study of its kind; the major United Kingdom study of Neolithic axe sourcing mentioned earlier did not get underway until the following year (Keiller et al. 1941). Turner's paper was not, however, as far as I can see, referenced in the United Kingdom for another 30 years (Clark 1965).

New Guinea petrographic analyses followed soon after in 1936 when Moyne and Haddon published a summary of thin section analyses of Mount Hagen and Aiome stone axes conducted by Phemister (Moyne and Haddon 1936:272). There had been earlier petrological interest in New Guinea adzes and axes, not least by Dr John E Marr and Mr WG Fearnsides of Cambridge University, who examined the products of the Suloga Quarry on Woodlark Island in the Massim and adzes from Collingwood Bay on the mainland for Seligmann around 1906 (Seligmann and Joyce 1907:331; Seligmann and Strong 1906:353–354; cf. Seligmann 1910:517). It is not clear, however, that Marr's examination extended beyond hand specimens. Similarly, Malinowski (1934:190) credits Dr EW Skeats, Professor of Geology at Melbourne University, for petrological examination of eastern New Guinea stone artefacts, but again gives no details of the actual analyses conducted.

Petrological thin section analysis seems to have been applied systematically only from the 1960s in the Pacific, in Melanesia at least as early as in the rest of the region.[10] When Golson moved from Auckland to ANU in 1961, an early priority of his was the establishment of a petrological laboratory there for the analysis of stone and pottery artefacts (Golson 1962). Brookfield and Brown (1963:65) reported thin section analysis of five PNG Highlands adzes by WR Morgan of the Bureau of Mineral Resources in Canberra and by GA Joplin of ANU. The *annus mirabilis* for the technique seems to have been 1966: Chappell and Strathern (1966) on PNG Highlands material, Verhofstad (1966) on West Papuan Highlands adzes, and a 1966 report for Jens Poulsen's Tongan thesis on stone adzes from Tongatapu by AJR White of the Geology Department of ANU (published in Poulsen 1987).

Thin section analysis has not proved very popular in the study of Pacific adzes as it requires a slice or plug to be cut out of the adze (see Adam (1953:414 fn.) in relation to PNG Highlands specimens, for instance). Other minimal or non-destructive techniques were adopted later, most

---

9   Turner had earlier conducted a petrological analysis of a piece of greenstone, possibly an axe fragment, from Aitutaki in the Cook Islands. He sourced it to Milford Sound in New Zealand, noting that he had recently completed the paper which was eventually published in 1935 (quote by Skinner 1933:225–226). For a short history of the Otago Geology Department see www.otago.ac.nz/geology/about/history.html.

10   Parker and Sheppard (1997) give primacy at Auckland University to Eleanor Crosby's (1963) alleged thin section analysis of New Zealand basalt artefacts, although this is a misattribution (Eleanor Crosby pers. comm. January 2019). They list the many contributions—not least John Chappell's—to adze geochemistry emanating from Auckland University, perhaps inspired at least in part by Roger Green's undergraduate background in geology. Chappell's original New Guinea petrological report, however, also dates to 1963, as reported by Susan Bulmer (1964b). Otago University can claim the earliest Pacific interest, as noted above. Turner's interest there was continued by his successor at Otago from 1947, Prof. DS Coombs of the Geology Department who used the 'X-ray powder method' on a small fragment of an argillite adze from Taranaki to source it tentatively to the Nelson district (Skinner 1953). Coombs gave a paper at the New Zealand Archaeological Association's 1957 second conference, on 'The use of petrology in delimiting the sources of the stone materials of the Moa hunters', based on thin section analysis of flakes from Leslie Lockerbie's excavation at Pounawea (summarised in Golson 1957a:271, 284–285; see also Lockerbie 1959). While Gifford thanks Prof. Howel Williams of University of California, Berkeley, for mineralogical identification of adzes and other stone from Fiji, New Caledonia and Yap, his analysis does not appear to have extended beyond examination of hand specimens (Gifford 1951:221; Gifford and Shutler 1956:68; Gifford and Gifford 1959:193–194). Firth (1959:153) reports on thin section characterisation of Tikopian (Solomon Islands) stone adzes carried out by Dr W Campbell Smith of the Department of Mineralogy, British Museum (Natural History), but with no comparative work undertaken to provenance them.

recently pXRF because of its portability. The range of chemical characterisation techniques available has been deployed much more systematically in Polynesia than in Melanesia (see papers in Weisler 1997). It is fair to say that outside mainland New Guinea there has been much less interest in adze sourcing in Melanesia compared to the rest of the Pacific, despite the promising start in the mid-1960s and continued attention from Roger Green and his associates on the South-East Solomons Culture History Project (Green 1978; Kirch and Yen 1982:232–237; Leach and Davidson 2008; Moore 1978; Sheppard 1996) and in Fiji (Best 1989 [orig. 1984]). The aforementioned research on Polynesian Outliers and some other sites by Green and his associates turned up adzes of Samoan origin in later prehistoric contexts; apart from language these remain the only certain link between the Outliers and their presumed easterly Polynesian cultural source.

The deployment of these techniques for the characterisation and provenance of pottery and stone artefacts has largely created the study of prehistoric exchange. Until their deployment, all that could be done at best was recognition that certain materials were exotic to the place in which they were found, and an appeal in places such as the Pacific to ethnohistorically documented exchange systems as illustrating the kinds of social relations possibly entailed by the archaeological evidence.

Practices and productivities: Manufacture, palaeoenvironments and the archaeology of death

Manufacture

The chances to observe the making of stone artefacts, as opposed to sourcing where they may have come from, were taken up to some extent in Melanesia; almost solely, however, in New Guinea. The major opportunity was afforded by the fact that the relatively isolated Highlands region was not penetrated by Europeans until the 1930s, when only a few worn steel axes had reached there through traditional exchange routes with lowlands societies who had had access to metal since the previous century. Thus, Seligmann complained upon his visit to the Suloga Adze quarry on Woodlark Island in 1904 that the quarry had been abandoned for a generation and the adze makers had died out through introduced diseases (Seligmann and Strong 1906:350).

Missionaries and anthropologists were quick to get into the Highlands but generally were not much interested in technology and artefact production, although traditional exchange, including of stone adzes/axes, did gain their early attention. An exception was LG Vial (1940) who visited two stone quarries in 1938 and 1939 and provided a description and photographs of how they were worked. Clark (1965:19) complains of the general lack of attention by early visitors to the Highlands, and Chappell, who visited many of the adze quarries between 1963 and 1965, encountered only one man whom he considered a skilled maker of stone tools (Chappell and Strathern 1966:103, 105). John Burton, however, was able to conduct a detailed study of adze manufacture from the memory of men in the early 1980s who had been among the last generation to have seen the quarries in operation (Burton 1987). Stone adze/axe procurement and manufacture using traditional practices continued much longer in the Highlands of West Papua, and the Pétrequins were able to take movie film of axe makers and record in detail their techniques at various remote locations in the 1980s (Pétrequin and Pétrequin 1993).

For flaked stone the situation was somewhat better in the PNG Highlands and J Peter White was able to produce a detailed record of production techniques in the 1960s (1967, 1968; White et al. 1977), as was Maurice Godelier (Godelier with Garanger 1973). Traditional pottery making throughout Melanesia lasted much longer than stone artefact production; indeed in some areas it remains vibrant today and has been subject to many studies (for PNG see particularly May and Tuckson 1982). It died out early, however, in New Caledonia at the turn of the 20th century but was recorded in place by various savants (as summarised by Sarasin 2009 [orig. 1929]:116–119). Ways of working shell for tools and ornaments have also received sustained levels of attention over the years.

Understanding prehistoric technologies allows one to examine questions of craft specialisation and potential levels of production, and assess whether particular craft skills were easily acquired or would have required long apprenticeships.

Palaeoenvironments and human impacts

Ideas of environmental change and human impacts upon landscape during human occupation of the Pacific Islands were strongly taken up by scholars working in Melanesia, as elsewhere in the Pacific. The general influence came from what would now be called historical ecology, and Kirch (1997) has summarised its development, particularly from an American perspective. In Australia it was more the demonstration of human impacts on the environment by palynologists working in New Guinea from the beginning of the 1970s and the work of geomorphologists such as Philip Hughes (for instance Hughes et al. 1979) that were particularly influential. The papers in Kirch and Hunt (1997) that relate to Melanesia show these more immediate influences, rather than those that inform most of the Polynesian studies in that volume.

The Pacific featured very early in discussion of 'megafaunal' extinctions, with the first New Zealand reports of bones of extinct giant birds later to be known as 'moa' published in 1838, and the first palaeontological description of the bones in 1839 by the brilliant anatomist Richard Owen. Moa-hunting sites were described from 1843 onwards (see Anderson 1989 for references). The extent of bird extinctions from the rest of Polynesia, although none of the species was as large as the largest moas, only became fully apparent from the 1980s onwards (Steadman 2006).

New Guinea's megafauna were first described as potentially associated with human occupation in the 1970s at the site of Nombe (Mountain 1979; White and O'Connell 1982:91). Flannery's (1995) contention that the Pleistocene megafauna of New Guinea were 'almost entirely unknown' (1995:48) until his own publications from 1983 onwards is not completely accurate. He in fact provides references to significant earlier research, although he seems to have missed an archaeologically related study by Plane (1972). That there was a major advance in knowledge of the New Guinea megafauna in the 1980s is certainly true, however, not least through Flannery's own studies of the Nombe fauna and that from other locations (summarised in Flannery 1995:48–54).

New Caledonia's extinct birds and reptiles were first reported in detail during the decade of the 1980s by Balouet and his colleagues, initially from fossil sites yielding remains of large birds, land crocodiles and tortoises. Remains from archaeological as opposed to fossil sites were first reported by Balouet and Olson at the end of the decade (1989). Solomon Islands' large extinct rats were reported from Pleistocene through mid-Holocene occupation deposits from Buka soon afterwards (Flannery and Wickler 1990), while Vanuatu's extinct land crocodiles, tortoises and birds had to wait until the 21st century before they were reported from archaeological sites there (Mead et al. 2002; White et al. 2010; Worthy et al. 2015). Steadman (2006:111–159) presents a comprehensive overview of human-induced avian extinctions in Melanesia known to that time.

From the above it can be seen that with the notable exception of New Zealand, where the ubiquitous bones of various moa species were hard to ignore, it would have been impossible to discuss the major human role in Pacific vertebrate extinctions until after 1980; before then there were precious few palaeontological and archaeozoological data on which to hang a story. A whole bestiary of fauna has since been revealed, evidence of some of the 'pull' factors that may have encouraged early exploration and settlement. Sadly, it also documents the major human-induced impacts on a 'naïve' fauna, that in some cases would have included 'keystone' species vital to the environmental balance on islands (Kirch 2017:229–231). Once that fragile balance was upset, environmental degradation was inevitable on small, and often otherwise depauperate island groups.

The archaeology of death

Funerary archaeology in the Pacific has a long history, with some major early excavations in Hawaii and New Zealand (Kirch 2017). In Melanesia it has been most spectacularly investigated at the Roi Mata burial site on Eretoka or Hat Island off the coast of Efate, now part of the World Heritage Site of Chief Roi Mata's Domain. Garanger's excavation of a mass chiefly grave there, linked to oral traditions, was published in 1972, along with other graves associated with detailed traditions also excavated by him on Tongoa Island in the same period (Garanger 1972). Central Vanuatu is also the location of the largest Lapita-phase cemetery recorded, at Teouma on Efate itself, excavated between 2004 and 2010 (Bedford et al. 2006, 2010). It was at this site that the innovative French forensic approach, infelicitously labelled *anthropologie de terrain* was first applied in the Pacific (Valentin et al. 2010a). Until the excavation of Teouma, this major strand of Lapita archaeology was virtually unknown, hindering discussion of important questions about Lapita ritual and of comparison with the comparatively rich Island South-East Asian funerary record from sites like Niah, and various Taiwanese Neolithic sites (Bellwood 2017).

The SAC site on Watom, off the coast of New Britain (Petchey et al. 2016 and references therein), and the Sigatoka Dune Site on Viti Levu in Fiji (Marshall et al. 2000) are the only other major Lapita and immediately post-Lapita open funerary sites in Melanesia where information on funerary practice has been published from more than a handful of burials. At the Watom site, as at Teouma, a range of isotopic and skeletal pathology studies have also been carried out (see Petchey et al. 2016 for the most recent summary of work there). Also of note is a large series of second millennium CE burials investigated on the Polynesian Outlier island of Taumako in the Solomons (Leach and Davidson 2008:133–253; see also Buckley 2001; Kinaston and Buckley 2017). Apart from this, there is a long history of Melanesian funerary studies of cave burials, some placed inside pottery vessels, going back to the early decades of the 20th century in the archaeological literature (see for instance Austen 1939; Lyons 1922; Seligmann 1910:731).

Before the recent discovery and scientific analysis of Lapita and later cemetery data in Melanesia, there were whole areas of ritual and symbolic life, and of the health and genetic affinities of early Pacific populations that were inaccessible to archaeologists. For example, we can now examine the human health 'costs' of colonisation of previously uninhabited island groups (Buckley et al. 2008, 2014; Foster et al. 2018), aspects of Lapita diet breadth (Kinaston et al. 2014; Valentin et al. 2010b) and changes in both through time (Valentin et al. 2014).

Concluding discussion

As can be seen from the examples given above, scientific applications and practices developed in America and Europe have generally been very quickly taken up in the Pacific, including in Melanesia. No significant lags can be identified between their development and general use in the metropoles and in our region. This can be explained by the fact that there was never an isolated development of archaeological practice in the Pacific. It was a European and American transplant, at first of interest to museum and, to a lesser extent, university scholars. All of these had access in their institutions or through international networks to a range of expertise beyond their own disciplines, initially calling upon geologists and biologists and later upon chemists and nuclear physicists. The widespread exchange of publications between museums and learned societies worldwide played a not insignificant role in such rapid dissemination.

Pacific archaeologists were among the first to recognise the immense promise of radiocarbon dating, and a radiocarbon dating laboratory was established in New Zealand within a couple of years of the availability of this revolutionary technique to archaeologists anywhere in the world. Characterisation and provenance studies of Pacific stone axes/adzes using thin section petrology were in use within a decade or so of their regular deployment in the United Kingdom, and other techniques of sourcing pottery and stone were also rapidly taken up in the region. This is particularly true of developments in obsidian characterisation, where deployment in New Zealand was almost simultaneous with the announcement of the first results in Anatolia and the Eastern Mediterranean.

Broader-scale practices such as the development of settlement pattern studies and landscape archaeology, backed by the use of aerial photographic analysis, were also deployed in a timely manner in the Pacific and Melanesia. Developments in both British and American traditions in these areas were quickly disseminated, as were the somewhat separate but complementary approaches used in palaeoenvironmental reconstruction and a consciousness of the role of human impacts in shaping Pacific environments. The latest developments in funerary archaeology as well, particularly the forensic techniques of *anthropologie de terrain*, have also been eagerly adopted in Melanesia. LiDAR surveys, which will further revolutionise our knowledge of settlement patterns in the region, are also now starting to become widely available.

Entire topics of study that are now considered central to archaeological practice could barely be considered before the development of some of the techniques listed above. Before radiocarbon dating in the 1950s there was no chronological framework available in the Pacific for periods before European contact apart from genealogically-linked oral traditions. These could only be used to go back a few hundred years in most cases. The archaeological study of exchange systems could not go beyond the ethnohistorical record and ethnographic analogy until artefact petrology and later characterisation techniques could be brought to bear on the problem. The impoverished biogeography of the Pacific at European contact was not recognised, beyond the question of the New Zealand moas, until palaeontological and archaeozoological research from the 1980s onwards revealed the past diversity of species, and the terrible effects that human settlement of the Pacific Islands had upon them.

The characterisation of phases or stages of Pacific archaeology often privileges developments in theory, the professionalisation of archaeology in the post–World War II period or the deployment of 'scientific' excavation techniques to key sites. These are all important markers for the history of the discipline in the Pacific that we attempt to understand. Knowing about the availability and procurement of particular archaeological science practices and techniques provides the possibility of other ways of organising disciplinary history that allow us to understand what it was possible to know at any particular moment about the region's past.

Acknowledgements

The Collective Biography of Archaeology in the Pacific (CBAP) project is funded by the Australian Research Council (ARC) as grant FL140100218 and by ANU. Thanks to my CBAP colleagues for discussions and to Catherine Fitzgerald for administrative support. Particularly fruitful discussions in relation to the paper have been had with Wal Ambrose, Stuart Bedford, Dave Burley, the late Bill Dickinson, Jack Golson and the volume editors. Wal Ambrose also provided some vital published and unpublished sources. The paper was finished at the Vila Rose Hotel, Port Vila, Vanuatu and, as ever, the extreme patience of Rosemary Leona during its production is gratefully acknowledged.

References

Adam, L. 1953. 'The discovery of the Vierkantbeil or quadrangular adze head in the Eastern Central Highlands of New Guinea'. *Mankind* 4:411–423.

Allen, J and C Gosden (eds). 1991. *Report of the Lapita Homeland Project*. Occasional Papers in Prehistory 20. Canberra: Department of Prehistory, Research School of Pacific Studies, The Australian National University.

Ambrose, W and R Green. 1962. 'Obsidian dating: Preliminary results'. *New Zealand Archaeological Association Newsletter* 5:247–248.

Ambrose, W and R Green. 1972. 'First millennium BC transport of obsidian from New Britain to the Solomon Islands'. *Nature* 237:31. doi.org/10.1038/237031a0.

Anderson, A. 1989. *Prodigious birds: Moas and moa-hunting in prehistoric New Zealand*. Cambridge: Cambridge University Press.

Austen, L. 1939. 'Megalithic structures in the Trobriand Islands'. *Oceania* 10 (1):30–53. doi.org/ 10.1002/j.1834-4461.1939.tb00255.x.

Ballard, C. 1994. 'The centre cannot hold: Trade networks and sacred geography in the Papua New Guinea Highlands'. *Archaeology in Oceania* 29:130–148. doi.org/10.1002/arco.1994.29.3.130.

Balouet, JC and S Olson. 1989. *Fossil birds from late Quaternary deposits in New Caledonia*. Smithsonian Contributions to Zoology 469. Washington, DC: Smithsonian Institution Press.

Barnes, I. 2003. 'Aerial remote-sensing techniques used in the management of archaeological monuments on the British Army's Salisbury Plain Training Area, Wiltshire, UK'. *Archaeological Prospection* 10:83–90. doi.org/10.1002/arp.197.

Bedford, S and M Spriggs. 2008. 'Northern Vanuatu as a Pacific crossroads: The archaeology of discovery, interaction and the emergence of the "ethnographic present"'. *Asian Perspectives* 47 (1):95–120.

Bedford, S, M Spriggs and R Regenvanu. 2006. 'The Teouma Lapita Site and the early human settlement of the Pacific Islands'. *Antiquity* 80:812–828. doi.org/10.1017/S0003598X00094448.

Bedford, S, M Spriggs, H Buckley, F Valentin, R Regenvanu and M Abong. 2010. 'A cemetery of first settlement: Teouma, South Efate, Vanuatu/ Un cimetière de premier peuplement: le site de Teouma, sud d'Efate'. In *Lapita: Ancêtres Océaniens / Oceanic ancestors*, edited by C Sand and S Bedford, 140–161. Paris: Musée de Quai Branly and Somogy Éditions d'Art.

Bedford, S, P Siméoni and V Lebot. 2018. 'The anthropogenic transformation of an island landscape: Evidence for agricultural development revealed by LiDAR on the island of Efate, Central Vanuatu, South-West Pacific'. *Archaeology in Oceania* 53 (1):1–14. doi.org/10.1002/arco.5137.

Bellwood, P. 2017. *First islanders: Prehistory and human migration in Island Southeast Asia*. Hoboken, NJ: Wiley Blackwell. doi.org/10.1002/9781119251583.

Best, S. 1989 [orig. 1984]. *Lakeba: The prehistory of a Fijian island*. Ann Arbor, Michigan: University Microfilms.

Bewley, R. 2003. 'Aerial survey for archaeology'. *Photogrammetric Record* 18 (104):273–292. doi.org/ 10.1046/j.0031-868X.2003.00023.x.

Bewley, R, S Crutchley and C Shell. 2005. 'New light on an ancient landscape: LiDAR survey in the Stonehenge World Heritage Site'. *Antiquity* 79 (305):636–647. doi.org/10.1017/ S0003598X00114577.

Blake-Palmer, G. 1947. 'New Zealand archaeology and air photography'. *Journal of the Polynesian Society* 56 (3):233–241.

Bonnemaison, J. 1974. 'Espaces et paysages agraires des Nouvelles-Hébrides'. *Journal de la Société des Océanistes* 44–45:163–232, 259–281.

Bonnemaison, J. 1979. 'Les voyages et L'enracinement: Formes de fixation et de mobilité dans les sociétés traditionelles des Nouvelles-Hébrides'. *L'Espace Géographique* 4:303–318. doi.org/10.3406/ spgeo.1979.1937.

Boyer, WW and P Robinson. 1955. 'Obsidian artifacts of Northwestern New Mexico and their correlation with source material'. *El Palacio* 63:333–345.

Britton, D and E Richards. 1969. 'Optical emission spectroscopy and the study of metallurgy in the European Bronze Age'. In *Science in Archaeology*, edited by D Brothwell and E Higgs, 2nd edn, 603–613. London: Thames and Hudson.

Brookfield, H and P Brown. 1963. *Struggle for land: Agriculture and group territories among the Chimbu of the New Guinea Highlands*. Melbourne: Oxford University Press.

Brookfield, H and D Hart. 1971. *Melanesia: A Geographical Interpretation of an Island World*. London: Methuen.

Buckley, H. 2001. 'Health and disease in the prehistoric Pacific Islands'. Unpublished PhD thesis, Otago University, Dunedin.

Buckley, H, N Tayles, M Spriggs and S Bedford. 2008. 'A preliminary report on health and disease in Early Lapita skeletons, Vanuatu: Possible biological costs of island colonization'. *Journal of Island and Coastal Archaeology* 3 (1):87–114. doi.org/10.1080/15564890801928300.

Buckley, H, R Kinaston, S Halcrow, A Foster, M Spriggs and S Bedford. 2014. 'Scurvy in a tropical paradise? Evaluating the possibility of infant and adult Vitamin C deficiency in the Lapita skeletal sample of Teouma, Vanuatu, Pacific Islands'. *International Journal of Paleopathology* 5:72–85. doi.org/10.1016/j.ijpp.2014.03.001.

Bulmer, S. 1964a. 'Radiocarbon dates from New Guinea'. *Journal of the Polynesian Society* 73:327–328.

Bulmer, S. 1964b. 'Prehistoric stone implements from the New Guinea Highlands'. *Oceania* 34 (4):246–268. doi.org/10.1002/j.1834-4461.1964.tb00268.x.

Burley, D and M Weisler. 2016. 'William R. Dickinson: Our appreciation of an archaeologist's geologist'. *Archaeology in Oceania* 51 (2):81–83. doi.org/10.1002/arco.5092.

Burton, J. 1987. *Axe makers of the Wahgi: Pre-colonial industrialists of the Papua New Guinea Highlands*. Ann Arbor, Michigan: University Microfilms.

Cann, J and C Renfrew. 1964. 'The characterization of obsidian and its application to the Mediterranean Region'. *Proceedings of the Prehistoric Society* 30:111–133. doi.org/10.1017/S0079497X00015097.

Cann, J, J Dixon and C Renfrew. 1969. 'Obsidian analysis and the obsidian trade'. In *Science in Archaeology*, edited by D Brothwell and E Higgs, 2nd edn, 578–591. London: Thames and Hudson.

Chang, K-C. 1958. 'Study of the Neolithic social grouping: Examples from the New World'. *American Anthropologist* 60:298–334. doi.org/10.1525/aa.1958.60.2.02a00080.

Chang, K-C. 1972. *Settlement Patterns in Archaeology*. Reading, Mass.: Addison-Wesley Publishing.

Chapman, F. 1891. 'On the working of greenstone or nephrite by the Maoris'. *Transactions of the New Zealand Institute* 24:479–539.

Chappell, J and M Strathern. 1966. 'Stone axe factories in the Highlands of East New Guinea, with a note on linguistic boundaries and the axe quarries'. *Proceedings of the Prehistoric Society* 32:96–121. doi.org/10.1017/S0079497X00014365.

Chappell, J, A Omura, M McCulloch, T Esat, Y Ota and J Pandolfi. 1994. 'Revised late Quaternary sea levels between 70 and 30 Ka from coral terraces at Huon Peninsula'. In *Study on Coral Reef Terraces of the Huon Peninsula, Papua New Guinea: Establishment of Quaternary Sea Level and Tectonic History*, edited by Y Ota, 155–165. Yokohama: Department of Geography, Yokohama National University.

Chase, A, D Chase, C Fisher, S Leisz and J Weishampel. 2012. 'Geospatial revolution and remote sensing LiDAR in Mesoamerican archaeology'. *Proceedings of the National Academy of Sciences* 109 (32):12916–12921. doi.org/10.1073/pnas.1205198109.

Clark, D. 1961. 'The obsidian dating method'. *Current Anthropology* 2(2):111–114. doi.org/10.1086/200172.

Clark, G. 1965. 'Traffic in stone axe and adze blades'. *Essays in Economic History Presented to Professor M.M. Postan. The Economic History Review* (new series) 18 (1):1–28. doi.org/10.2307/2591871.

Clarke, D. 1973. 'Archaeology: The loss of innocence'. *Antiquity* 47:6–18. doi.org/10.1017/S0003598X0003461X.

Clarkson, C [and 27 others]. 2017. 'Human occupation of Northern Australia by 65,000 years ago'. *Nature* 547:306–310. doi.org/10.1038/nature22968.

Crane, HR. 1956. 'University of Michigan radiocarbon dates 1'. *Science* 124 (3324):664–672. doi.org/10.1126/science.124.3224.664.

Crawford, OGS. 1928. *Air survey and archaeology*. London: HMSO.

Crawford, OGS. 1953. *Archaeology in the field*. London: Phoenix House.

Crosby, E. 1963. 'Preliminary report on Whiritoa'. *New Zealand Archaeological Association Newsletter* 6:46–49.

Damour, A. 1865. 'Sur la composition des haches en pierre trouvées dans les monuments Celtiques et chez les tribus sauvages'. *Comptes Rendus Hebdomadaires des Séances de l'Académie des Sciences* 60:313–321, 61:357–368.

Daniel, G. 1975. *A hundred and fifty years of Archaeology*. 2nd edn. London: Duckworth.

Devereux, B, G Amable, P Crow and A Cliff. 2005. 'The potential of airborne lidar for detection of archaeological features under woodland canopies'. *Antiquity* 79 (305):648–660. doi.org/10.1017/S0003598X00114589.

Dickinson, P and M Sykes. 1965. 'Kuro manufacture in Yavulo Village'. *Records of the Fiji Museum* 1 (1):69–72.

Dickinson, WR. 1969. 'Temper sands in prehistoric potsherds from Vailele and Falefa'. In *Archaeology in Western Samoa*, Volume 1, edited by R Green and J Davidson, 271–273. *Auckland Institute and Museum Bulletin* 6. Auckland: Auckland Institute and Museum.

Dickinson, W. 1971. 'Petrography of some temper sands in prehistoric pottery from Viti Levu, Fiji'. *Records of the Fiji Museum* 1 (5):107–121.

Dickinson, W. 2006. *Temper sands in prehistoric Oceanian pottery: Geotectonics, sedimentology, petrography, provenance*. The Geological Society of America Special Paper 406. Boulder, Colorado: The Geological Society of America.

Dickinson, WR and R Shutler Jr. 1968. 'Insular sand tempers of prehistoric pottery from the Southwest Pacific'. In *Prehistoric culture in Oceania*, edited by I Yawata and Y Sinoto, 29–37. Honolulu: Bishop Museum Press.

Evans, D, R Fletcher, C Pottier, J-B Chevance, D Soutif, BS Tan, S Im, D Ea, T Tin, S Kim, C Cromarty, S de Greef, K Hanus, P Baty, R Kuszinger, I Shimoda and G Boornazian. 2014. 'Uncovering archaeological landscapes at Angkor using LiDAR'. *Proceedings of the National Academy of Sciences* 110 (31):12595–12600.

Firth, R. 1959. 'Ritual adzes in Tikopia'. In *Anthropology in the South Seas: Essays Presented to H.D. Skinner,* edited by JD Freeman and WR Geddes, 149–159. New Plymouth, NZ: Thomas Avery and Sons.

Flannery, T. 1995. *Mammals of New Guinea*. Revised and updated edition. Chatswood, NSW: Reed Books.

Flannery, T and S Wickler. 1990. 'Quaternary murids (Rodentia: Muridae) from Buka Island, Papua New Guinea, with descriptions of two new species'. *Australian Mammalogy* 13:127–139.

Foster, A, R Kinaston, M Spriggs, S Bedford, A Gray and H Buckley. 2018. 'Possible diffuse idiopathic skeletal hyperostosis (DISH) in a 3000-year-old Pacific Island skeletal assemblage'. *Journal of Archaeological Science: Reports* 18:408–419. doi.org/10.1016/j.jasrep.2018.01.002.

Fox, C. 1923. *The archaeology of the Cambridge region: A topographical study of the Bronze, Early Iron, Roman and Anglo-Saxon Ages, with an introductory note on the Neolithic Age*. Cambridge: Cambridge University Press.

Freeland, T, B Heung, D Burley, G Clark and A Knudby. 2016. 'Automated feature extraction for prospection and analysis of monumental earthworks from aerial LiDAR in the Kingdom of Tonga'. *Journal of Archaeological Science* 69:64–74. doi.org/10.1016/j.jas.2016.04.011.

Friedman, I, R Smith, C Evans and B Meggers. 1960. 'A new dating method using obsidian'. *American Antiquity* 25:476–537. doi.org/10.2307/276634.

Garanger, J. 1972. *Archéologie des Nouvelles-Hébrides: Contribution à la connaissance des îles du Centre*. Publications de la Société des Océanistes 30. Paris: Société des Océanistes, Musée de l'Homme. doi.org/10.4000/books.sdo.859.

Gifford, E. 1951. *Archaeological Excavations in Fiji*. Anthropological records 13(3). Berkeley and Los Angeles: University of California Press.

Gifford, E. 1952. 'A carbon-14 date from Fiji'. *Journal of the Polynesian Society* 61:237.

Gifford, E. 1955. 'Six Fijian radiocarbon dates'. *Journal of the Polynesian Society* 64:240.

Gifford, E and D Gifford. 1959. *Archaeological excavations in Yap*. Anthropological Records 18(2). Berkeley and Los Angeles: University of California Press.

Gifford, E and R Shutler Jr. 1956. *Archaeological excavations in New Caledonia*. Anthropological Records 18(1). Berkeley and Los Angeles: University of California Press.

Godelier, M with J Garanger. 1973. 'Outils de pierre, outils d'acier chez les Baruya de Nouvelle-Guinée: Quelques données ethnographiques et quantitatives'. *L'Homme* 13:187–220. doi.org/10.3406/hom.1973.367374.

Golson, J. 1957a. 'New Zealand archaeology, 1957'. *Journal of the Polynesian Society* 66(3):271–290.

Golson, J. 1957b. 'Field archaeology in New Zealand'. *Journal of the Polynesian Society* 66(1):64–109.

Golson, J. 1962. 'Submissions on the development of prehistory at The Australian National University, Canberra. Submitted to the Universities Commission 1962'. Unpublished typescript in possession of the author. ANU, Canberra.

Golson, J. 1986. 'Old guards and new waves: Reflections on Antipodean archaeology, 1954–1975'. *Archaeology in Oceania* 21 (1):2–12. doi.org/10.1002/j.1834-4453.1986.tb00120.x.

Golson, J and R Green. 1959. *A handbook to archaeological field recording in New Zealand*. NZAA Handbook 1. Auckland: New Zealand Archaeological Association.

Gosden, C and C Pavlides. 1994. 'Are islands insular? Landscape vs. seascape in the case of the Arawe Islands, Papua New Guinea'. *Archaeology in Oceania* 29:162–171. doi.org/10.1002/arco.1994.29.3.162.

Green, JH, J Harris, JWG Neuhaus, DKB Sewell and M Watson. 1965. 'University of New South Wales radiocarbon dates I'. *Radiocarbon* 7:162–165. doi.org/10.1017/S0033822200037140.

Green, R. 1962. 'Obsidian, its application to archaeology'. *New Zealand Archaeological Association Newsletter* 5:8–16.

Green, R. 1964. 'Sources, ages and exploitation of New Zealand obsidian: An interim report'. *New Zealand Archaeological Association Newsletter* 7:134–143.

Green, R. 1978. 'Notes on adze flakes, oven stones, pumice, muscovite-garnet schist and metamorphosed sandstone specimens from the main Reef/Santa Cruz Lapita Sites, Southeast Solomons'. *Oceanic Prehistory Records* 7:29–35. Microfiche. Auckland: University of Auckland Archaeological Society.

Green, R, R Brooks and R Reeves. 1967. 'Characterisation of New Zealand obsidians by emission spectroscopy'. *New Zealand Journal of Science* 10:675–682.

Grimes, W. 1979. 'The history of implement petrology in Britain'. In *Stone axe studies*, edited by TMcK Clough and W Cummins, 1–4. CBA Research Report 23. London: Council for British Archaeology.

Groube, L. 1965. *Settlement patterns in New Zealand*. Occasional Papers in Archaeology 1. Dunedin: Department of Anthropology, University of Otago.

Groube, L, J Chappell, J Muke and D Price. 1986. 'A 40,000 year-old human occupation site at Huon Peninsula, Papua New Guinea'. *Nature* 324:453–455. doi.org/10.1038/324453a0.

Harker, A. 1935. 'Herbert Henry Thomas 1876–1935'. *Obituary Notices of Fellows of the Royal Society* 1 (4):590–594.

Heine-Geldern, R. 1932. 'Urheimat und Früheste Wanderungen der Austronesier'. *Anthropos* 27:543–619.

Hughes, P, G Hope and M Latham. 1979. 'Prehistoric man-induced degradation of the Lakeba landscape: Evidence from two inland swamps'. In *Lakeba: Environmental change, population dynamics and resource use*, edited by H Brookfield, 93–110. UNESCO/UNFPA Population and Environment Project in the Eastern Outer Islands of Fiji, Island Reports 5. Canberra: UNESCO.

Keiller, A, S Piggott and F Wallis. 1941. 'First report of the sub-committee of the South-Western Group of Museums and Art Galleries on the petrological identification of stone axes'. *Proceedings of the Prehistoric Society* 7:50–72. doi.org/10.1017/S0079497X00020272.

Key, C. 1968a. 'Pottery manufacture in the Wanigela area of Collingwood Bay, Papua'. *Mankind* 6 (12):653–657. doi.org/10.1111/j.1835-9310.1968.tb00758.x.

Key, C. 1968b. 'Trace element identification of the source of obsidian in an archaeological site in New Guinea'. *Nature* 219:360. doi.org/10.1038/219360a0.

Key, C. 1969. 'The identification of New Guinea obsidians'. *Archaeology and Physical Anthropology in Oceania* 4:47–55.

Kidder, A and A Shepard. 1936. *The pottery of Pecos, Volume 2.* Papers of the Southwestern Expedition 7. New Haven: Yale University Press.

Kinaston, R and H Buckley. 2017. 'Isotopic insights into diet and health at the site of Namu, Taumako Island, Southeast Solomon Islands'. *Archaeological and Anthropological Sciences* 9 (7):1421–1437. doi.org/10.1007/s12520-016-0440-y.

Kinaston, R, HR Buckley, F Valentin, S Bedford, M Spriggs, S Hawkins and E Herrscher. 2014. 'Lapita diet in Remote Oceania: New stable isotope evidence from the 3000-year-old Teouma Site, Efate Island, Vanuatu'. *PLoS ONE* 9 (3):e90376. doi.org/10.1371/journal.pone.0090376.

Kirch, P. 1985. *Feathered gods and fishhooks: An introduction to Hawaiian archaeology and prehistory.* Honolulu: University of Hawai'i Press.

Kirch, P. 1997. 'Introduction: The environmental history of Oceanic islands'. In *Historical ecology in the Pacific Islands: Prehistoric environmental and landscape change*, edited by P Kirch and T Hunt, 1–21. New Haven and London: Yale University Press. doi.org/10.2307/j.ctt211qz1v.6.

Kirch, P. 2017. *On the road of the winds: An archaeological history of the Pacific Islands before European contact.* Revised and expanded edition. Oakland: University of California Press.

Kirch, P and T Hunt (eds). 1997. *Historical ecology in the Pacific Islands: Prehistoric environmental and landscape change.* New Haven and London: Yale University Press. doi.org/10.2307/j.ctt211qz1v.6.

Kirch, P and D Yen. 1982. *Tikopia: The prehistory and ecology of a Polynesian outlier.* B.P. Bishop Museum Bulletin 238. Honolulu: Bishop Museum Press.

Ladefoged, T, M McCoy, G Asner, P Kirch, C Puleston, O Chadwick and P Vitousek. 2011. 'Agricultural potential and actualized development in Hawai'i: An airborne LiDAR survey of the leeward Kohala field system (Hawai'i Island)'. *Journal of Archaeological Science* 38 (12):3605–3619. doi.org/10.1016/j.jas.2011.08.031.

Leach, F and J Davidson. 2008. *The archaeology of Taumako: A Polynesian outlier in the Eastern Solomon Islands.* New Zealand Journal of Archaeology Special Publication. Dunedin: New Zealand Journal of Archaeology.

Libby, W. 1951. 'Radiocarbon dates, II'. *Science* 114 (2960):291–296. doi.org/10.1126/science.114.2960.291.

Lockerbie, L. 1959. 'From moa-hunter to classic Maori in southern New Zealand'. In *Anthropology in the south seas: Essays presented to H.D. Skinner*, edited by JD Freeman and WR Geddes, 75–110. New Plymouth, NZ: Thomas Avery and Sons.

Lyons, AP. 1922. 'Sepulchral pottery of Murua, Papua'. *Man* 22 (Article 93):164–165.

Malinowski, B. 1934. 'Stone implements in Eastern New Guinea'. In *Essays presented to C.G. Seligman*, edited by E Evans-Pritchard, R Firth, B Malinowski and I Schapera, 189–196. London: Kegan Paul, Trench, Trubner & Co.

Marshall, Y, A Crosby, S Mataraba and S Wood. 2000. *Sigatoka: The shifting sands of prehistory.* Oxford: Oxbow Books.

Matson, F. 1969. 'Some aspects of ceramic technology'. In *Science in archaeology*, edited by D Brothwell and E Higgs, 2nd edn, 90–602. Thames and Hudson, London.

May, P and M Tuckson. 1982. *The traditional pottery of Papua New Guinea.* Bay Books, Sydney.

McCoy, M, G Asner and M Graves. 2011. 'Airborne lidar survey of irrigated agricultural landscapes: An application of the slope contrast method'. *Journal of Archaeological Science* 38 (9):2141–2154. doi.org/10.1016/j.jas.2011.02.033.

Mead, J, D Steadman, S Bedford, C Bell and M Spriggs. 2002. 'New extinct Mekosuchine crocodile from Vanuatu, South Pacific'. *Copeia* 2002 (3):632–641. doi.org/10.1643/0045-8511(2002)002 [0632:NEMCFV]2.0.CO;2.

Moore, P. 1978. 'Petrography of adzes from the Southeast Solomons'. *Oceanic Prehistory Records* 7:8–28. Microfiche. Auckland: University of Auckland Archaeological Society.

Mountain, MJ. 1979. 'The rescue of the ancestors in Papua New Guinea'. *Institute of Archaeology, University of London, Bulletin* 16:63–80.

Moyne, Lord and K Haddon. 1936. 'The pygmies of the Aiome Mountains, Mandated Territory of New Guinea'. *Journal of the Royal Anthropological Institute* 66:269–290.

Mulvaney, DJ. 1993. 'From Cambridge to the bush'. In *A community of culture: The people and prehistory of the Pacific*, edited by M Spriggs, D Yen, W Ambrose, R Jones, A Thorne and A Andrews, 18–26. Occasional Papers in Prehistory 21. Canberra: Department of Prehistory, Research School of Pacific Studies, The Australian National University.

Mulvaney, DJ. 2011. *Digging up a past*. Sydney: UNSW Press.

Osborne, D. 1966. *The archaeology of the Palau Islands: An intensive survey*. B.P. Bishop Museum Bulletin 230. Honolulu: Bishop Museum Press.

Parker, R and P Sheppard. 1997. 'Pacific Island adze geochemistry studies at the University of Auckland'. In *Prehistoric long-distance interaction in Oceania: An interdisciplinary approach*, edited by M Weisler, 205–211. NZAA Monograph 21. Auckland: New Zealand Archaeological Association.

Parry, J. 1977. *Ring-ditch fortifications in the Rewa Delta: Air photo interpretation and analysis*. Bulletin of the Fiji Museum 7.

Parry, J. 1997. *The north coast of Viti Levu, Ba to Ra: Air photo archaeology and ethnohistory*. Bulletin of the Fiji Museum 10.

Parsons, J. 1972. 'Archaeological settlement patterns'. *Annual Review of Anthropology* 1:127–150. doi.org/10.1146/annurev.an.01.100172.001015.

Petchey, P, H Buckley, R Walter, D Anson and R Kinaston. 2016. 'The 2008–2009 excavations at the SAC Locality, Reber-Rakival Lapita Site, Watom Island, Papua New Guinea'. *Journal of Indo-Pacific Archaeology* 40:12–31. doi.org/10.7152/jipa.v40i0.14928.

Pétrequin, P and A-M Pétrequin. 1993. *Ecologie d'un outil: La hache de pierre en Irian Jaya (Indonésie)*. Monographe du CRA 12. Paris: CNRS Editions.

Phillips, C and M Campbell. 2004. 'From settlement patterns to interdisciplinary landscapes in New Zealand'. In *Change through time: 50 years of New Zealand archaeology*, edited by L Furey and S Holdaway, 85–104. NZAA Monograph 26. Auckland: New Zealand Archaeological Association.

Plane, M. 1972. 'Fauna from the basal clay of Kafiavana'. In *Ol Tumbuna: Archaeological excavations in the eastern Central Highlands, Papua New Guinea*, edited by JP White, 168. Terra Australis 2. Canberra: Department of Prehistory, Research School of Pacific Studies, The Australian National University.

Poulsen, J. 1987. *Early Tongan prehistory*, Volume 1. Terra Australis 12. Canberra: Department of Prehistory, Research School of Pacific Studies, The Australian National University.

Quintus, S, J Clark, S Day and D Schwert. 2015. 'Investigating regional patterning in archaeological remains by pairing extensive survey with a lidar dataset: The case of the Manu'a Group, American Samoa'. *Journal of Archaeological Science: Reports* 2:677–687. doi.org/10.1016/j.jasrep.2014.11.010.

Rae, ID. 2018. 'Radiocarbon dating at the Museum of Applied Science Victoria 1952–70: A pioneer venture'. *Historical Records of Australian Science* 29:14–27. doi.org/10.1071/HR17019.

Reimer, P [and 27 others]. 2009. 'Intcal09 and Marine09 radiocarbon age calibration curves, 0–50,000 years cal BP'. *Radiocarbon* 51 (4):1111–1150. doi.org/10.1017/S0033822200034202.

Riesenfeld, A. 1952. 'Was there a Palaeolithic period in Melanesia?' *Anthropos* 47:405–446.

Roberts, R, R Jones and M Smith. 1990. 'Thermoluminescence dating of a 50,000-year-old human occupation site in Northern Australia'. *Nature* 345:153–156. doi.org/10.1038/345153a0.

Roberts, R, R Jones and M Smith. 1993. 'Optical dating at Deaf Adder Gorge, Northern Territory, indicates human occupation back to between 53,000 and 60,0000 years ago'. *Australian Archaeology* 37:58–59. doi.org/10.1080/03122417.1993.11681497.

Roux, J. 1990. 'Traditional Melanesian agriculture in New Caledonia and pre-contact population distribution'. In *Pacific production systems: Approaches to economic prehistory*, edited by D Yen and J Mummery, 161–173. Occasional Papers in Prehistory 18. Canberra: Department of Prehistory, Research School of Pacific Studies, The Australian National University.

Santayana, G. 1905. *The life of reason, volume 1: Reason in commonsense.* New York: Charles Scribner.

Sarasin, F. 2009 [orig. 1929]. *Ethnographie des Kanak de Nouvelle-Calédonie et des Iles Loyauté.* Paris: Ibis Press [Originally published as *Ethnologie der Neu-Kaledonier und Loyalty-Insulaner.* Munich: C.W. Kreidel's Verlag].

Scarlett, R. 1958. 'Obsidian'. *New Zealand Archaeological Association Newsletter* 2 (1):3.

Seligmann, C. 1910. *The Melanesians of British New Guinea.* Cambridge: Cambridge University Press.

Seligmann, C and TA Joyce. 1907. 'On prehistoric objects in British New Guinea'. In *Anthropological essays presented to Edward Burnett Tylor in honour of his 75th birthday Oct. 2 1907*, 325–341. Oxford: Clarendon Press.

Seligmann, C and W Strong. 1906. 'Anthropogeographical investigations in British New Guinea'. *Geographical Journal* 27 (3):225–242, 27 (4):347–369.

Sheppard, P. 1996. 'Hard rock: Archaeological implications of chert sourcing in Near and Remote Oceania'. In *Oceanic culture history: Essays in honour of Roger Green*, edited by J Davidson, G Irwin, F Leach, A Pawley and D Brown, 99–115. *New Zealand Journal of Archaeology Special Publication.* Dunedin: New Zealand Journal of Archaeology.

Skinner, H. 1933. 'Greenstone in the Cook group'. *Journal of the Polynesian Society* 42 (3):225–226.

Skinner, H. 1953. 'An argillite adze from Taranaki'. *Journal of the Polynesian Society* 62 (1):81–83.

Smith, WC. 1963. 'Jade axes from sites in the British Isles'. *Proceedings of the Prehistoric Society* 34:133–172. doi.org/10.1017/S0079497X00015371.

Specht, J, I Lilley and J Normu. 1981. 'Radiocarbon dates from West New Britain, Papua New Guinea'. *Australian Archaeology* 12:13–15.

Specht, J, I Lilley and J Normu. 1983. 'More on radiocarbon dates from West New Britain, Papua New Guinea'. *Australian Archaeology* 16:92–95.

Spoehr, A. 1957. *Marianas prehistory: Archaeological survey and excavations on Saipan, Tinian and Rota.* Fieldiana Anthropology 48. Chicago: Field Museum of Natural History.

Spriggs, M. 1985. '"A school in every district": The cultural geography of conversion on Aneityum, Southern Vanuatu'. *Journal of Pacific History* 20 (1 & 2):51–64. doi.org/10.1080/0022334850857 2503.

Spriggs, M. 1987 [orig. 1981]. *Vegetable kingdoms: Taro irrigation and Pacific prehistory*. Ann Arbor, Michigan: University Microfilms.

Steadman, D. 2006. *Extinction and biogeography of tropical Pacific birds*. Chicago and London: University of Chicago Press.

Stuiver, M and P Reimer. 1993. 'Extended ^{14}C data base and revised CALIB 3.0 ^{14}C age calibration program'. *Radiocarbon* 35:215–230. doi.org/10.1017/S0033822200013904.

Summerhayes, G. 2009. 'Obsidian network patterns in Melanesia: Sources, characterisation and distribution'. *Indo-Pacific Prehistory Association Bulletin* 29:109–123.

Summerhayes, G, J Bird, R Fullagar, C Gosden, J Specht and R Torrence. 1998. 'Application of PIXE-PIGME to archaeological analysis of changing patterns of obsidian use in West New Britain, Papua New Guinea'. In *Archaeological obsidian studies: Method and theory*, edited by M Shackley, 129–158. New York: Plenum Press. doi.org/10.1007/978-1-4757-9276-8_6.

Summerhayes, G, M Leavesley, A Fairbairn, H Mandui, J Field, A Ford and R Fullagar. 2010. 'Human adaptation and plant use in Highland New Guinea 49,000 to 44,000 years ago'. *Science* 330:78–81. doi.org/10.1126/science.1193130.

Thomas, H. 1923. 'The source of the stones of Stonehenge'. *Antiquaries Journal* 3:239–260. doi.org/10.1017/S0003581500005096.

Thorpe, W. 1929. 'Evidence of Polynesian culture in Australia and Norfolk Island'. *Journal of the Polynesian Society* 38 (2):122–126.

Torrence, R [and 11 others]. 2004. 'Pleistocene colonisation of the Bismarck Archipelago: New evidence from West New Britain'. *Archaeology in Oceania* 39:101–130. doi.org/10.1002/j.1834-4453.2004.tb00568.x.

Turner, F. 1935. 'Geological investigation of the nephrites, serpentines, and related "greenstones" used by the Maoris of Otago and South Canterbury'. *Transactions of the Royal Society of New Zealand* 65:187–210.

Valentin, F, S Bedford, H Buckley and M Spriggs. 2010a. 'Lapita burial practices: Evidence for complex body and bone treatment at the Teouma Cemetery, Vanuatu, Southwest Pacific'. *Journal of Island and Coastal Archaeology* 5:1–24. doi.org/10.1080/15564891003648092.

Valentin, F, H Buckley, E Herrscher, R Kinaston, S Bedford, M Spriggs, S Hawkins and K Neal. 2010b. 'Lapita subsistence strategies and food consumption patterns in the community of Teouma (Efate, Vanuatu)'. *Journal of Archaeological Science* 37:1820–1829. doi.org/10.1016/j.jas.2010.01.039.

Valentin, F, E Herrscher, S Bedford, M Spriggs and H Buckley. 2014. 'Evidence for social and cultural change in Central Vanuatu during the first millennium BC: Comparing funerary and dietary patterns of the first and later generations at Teouma, Efate'. *Journal of Island and Coastal Archaeology* 9 (3):381–399. doi.org/10.1080/15564894.2014.921958.

Verhofstad, J. 1966. 'Glaucophanitic stone implements from West New Guinea (West Irian)'. *Geologie en Mijnbouw* 45:291–300.

Vial, L. 1940. 'Stone axes of Mount Hagen, New Guinea'. *Oceania* 11:158–163. doi.org/10.1002/j.1834-4461.1940.tb00282.x.

Warren, SH. 1919. 'A stone axe factory at Graig-Lwyd, Penmaenmawr'. *Journal of the Royal Anthropological Institute* 49:342–365.

Warren, SH. 1921. 'Excavations at the stone axe factory of Graig-Lwyd, Penmaenmawr'. *Journal of the Royal Anthropological Institute* 51:165–199.

Weisler, M (ed.). 1997. *Prehistoric long-distance interaction in Oceania: An interdisciplinary approach*. NZAA Monograph 21. Auckland: New Zealand Archaeological Association.

White, A, T Worthy, S Hawkins, S Bedford and M Spriggs. 2010. 'Megafaunal Meiolaniid horned turtles survived until early human settlement in Vanuatu, Southwest Pacific'. *Proceedings of the National Academy of Sciences* 107:15512–15516. doi.org/10.1073/pnas.1005780107.

White, JP. 1967. 'Ethnoarchaeology in New Guinea: Two examples'. *Mankind* 6:409–414.

White, JP. 1968. 'Fabricators, outils écaillés or scalar cores?' *Mankind* 6:658–666.

White, JP. 1972. *Ol Tumbuna: Archaeological excavations in the eastern Central Highlands, Papua New Guinea*. Terra Australis 2. Canberra: Department of Prehistory, Research School of Pacific Studies, The Australian National University.

White, JP and J O'Connell. 1982. *A prehistory of Australia, New Guinea and Sahul*. Sydney: Academic Press.

White, JP, K Crook and B Ruxton. 1970. 'Kosipe: A Late Pleistocene site in the Papuan Highlands'. *Proceedings of the Prehistoric Society* 36:152–170. doi.org/10.1017/S0079497X00013128.

White, JP, N Modjeska and I Hipuya. 1977. 'Group definitions and mental templates: An ethnographic experiment'. In *Stone tools as cultural markers: Change, evolution, complexity*, edited by R Wright, 380–390. Canberra: Australian Institute of Aboriginal Studies.

Wickler, S and M Spriggs. 1988. 'Pleistocene human occupation of the Solomon Islands, Melanesia'. *Antiquity* 62 (237):703–706. doi.org/10.1017/S0003598X00075104.

Willey, G. 1953. *Prehistoric settlement patterns in the Viru Valley, Peru*. Bureau of American Ethnology Bulletin 155. Washington DC: Bureau of American Ethnology.

Worthy, T, S Hawkins, S Bedford and M Spriggs. 2015. 'Avifauna from the Teouma Lapita Site, Efate Island, Vanuatu, including a new genus and species of megapode'. *Pacific Science* 69 (2):205–254. doi.org/10.2984/69.2.6.

Landscapes and complexities

3

Saltwater and bush in New Georgia, Solomon Islands: Exchange relations, agricultural intensification and limits to social complexity

Tim Bayliss-Smith, Matthew Prebble and Stephen Manebosa

The wet and the dry in Island Melanesia

Before European contact and its various effects, the cultivation of taro (*Colocasia esculenta*) was widespread in Island Melanesia. Taro was grown alongside yams, bananas and vegetables in dryland swiddens, and also in irrigated or wetland sites (Rivers 1926:264). Matthew Spriggs (1990:175) divided the ecological contexts for wetland cultivation into (1) swampland cultivation, where water tables were lowered by digging drainage ditches, which enabled taro to be cultivated in 'island beds'; (2) pit cultivation to tap ground water, a practice developed mainly on coral islands and atolls; and (3) true irrigation in which water was diverted to fields by canals or pipes, being delivered to the crop by simple flooding, in furrows, within pondfields or by flowing around island beds.

It was true irrigation that was often noted by early European visitors like de Queirós in Santo, Vanuatu (Purchas [1625] 1906:221–225; Spriggs 2012; Yen 1976). Although irrigation and water control was extensive on Santo, Rivers (1926:265–266) noted that these practices were not universal in the islands, being sometimes absent even where streams or springs were abundant. Today in Vanuatu, dryland cultivation in swiddens is much more widespread than wetland management (Kirch 1994; Weightman 1989:88), and everywhere disease problems have resulted in a massive decline in taro and its replacement in the diet by sweet potato, cassava and purchased grain foods (Bourke 2012).

Irrigated taro in Solomon Islands

Rivers (1926:269, 283) noted that irrigated taro in Solomon Islands was 'extensive' on Kolobangara but altogether absent from other islands; for example Santa Isabel and Guadalcanal. This patchy distribution in the post-contact period has been confirmed by later scholars, although parts of north Guadalcanal were a different landscape when Mendaña visited in 1568 (Amherst and Thompson 1901:306; Roe 1993, 2000).

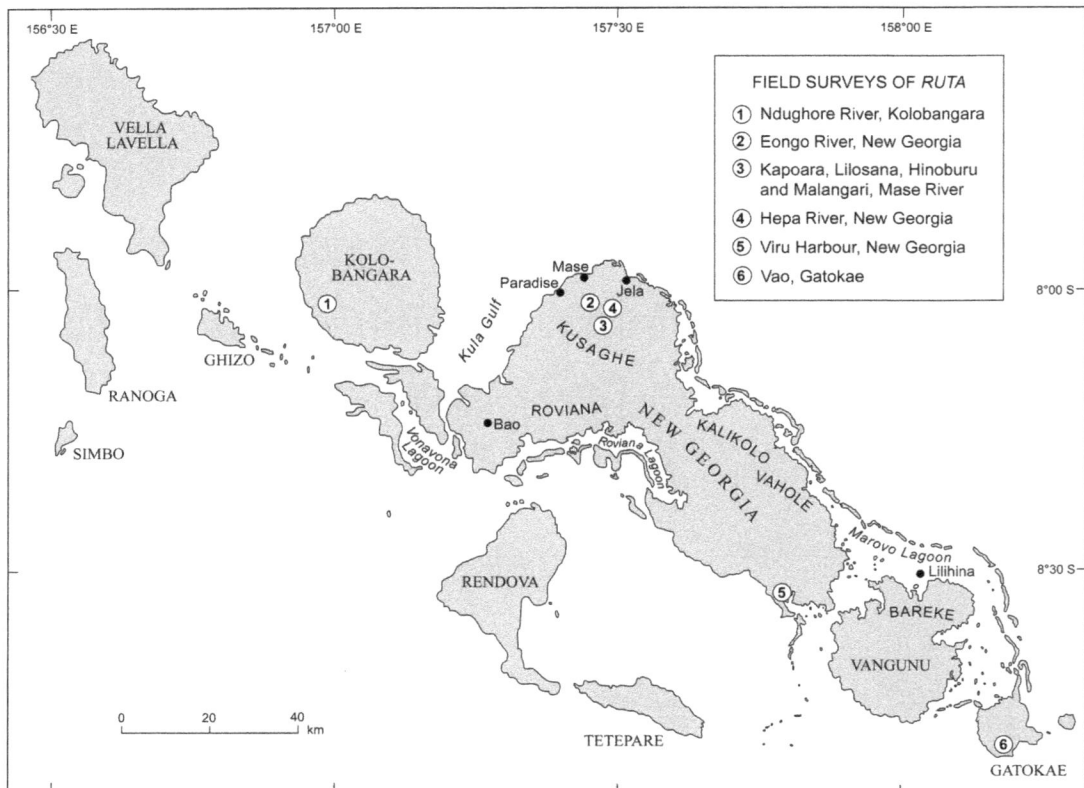

Figure 3.1. Localities in the western Solomons where terraced irrigated taro (*ruta*) has been reported and surveyed.

Source: Tim Bayliss-Smith, using the following data sources: (1) Kolobangara—Yen 1976, 2009; Scales 2003; (2) and (3) Kusaghe, Eongo and Mase—M Tedder with Barrus 1976; Bayliss-Smith and Hviding 2015; this paper; (4) Kusaghe, Hepa—J Tedder 1968; (5) Viru Harbour—Miller 1979; (6) Gatokae—Bayliss-Smith and Hviding 2012, 2014, 2015.

Cultivation using irrigated terraces was a practice most fully developed in the New Georgia group and Kolobangara, but may have been present on other islands (Bayliss-Smith and Hviding 2012, 2014, 2015; Bayliss-Smith et al. 2003; Hviding and Bayliss-Smith 2000; M Tedder with Barrus 1976). The map showing known sites with terraced irrigated taro (*ruta*) is based on published records and no doubt could be extended through oral testimony or fieldwork (Figure 3.1).

In the 1960s abandoned systems of taro terracing were reported in the western Solomons, especially Kolobangara and the New Georgia group (Miller 1979). In the interiors of these large forested islands, reports described a relict landscape of terraced pondfields, stone-backed terraces and irrigation channels (Chikamori 1966). It appeared that valley cultivation had been linked to settlements on nearby ridgetops and to sacred sites with megaliths or standing stones (J Tedder 1968). In some places logging, mineral prospecting and field surveys began to reveal widespread evidence for a substantial bush population (Page 1964).

Margaret Tedder in 1974 and Susan Barrus in 1975 carried out surveys of the Mase Crater in north New Georgia, combining their maps and observations in a joint publication (M Tedder with Barrus 1976). As well as taro grown mostly in irrigated terraces, their informants mentioned several other sources of plant food including nuts from *Canarium* groves, wild bananas, wild yams, and cultivated bananas and sugar cane from swiddens. Already it was too late to recover much oral history, as the old men had been small boys when the last of the Mase *ruta* had been abandoned in 1917 after the surviving population all moved down to coastal villages such as Paradise, Mase and Njela (Jela).

The fieldwork of Tedder and Barrus focused on the upper basin of the Mase river, in the area they called 'Old Kusaghe'. They surveyed in detail two complete *ruta* systems and mapped the total extent of *ruta* in the Mase Crater. They recorded 15 settlement sites marked by house platforms and standing stones, and connected by graded 'roads' 2–5 m wide. They also discovered rock art and sacred sites containing skull shrines, shell valuables (*poata*) and, on occasion, evidence for 19th-century trade goods such as clay pipes, a musket and blue-figured glazed pottery. Ceremonial feasting with taro puddings was suggested by the discovery at Kokorapa of a large, upturned, canoe-shaped food bowl (*horete*) in a rotten state, within a rock shelter that also contained skulls, shell valuables and some trade goods. The food bowl was said by informants to have been 'used to bring taro and *ngali* nut pudding … as an offering to the spirits' (M Tedder with Barrus 1976:83).

Tedder and Barrus estimated that the total area in Mase Crater with *ruta* terracing was 100 hectares, requiring work inputs from a substantial population. From her work in the archives of the British Solomon Islands Government, Tedder knew that the whole region experienced severe depopulation in the decades before and after 1900. Pioneer missionary Rev. JF Goldie told the Phillips Land Commission in 1923 that after migrating to the coast in 1917, the surviving population of Kusaghe District numbered only 300 people. Goldie estimated that in the past each inland village had 40–50 inhabitants, which suggested to Tedder a former bush population of about 600–750 people (M Tedder with Barrus 1976:47).

Our maps now show at least 19 sites of villages in the Mase Crater. Of course, the population of each could have been larger than '40–50 people' if numbers in the 19th century were already being affected by depopulation. Tedder calculated the total area of the Mase basin was 24 km² and she estimated that about one third was potentially arable land. Using multipliers for the carrying capacity of taro swiddens derived from Barrau (1958) and Brookfield with Hart (1971), she estimated that taro cultivation on this land could have supported at least 1000 people (M Tedder with Barrus 1976:48).

Using vegetation maps based on 1960s aerial photography, these estimates could be tested further (Bayliss-Smith et al. 2003). In the Kusaghe area the various 'disturbance forests' that had been mapped totalled 10.2 km² in area. With an assumed economy of swiddening and using conservative assumptions for yield and fallow length, this land could have supported a population of 1100. The calculated number rises to 2400 people if one assumes 10 per cent of the disturbance forests were once under wet taro, cultivated more intensively than swiddens and without fallow periods. A population of 2400 implies an overall density of 7.5 persons per km², a density comparable to populations in inland areas of south Bougainville and north Malaita in the mid-20th century (Bayliss-Smith et al. 2003:350).

Ruta in the Eongo Valley

We now turn to field evidence for the layout and functioning of one particular *ruta* system along the Eongo River, north New Georgia, based on our joint fieldwork in 2016. The whole Eongo Valley has been logged in recent years by Pacific Everest Company and some *ruta* have been damaged or destroyed, but enough evidence survives to show that taro terraces once extended from the Eongo's headwaters to its confluence with the Mase. We hope that our excavations from two *ruta* sites in the upper Eongo and another site in the Mase Crater will provide inferences about the building of *ruta* walls, the control of water and connections to nearby habitation sites. Here we focus on the physical evidence that survives at Eongo Ruta 1 and 2 (altitude 450 m), with two radiocarbon dates that provide insights about when this landscape of intensification was first initiated.

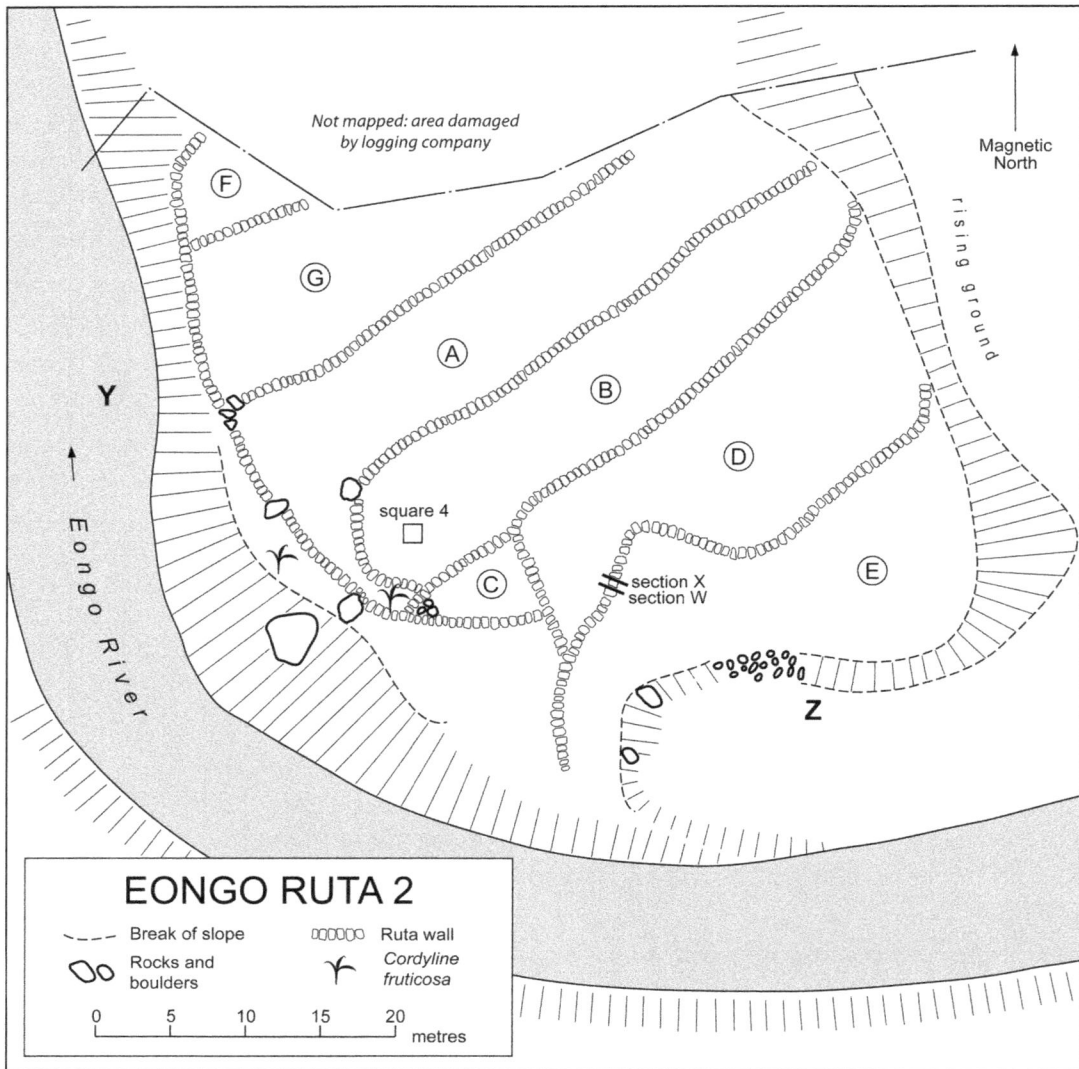

Figure 3.2. Eongo Ruta 2 showing the seven pondfields surviving after damage by loggers, and the location of the first excavation (Square 4).

Source: Stephen Manebosa, field mapping, redrawn.

We have analysed the stratigraphy of seven 1x1 m squares that we excavated at these two sites, plus the evidence from adjacent river banks and cores taken in *ruta* pondfields. These all provide evidence for forest clearance in the Eongo catchment with peaks on at least two separate occasions. A side effect of clearance was the deposition of alluvial gravel, sand, silt and charcoal on the river terrace. The sediments were spread by overbank flooding and resulted from accelerated erosion in the Eongo headwaters. At a later stage, *ruta* walls were constructed on both sites, some of which are visible today, and the flow of water between adjacent pondfields was regulated (Figure 3.2).

It may be possible to match the history of Eongo forest disturbance to the chronology of climate change, in particular the lower rainfall experienced during the Little Ice Age, a period which began around 1300 CE and peaked in the 18th century. Since that time the western Solomons has experienced higher and less seasonal rainfalls, as shown by ongoing work on lake cores from Rendova (Prebble ms.). In the current rainfall regime it is difficult to imagine forest clearing and burning being possible in the New Georgia bush except sometimes during El Niño episodes.

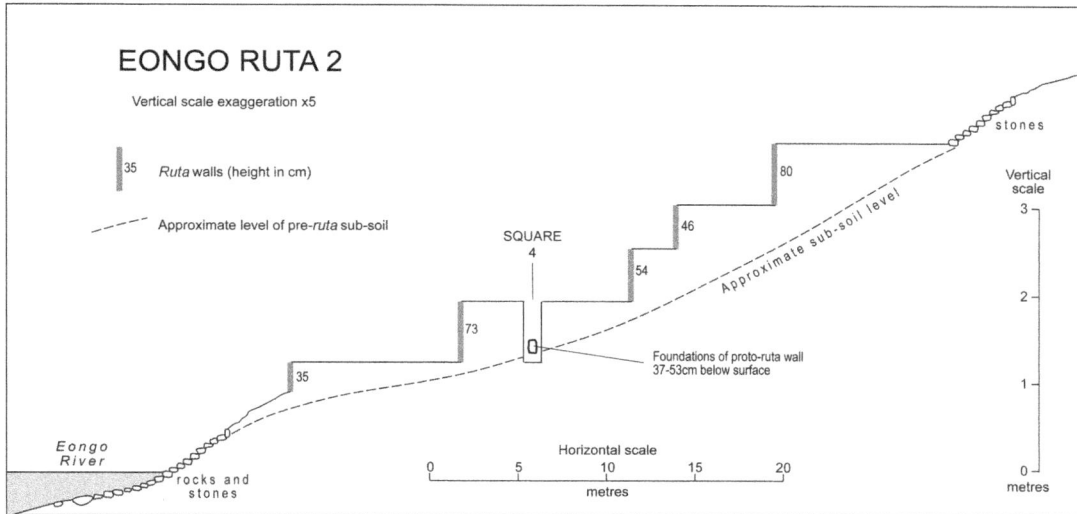

Figure 3.3. Cross-section through five pondfields in Eongo Ruta 2, from point Y to point Z in Figure 3.2.

The vertical scale is exaggerated five times. Excavation in Square 4 revealed part of the buried linear feature shown in Figure 3.5. Source: Tim Bayliss-Smith, field mapping.

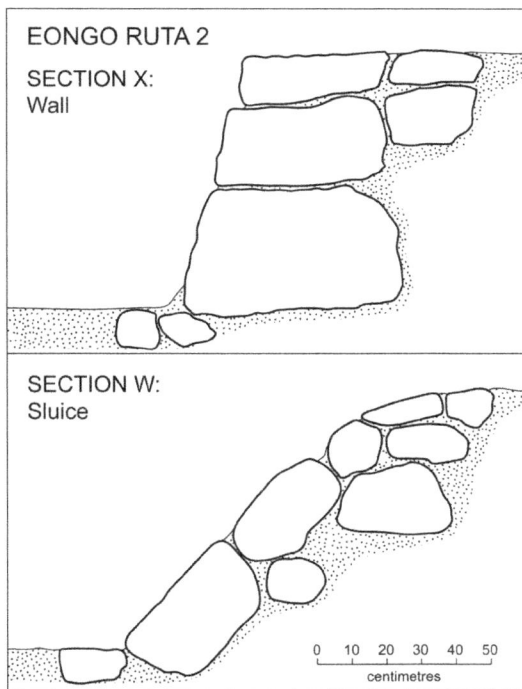

Figure 3.4. Cross-sections through the *ruta* terrace walls at points W and X of Eongo Ruta 2 (see Figure 3.2).

The wall at X, like most *ruta* walls, is almost vertical (75–80 degrees), whereas at the overflow (section W) the gradient of the sluice is 52 degrees from the horizontal. Its design minimises the erosive impact of the water overflowing from pondfield E to pondfield D, with a fall of 0.75 m from one level to the next.

Source: Tim Bayliss-Smith, field mapping.

A cross-section through Eongo Ruta 2 shows stone-built terrace walls up to 1.1 m high separating adjacent pondfields (Figure 3.3). Overflow channels or sluices were constructed in some walls to control the flow of water between adjacent pondfields. When drawn in cross-section, one well-preserved example shows the care that was taken to prevent surplus water from flowing over the wall thereby eroding or undermining it (Figure 3.4). Whereas the main terrace walls mostly rise at an angle of 75–80 degrees from the horizontal, at the overspill or sluice the wall rises more gently at 52 degrees. At its base the overflowing water was channelled on to flat stones in order to further reduce its erosive potential.

The four squares excavated in Eongo Ruta 2 all revealed a linear feature running parallel to the *ruta* walls that are visible above ground today. We interpret this linear feature as the remains of a former wall now buried 0.4 m beneath the silty clay soils of the *ruta* pondfield and dating from an earlier phase of *ruta* construction. After it was abandoned most of the stones of the earlier wall were re-used elsewhere, but some foundation stones were left in place. Stones from this earlier terrace wall were probably used in the construction of a new and higher wall 2 m further downslope, thus extending the area of the pondfield (Figure 3.5).

Radiocarbon dates on charcoal recovered from below this 'proto-*ruta*' feature, and from lower soil levels below the major phase of colluvial input, help us to constrain the chronology of these events (Figure 3.6). Fragments of charred *Canarium* nut came from bulk sieved samples excavated from Spit 6 (50–60 cm) and Spit 8 (70–80 cm) from the west wall of Square 4. As the section drawing shows, these samples effectively bracket the construction of the abandoned wall of the proto-*ruta*. The AMS (accelerated mass spectrometry) date on Spit 8 is 693 +/- 26 years (1267–1385 cal CE), and from Spit 6 is 638 +/- 24 years (1286–1394 cal CE).

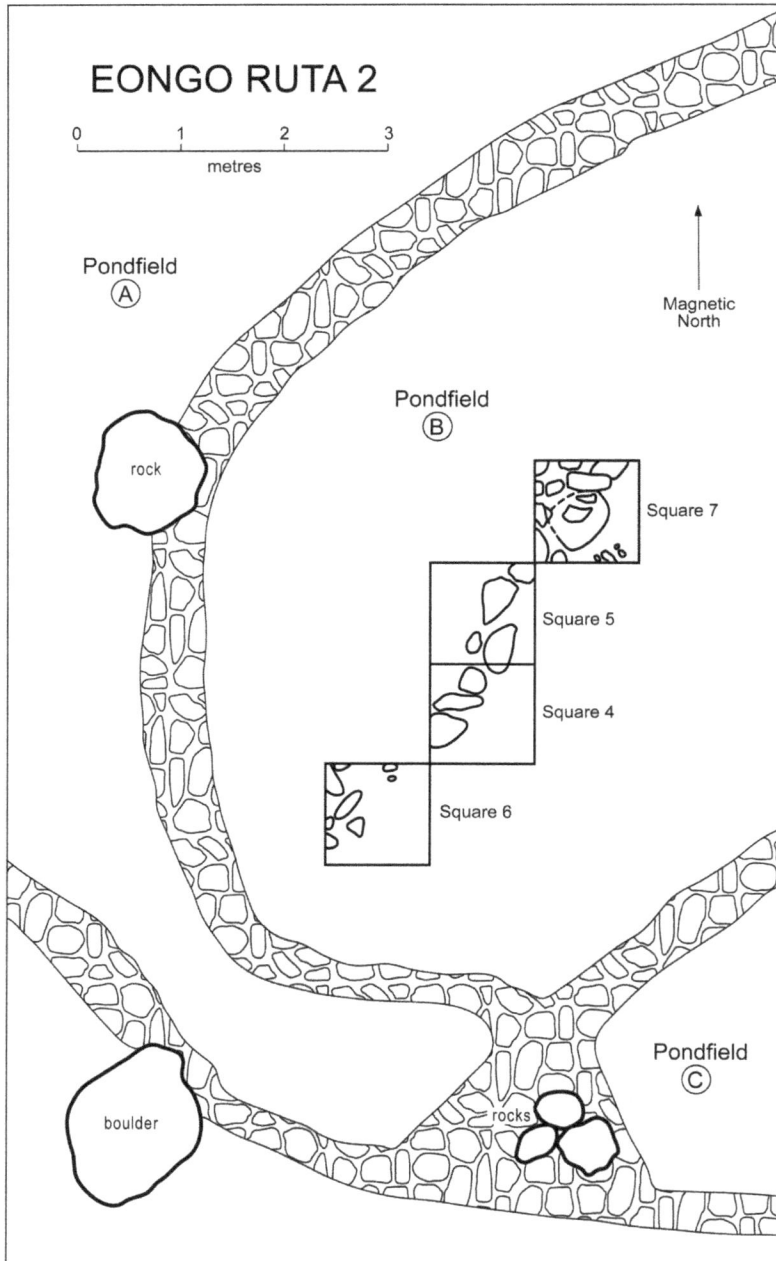

Figure 3.5. Detail of the map of Eongo Ruta 2 showing a buried linear feature that we interpret as the foundations of a 'proto-*ruta*' wall.

Radiocarbon dating of the charcoal-rich horizon that underlies this feature enables us to date its initial construction to the 14th century CE (see Figure 3.6).

Source: Stephen Manebosa, field mapping.

EONGO RUTA 2, SQUARES 4 & 5, WEST FACE Scale 1:10

A. 0–7 cm Light brown clayey silt
with abundant small roots
B. 7–20 cm Brown clayey sandy silt
with abundant small roots
C. 20–33 cm Reddish brown sandy silt with charcoal
D. 33–47 cm Light brown clayey silt with
some charcoal
E. 47–80 cm Dark-brown silty clay with charcoal
Excavation ceased before reaching bedrock

Notes: Charcoal sample taken from near East Face of the NE corner
Stone at base of SQUARE 4 is a basal stone of an earlier generation
ruta wall (proto-*ruta*)

638+/-24
(1286-1394 cal. AD)

693+/-26
(1267-1385 cal. AD)

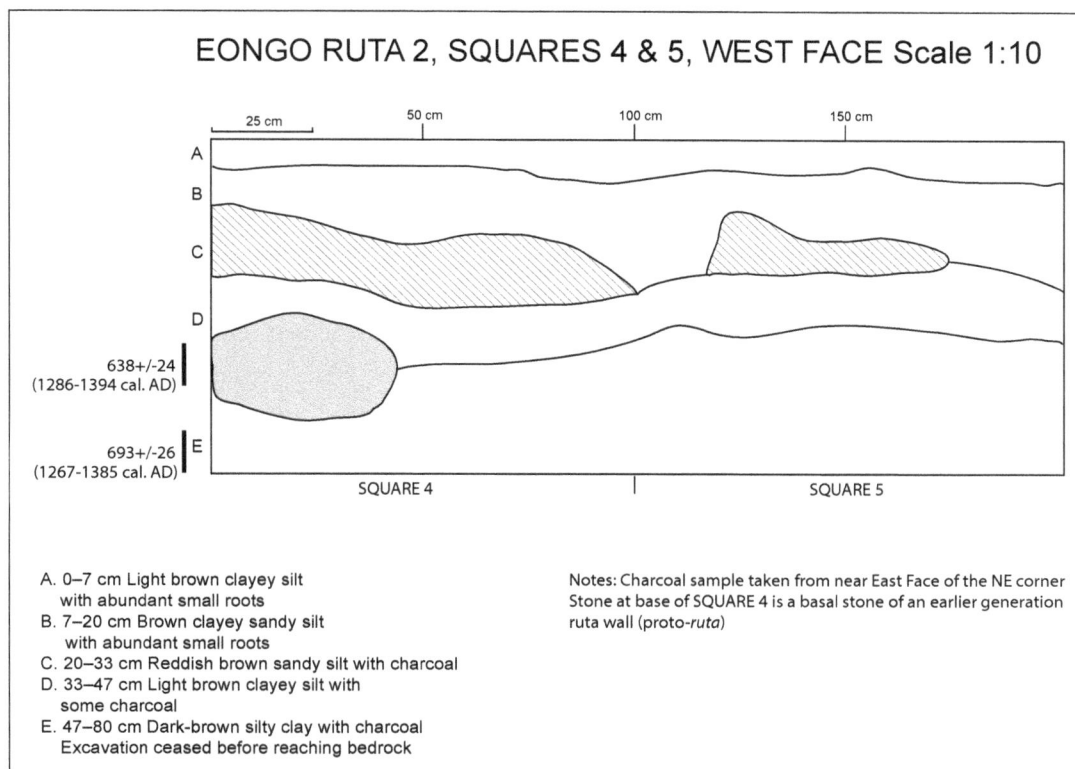

Figure 3.6. West-face stratigraphic diagram of the Eongo Ruta 2 Squares 4 and 5, showing two similar AMS dates based on charred *Canarium* nut from bulk sieved samples taken from Spit 6 (50–60 cm) and Spit 8 (70–80 cm).

S-ANU# 55010 provides a date for Spit 8 and S-ANU# 55011 for Spit 6. These two dates indicate the construction of the proto-*ruta* was in the 14th century CE.

Source: Matthew Prebble, field survey, with details added of the two AMS dates.

If we generalise to Eongo Ruta 2 as a whole, this terraced agricultural system was probably constructed in the 14th century CE. If so, then it pre-dates several coastal sites associated with the expansion of the Roviana chiefdoms in south-west New Georgia (Aswani and Sheppard 2003). Eongo Ruta 2 appears instead to be contemporary with the large earth platforms faced with basalt slabs that are found on the Bao ridge inland from Roviana. These platforms belong to the so-called Bao Period of 1200–1550 CE and are described today as shrines used in rituals of land clearance and fertility, being associated with speakers of the now extinct Kazukuru language (Thomas 2009:123; Walter and Sheppard 2006). The earliest of the ones excavated is Site 145 on the Bao ridge, 4 km inland from the lagoon and about 160 m above sea level. All these sites are situated some distance from the presumed habitation and gardening zones (Walter and Sheppard 2017:142). Apart from the Bao shrines, prior to our fieldwork in the Kusaghe region of north New Georgia no inland sites had been excavated or dated.

We have no information yet about the date of abandonment of the Eongo River *ruta* system, but it may be significant that we found still growing by the riverside nearby several plants of feral taro (*Colocasia esculenta*). On the site itself there were two *zipolo* plants (*Cordyline fruticosa*), still planted today in gardens for their spiritual qualities. These plants must be survivors from the last time this site was cultivated, possibly in the late 19th or early 20th century.

The ethnography of *ruta* on Kolobangara

The first written account of *ruta* in cultivation comes not from New Georgia but from the neighbouring island of Kolobangara, where a young English anthropologist Arthur Hocart spent two weeks in December 1908 based at Ghatere. With his Ghatere guides Hocart walked inland to Aghara to see taro cultivation in walled pondfields called *lologha*, a word translated by Hocart as 'Roviana: *ruta*'. Transcribed by Ian Scales (2003:262, 334), his field notes read as follows:

> *Ruta*. In Aghara beside river that has no name. *Ruta* consists of a series of terraces about 5 by 10 m or thereabouts; each terrace about 50 cm above the other: all dammed with stones through which water trickles. Taro planted in rich mud with about 1 cm of water upon it. One lot belongs to Pizhaka, another to Tandi.

This appears to be the first and only eye-witness account of *ruta* in cultivation. Hocart's precise descriptions of the width of pondfields, height of walls and depth of water ('about 1 cm') are important details. It would appear that water management required the damming of inlets and outlets and was designed to flood the taro field with just enough water to fertilise the crop and discourage weed growth.

Hocart questioned his guides about the inheritance and ownership of taro pondfields (Scales 2003:262, 334). He was told that each *ruta* was the property of an individual, and once built it became a permanent feature: 'a *lologha* [*ruta*] does not and is never changed'. The taro grown there was replanted immediately after harvest ('the same day'), having taken 13 months to reach maturity (Scales 2003:310). Hocart makes frequent mention of persons from an older generation as being the earlier owners or builders of individual pondfields, and Scales comments that this genealogy 'suggests continuous use of the fields since at least the 1880s' (Scales 2003:262).

Some Kolobangara *ruta* were probably constructed much earlier than the 1880s. In 1971 Kirch, Rosendahl and Yen surveyed archaeological sites in the Ndugore valley in south-east Kolobangara and obtained charcoal from behind the terrace wall of a *ruta* built on a tributary stream (Yen 1976:69). The sample was taken from 40 cm below the soil surface and gave a calibrated date in the range 1630–1820 CE (Yen 2009:173).

In the 1970s all the inland *ruta* pondfields on Kolobangara were lying abandoned, but all were still claimed in ownership by individuals living in the coastal villages (Yen 1976:70). Today logging has extended across most of the island, and probably most of the archaeological evidence for *ruta* on Kolobangara has now been damaged or destroyed.

Oral history of *ruta* in Marovo, New Georgia

In New Georgia there has also been extensive logging, but in the Mase Crater and elsewhere there is still much field evidence that survives. As on Kolobangara, in New Georgia some knowledge of *ruta* has been maintained by people now living in coastal villages, although many have never seen the inland sites. Even so, the vocabulary used in New Georgia languages shows that 'taro gardens are different from all other gardens', as the Marovo people explain it (Hviding and Bayliss-Smith 2000:120–122). Terms used for the cultivation of sweet potato (since the late 19th century) and cassava (since the 20th century) were taken from the existing vocabulary for yam cultivation, whereas the distinct vocabulary for taro cultivation, conferring a special status on this crop, was retained.

This distinctive taro vocabulary still remains active, especially among the few people trying to retain or revive *ruta* cultivation. For example, in Vahole in the 1990s some old couples maintained small relict *ruta* along tributaries of the Piongo Lavata River (Hviding and Bayliss-Smith

2000:117). These were merely shallow pools along streams where the water flow was regulated by means of a few logs. The attachment of these people to their *ruta* was not primarily materialistic, having also an emotional dimension. Taro cultivation was seen as an aspect of a 'good life', the flourishing pondfield and its environs representing a symbolic interconnection between land, water, useful trees and esteemed plant life, all under careful human cultivation to provide the most prized of all root crops. *Ruta* embodies the practical, the magical and the aesthetic, and thus constitutes the essence of what *mana* was, and is, supposed to be all about (Bayliss-Smith and Hviding 2012:238).

In the 1990s some of the former practices for making and cultivating *ruta* could be reconstructed from interviews with old people, for example those from the Bareke Bush in Marovo whom we consulted. According to their testimony, taro was planted in pondfields into which water was led from small streams, the planted beds being surrounded by wooden fences or stone walls to retain the water. The channels thus created were sloping and compartmentalised in order to manipulate the water flow. Generally the *ruta* that were remembered were quite elaborate constructions with relatively large field spaces devoted to taro plants in three different growth stages, but *ruta* also existed in the form of smaller fields in places naturally amenable to irrigation. These taro beds needed little modification beyond simple logs for regulating the water flow from the shallow pools found in small tributary rivers and streams. On the Piongo Lavata River the terrace and channel walls were mainly built with stones, but timbers resistant to waterlogging and decay were also needed for *ruta* construction (Bayliss-Smith and Hviding 2012:238; Hviding and Bayliss-Smith 2000:90).

Oral histories from Kusaghe, New Georgia

Further information about the former bush diet is available for Kusaghe from Margaret Tedder's interviews in 1974 with the people of Paradise Village. They said that before they moved to the coast, taro and yams were supplemented with meat from feral and domestic pigs, freshwater shellfish, fruits and nuts, especially *Canarium* spp. Each village or group of hamlets had as its focus a sacred site on a hilltop or ridge where chiefs were buried, with the taro gardens situated in the valleys below. It was said that each family had more than one house and moved up and down the Mase Valley working different gardens (M Tedder with Barrus 1976:48).

Oral histories collected by Hviding suggest that the bush people in Old Kusaghe had exchange and marriage relations with Kazukuru and the coastal people of Roviana to the south, and with the neighbouring bush dwellers of Kalikolo to the east. The Mase Crater provided the Kusaghe with a circumscribed space, but they were not an isolated society. Histories of intermarriage and the existence of several closely related bush languages along the northern slopes of New Georgia indicate a rather homogeneous, inland, taro-cultivating society of wide extent, with solidarity maintained through kinship, exchange and feasts (Bayliss-Smith et al. 2003:350).

The actual techniques of *ruta* cultivation were described in 1968 by Silas Eto (1968a, 1968b) in two interviews with James Tedder, the District Commissioner. Silas Eto was the 'Holy Mama' or spiritual leader of the Christian Fellowship Church. He was born in 1902 in Hoava, north-west Marovo, but he moved in 1912 to Kolobaghera in eastern Kusaghe before being sent to Goldie College at Kokeqolo and later becoming a Methodist catechist (Aseri Yalangono, interview, Honiara, 26 October 2016).

As a boy Silas Eto would have seen the various operations needed to maintain the family's irrigated taro gardens (*ruta*). His father Leti, a prominent chief, owned two *ruta* systems made along streams (*ruta bukaha*), each having 11 plots. Clearly *ruta* was a form of cultivation still in operation in both of his childhood homes, and the information he gave to Tedder is essentially an eye-witness account. The second interview goes beyond horticultural matters to place *ruta* into a wider social and cultural context (Eto 1968b).

Silas Eto stated that wet gardens could be divided into two kinds, *ruta gineli* (terraced fields irrigated from streams) and *ruta bukaha* (irrigation of flat land on valley floors). A *ruta bukaha* could be planted and left for a few months 'as they don't need to be looked after', but *ruta gineli* needed constant maintenance and were therefore always made close to the villages where people lived. A *ruta gineli* was constructed by digging up the soil to make it soft and by heaping stones into lines forming walled terraces. In this way many separate plots (pondfields) were made for planting. People then dug a trench from a big stream to allow each plot to be irrigated. The plots were very easy to plant, 'just push young shoots down into the mud with your hand or a stick'. When the taro needed water the bottom gate would be closed and the top gate opened to allow water in from the stream, enabling one plot after another to be irrigated, 'filled with water, but not deep'. After three or four days the bottom gate would be opened, every interconnected plot would drain, and then new water would be let in. The *ruta gineli* was checked morning and evening and if a flood was coming the top gate could be closed. This regime of water management continued until it was time to harvest the taro (Eto 1968b).

In contrast the *ruta bukaha* that Silas Eto described were on flat land (*hapanggala*, swampy). Some were constructed close to the villages but often they were made 'very far distant in the bush'. After planting, a *ruta bukaha* was sometimes left for 3 to 6 months before being revisited. It could be left untended as the water entered it continually and directly from the flowing stream, not along man-made trenches. A new site would be first cleared of trees, then cleaned up, and then divided by constructing walls: 'each stone boundary was like a path and people could walk on them. On the tops of the stone boundaries people planted betel nut and bananas'. This type of *ruta* could be filled with water by blocking the lower gate. Later, after harvesting and weeding, it could be cleared of debris by making the stream flow right through the pondfields. After that the top dam was shut again and the *ruta* could be replanted with taro (Eto 1968a).

The rationale for terraced irrigated taro

The 'wet' form of cultivation, described by Bareke informants in the 1990s and by Silas Eto in the 1968 interviews, was a technique for taro cultivation that has unknown origins. Our finding that the building of terrace walls in Eongo Ruta 2 took place in the late 13th or 14th century CE suggests a phase of intensification of taro production, but this particular *ruta* wall may not date the initiation of terracing in the Eongo Valley.

In recent papers Bayliss-Smith and Hviding have tried to explain the origins of *ruta* within the broader context of exchange, food storage and agricultural intensification in Island Melanesia. They have argued that inland ('bush') populations developed *ruta* cultivation as a result of their contacts with coastal ('saltwater') populations engaged in predatory inter-island warfare and headhunting. By the late 19th century the relationship had become unequal, especially after coastal groups monopolised access to European trade goods. Arguably these interactions originally took place through a more balanced exchange system in which fish and shell valuables moved inland in exchange for taro, nuts and meat derived from *ruta* terraces, groves of *Canarium* trees and hunting respectively. There was also seasonal tribute whereby inland people provided taro for large feasts on the coast.

Despite its potential for escalation because of *ruta*'s capacity to store and accumulate food energy, the outcome of saltwater/bush exchange was not the growth of population nor the emergence of more centralised polities (Bayliss-Smith and Hviding 2015). *Ruta* could have been an engine for regional expansion, but instead this system remained a localised and perhaps fragile form of intensification.

While the evidence does not suggest an inexorable process of growth and political expansion, it may be possible to match the onset and intensification of inland *ruta* to changes in the wider political economy, as reconstructed from archaeological evidence. After c. 1600 CE there were changes in the sacred sites of Nusa Roviana, which became the paramount chiefdom of Roviana Lagoon. The chiefdom of Tusu Marovo in Marovo lagoon probably emerged at this time too. In both cases it is thought that the dramatic expansion of chiefdoms only took place after regular European contact in the 19th century (Thomas et al. 2001). As late as 1900 Kazukuru, the language of the bush people who lived inland of Roviana Lagoon, was still being spoken. It only died out after the last Kazukuru communities moved to the coast, abandoning their inland taro swiddens and *ruta* (Sheppard et al. 2004:130).

Bayliss-Smith and Hviding (2012) identified various constraints in the western Solomons on the expansion of bush/saltwater exchange based on surplus production from *ruta*. Elsewhere in the Pacific these interactions between transformed ecology, surplus production and intensified exchange escalated towards the formation of regional chiefdoms and radically transformed landscapes, as in Fiji and Polynesian high islands, but in New Georgia the evidence suggests that an expansion of *ruta*-based polities was somewhat limited.

According to this argument, three main factors acted in combination to limit growth. Taken together, they can explain the paradox of large islands (for example the New Georgia group) and high potential for expanded production of surplus taro but no evidence for sustained political expansion and centralisation. The three limiting factors are: (1) a diverse cultural geography derived from the mosaic of Non-Austronesian and intrusive post-Lapita peoples and cultures; (2) perpetually unstable politics within a social landscape of persistent inter- and intra-island warfare; and (3) epidemiological constraints, particularly endemic malaria, which made problematic the growth and mobility of population. Acting in combination, we believe these constraining factors encouraged the coexistence of diverse Non-Austronesian and Austronesian languages and cultures, and discouraged the political expansion of any particular group (Bayliss-Smith and Hviding 2012, 2014, 2015).

Inland Kusaghe before its collapse

Our field evidence from the Eongo River and Mase Crater shows the scale of investment into intensive wet taro production made by bush people, before their society and economy were undermined by the events of the 19th century. The end result was population decline and the eclipse of the inland production system, probably because both its demographic and its sociopolitical rationale had been destroyed by new diseases, new tools and weapons, and new concepts of value. Complete collapse of the bush people's society was signalled by the move to the coast of the few survivors, and their construction of new villages (Paradise, Mase, Njela and others) based on copra as a cash crop and Christianity as a new religion. By 1950, despite being a large and fertile island, New Georgia was mainly covered in rainforest with a sparse population living in small coastal villages. They sometimes visited the extensive forests and mountains of the island's interior for valuable resources like *Canarium* nuts, wild pigs or timber for canoes, but to the outside world the unknown bush appeared to be largely empty.

The evidence from Kusaghe suggests that the landscape of the New Georgia bush was very different in the early or mid-19th century. We get some glimpses of coastal communities from traders' accounts of 1844 and 1851 (Bradley 1860:22; Shineberg 1971:305). It seems there were frequent contacts between New Georgians and European whaling and trading ships exchanging turtle shell or food for tomahawks, but these brief encounters are seldom documented. Coastal people obtained from these exchanges the various commodities that Jared Diamond (1997) famously summarised as 'guns, germs and steel', whereas the bush people received these things later, second-hand, or not at all. In Bougainville, for example, Carl Ribbe (1903:96) commented that although the merchandise exchanged by the traders went far into the mountains, moving from tribe to tribe, the transactions became more costly. As a result, bushmen in the interior had to pay the equivalent of 300–400 coconuts for a hatchet that was priced at only 100 coconuts on the coast.

Accompanying this process of marginalisation, by the mid-19th century hostility seems to have become the dominant pattern in bush/saltwater relations. The period after 1850 saw a steady decline in the status of bush communities in the western Solomons. At the same time as their cultures and economies had been marginalised, their populations were being destroyed by disease and warfare. Reflecting their marginal position in the new political economy of colonial contact, Europeans began to describe the cultures of bush people in unfavourable terms, and even denigrated their supposed racial characteristics.

Case study: The Bareke Bush, Vangunu Island

By the 1880s the 'primitive' character of bush populations in Solomon Islands had become the dominant narrative. The visiting English naturalist Charles Woodford, for example, was at Lilohina Island in Marovo Lagoon in October 1886, where he found himself among the saltwater people living adjacent to the inland settlements of Voge and Vavae on the Bareke side of Vangunu Island. In his diary he combines local information with his own observations and conjectures:

> There are abreast of this place [Lilohina Island] several bush villages on the tops of the range while the existence of others is shown by wreaths of smoke. I am told they are a different race and speak another language to the coastal natives, they are probably earlier inhabitants of the island driven inland by the later arriving coast tribes. They and the coast natives hold little communication and the former rarely come down to the coast. Occasionally the coast people capture a head or two from the bushmen. (Woodford 1886)

Only one foreigner, Lieutenant Somerville of the Royal Navy survey ship HMS *Penguin*, saw life in the New Georgia bush first-hand and recorded his observations. In 1893 Somerville led a surveying party inland on Vangunu, but by travelling with coastal guides along ridgetop paths he was unable to observe the presence of *ruta* cultivation in the valley floors. In his report to Commander AJ Balfour he stated it was perfectly safe ('for men of war folk at least') to travel into the New Georgia interior 'provided that sufficient warning be given so as not to alarm the bush natives by a sudden appearance in their villages' (Somerville 1893).

Somerville sought to extend his general conclusion to other bush populations in New Georgia, suggesting that:

> This small expedition into the bush thus points out that (1) Most of the people of this district live away from the sea coast. (2) That, however, they are probably in the habit of visiting the coast for trade, etc. (Somerville 1893:9)

Oral histories collected by Hviding confirm that there were formerly significant numbers of people in the area that Somerville visited. According to late-20th-century informants they were swidden cultivators but also had irrigated taro (*ruta*) in the valleys (Bayliss-Smith and Hviding 2012; Bayliss-Smith et al. 2003:250).

Somerville's theodolite survey station was established on a ridge about 450 m in altitude and close to a hamlet of six inhabited huts and a large house, but with only three or four old men and women in residence. He was impressed by the evidence of European goods ('pipes, tobacco and trade axes') showing that the bush people made regular visits to the coast for trade (Somerville 1893:6). A majority of the population, he believed, lived inland not on the coast (Somerville 1897). On the Admiralty chart based on the surveys of Somerville and others are marked houses on the ridgetops and plateaus of the Bareke Bush covering those areas where Somerville travelled, but none are marked in areas where he did not travel (Admiralty 1896). Inland there are 23 house symbols marking 11 different sites (i.e. hamlets). The six inhabited huts in the ridgetop hamlet where Somerville's party stopped are represented by two symbols. The chart also marks saltwater settlements. There are 33 house symbols along the adjacent coastline, showing settlements at Repi on the Vangunu Coast (total nine symbols), on Marovo Island (13) and elsewhere. Each site is marked with clusters of up to five symbols, and they are shown in places that match the locations of present-day villages. We can conclude that in the 1890s bush settlements in Bareke were still numerous, but they were smaller in size than the coastal villages.

Somerville's observations from 1893 point to both the separation and the integration of saltwater and bush peoples in this Ulusaghe region of New Georgia. The quality of the footpaths that Somerville followed indicates constant use as well as the ability of bush people to organise substantial labour for the construction and maintenance of what were described as 'roads'. These well-maintained tracks running between seashores and mountain ridges allowed frequent contact between bush and coast, which is consistent with regularised food barter between the two groups. A major item in this barter was the taro produced from irrigated terraces (*ruta*) in inland valleys.

There are almost no other accounts on which to base an ethnography of these inland populations. All transactions between Europeans and local populations were conducted on the beach or in coastal villages, with saltwater people usually acting as the middlemen. Did the saltwater people often venture inland? It would appear that Somerville's coastal guides were reluctant to do so, an attitude reflected in oral traditions about the dangers posed by special snakes, crocodiles and other creatures of the inner lands, as well as dangers from the local spirits that inhabited certain places (Bayliss-Smith and Hviding 2012).

With the arms trade, headhunting and expanding warfare, few Europeans dared to travel far from the coast, and the incentive to do so was further reduced after 1900 when the few remaining bush populations, already decimated in numbers by warfare and disease, relocated their settlements to coastal sites (Hviding and Bayliss-Smith 2000:149–152). Their declining numbers, diminished political role and isolation from colonial trade removed any incentive to live inland. With the end of endemic warfare around 1900, it became possible for bush people to live in coastal settlements and cultivate coconuts, and thereby to gain direct access to European trade goods.

The wider political economy of bush collapse

An important factor in the decline of inland populations on New Georgia was the increasing pressure put upon them by coastal chiefdoms, centred on Nusa Roviana and Tusu Marovo. The escalation in headhunting voyages overseas has been attributed to the acquisition in the early 19th century of steel tools, tomahawks and later firearms by certain coastal groups in Simbo, Roviana and Marovo (Hviding 1996; McKinnon 1975). We know much less about the escalating violence between coastal chiefdoms and inland groups, but there are indications that in the 19th century the Roviana chiefs began to have more aggressive relations with their trading partners in the Kusaghe Bush (Aswani and Sheppard 2003:S59). Roviana oral traditions describe conflicts with neighbouring Kusaghe and also disease epidemics, which together persuaded another inland group, the Kazukuru, to abandon their inland settlements on the Bao ridge, 4–5 km inland and above 150 m in altitude. Roviana traditions say that the Kazukuru migrated southwards and moved to small islands on the coast such as Nusa Roviana.

A Kusaghe perspective on these turbulent events can be gained from the evidence collected by Judge FB Phillips in 1923, in the course of his investigations into the validity of claims to land alienated to foreigners across a wide swathe of coastal land in north New Georgia (Phillips 1923:105–135). The question for Phillips to decide was whether these lands had been occupied and used at the time of the Pacific Islands Company land grab in 1903, and therefore to what extent they were really 'wasteland' suitable for land alienation. In this connection a man called Lai testified that as a child he and all the Kusaghe people had lived in the bush 'at Gegeri, Kusagi, Senga, Harena'. Nggenggere and Sengga (modern spellings) are both places in the Mase Crater. Lai said they did not live on the coast because of headhunting raids especially by warriors from Roviana Lagoon, although they still fished and collected coconuts, for example those planted at Menasakapa, today's Paradise (Phillips 1925:137–154).

These accounts also indicate that warriors from Marovo Lagoon were becoming more aggressive towards their exchange partners in the Kusaghe Bush (Phillips 1923:107–112). The testimony of Lai appears to corroborate Roviana accounts that suggest the Kazukuru people were pushed southwards towards Roviana (Aswani and Sheppard 2003:S59). This movement may perhaps have been the result of epidemics (Roviana oral histories) or perhaps because of defeat and massacre by the Kusaghe from the north (Lai's account). Eventually the Kazukuru intermarried and became absorbed into coastal Roviana groups, and their language later became extinct.

Clearly the 19th century was a time of growing political unrest and escalating violence in New Georgia, continuing up until to 1900 and forcing the Kusaghe to abandon the coast. Increasingly they were confined to remote inland areas, especially the Mase Crater. Perhaps this confinement of bush populations like the Kusaghe to inland areas was one factor that encouraged further agricultural intensification. According to this model the expansion of *ruta* in the 19th century would be a response to the marginalisation of bush peoples in the new economy of tomahawks, headhunting and copra trading. In order to compete in this brave new world they had to produce more taro from an expansion of their *ruta*.

Conclusion

The field evidence from the Eongo River suggest that agricultural intensification in inland New Georgia was a dynamic and sustained process. We have evidence for forest clearance and burning in the past, and on a scale difficult to envisage in the present climate of high and non-seasonal rainfall. It appears that the steep valley-side slopes of the Eongo catchment were subject to widespread slash-and-burn for the purposes of 'dry' swidden cultivation, presumably for yams as well as taro. On less steep slopes with a potential for water supply this clearance phase was followed by an intensification of taro production, involving the construction of stone walls to support terraced pondfields (*ruta*). In one case that we excavated we see evidence for an earlier wall being reconstructed to enlarge the cultivated area.

It is not valid to interpret the 'rise of *ruta*' entirely through an understanding of its fall in the decades just before and after 1900, in the face of colonial impacts and opportunities. There were certain unique features of colonialism, such as the epidemics that rapidly undermined the viability of inland societies and their production systems. At the general level of political economy, however, there may be lessons that we can learn from *ruta*'s collapse.

In particular, it is tempting to see the advantaged position of coastal groups c. 1850, following their privileged access to new trade goods (steel axes, firearms, tobacco), as a suitable analogue for saltwater/bush relationships in earlier times, following coastal innovations in ideology and wealth. By 1600 there is archaeological evidence from Roviana for the building of new types of shrine and the production of new shell valuables, alongside (it is assumed) the emergence of a more ranked saltwater society of paramount chiefs, commoners and slaves (Aswani and Sheppard 2003; Sheppard et al. 2000; Walter and Sheppard 2000, 2017).

Were these coastal innovations around 1300 and/or 1600 a sufficient stimulus for a process inland of agricultural intensification and the expansion of *ruta*? As an alternative, the reverse scenario is equally possible. Perhaps the real driver of change was the surplus taro that became available from an expanding population living inland in the malaria-free uplands. Was it this food surplus that encouraged saltwater communities to innovate so they could maintain some leverage in these vital bush/saltwater exchanges? Only when we obtain a fuller chronology for the rise of inland *ruta* can we hope to resolve some of these tantalising questions.

Acknowledgements

For their help with the fieldwork we thank, in Honiara: Aseri Yalangono, James Bosamata (Ministry of Education), Tony Heorake and Lawrence Kiko (Solomon Islands National Museum); in Gizo: Kenneth George Nginabule, Nixon Tigina and Adrian Toni (Provincial Secretary); in Paradise: Rooseman Ruriti; in Mase: Lidly George, Melva George, Randall Reke and numerous field assistants. For help with archival work in Canberra and Sydney we thank Jean Kennedy, Bernadette Hince, Kylie Moloney, Leela Smith and Bob Debus. Discussions in Cambridge with Edvard Hviding in 2017 and 2018 were also an important stimulus. For administrative and logistic support in the University of Cambridge Department of Geography, we thank Bill Adams, Ash Amin, Danielle Feger, Yasmiena Jones, Chris Rolfe and Philip Stickler. The research by Author #1 received financial support from a Leverhulme Emeritus Fellowship, from the Smuts Fund, University of Cambridge, and from St John's College, Cambridge.

References

Published

Admiralty. 1896. South Pacific, Anchorages in the Solomon Islands. Surveyed by Commander AF Balfour, HMSS *Penguin* 1894. 1. New Georgia, Vangunu Island, North and North-east Coast Marovo Lagoon. Map, scale circa 1:75,000. London: British Admiralty.

Amherst, Lord, of Hackney and B Thomson (eds). 1901. *The discovery of the Solomon Islands by Alvaro de Mendaña in 1568*. Vol. 2. London: Hakluyt Society.

Aswani, S and P Sheppard. 2003. 'The archaeology and ethnohistory of exchange in precolonial and colonial Roviana. Gifts, commodities and inalienable possessions'. *Current Anthropology* 44 (supplement):S51–S78. doi.org/10.1086/377667.

Barrau, J. 1958. *Subsistence agriculture in Melanesia*. B.P. Bishop Museum Bulletin 219. Honolulu: Bishop Museum.

Bayliss-Smith, T and E Hviding. 2012. 'Irrigated taro, malaria and the expansion of chiefdoms: Ruta in New Georgia, Solomon Islands'. In *Irrigated taro (Colocasia esculenta) in the Indo-Pacific. Biological, social and historical perspectives*, edited by M Spriggs, D Addison and PJ Matthews, 219–254. Senri Ethnological Studies no. 78. Osaka: National Museum of Ethnology.

Bayliss-Smith, T and E Hviding. 2014. 'Taro terraces, chiefdoms and malaria: Explaining landesque capital formation in Solomon Islands'. In *Landesque capital: The historical ecology of enduring landscape modifications*, edited by T Hakansson and M Widgren, 75–97. Walnut Creek, California: Left Coast Press.

Bayliss-Smith, T and E Hviding. 2015. 'Landesque capital as an alternative to food storage in Melanesia: Irrigated taro terraces in New Georgia, Solomon Islands'. *Environmental Archaeology* 20 (4):425–436. doi.org/10.1179/1749631414Y.0000000049.

Bayliss-Smith, T, E Hviding and T Whitmore. 2003. 'Rain forest composition and histories of human disturbance in Solomon Islands'. *Ambio* 32 (5):346–352. doi.org/10.1579/0044-7447-32.5.346.

Bourke, M. 2012. 'The decline of taro and taro irrigation in Papua New Guinea'. In *Irrigated taro (Colocasia esculenta) in the Indo-Pacific. Biological, social and historical perspectives*, edited by M Spriggs, D Addison and PJ Matthews, 255–264. Senri Ethnological Studies no. 78. Osaka: National Museum of Ethnology.

Bradley, J. circa 1860. *A nine month's cruise in the 'Ariel' schooner from San Francisco, in company with the 'Wanderer' of the Royal Yacht Squadron, belonging to Benjamin Boyd Esq.* Church Street, Parramatta, New South Wales: J.J. Beukers, General Printer.

Brookfield, HC with D Hart. 1971. *Melanesia: A geographical interpretation of an island world*. London: Methuen.

Diamond, J. 1997. *Guns, germs and steel: A short history of everybody for the last 13,000 years*. London: Jonathan Cape.

Hviding, E. 1996. *Guardians of Marovo Lagoon: Practice, place and politics in maritime Melanesia*. Pacific Islands Monograph Series 14. Honolulu: University of Hawai'i Press.

Hviding, E and T Bayliss-Smith. 2000. *Islands of rainforest: Agroforestry, logging and eco-tourism in Solomon Islands*. Aldershot: Ashgate. Reprinted 2019, London: Routledge [citations refer to the 2000 edition].

Kirch, P. 1994. *The wet and the dry: Irrigation and agricultural intensification in Polynesia*. Chicago: University of Chicago Press.

McKinnon, JM. 1975. 'Tomahawks, turtles and traders: A reconstruction of the circular causation of warfare in the New Georgia Group'. *Oceania* 45 (4):290–307. doi.org/10.1002/j.1834-4461.1975.tb01872.x.

Miller, D. 1979. *Solomon Islands national sites survey summary report*. Honiara: National Museum.

Purchas, S. [1625] 1906. *Hakluytus posthumus or Purchas his pilgrimes in twenty volumes*. Vol. 17. Glasgow: James MacLehose & Sons.

Ribbe, C. 1903. *Zwei Jahre unter den Kannibalen der Salamo-Inseln*. Dresden-Blasewitz: Hermann Bayer.

Rivers, WHR. 1926. 'Irrigation and the cultivation of taro'. In *Psychology and ethnology*, edited by G Elliot Smith, 262–287. London: Kegan Paul, Trench, Trubner & Co.

Roe, D. 2000. 'Maritime, coastal and inland societies in Island Melanesia: The bush-saltwater divide in Solomon Islands and Vanuatu'. In *East of Wallace's Line: Studies of past and present maritime cultures in the Indo-Pacific region*, edited by S O'Connor and P Veth, 197–222. Rotterdam: Balkema, and Vermont: Brookfield.

Sheppard, PJ, R Walter and T Nagaoka. 2000. 'The archaeology of head-hunting in Roviana Lagoon, New Georgia, Solomon Islands'. *Journal of the Polynesian Society* 109 (1):9–37.

Shineberg, D (ed.). 1971. *The trading voyages of Andrew Cheyne, 1841–1844*. Canberra: Australian National University Press.

Somerville, HBT. 1897. 'Ethnographical notes in New Georgia, Solomon Islands'. *Journal of the Royal Anthropological Institute of Great Britain and Ireland* 26:357–413. doi.org/10.2307/2842009.

Spriggs, MJT. 1990. 'Why irrigation matters in Pacific prehistory'. In *Pacific production systems: Approaches to economic prehistory*, edited by DE Yen and J Mummery, 174–189. Occasional Papers in Prehistory 18. Canberra: Department of Prehistory, Research School of Pacific Studies, The Australian National University.

Spriggs, MJT. 2012. 'From Mendana to Riesenfeld: Early account of and speculation on taro irrigation in the Asia-Pacific area'. In *Irrigated taro (Colocasia esculenta) in the Indo-Pacific. Biological, social and historical perspectives*, edited by M Spriggs, D Addison and PJ Matthews, 1–19. Senri Ethnological Studies no. 78. Osaka: National Museum of Ethnology.

Tedder, M with S Barrus. 1976. 'Old Kusaghe'. *Journal of the Cultural Association of the Solomon Islands* 4:41–95.

Thomas, T. 2009. 'Communities of practice in the archaeology of New Georgia, Rendova and Tetepare'. In *Lapita: Ancestors and descendants*, edited by PJ Sheppard, T Thomas and G Summerhayes, 119–145. NZAA Monograph 28. Auckland: New Zealand Archaeological Association.

Thomas, T, PJ Sheppard and R Walter. 2001. 'Landscape, violence and social bodies: Ritualized architecture in a Solomon Islands society'. *Journal of the Royal Anthropological Institute* NS 7:545–572. doi.org 10.1111/1467-9655.00077.

Walter, R and PJ Sheppard. 2000. 'Nusa Roviana: The archaeology of a Melanesian chiefdom'. *Journal of Field Archaeology* 27:295–318. doi.org/10.1179/jfa.2000.27.3.295.

Walter, R and PJ Sheppard. 2006. 'Archaeology in Melanesia: A case study from the Western Province of the Solomon Islands'. In *Archaeology of Oceania, Australia and the Pacific Islands*, edited by I Lilley, 137–159. London: Blackwell. doi.org/10.1002/9780470773475.ch7.

Walter, R and PJ Sheppard. 2017. *Archaeology of the Solomon Islands*. Dunedin: Otago University Press.

Weightman, B. 1989. *Agriculture in Vanuatu: A historical review*. Cheam, Surry, UK: British Friends of Vanuatu.

Yen, DE. 1976. 'Agricultural systems and prehistory in Solomon Islands'. In *South east Solomon Islands cultural history*, RC Green and MM Cresswell, 61–74. Wellington: Royal Society of New Zealand.

Yen, DE. 2009. 'Ethnobotany of the Southeast Solomons cultural history project'. In *Lapita: Ancestors and descendants*, edited by PJ Sheppard, T Thomas and G Summerhayes, 173–179. NZAA Monograph 28. Auckland: New Zealand Archaeological Association.

Unpublished

Chikamori, M. 1966. 'Preliminary report on archaeological and ethnological research in the Western Solomon Islands' [in Japanese with English summary]. Tokyo: Kaimedo. Unpublished typescript of summary. In James LO Tedder, Solomon Islands Papers, Pacific Manuscripts Bureau, The Australian National University, PMB 1365, Canberra.

Eto, S. 1968a. 'Interview Holy Mama, description of gardening, March 1968'. Unpublished typescript, pp. 1–3. In James LO Tedder, Solomon Islands Papers, Pacific Manuscripts Bureau, The Australian National University, PMB 1365, Canberra.

Eto, S. 1968b. 'Interview Holy Mama, on gardening, April 1968'. Unpublished typescript, pp. 1–5. In James LO Tedder, Solomon Islands Papers, Pacific Manuscripts Bureau, The Australian National University, PMB 1365, Canberra.

Page, B. 1964. Bill Page to Margaret Tedder, unpublished letter dated October 30, 1964. In James LO Tedder, Solomon Islands Papers, Pacific Manuscripts Bureau, The Australian National University, PMB 1365, Canberra.

Phillips, FB. 1923. 'Report of the proceedings at Inquiry 34'. Honiara: Solomon Islands National Archives (item missing in 2016). Unpublished notes on Inquiry 34. In James LO Tedder, Solomon Islands Papers, Pacific Manuscripts Bureau, The Australian National University, PMB 1365, Canberra.

Phillips, FB. 1925. 'Land Commissioner's report for native claims 30–37, 50, &c. (Lever's certificate of occupation, etc.)'. Unpublished. Solomon Islands National Archives, BSIP 18/1/26, Honiara.

Roe, D. 1993. 'Prehistory without Pots: Prehistoric settlement and economy of Northwest Guadalcanal, Solomon Islands'. Unpublished PhD thesis, The Australian National University, Canberra.

Scales, IA. 2003. 'The social forest: Landowners, development conflicts and the state in Solomon Islands'. Unpublished PhD thesis, The Australian National University, Canberra.

Sheppard, PJ, M Busse, C Dureau and J Dodson. 2004. 'Contract UOA312, Annual report 2004'. Unpublished report. Auckland: Department of Anthropology, University of Auckland.

Somerville, HBT. 1893. 'Report concerning the bush in the vicinity of Lihihina Island, Marovo Lagoon, New Georgia, Solomon Islands'. Unpublished report to Commander AJ Balfour, HMS *Penguin*, pp. 1–10. In Balfour Collection, Royal Geographical Society, London.

Tedder, JLO. 1968. 'Trip into Lupa country up ridge paralleling Hepa River'. Unpublished typescript. In James LO Tedder, Solomon Islands Papers, Pacific Manuscripts Bureau, The Australian National University, PMB 1365, Canberra.

Woodford, CM. 1886. Diary from 4th August 1886 to November 10th 1886. Chas. M. Woodford, F.R.G.S., Gravesend, England. Unpublished. Pacific Manuscripts Bureau, The Australian National University, PMB 1290, Canberra.

4

From test pits to big-scale archaeology in New Caledonia, southern Melanesia

Christophe Sand, David Baret, Jacques Bolé, Stéphanie Domergue, André-John Ouetcho and Jean-Marie Wadrawane

Introduction

Following on from pioneering projects (Allen and Gosden 1991; Garanger 1972; Green and Cresswell 1976), Melanesian archaeology has, during the last three decades, seen massive developments. In every archipelago, a number of ambitious research programs were initiated in the 1990s (e.g. Bedford et al. 1999; Clark and Anderson 2009; Sand 1996; Sheppard et al. 2000; Summerhayes 2000) and carried on in the following decades, allowing us to broaden, sometimes exponentially, our knowledge of the long past of this part of Oceania. Sadly, in a period characterised by important economic development in the region with the construction of numerous international hotels and tourism-related facilities, new roads and airstrips, extensions of townships, factories and housing, and logging and mining, very few large-scale archaeological rescue excavations in the form of cultural resource management (CRM) programs have been carried out. Impact studies are non-compulsory or mostly neglected in Oceania. In this regard, clear differences can be identified between the archipelagos of the region. Some nation-states have at times allowed highly destructive economic projects like logging or mining without any previous archaeological studies, while in other instances, multimillion dollar development projects by international companies include a multi-year archaeological assessment of the heritage landscapes before development (e.g. Richards et al. 2016).

As elsewhere in the Pacific, archaeology was considered problematic in New Caledonia for a long time and was consequently left to be dealt with by foreign research institutions. The political changes witnessed by the archipelago since the end of the 1980s, as part of a political decolonising dynamic, have fostered the creation of a local team of archaeologists and a slow rise in the occurrence of CRM excavations as part of some major development projects. In this paper we present the main steps that have led to positioning the archipelago as one of the regional leaders in CRM over the last decade (Figure 4.1), as well as an example of the type of archaeological results this approach has generated.

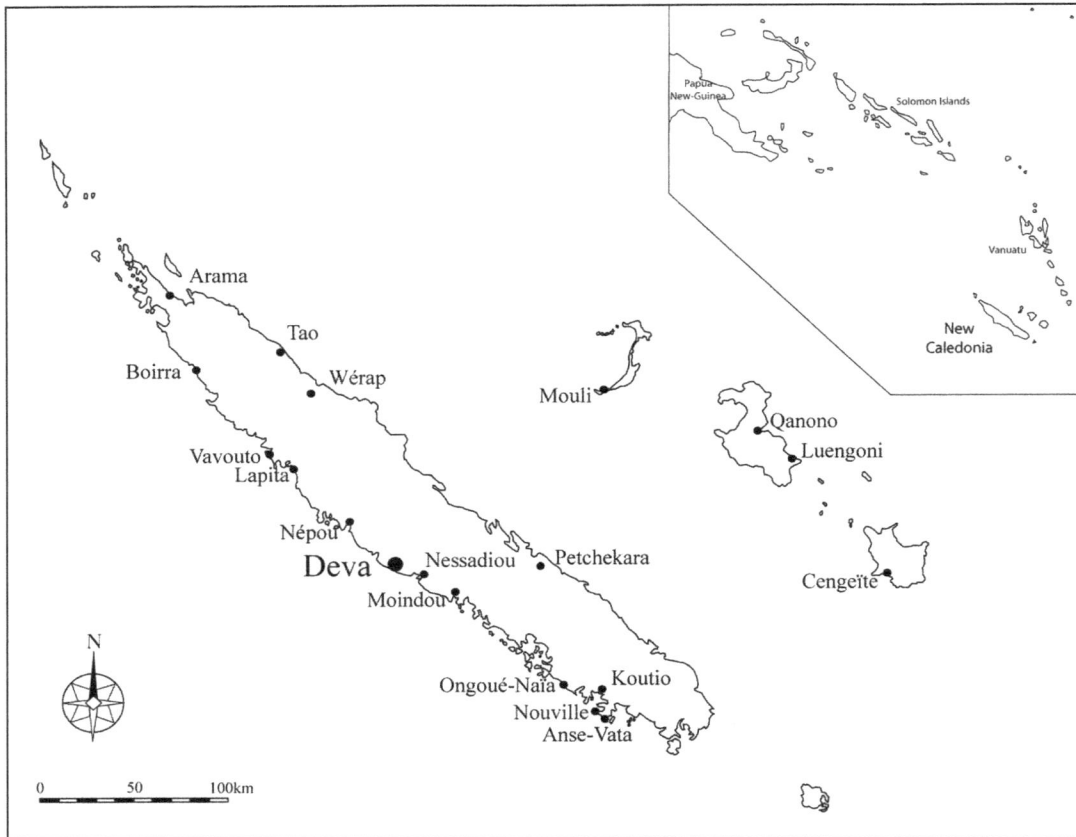

Figure 4.1. Location of sites where major rescue archaeology and CRM projects have been undertaken in New Caledonia.
Source: The authors.

From small-scale rescue excavations to CRM: A synopsis for New Caledonia

As in most of Melanesia, the insertion of archaeological heritage into impact studies for the development of economic projects has been slow to appear in New Caledonia. The political choice of negating archaeological remains that could potentially highlight indigenous history was one of the main drivers of the destruction of old sites during the colonial period of the archipelago (Sand et al. 2011a). Another significant aspect was that there was no dedicated local team to undertake excavations on development projects until the most recent decades. Consequently, professional archaeological programs in New Caledonia—which started in the 1950s—remained mainly research-based and the few rescue excavations were, for a long time, fulfilled as real 'rescue' operations, with often small-scale excavations opened during or after an archaeological site had already been severely disturbed.

Aside from observations done by local amateur archaeologists, the first real scientific project that incorporated the use of rescue excavation procedures in New Caledonia was Colin Smart's PhD project in 1966–67 on the site of Naïa in the south of Grande Terre. This beach location was heavily used as a sand quarry and Smart took this opportunity to open a number of trenches and a few larger-scale excavations (Figure 4.2). The varied data recovered, including a number of structures such as alignments of postholes, earth ovens and burials, allowed him to establish a ceramic chronology for the southern part of the archipelago (Green and Mitchell 1983; Smart n.d.). Another example of early rescue operation is the work of D Frimigacci at the site of Nessadiou in the 1970s, where he excavated a number of structures in what remained of the archaeological fill at the bottom of a sand quarry that had yielded Lapita sherds (Frimigacci 1999).

Figure 4.2. Large-scale excavation underway on site TON6 of Naïa by Colin Smart in 1966–67.
Source: Colin Smart; picture courtesy The Australian National University.

The 1980s were a time of political turmoil in New Caledonia, which hindered the development of field archaeology in the archipelago. Rescue excavations were mainly restricted to opening a few test pits on seashore locations that were under threat of economic development, especially around the capital Nouméa (Galipaud 1997). Things changed markedly in the 1990s, with the return of peace associated with a major phase of economic development that boosted the number of archaeological sites under threat. The creation of a local Department of Archaeology at the New Caledonia Museum in 1991, composed of three people, allowed archaeologists to work on some of these projects, mainly through publicly funded rescue excavations and low-scale archaeological impact studies. Rescue excavations were opened before the construction of hotels on each of the main islands of the Loyalties (Sand 1998a), while on Grande Terre it was mainly sand quarries and shrimp farm projects that prompted interventions (Sand 1998b; Sand and Ouetcho 1993; Sand et al. 1996). The main characteristic of the rescue programs undertaken during this decade is probably that the excavations remained mostly confined to a few square metres, in part due to the low funding provided. Nonetheless, these studies produced information that enhanced the understanding of some of the understudied periods of New Caledonia's chronology and allowed for the analysis of new topics (Sand 1996). Unfortunately, since impact studies were not compulsory, this period also witnessed a massive phase of destruction of important archaeological sites without any study.

A change in local procedures for impact studies emerged at the beginning of the 2000s, mainly driven by ecological lobbying. This had a positive effect on the development of archaeological interventions before economic projects. From then on, in a number of cases large-scale provincial projects in partnership with international companies—such as nickel smelters and multi-star hotels—had to be preceded by a comprehensive set of impact studies. International regulations certainly fostered this new approach, but it must be highlighted in the case of New Caledonia that local Kanak communities were also very much instrumental in the final incorporation of impact studies as part of the overall agreement to see these projects completed. In the early days of this new era, heritage was generally a poorly financed component of these studies, but the importance of the archaeological data recovered prompted in some cases a multi-year phasing of archaeological involvement, allowing for the emergence of a proper CRM methodology. This was characterised by the use of a backhoe and other heavy machinery to excavate large perimeters and by the development of trench digs to crisscross extensive surfaces. The need for large teams for these projects highlighted the difficulty of having CRM programs organised by the administratively constrained structure of the local Department of Archaeology. This prompted an experiment with the creation of private archaeological entities that was short-lived. In 2009 the New Caledonian government decided to preserve a public monopoly on archaeological digs.

One of the main archaeological CRM projects during this period was connected to the construction of a nickel smelter on the Vavouto Peninsula between the townships of Koné and Voh in the Northern Province (north-west coast of Grande Terre). Over the three phases, between 2002 and 2005 (Baret et al. 2000; Barp 2006; Carson 2003), a total of nearly 1600 m^2 was excavated, mainly in trenches, uncovering many different sites and features ranging from a Lapita site to traditional pre-contact Kanak hamlets and horticultural field structures. Another important CRM project occurred in the Southern Province where the destruction of burials as part of a controversial housing project on the Poé dunes (central west coast of Grande Terre) led to extensive trenching of the affected site in different phases between 2006 and 2008. This led to the discovery of deep stratified deposits and other burials (Barp 2009; Sand et al. 2008, 2012).

Switching to a larger scale: The Deva project

These first cases of proper CRM experiments led to a change of paradigm. The significant public impact of the Poé excavations prompted the Kanak stakeholders of the central west coast region of Grande Terre and the municipality of Bourail to include a compulsory archaeological impact assessment component in the general protocol of the economic development project of the nearby provincial property of Deva. The project included the construction of a 5-star hotel and an 18-hole international golf course on the seashore plains of Deva, facing one of the reef/lagoon marine clusters of New Caledonia, which were inscribed on the UNESCO World Heritage List in 2008. The start of the project coincided with a boost in the number of archaeologists working at the Department of Archaeology, soon to be transformed into the Institute of Archaeology of New Caledonia and the Pacific (IANCP). There was thus for the first time enough trained personnel to envision a long-term CRM project in New Caledonia through a public research institution, something that, to this day, is still unique in the Melanesian context.

The extent of the Deva excavations

The scale of the project meant that we had to adapt our methodology to be able to cover huge areas (cf. Sand et al. 2013:15–25). The Deva property, owned by the Southern Province, covers a surface of about 7450 hectares, encompassing a 15 km strip of coastal plain and a series of inland valleys and hills stretching up to 5 km from the coast. Although very depopulated at French colonisation, the Deva region is identified in Kanak oral traditions as an important traditional nexus during the centuries before first European contact. A general survey of the property allowed us to record over 200 Kanak sites, mainly in the plains and hilltops (Domergue 2009).

At first, the development projects were concentrated mainly on some parts of the seashore plain, where the hotel complex planned to occupy about 45 hectares and where 110 hectares were devoted to the golf course.

Since surface surveys had identified only minimal traces of archaeological occupations on the seashore plain, it was decided to begin the archaeological study by opening trenches with a backhoe in order to get a general understanding of the stratigraphy. The backhoe bucket was positioned to remove about 10 cm of sediment at every pass in order to observe and record any change in stratigraphy and to identify the appearance of archaeological features (ovens, burials, etc.). In 2008, a set of 152 10 m trenches were excavated every 50 m. In 2010, another set of 108 trenches were positioned more precisely on the location of the future bungalows of the hotel and on the area planned to receive the larger buildings for the hotel rooms. In 2012, 71 trenches covering 600 m² were excavated over an area of about 8 hectares at the north-west extremity of the coastal development area, where the golf course was soon to be located.

The excavations identified a sand-fill up to about 300–400 m away from the present beach, marked on the ground by successions of low dunes positioned parallel to the coast. This fill is replaced by marshy deposits or in situ basal rock formations towards the hillside. In the sand dunes, the archaeological fill was not deeper than about 65 cm regardless of the location where the trenches were excavated. The main stratigraphy was composed of a light terrigenous surface layer overlying usually one to three sandy deposits with pottery, shells, occasional stone artefacts and, in some instances, stone ovens, small post holes or human burials.

Aside from the trenching program, two large-scale archaeological excavations were opened as part of the hotel and golf course development projects. The first was 656 m² and was located in the back part of the dune area, where a concentration of archaeological remains, including stone ovens and burials, had been identified during trenching. As this was the planned location of one of the large hotel buildings, we decided to investigate the archaeological significance of the area. The excavations highlighted the presence of a well-preserved layer dated from 600–400 BCE with some large stone ovens as well as a number of postholes, but without any sign of large habitation structures. A total of seven burials, all dated from the second millennium CE, were also excavated. They were distributed randomly across the site and did not show any indication of a deliberate 'burial ground'. In consequence of the discovery of the burials, the hotel promoters decided—at the explicit demand of the Kanak stakeholders—to move the planned hotel building to a new location in order to prevent the disturbance of the skeletons.

The presence of other burials in different trenches opened in the golf course area fostered the second large-scale excavation of Deva. In order to prevent the possible destruction of burials in the course of quarrying sand for the bunkers of the golf course, the Kanak customary leaders asked the Southern Province to agree to the complete excavation of a nearly one-hectare block. This led to what is probably to this date the largest open area (about 130 m by 65 m) excavation ever undertaken in Melanesia, with a total area of just under 8000 m² (Figure 4.3). The study highlighted the absence of deeply buried remains over a large surface and confirmed the patterns exposed by the trenching program regarding settlement patterns and chronologies.

Figure 4.3. The nearly 1-hectare excavation of the Deva sand quarry at the end of the CRM project.
Source: Photograph Christophe Sand, IANCP.

Deva's settlement pattern data

The extensive set of excavations opened in the seashore dunes of Deva as part of the CRM project have allowed us to gain a unique understanding of the formation processes of this coastal strip of Grande Terre, facing the area of the lagoon where the reef is closest to land (about 2–3 km). The identification of a massive change in the coastal environment over the past 3000 years, which corresponds to the period of human settlement, is probably the most significant result in terms of environmental setting (Figure 4.4). The excavations have clearly demonstrated that at the end of the last ocean highstand, around 4000–3500 years ago, the seashore was located about 300–400 metres further inland from its present position. The drop of the sea level to its present level over the centuries led to the formation of small dunes, on which the first Lapita occupants of the area known today as Deva settled between 950 and 850 BCE. At that time, the actual surface for settlement was in most places probably less than 50 metres wide, since the land behind the narrow dunes was marshy. Through the following millennium, new dunes progressively formed in front of the original sand spit, resulting in the expansion of the area by about 100 metres. This prompted the occupants to constantly move their dwellings to the most recently formed dunes, in order to keep direct access to the seashore and created what we have termed a 'horizontal stratigraphy'. This process of repetitive seaward moves sealed most of the previous archaeological remains, prevented massive disturbances by later occupations and explains the absence of deep stratigraphy anywhere in the hotel and golf course areas. During the first and second millennia CE, the continuing natural process of dune formation—linked to natural sand production but without any tectonic process involved—led to the further expansion of the width of the area by up to 200 m in some places.

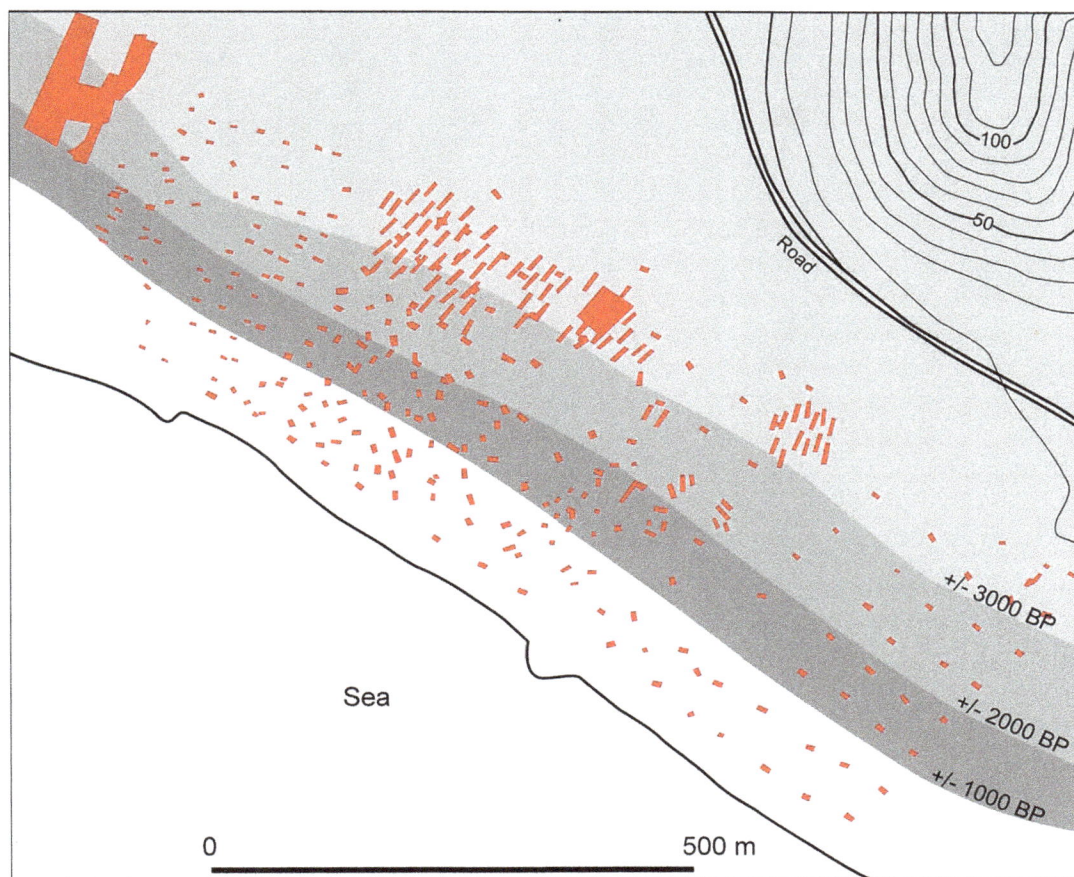

Figure 4.4. Synthesis map of the different excavations undertaken between 2008 and 2012 on the hotel and golf course settings of Deva, with the general chronological progression of the coastal dunes over the last 3000 years.

Source: The authors.

The fairly low amount of archaeological material uncovered for such a long chronology, as well as the low density of shell remains and the limited number of cooking and heating structures in most excavated zones, are clear testimonies to the discontinuous occupation of this coastal strip over a significant part of its human occupation. For nearly two millennia, the groups foraging the seashore of this easily accessible lagoon environment appear to have been living a semi-nomadic lifestyle, moving up and down the coast, possibly to prevent overharvesting the lagoon's limited ecological environment. Nowhere in the excavations has it been possible to identify any trace of permanent housing structures. While a number of clear postholes were uncovered on a regular basis, they never formed a coherent set of housing patterns. They appeared more like components of simple shelters. In a number of instances, postholes were covered by stone ovens, indicating resettlement after a period of abandonment.

Data allow us to subdivide this general scheme of occupation into different phases. The first millennium BCE is characterised by few occupations of groups that were probably mainly seashore foragers with a low-level reliance on horticulture. This general hypothesis is supported by the near-absence of sites related to this time period in the valleys behind the beach. A change in demography is clearly apparent during the first millennium CE, with the progressive increase of the number of burials, mainly positioned in the dunes that were at the back of the beachfront at that time. Of the 25 skeletons excavated, 15 are dated to the central part of the first millennium

CE. This time period saw on Grande Terre a crisis possibly linked to demographic growth and environmental factors, but also saw the slow appearance of new intensified horticultural techniques that contributed to the emergence of the 'Traditional Kanak Cultural Complex' at the beginning of the second millennium CE (Sand et al. 2003). The last millennium of occupation was characterised by sedentary multi-secular hamlet occupations. Significantly, only a few scarce signs of Kanak occupation have been uncovered in the more recent dunes, located in the first 100 metres behind the present beach. This clearly sets apart the settlement pattern of this recent period compared to the multiple remains of the two preceding millennia excavated in the Deva dunes (Sand et al. 2018). The archaeological data do not suggest that there were no coastal settlements during the traditional Kanak period, but rather that these were mainly restricted to clearly defined hamlets, probably positioned at the estuaries of the permanent creeks of Deva which are outside the area excavated by our CRM project. Numerous indications of densified Kanak settlements, with some extensive villages and associated horticultural structures, have been identified in the inner valleys of Deva (Sand et al. 2013:9–14).

The cultural chronology of the central west coast of Grande Terre

This project allowed us to study for the first time the whole cultural chronology of this central portion of the west coast of Grande Terre, at the border between the northern and southern ceramic regions of the archipelago (Sand et al. 2011b). The process of horizontal stratigraphy permitted by the progressive building of new sand dunes over a 3000–year period, and its consequent low mixing of material from different chronological periods, resulted in a clarification of a number of typological uncertainties for the local ceramic sequence (see Sand et al. 2013:38–49 for details). This has been achieved thanks to more than 350 radiocarbon dates obtained during the multi-year program.

Pottery

The amount of dentate-stamped vessels related to the first Lapita settlement is limited to a few sherds. This is not surprising as the oldest dates obtained are calibrated around 950–850 BCE, at the end of the Lapita period. These are associated with a great number of paddle-impressed sherds of the Podtanean tradition, some also bearing decorations from shell impressions or incisions. The rim profiles that could be reconstructed for some of these vessels in Deva show outcurved rims and poorly angled carination at the beginning of the occupation, with a progressive disappearance of the carination and increasing numbers of vessels with straighter rims. The chronological overlap between Podtanean and the succeeding incised Puen wares is clearly visible in the layers dated to the second half of the first millennium BCE. Puen pots show a significant diversity in form, size and decoration, but retain the mainly globular profile with simple incurved rim.

The start of the first millennium CE saw the progressive emergence of the handled Plum tradition pots, which becomes the main pottery type during most of the millennium. The Deva excavations have confirmed the parallel production of Puen and Plum pots during a few centuries in the Bourail region. They have also shown that, unlike in the southern part of Grande Terre, Plum vessels in this central region, while poorly decorated, have a unique type of tenon beside the usual horizontal handles. This consists of a bulky kind of rounded nubbin, known until now only through museum collections (Chevalier 1966–70). The last ceramic period, characterised by the Nera tradition of oval pots with incurved rims and alignments of raised nubbins, is the least represented in the excavated areas. A few Oundjo sherds at Deva indicate that some pots produced in the northern half of Grande Terre were brought to the site, probably through exchange.

Shell ornaments

A significant quantity of shell ornaments has been retrieved during the Deva excavations. They display a diversity of production types, ranging from mainly *Conus* armbands and discs, to numerous small beads extracted from *Conus leopardus* and *Conus eburneus* shells. *Tridacna* ornaments are restricted to the first millennium BCE. In regards to shell artefacts, two outcomes can be highlighted. The first is related to the in situ production of these items, as numerous grinding and polishing plaques of diverse sizes were used during the manufacturing process. The second relates to the site itself; Deva being known in Kanak oral traditions as one of the important places of traditional shell money manufacture, with people coming even from the east coast of Grande Terre to collect specific shells in the lagoon. The excavation at the sand quarry uncovered the working floor of an area where shell beads were produced dated to about 2400 years ago. The archaeological data for New Caledonia supports the hypothesis that beads were used as shell money during that time period, but this is the first time an actual production centre has been identified. Significantly, shell money typology changed with the advent of the 'Traditional Kanak Cultural Complex', something that has been clearly documented in Deva. Again for the first time for the archipelago, remains of a complete shell money kit was excavated just over the wrapped bones of an adult dated to the early 19th century. It consisted of a series of finely carved oyster shell pendants, each between 20 mm and 30 mm long, that were probably attached to a vegetal packet as is known through museum specimens.

Stone artefacts

Compared to the shell artefacts, the number of stone artefacts uncovered during the Deva excavations is low. This is probably partly due to the poor quality of the rocks that could be extracted for flaking and polishing in the immediate geological area surrounding this portion of the west coast. Excavations have nonetheless allowed us to uncover a few adzes dating from the central part of the Koné period (second half of the first millennium BCE), filling a void in our chronology of polished items. Of interest was also the discovery of a large fragment of a drilled nephrite polished axe, clearly similar to the Kanak ceremonial 'ostensoir axes', in a layer dated to the 15th century CE. This is only the third occurrence of such an item in a datable stratigraphic context in New Caledonia.

Burials

The last major contribution of the CRM excavations at Deva relate to burial customs. In total, 25 burials were excavated. The agreement with the Kanak customary authorities was that we were allowed to excavate each identified skeleton and to map and photograph the in situ remains without removing the bones. We got the permission to collect three small bones, one used for dating, one for isotope studies and one for possible DNA analysis in the future. After completion of the archaeological study, each skeleton was reburied in sand. A diversity of funerary practices only partly related to chronological changes was identified throughout the site (Sand et al. 2013:66–69). During the period corresponding with the most intense use of the area as a burial place from the first millennium CE to the beginning of the second millennium CE, most bodies were placed in a pit in a flexed seated position (Figure 4.5). Some bodies show clear signs of wrapping, possibly with a mat or some sort of rope. The few burials from the later part of the second millennium CE show more significant body manipulation in some instances, with the presence of partly reorganised remains wrapped in square packs.

Figure 4.5. Example of flexed burials in pits, excavated in the south-western area of Deva's sand quarry.
Source: Photograph Jacques Bolé, IANCP.

Conclusion

By highlighting the CRM case study of Deva in New Caledonia, this paper has discussed a neglected aspect of archaeological potential in Melanesia. The slow emergence of a proper interest in archaeological impact studies in the archipelago over the last few decades has been linked to the unique historical and political situation of this southern Melanesian archipelago. While the international regulations were implemented as part of the preparatory process in the case of the two large multimillion dollar nickel smelter projects, Kanak customary pressure was unquestionably instrumental in the imposition of archaeological impact studies for the Deva property development (Sand 2015). One of the direct outcomes of the CRM programs for the Deva hotel and golf course projects has been to move one of the main buildings to a new location and to limit the extent of the sand quarry surface in order to protect a set of burials. Moreover, each identified burial of the coastal dune area is now protected by a 4 m² perimeter, on which nothing can be built.

It can be asked if the same development of archaeological impact studies is to be expected elsewhere in Island Melanesia in the near future. To this day, the only direct parallel in terms of scale is the archaeological research at Caution Bay near Port Moresby on mainland New Guinea (Richards et al. 2016), where a well-funded archaeological CRM program was undertaken ahead of the construction of a liquefied natural gas plant and pipeline. In this case, the work was done by an international team, with only some local expert input. The main challenge to the future development of CRM programs appears to be in the field of local archaeological expertise in the Melanesian countries. As long as local governments do not promote training, including postgraduate education, and support for permanent archaeological staff in their museums and cultural centres, archaeology will continue to remain mainly an outsider-driven topic in the region. Only well trained and well equipped teams will have the capacity and the administrative power to promote effective archaeological resource management and rescue archaeology ahead of development in Island Melanesia. Economic pressure as well as political constrains will continue to dominate the agenda and local archaeologists will have to maintain their lobbying to see any progress in this domain in the years to come.

The progressive shift of the administrative understanding of what should be the mandate of archaeology in New Caledonia is a less obvious consequence of the rise of CRM programs that has major negative implications. Like other developed regions around the world, the rise of archaeological impact studies has sadly led decision-makers to think that archaeology is mainly devoted to this type of economically driven fieldwork for the sake of 'clearing the site' for development (Hutchings and La Salle 2015). Consequently in New Caledonia, the emergence of CRM has gone hand in hand with the massive drop in public finances for archaeological projects associated with research questions. Over the last years, the program of the IANCP has been nearly entirely devoted to CRM activities, trapping the local archaeological team into a never-ending series of archaeological impact studies. The saddest outcome of this change of focus is that the amount of archaeological data recovered though CRM has become so extensive, and the time that can be devoted to its study has shrunk so much, that publications are limited to 'grey literature' reports for the developers. This progressive change in paradigm highlights the slow move of CRM archaeology towards the private sector, something that is today promoted by the provincial cultural services. This will undoubtedly reinforce the trend towards 'grey literature' publications, depriving the local populations as well as the archaeologists working in Melanesia of the massive amount of new data that CRM will continue to generate in the decades to come.

Acknowledgements

The archaeological research programs and CRM projects on the Deva property have been fulfilled through the financial support of the Southern Province and the Government of New Caledonia to the authors' institute. The fieldwork presented here was undertaken by the authors under the direction of the first author, who wrote the present paper. The SEM (Société d'économie mixte) Mwé Ara, who is in charge of the management of the property, has given all the help possible during the fieldwork. The traditional Kanak landowner families and clans related to Deva, grouped in the GDPL (Groupement de Droit Particulier Local) Mwé Ara, have given their permission for the surveys and excavations.

References

Allen, J and C Gosden (eds). 1991. *Report of the Lapita Homeland Project*. Occasional Papers on Prehistory 20. Canberra: Department of Prehistory, Research School of Pacific Studies, The Australian National University.

Baret, D, J Bolé, A-J Ouetcho and C Sand. 2000. *Etude de potentiel et pré-inventaire des ressources patrimoniales du milieu*. Etude environnementale de base. Koné: Projet Koniambo.

Barp, F. 2006. *Etude archéologique phase 3. Rapport final d'opération*. Nouméa: Project Koniambo.

Barp, F. 2009. *Site 'Ecrins de Poé', WBR047, Commune de Bourail, Province Sud, Nouvelle-Calédonie*. Nouméa: Rapport de 'Strates, archéologie préventive, Nouvelle-Calédonie' pour le compte de la province Sud de la Nouvelle-Calédonie.

Bedford, S, M Spriggs and R Regenvanu. 1999. 'The Australian National University–Vanuatu Cultural Centre Archaeology Project 1994–97: Aims and results'. *Oceania* 70 (1):16–24. doi.org/10.1002/j.1834-4461.1999.tb02986.x.

Carson, M. 2003. *Phase two archaeological study, Koniambo Project, regions of Voh, Koné, and Pouembout, Northern Province, New Caledonia.* Honolulu: International Archaeological Research Institute, Inc.

Chevalier, L. 1966–70. 'Les éléments de préhension de la poterie calédonienne'. *Etudes Mélanésiennes* 21–25:45–54.

Clark, G and A Anderson. 2009. *The early prehistory of Fiji.* Terra Australis 31. Canberra: ANU E Press. doi.org/10.22459/TA31.12.2009.

Domergue, S. 2009. *Mission Deva 2006. Premier inventaire des vestiges archéologiques.* Nouméa: Département archéologie de la direction des affaires culturelles et coutumières.

Frimigacci, D. 1999. 'Où sont allés les potiers Lapita de Bourail? Remarques sur le site WBR001'. In *Le Pacifique de 5000 à 2000 avant le présent. Suppléments à l'histoire d'une colonisation*, edited by J-C Galipaud and I Lilley, 63–84. Paris: Editions de l'IRD.

Galipaud, J-C. 1997. 'A revision of the archaeological sequence of Southern New Caledonia'. *New Zealand Journal of Archaeology* 17 (1995):77–109.

Garanger, J. 1972. *Archéologie des Nouvelles-Hébrides: Contribution à la connaissance des îles du Centre.* Publications de la Société des Océanistes 30. Paris: Société des Océanistes, Musée de l'Homme. doi.org/10.4000/books.sdo.859.

Green, RC and MM Cresswell. 1976. *Southern Solomon Islands cultural history: A preliminary report.* Bulletin 11. Wellington: Royal Society of New Zealand.

Green, RC and J Mitchell. 1983. 'New Caledonian culture history: A review of the archaeological sequence'. *New Zealand Journal of Archaeology* 5:19–68.

Hutchings, R and M La Salle. 2015. 'Archaeology as disaster capitalism'. *International Journal of Historical Archaeology* 19 (4):699–720. doi.org/10.1007/s10761-015-0308-3.

Richards, T, B David, K Aplin, and I McNiven. 2016. *Archaeological research at Caution Bay, Papua New Guinea: Cultural, linguistic and environmental setting.* Caution Bay Studies in Archaeology 1. Oxford: Archaeopress.

Sand, C. 1996. 'Recent developments in the study of New Caledonia's prehistory'. *Archaeology in Oceania* 31:47–71. doi.org/10.1002/j.1834-4453.1996.tb00349.x.

Sand, C. 1998a. 'Recent archaeological research in the Loyalty Islands of New Caledonia'. *Asian Perspectives* 37:194–223.

Sand, C. 1998b. 'Archaeological report on localities WKO013A and WKO013B of the site of Lapita (Koné, New Caledonia)'. *Journal of the Polynesian Society* 107:7–33.

Sand, C. 2015. 'On the edge of a World Heritage Site: Local communities and archaeological practice related to the nomination of the New Caledonia Reef'. In *Second International Conference on Best Practices in World heritage: People and Communities*, edited by AC Mena, 874–887. Madrid: Universidad Complutense de Madrid.

Sand, C, J Bolé and A-J Ouetcho. 1996. *Le début du peuplement austronésien de la Nouvelle-Calédonie. Données archéologiques récentes.* Les cahiers de l'archéologie en Nouvelle-Calédonie 6. Nouméa: Service territorial des musées et du patrimoine.

Sand, C, J Bolé and A-J Ouetcho. 2003. 'Prehistory and its perception in a Melanesian Archipelago: the New Caledonia example'. *Antiquity* 77 (297):505–519. doi.org/10.1017/S0003598X00092565.

Sand, C, J Bolé and A-J Ouetcho. 2011a. 'Evolutions du discours archéologique sur 150 ans d'histoire colonial et postcoloniale en Nouvelle-Calédonie. Un cas d'école'. *Les nouvelles de l'Archéologie* 126:37–40.

Sand, C, J Bolé and A-J Ouetcho. 2011b. 'A revision of New Caledonia's ceramic sequence'. *Journal of Pacific Archaeology* 2:56–68.

Sand, C, JA Grant-Mackie, HJ Campbell and J Turnbull. 2018. 'Seashore settlement patterns in the Koné and Naïa Periods: Case studies from Southwestern New Caledonia'. *Journal of Island & Coastal Archaeology* 13 (4):1–13. doi.org/10.1080/15564894.2018.1513101.

Sand, C, and A-J Ouetcho. 1993. 'Three thousand years of settlement in the south of New Caledonia: Some recent results from the region of Païta'. *New Zealand Journal of Archaeology* 15:107–130.

Sand, C, A-J Ouetcho, J Bolé, D Baret, L Lagarde and F Valentin. 2012. 'Archéologie en Mélanésie: Données du site côtier WBR047 des "Ecrins de Poé" (Bourail, Nouvelle-Calédonie)'. *Bulletin de la Société préhistorique française* 109 (3):495–512. doi.org/10.3406/bspf.2012.14172.

Sand, C, A-J Ouetcho, J Bolé, D Baret and F Valentin. 2008. *Données archéologiques sur le site WBR047 des 'Ecrins de Poé' (Commune de Bourail, province Sud): Tentative de synthèse sur l'intervention de 2007.* Nouméa: Département archéologie de la direction des affaires culturelles et coutumières.

Sand, C, M Terebo and L Lagarde (eds). 2013. *La passé de Deva. Archéologie d'un domaine provincial calédonien.* Archeologia Pasifika 2. Nouméa: Institut d'archéologie de la Nouvelle-Calédonie et du Pacifique.

Sheppard, P, R Walter and T Nagaoka. 2000. 'The archaeology of head-hunting in Roviana Lagoon, New Georgia, Solomon Islands'. *Journal of the Polynesian Society* 109:9–37.

Smart, C. n.d. 'Notes on the pottery sequence obtained for southern New Caledonia' (Report confidential 1969) (ms).

Summerhayes, G. 2000. *Lapita interaction.* Terra Australis 15. Canberra: Department of Archaeology and Natural History and Centre for Archaeological Research, The Australian National University.

5

The complexity of monumentality in Melanesia: Mixed messages from Vanuatu

Stuart Bedford

Introduction

This paper revisits the concept of monumentality through the lens of grand communal ceremonies on three separate islands, with contrasting chiefly systems, in the archipelago of Vanuatu (Figure 5.1). One is the island of Malakula in the north where substantial stone structures associated with a range of ceremonies can be found right across the landscape. Further south on Efate the use of stone is limited but grand ceremony and monumentality is spectacularly demonstrated in the archaeological record. Lastly, large ceremonies involving thousands of people occur on a regular basis on the island of Tanna in the south, yet the material remains of such events are almost completely absent (Bonnemaison 1994). This striking variance across a single archipelago leads to some questions regarding the whole concept and significance of monumentality (Ballard and Wilson 2014) and particularly to its importance in relation to processes of social transformation in the Pacific. However, it needs to be emphasised that the wider debate is somewhat handicapped by the fact that the study of monumentality across the broader Pacific is extremely uneven in its coverage, at least in archaeological focus, in terms of both even basic information and a lack of targeted research (Walter and Sheppard 2006). While the trajectory of sociopolitical complexity and its associated proxies have been tracked on almost literally every major Polynesian island group, along with many in Micronesia, the archaeology of social systems of the South-West Pacific are rare (Allen 1985; Garanger 1972; Irwin 1985; Sand 1995; Spriggs 1986) and specifically those associated with ritual architecture, or monumentality generally, remain remarkably few (Bickler 2004; Byrne 2013; Field 2004; Sand 1995; Spriggs 1986; Thomas 2009; Walter and Sheppard 2006).

Pacific Island societies have long played a special role in influencing Western theoretical discourse relating to the form and development of sociopolitical structures and their evolution on a world-scale (Kirch 1984, 2010; Spriggs 2008). Right from the very beginnings of European and Pacific encounters, as the accounts of the early explorers surfaced in Europe, debate was inspired regarding the nature of human society (Smith 1989, 1992). It did not take long for Pacific societies to be drafted into theories relating to the emerging 19th-century ladder-like structures of social evolution as exemplars of the lower rungs (Golson 1977). When the region was carved up on maps into Melanesia, Micronesia and Polynesia by the French explorer Dumont d'Urville in 1832, insidious racial categories became formalised (Dumont d'Urville 2003). Apparent forms of social organisation were particularly influential in the ordering of a region's position on the evolutionary scale. Polynesians at the apex were admired for having sophisticated sociopolitical structures and light skin colour, while at the other end of the scale, Melanesians were described as having 'no governing bodies, no laws, and no formal religious practices' concomitant with their darker skin colour (Dumont d'Urville 2003).

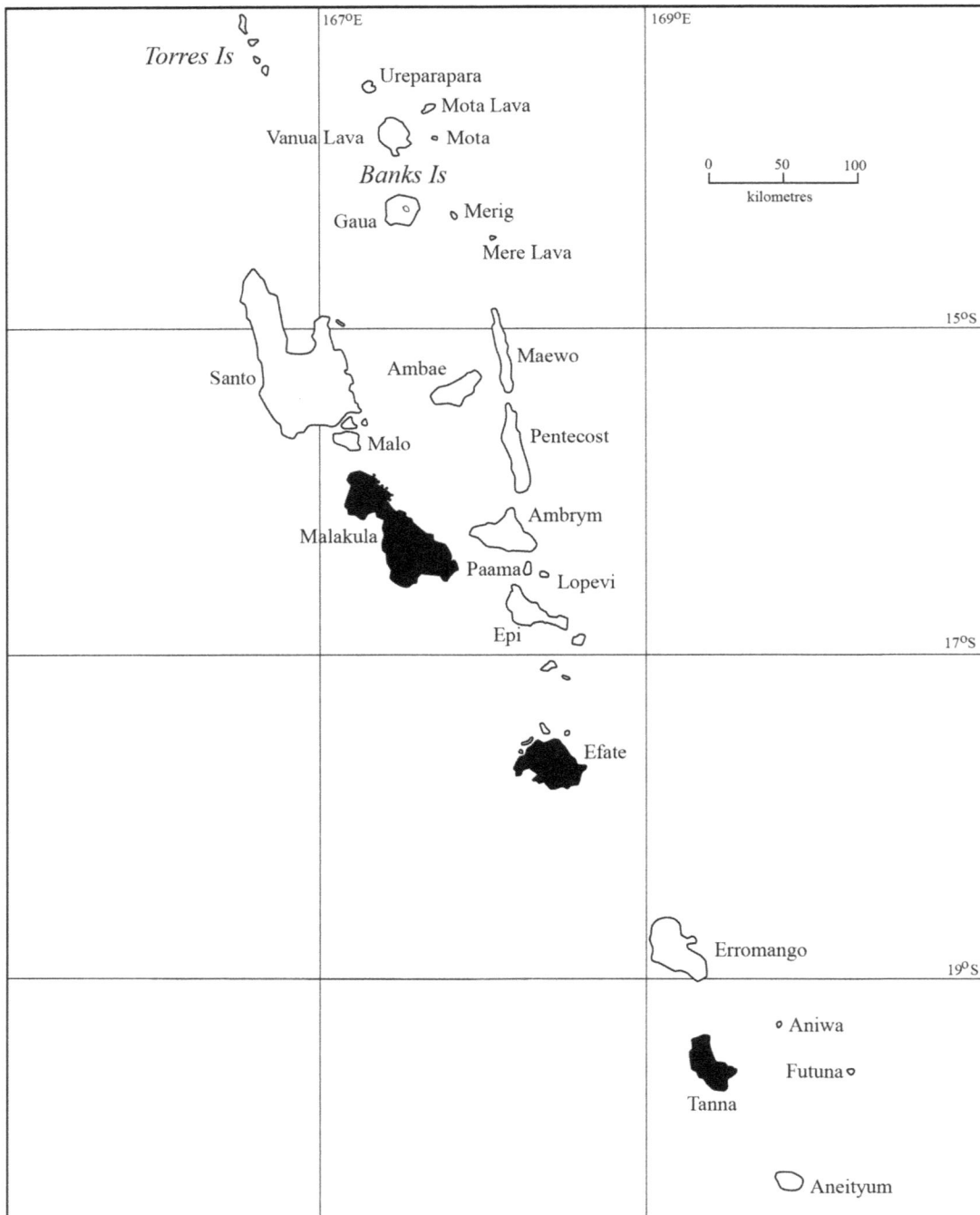

Figure 5.1. Vanuatu archipelago (Malakula, Efate and Tanna infilled).
Source: Stuart Bedford.

Despite these divisions and their subsequent influence having been repeatedly criticised on a whole series of levels (e.g. Clark 2003; Douglas 1979; Golson 1977; Green 1991; Lilley 1985; Sand 2002; Spriggs 2008; Tcherkézoff 2003; Thomas 1989; see also David and Denham 2006 for a critique of Australian Aboriginal categorisation), they still retain considerable authority, entrenched in the wider public consciousness and in contemporary discourse.

A range of material signals or proxies for social transformation, most often assumed to be associated with increasing social stratification, have been identified from archaeological research in the Pacific. These include population growth; extensive modification of island ecosystems; intensification of agriculture or other productive systems; increased economic specialisation; development of ceremonial or public architecture and increasing territoriality often reflected in more frequent construction of fortifications (Kirch 1984:13–15). Most researchers today agree that there are no universal 'prime movers' in terms of drivers of cultural change but rather a varied combination of environmental contexts and long-term processes influenced by human agency which can produce divergent historical trajectories (Earle 1989; Kirch 2010).

However, discussions of monumentality in general in the Pacific and more specifically monumental architecture in stone, tends to be fixed in association with hierarchically organised chiefdoms, and that such activity would not have occurred if such social frameworks were not in place. These assumptions can clearly be challenged across much of the Melanesian region and very strikingly so in the archipelago of Vanuatu. Various islands in Vanuatu exhibit a similar range of proxies that are associated with social transformation and increasing hierarchy elsewhere, but ultimately arrived at radically different forms of social organisation and expressions of 'monumentality'.

The travelling stones of Malakula

Malakula is located in the north of the Vanuatu archipelago (Figure 5.1), the second largest island of the group at 2051 km², along with 15 small islands off its north-east and south coasts (Siméoni 2009:55–61). Its reputation for an island where monumental stone architecture was widely practised has been well known for more than 100 years, to the point where it is often seen as the island's most characteristic cultural feature. Riesenfeld, for example, in his exhaustive tome, *The Megalithic Culture of Melanesia*, commented that 'it is no exaggeration to consider Malekula as the best-known place in Melanesia as regards megaliths' (Riesenfeld 1950:35). The ethnographers Speiser, Layard and Deacon, who spent time on the islands in the first part of the 20th century, recorded these sites, generally known as *nasara*, and associated ceremonial practice in lengthy detail (Deacon 1934; Layard 1942; Speiser 1996). The layout and form of the stone in these structures takes a wide range of forms. In the south, lines or large circles of standing stones tend to be most common, although small dolmens have also been recorded. In some areas, the standing stones are worked into a tubular form. This is seen particularly in the South-West Bay area where a majority of standing stones in any *nasara* are tubular, but examples can also be found amongst large *nasara* right up the west coast and into the interior of the north and centre (Figure 5.2a). In the central and northern part of the island, *nasara* comprise standing stones displaying limited dressing, and stone platforms and tables that are arranged in linear or curvilinear, amphitheatre-like, plan (Figure 5.2b). A very distinctive feature found across the islands in almost all *nasara* is the marking of a single stone, or in rarer cases several stones, with cupules (Figure 5.2c). Although rarer still, standing stones are also carved with anthropomorphic designs and profiles, an aspect that appears to be more common in the south (Figure 5.2d), although the trading and collecting of these items that has occurred over the last 100 years or more may well have skewed their currently understood distribution.

Figure 5.2. Range of stone features found in *nasara*: (a) tubular standing stones, Vao mainland, north Malakula; (b) stone platforms and standing stones, Tenmiel, north-west Malakula; (c) standing flat slab of beach rock with cupules, Lamap, south-east Malakula; (d) carved tubular standing stone, South-West Bay, Malakula.

Source: Stuart Bedford.

The primary materials that are used in construction are beach rock and limestone from the uplifted reef terraces that are present right up into the interior of the island. *Acropora* table coral, broken from fringing reefs, has also been used, particularly so in those *nasara* relatively close to source. They were planted on their side to form wide standing features or sections of wall or more commonly as the flat tops of dolmens or tables (Figure 5.3a). At many of these sites, the beach rock or coral material could be sourced relatively close to hand but even then, the transport and positioning of some of the largest slabs, which might weigh upwards of several tons, would have required significant labour input and engineering skill (Layard 1942:363–408). There are few ethnographic accounts of construction, but Speiser was on the island of Vao when one large slab of beach rock was being hauled to a *nasara* on a sledge built of logs (see Speiser 1996:Plate 63, 64).

Although Layard did not witness any of the procedures associated with erecting the stones, he recorded oral traditions associated with *nasara* construction. It was a complicated and lengthy multi-year process, even for single stones, which involved a whole series of ceremonies at every stage and could involve the participation of labour from nearby villages (1942:363–408).

While much stone could be sourced locally (Layard 1942:417–418), there are almost always stones at these sites that have been sourced from much further afield. For example, the *Acropora* coral is found associated with dolmens built as shrines in many *nasara* across the entire central and north of Malakula. In these cases, their transport would have been undertaken across many kilometres and hundreds of metres above sea level. Very large tubular-shaped sections of limestone have been regularly recorded many kilometres from any source, and in one case at one of the highest points (355 m) in the north of the island (Figure 5.3b). Water-worn stone sourced from rivers on Malakula have also been recorded in *nasara* on the small islands of the north-east. Further complicating the picture of establishing the origins of stone in any *nasara* complex was a practice where participants in various ceremonies, including some who had come some distance, would contribute stones themselves. Once erected, particular stones remained associated with that individual who may have participated in ceremonies at a number of *nasara* over their lifetime (Layard 1942:17).

Figure 5.3. (a) *Acropora* coral sourced directly from the reef and incorporated into the *nasara* structure, Uripiv Island; (b) tubular stone at *nasara* on the high point of northern Malakula.
Source: Stuart Bedford.

These *nasara* sites were central to community life where a whole host of ceremonies took place. The most frequent and most important in terms of local political structure were the grade-taking ceremonies where men attempted to achieve status through ritual and economic tests, rather than hereditary title (Layard 1942:12–19). The chiefly structure on Malakula demonstrated limited hierarchy, certainly in terms of wider community influence, and was only consolidated through the accumulation of grades that involved individuals sponsoring various forms of public ceremony. Grade-taking ceremonies were associated with accumulation and distribution of wealth, most often pigs but also yams. Debt could be accumulated over a generation and organisational aspects of a single ceremony could take 12 months or more to prepare (Bonnemaison 1996; Deacon 1934; Layard 1942). The scale of the largesse associated with these occasions is exemplified by a report from 1892 where 1500 pigs were sacrificed during one ceremony on the small island of Vao, Malakula (population then 2500) (Beaune 1894).

From the start of the 20th century, increasing depopulation in combination with missionisation generally led to a radical reduction in the number of ceremonies undertaken and in many areas they were discontinued. However, these sites remain durable and highly visible artefacts of ceremony and ritual and represent the material archive containing details of the sociopolitical development of the islands. Even today these ritual structures remain central to peoples' lives, relating to origins, identity and land ownership (Bedford et al. 2017a). In that respect, *nasara* have retained a continuum of use and a connection with those first generations who established them.

Malakula then, is an island where large ceremonial structures in stone are a widespread feature of the cultural and political landscape, but one that was developed within a minimally stratified social system.

Efate: Monumentality in earth and ceremony

In contrast, stone architecture was not generally a feature of ceremonial activity on the island of Efate in central Vanuatu. In some cases, standing stones were used to mark chiefly graves but these tended to be few in number and relatively small, no higher than 1 m above the ground surface (Garanger 1972:Figure 149). However, as demonstrated through the 1960s excavations of José Garanger on the island of Retoka, the use and/or size of stones on Efate is not a reliable marker of ceremonial significance or importance. The 12 small basaltic standing stones (some of which now lie flat) at the site in fact mark the communal burial of more than 50 individuals (Figure 5.4a), who are related to one of the most significant historical ceremonial events on that island for the last 500 years. Apart from these few small standing stones, there was actually very little to be seen on the surface at the site in the 1960s, when excavated, and that remains the case today. The site on Retoka, inscribed in 2008 on the UNESCO World Heritage List, thanks primarily to Garanger's archaeological excavations, is associated with the culmination of a grand ceremony marking the death of the revered high chief Roi Mata in c. 1600 CE (Garanger 1972:59–77). Retoka remains one of the few cultural sites in the Pacific that corresponded to the rich oral traditions (Ballard and Wilson 2012; Garanger 1996).

Roi Mata is credited with introducing peace to the region after an extended period of conflict with his establishment or perhaps reinvigoration of the matrilineal *naflak* system. According to oral traditions, he became ill at a competitive feast and due to his very high status was buried with followers on the isolated island of Retoka (Ballard and Wilson 2012). This ceremony would have taken considerable time to prepare and involved people from all over Efate and the Shepherd Islands who were prepared to sacrifice a substantial number of high-status individuals as part of the funerary ritual. Grand feasts and displays of largesse would have been intimately associated with this process.

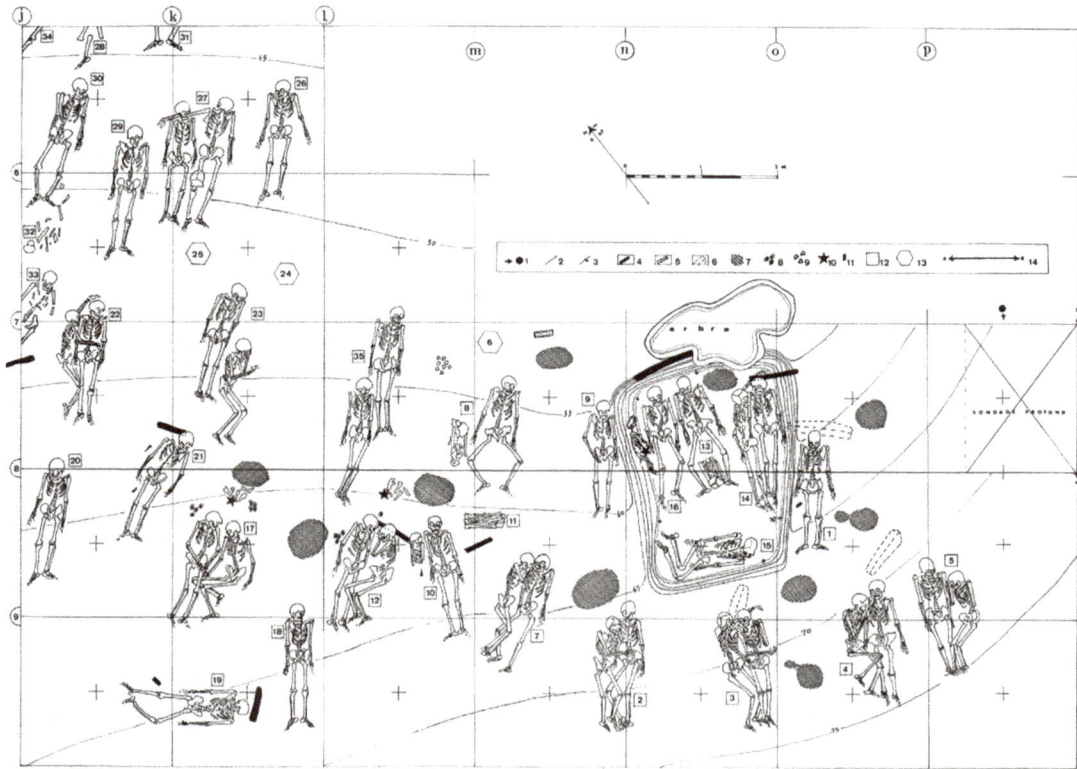

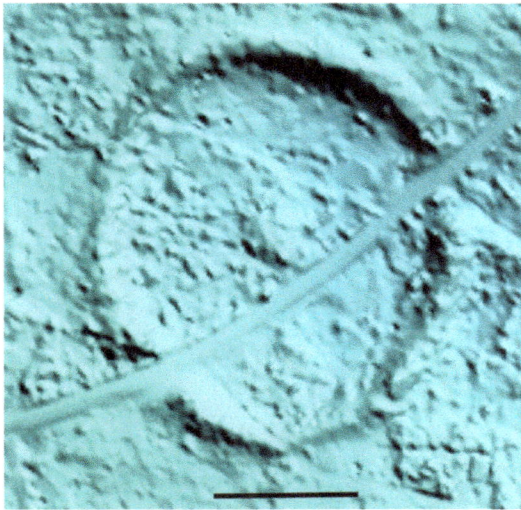

Figure 5.4. (a) Roi Mata burials, Retoka Island, Efate (Garanger 1972:Figure 153); (b) circular feature, 110 m in diameter, cut through by road, Eratap, Efate. Black bar is 50 m.

Source: Stuart Bedford.

More recent research has identified another very different form of monumentality on Efate. A light detection and ranging (LiDAR) survey of 32.4 per cent of the island has revealed that much of the landscape was completely modified by human activity prior to European contact (Bedford et al. 2017b). Features that dominate the landscape are a range of linear mounds that in some cases extend for several hundred metres or form enclosures of varying size in an irregular mosaic or grid pattern that are associated with agricultural activity. However, the most spectacular and unexpected of these features are massive circular depressions bounded by earth banks (Figure 5.4b). Seventy-one of these circular features have been identified (Bedford et al. 2017b:Figure 2). Their sizes vary greatly but the majority (51) are between 50 and 100 m in diameter, 15 are between 100 and 145 m in diameter, and one is substantially larger, at almost 200 m in diameter. They are found at all altitudes, from 10 m to 260 m above sea level, across the landscape. They appear to have been formed through soil being shifted from the inside of the feature and out to the exterior. The dimensions of the boundary walls vary, but they are between 1.5–2.0 m high (measured from the interior) and 3–4 m wide. The average diameter of these features is 84 m, a rough calculation of soil displacement for such a feature is more than 33 000 m[3].[1] While interpretation of the circular features remains speculative, they are without doubt truly monumental in terms of their size and the labour input associated with their construction.

What of the chiefly system of Efate? It is very different to that of Malakula in the north as it is essentially characterised by heredity within a hierarchical system where chiefs can exercise considerable authority over their territorial domains. Individuals receive customary names, which is a title within a structure of hierarchical titles (Bonnemaison 1996:212–216). It is also a chiefly system that demonstrates some time depth, as indicated from the oral traditions and archaeological record on Retoka.

Massive depopulation, land alienation and missionisation have all heavily impacted on traditional cultural and political activities on Efate. However, monumentality is clearly seen most visibly today both in the massive earthwork remains across the landscape but also in the 400-year-old ceremony represented by the Roi Mata burials on Retoka that has been preserved within oral traditions.

Tanna: Monumental ritual exchange

Finally, to the south of the archipelago and the island of Tanna. This is the sixth largest island (570.7 km[2]) in Vanuatu and one of the most densely populated (46.1 per km[2]). Tanna is well known for its retention of aspects of a 'traditional' way of life which revolves around regular all-year-round ceremonies of ritual exchange that encompass all parts of the life cycle and are integral to Tannese social and political life (Bonnemaison 1996:214–216; Lindstrom 1996:123–128). Some of these ceremonies of exchange, based on a system of reciprocity, can take years to prepare, involve thousands of people and abundant displays of largesse, often in the form of pigs and yams (Figures 5.5a and b).

Figure 5.5. Exchange items at a *Nial* (food exchange) ceremony, Tanna, July 2017: (a) a wall of yams stacked more than 2 m high; (b) pigs and kava.

---

1   Volume = π×84[2]×1.5 = 33250.61 m[3]. This does not take into account the small mound in the centre of most circular features, but the calculation uses the minimal exterior wall height.

Source: Photographs by Joel Simo.

The population of Tanna is generally scattered across the landscape in small hamlets, with a ceremonial open space of c. 2000–3000 m^2 located nearby (Bonnemaison 1994:106–112). These spaces, which are regularly cleaned, generally display nothing exceptional apart from a mature banyan tree on one side of the open area.[2] However, it is here that the ceremonies of ritual exchange take place, whether they be the nightly exchange of kava between men of the same village or seasonal grand exchanges of agricultural largesse involving a number of tribes that serve to establish or maintain political alliances. Months after these large ceremonies have finished, there is nothing to show but well-stamped open spaces and it is only oral traditions that essentially keep the memory of such events alive. The open space continues to be recognised and restricted as a zone for a range of ongoing ceremonial activities, but beyond the open space and the banyan no other permanent features are added. It is the open space and the repeated ritual exchanges that are the monuments.

The chiefly system on Tanna, although hereditary, is like that of Malakula in that it displays minimal hierarchy and very localised control. James Cook described his initial impressions in relation to the Tannese political structure as follows: 'Chiefs they seem to have amongst them; at least some were announced as such, but they appeared to have little authority over the rest of the people' (Beaglehole 1961:497). However, the apparent egalitarian political nature of the chiefly system on Tanna should not be confused with simplicity, as any claims or conferred rights are open to constant public debate and negotiation and include assessments of individual accomplishment during ritual exchange (Lindstrom 1996:123).

Discussion

In his summary of traditional Vanuatu political power, Bonnemaison explains that there are very broadly two types of political power found across the archipelago. There are those where chiefdoms are based on a hierarchy of grades and where men come to power through competitive economic display; while the other system is based on heredity and titles. However, he warned against oversimplification, suggesting that neither system was as straightforward as these broad categories might suggest, adding that:

> it is as if it were part of the Melanesian genius to take the model it receives, as it spreads from place to place, and complicate it as much as possible to put a local stamp on it. (Bonnemaison 1996:200)

The same complex variation in forms and establishment of chiefly power in Vanuatu is, not surprisingly, also found in the various representations and expressions of monumentality. A common theme related to political power and its material manifestations across the archipelago is in fact diversification. There exists in Vanuatu a range of elements that are seen as proxies for social transformation, that have led to increased hierarchy in other regions of the Pacific: high levels of population density; extensive modification of the ecosystem; development of ceremonial architecture; intensification of agriculture or other productive systems; and in some cases increased economic specialisation. However, the three islands highlighted here, Malakula, Efate and Tanna, all of which display aspects of potential drivers of social transformation, appear to have ultimately arrived at very different forms of social organisation and representations of monumentality. While the three islands hosted regular large ceremonies often involving thousands of people that could take years of preparation, the material legacy of those events is vastly different. Chiefly systems

---

2   Although there is very limited use of transported or manipulated stone as such in association with any ceremony on Tanna, metaphorical 'stones' are an integral component of Tannese identity and cosmology. They are almost exclusively natural features such as outcrops, mountain tops or ridge crests spread across the landscape (Bonnemaison 1994:116–122).

on two of the islands demonstrate minimal hierarchy and have very localised influence, yet monuments in the traditional Western sense, large structures in stone, are widespread on one of them. Conversely, the island with the most hierarchical chiefly system demonstrates almost no ceremonial effort with stone.

This extraordinary variation requires some questioning of the whole concept of monumentality in the Pacific. This was a point raised by Chris Ballard and Meredith Wilson, who were instrumental in the inscription of the Roi Mata site on the UNESCO World Heritage List, when they outlined in detail a challenge to the perception of monumentality in the Pacific. They suggest that largely Western concepts that equate monumental only with massive and highly visible construction, almost exclusively using stone, at distinct sites, is misguided. They argue:

> Pacific monumentalism is more often located in the elaboration of cosmologies, which are mapped across entire landscapes or seascapes, and which may or may not incorporate what we commonly define as monuments. (Ballard and Wilson 2014:77)

As illustrated by the data presented in this chapter, this is indeed an aspect that needs to be seriously considered when archaeologists are trying to reconstruct past societies. Highly visible individual monuments often play a central and dominant role in any interpretation of societal complexity, but while this may have some relevance in some parts of the Pacific, it clearly does not in others. In any archaeological interpretation of Pacific societies and their development we must be wary both of European-oriented categories and rigid concepts such as the ladder-like nature of social evolution (Denham 2004; Golson 1977) and the constraints imposed by the 19th-century artificial boundaries of Melanesia, Micronesia and Polynesia (Bedford 2014; Clark 2003).

Conclusion

While an increasingly sophisticated archaeology investigating social and political transformation has been developed in the Pacific over many decades, it has been strikingly region-specific, primarily focused on Polynesia and, to a lesser extent, Micronesia (Walter and Sheppard 2006). As yet, it remains barely nascent in Melanesia, comprising literally a handful of projects that have explored specialised trading systems, agricultural intensification, and increasing territoriality and social stratification. This dearth of research in Melanesia is due to a whole host of reasons both logistical and theoretical, but it has in many respects perpetuated both the boundaries set out in the 19th century and unilineal evolutionary social-ladder models of historical process. There needs to be a much greater focus on the archaeology of the Melanesian region, beyond Lapita and the Pleistocene, so that we can more fully appreciate the full complexity and diversity of the Pacific region and the diverse routes of societal transformation that have been followed.

Acknowledgements

Funding for research on Malakula came from an Australian Research Council grant (FT120100716). General thanks are due for the tolerance and collaboration of Malakula communities over two decades and more specifically during a recent project focusing on recording of *nasara*. Also thanks to James Flexner for presenting a much simpler version of this paper, in my absence, at the World Archaeological Congress meeting in Kyoto in 2016. Joel Simo of the Land Desk at the Vanuatu Cultural Centre provided the photos of the *Nial* ceremony on Tanna.

References

Allen, J. 1985. 'Comments on complexity and trade: A view from Melanesia'. *Archaeology in Oceania* 20 (2):49–56. doi.org/10.1002/j.1834-4453.1985.tb00102.x.

Ballard, C and M Wilson. 2012. 'Unseen monuments: Managing Melanesian cultural landscapes'. In *Managing cultural landscapes*, edited by K Taylor and J Lennon, 131–153. London and New York: Routledge.

Ballard, C and M Wilson. 2014. 'Pacific monumentalism'. In *Monuments and people in the Pacific*, edited by H Martinsson-Wallin and T Thomas, 77–98. Studies in Global Archaeology 20. Uppsala: Department of Archaeology and Ancient History, Uppsala University.

Beaglehole, JC (ed.). 1961. *The journals of Captain James Cook on his voyages of discovery: The voyage of the* Resolution *and* Adventure *1772–1775*. Volume II. Cambridge: The Hakluyt Society.

Beaune, G. 1894. *La terre australe inconnue: Onze croisières aux Nouvelles-Hébrides*. Lyon: Delhomme et Briguet.

Bedford, S. 2014. 'Melanesia'. In *The Cambridge world prehistory*, edited by C Renfrew and P Bahn, 622–631. Volume 1. Cambridge: Cambridge University Press.

Bedford, S, M Abong, R Shing and F Valentin. 2017a. 'From first encounters to sustained engagement and alienation: European and ni-Vanuatu contact from 1774 to 1915, Port Sandwich, Malakula, Vanuatu, Southwest Pacific'. In *Historical and archaeological perspectives on early modern colonialism in Asia-Pacific and the Pacific*, edited by MC Berrocal and C Tsang, 92–122. Volume 1. Florida: University of Florida Press. doi.org/10.5744/florida/9780813054759.003.0005.

Bedford, S, P Siméoni and V Lebot. 2017b. 'The anthropogenic transformation of an island landscape: Evidence for agricultural development revealed by LiDAR on the island of Efate, Central Vanuatu, South-West Pacific'. *Archaeology in Oceania* 53 (1):1–14. doi.org/10.1002/arco.5137.

Bickler, S. 2004. 'Prehistoric stone monuments in the northern region of the Kula Ring'. *Antiquity* 80 (307):38–51. doi.org/10.1017/S0003598X00093248.

Bonnemaison, J. 1994. *The Tree and the canoe: History and ethnography of Tanna*. Honolulu: University of Hawai'i Press.

Bonnemaison, J. 1996. 'Graded societies and societies based on title: Forms and rites of traditional political power in Vanuatu'. In *Arts of Vanuatu*, edited by J Bonnemaison, K Huffman, C Kaufmann and D Tryon, 200–216. Bathurst: Crawford House Press.

Byrne, S. 2013. 'Rock art as material culture: A case study on Uneapa Island, West New Britain, Papua New Guinea'. *Archaeology in Oceania* 48 (2):63–77. doi.org/10.1002/arco.5004.

Clark, G. 2003. 'Shards of meaning: Archaeology and the Melanesia–Polynesia divide'. *Journal of Pacific History* 38 (2):197–215. doi.org/10.1080/0022334032000120530.

David, B and T Denham. 2006. 'Unpacking Australian prehistory'. In *The social archaeology of Australian Indigenous societies*, edited by B David, B Barker and I McNiven, 52–71. Canberra: Aboriginal Studies Press.

Deacon, B. 1934. *Malekula: A vanishing people in the New Hebrides*. London: Routledge and Sons.

Denham, T. 2004. 'The roots of agriculture and aboriculture in New Guinea: Looking beyond Austronesian expansion, Neolithic packages and indigenous origins'. *World Archaeology* 36 (4):610–620. doi.org/10.1080/0043824042000303791.

Douglas, B. 1979. 'Rank, power, authority: A reassessment of traditional leadership in South Pacific societies'. *The Journal of Pacific History* 14 (1):2–27. doi.org/10.1080/00223347908572362.

Dumont d'Urville, JSC. 2003. 'On the islands of the great ocean'. *Journal of Pacific History* 38 (2):163–174. doi.org/10.1080/0022334032000120512.

Earle, T. 1989. 'The evolution of chiefdoms'. *Current Anthropology* 30 (1):84–88. doi. org/10.1086/203717.

Field, J. 2004. 'Environmental and climatic considerations: A hypothesis for conflict and the emergence of social complexity in Fijian prehistory'. *Journal of Anthropological Archaeology* 23 (1):79–99. doi.org/ 10.1016/j.jaa.2003.12.004.

Garanger, J. 1972. *Archéologie des Nouvelles-Hébrides: Contribution à la connaissance des îles du Centre.* Publications de la Société des Océanistes 30. Paris: Société des Océanistes, Musée de l'Homme. doi.org/10.4000/books.sdo.859.

Garanger, J. 1996. 'Tongoa, Mangaasi and Retoka—History of a prehistory'. In *Arts of Vanuatu*, edited by J Bonnemaison, K Huffman, C Kaufmann and D Tryon, 66–73. Bathurst: Crawford House Press.

Golson, J. 1977. *The Ladder of social evolution: Archaeology and the bottom rungs.* Sydney: University Press for the Academy of the Humanities.

Green, RC. 1991. 'Near and Remote Oceania—Disestablishing "Melanesia" in culture history'. In *Man and a half: Essays in Pacific anthropology and ethnobiology in honour of Ralph Bulmer*, edited by A Pawley, 491–502. Auckland: Polynesian Society.

Irwin, G. 1985. *The emergence of Mailu.* Terra Australis 10. Canberra: The Australian National University.

Kirch, PV. 1984. *The evolution of Polynesian chiefdoms.* Cambridge: Cambridge University Press.

Kirch, PV. 2010. *How chiefs became kings: Divine kingship and the rise of archaic states in ancient Hawai'i.* Berkeley: University of California Press. doi.org/10.1525/california/9780520267251.001.0001.

Layard, JW. 1942. *The stone men of Malakula: The small island of Vao.* London: Chatto and Windus.

Lilley, I. 1985. 'Chiefs without chiefdoms? Comments on prehistoric sociopolitical organization in western Melanesia'. *Archaeology in Oceania* 20 (2):60–65. doi.org/10.1002/j.1834-4453.1985.tb00104.x.

Lindstrom, L. 1996. 'Arts of language and space, south-east Tanna'. In *Arts of Vanuatu*, edited by J Bonnemaison, K Huffman, C Kaufmann and D Tryon, 123–128. Bathurst: Crawford House Press.

Riesenfeld, A. 1950. *The megalithic culture of Melanesia.* Leiden: E.J. Brill.

Sand, C. 1995. *'Le Temps d'avant' la préhistoire de la Nouvelle-Calédonie.* Paris: L'Harmattan.

Sand, C. 2002. 'Melanesian tribes vs Polynesian chiefdoms: Recent archaeological assessment of a classic model of sociopolitical types in Oceania'. *Asian Perspectives* 41 (2):282–296. doi.org/10.1353/asi. 2003.0010.

Siméoni P. 2009. *Atlas du Vanouatou (Vanuatu).* Port Vila: Géo-Consulte Publishing.

Smith, B. 1989. *European vision and the South Pacific.* Melbourne: Oxford University Press.

Smith, B. 1992. *Imagining the Pacific.* Melbourne: Melbourne University Press.

Speiser, F. 1996. *Ethnology of Vanuatu. An early twentieth century study.* Bathurst: Crawford House Press.

Spriggs, M. 1986. 'Landscape, land use, and political transformation in southern Melanesia'. In *Island Societies. Archaeological approaches to evolution and transformation*, edited by PV Kirch, 6–19. Cambridge: Cambridge University Press.

Spriggs, M. 2008. 'Ethnographic parallels and the denial of history'. *World Archaeology* 40 (4):538–552. doi.org/10.1080/00438240802453161.

Tcherkézoff, S. 2003. 'A long and unfortunate voyage towards the "invention" of the Melanesia/Polynesia distinction 1595–1832'. *Journal of Pacific History* 38 (2):175–196. doi.org/10.1080/0022334032000 120521.

Thomas, N. 1989. *Out of time: History and evolution in anthropological discourse*. Cambridge: Cambridge University Press.

Thomas, T. 2009. 'Communities of practice in the archaeology of New Georgia, Rendova and Tetepare'. In *Lapita: Ancestors and descendants*, edited by P Sheppard, T Thomas and G Summerhayes, 119–145. NZAA Monograph 28. Auckland: New Zealand Archaeological Association.

Walter, R and P Sheppard. 2006. 'Archaeology in Melanesia: A case study from the Western Province of the Solomon Islands'. In *Archaeology of Oceania: Australia and the Pacific Islands*, edited by I Lilley, 137–159. Oxford: Blackwell Publishing. doi.org/10.1002/9780470773475.ch7.

6

Reconsidering the 'Neolithic' at Manim rock shelter, Wurup Valley, Papua New Guinea

Tim Denham

Is the 'Neolithic' relevant to the highlands of Papua New Guinea?

> What needs to be pointed out at this stage is that there was no point at which a homogenous Neolithic 'package' of economic practice and material culture ever existed. (Thomas 1999:14)

> … in practice the evidence which is available to us relates to a more complex, messy and fragmented series of developments, and that any attempt to define a particular set of attributes as constituting the Neolithic will be arbitrary in the extreme. (Thomas 1999:13)

The term 'Neolithic' was proposed by Lubbock (1865) as a formal category to differentiate the Palaeolithic—namely, old flaked stone technologies—from new ground and polished stone technologies. Subsequently, a range of alternative meanings of the Neolithic have emerged (Trigger 2003). Childe (1925) shifted the emphasis from evolutionary perspectives on stone tool technology onto sets of culture-historic traits, albeit with temporal and geographical variation. During the 20th century, the concept of the Neolithic broadened to encompass agriculture (associated with domesticated plants and animals), sedentism, pottery and mortuary practices, as well as stone tool technology. Subsequently, Hodder (1990) drew attention to the social and symbolic aspects of the Neolithic, while Thomas (1999) considered the Neolithic to be more a way of 'Being'. Today, in both academic and public discourse, the Neolithic has become a signifier of social complexity, dynamism and progression (David and Denham 2006; Florin and Carah 2018).

It remains to be seen how relevant the concept of the Neolithic is outside Eurasia, the region of its original development and application. Does the concept reflect something fundamental about long-term social history, or is it chronologically and geographically specific? Indeed, does the concept have too much inherited baggage, which would make its relevance to the highlands of New Guinea problematic?

Here, the lithic assemblage at Manim, a rock shelter in the highlands of Papua New Guinea, is re-evaluated in terms of Lubbock's initial usage, namely in terms of the advent of ground stone tool technology. Subsequently, broader conceptions of the Neolithic, namely those that draw on a suite of cultural traits, are evaluated in terms of the multidisciplinary record for the highlands.

Taking another look at Manim

Ground stone axe-adzes were 'an important component of most tool kits in the Western Highlands' of Papua New Guinea by c. 7000–6000 cal BP and would greatly have increased the efficiency of forest clearance (Christensen 1975:33). Christensen based his interpretation on the results of his excavations at Manim rock shelter in the Wurup Valley, together with Bulmer's excavations at Kiowa and Yuku (Bulmer and Bulmer 1964:66). Tools with edge grinding dated to the early Holocene at Kafiavana (White 1972:195) and Kosipe (White et al. 1970:162), with less specific reports of ground artefacts dating to the Pleistocene at Kosipe (White et al. 1970:165) and Yuku (Bulmer 1975:31; cf. Bulmer 1977a:57). The only definite edge ground tool from the Pleistocene was an axe with butt modification from the earliest occupation at Nombe (Golson 2001:196). Christensen (1975:32; after White 1967) noted that the Kafiavana collection provided evidence of early Holocene grinding on the faces, sides and cutting edge. The marked increase in the frequency of ground stone tools from c. 7000–6000 cal BP loosely correlated with a decrease in the variety of other stone tools (Bulmer 1975:44).

Ground stone axe-adzes have become embroiled in debates concerning archaeological signatures of the 'Neolithic' (Denham 2003, 2006) and early agriculture in the highlands (Bulmer 1966, 1975, 1977a, 1977b, 1991, 2005; Gaffney et al. 2015a; Golson 2005). Although the ground stone axe-adzes at Manim are not the earliest in the highlands (Mountain 1991; White 1972; see reviews in Bulmer 2005 and Golson 2005), they are highly significant because of the site's proximity to wetlands preserving archaeological evidence of early agriculture on the floor of the Upper Wahgi Valley, including Kuk Swamp (Denham and Haberle 2008). Manim is located in the Wurup Valley, a tributary of the Upper Wahgi Valley, less than 20 km away from Kuk (Figure 6.1). The potential correlations between the adoption of ground stone axe-adzes at Manim, forest clearance on the valley floor, and the agricultural chronology at Kuk are significant for developing a regional understanding of human–environment interactions during the early to mid-Holocene (Denham and Haberle 2008), as well as of the emergence of agrarian societies in the Upper Wahgi Valley.

Despite the centrality of Christensen's excavations at Manim to debates concerning the antiquity and prevalence of ground stone tool technology in the highlands (Burton 1984:227–228; Christensen 1975; Golson 2005:469; Mangi 1984), there are problems with the previous radiocarbon dating. Previous conventional radiocarbon dates were derived from different test units to those containing key lithic materials and they were obtained on relatively large samples of wood charcoal. Here, a new accelerator mass spectrometry (AMS) dating program relies, where possible, on short-lived macrobotanical remains, primarily *Pandanus* sp. nut and kernel fragments, collected from the same excavation quadrant within one test unit (Test Unit I), which contained several significant stone artefacts. The new dating program has greater precision and a higher degree of chronostratigraphic control in terms of the association between dated materials and ground stone artefacts.

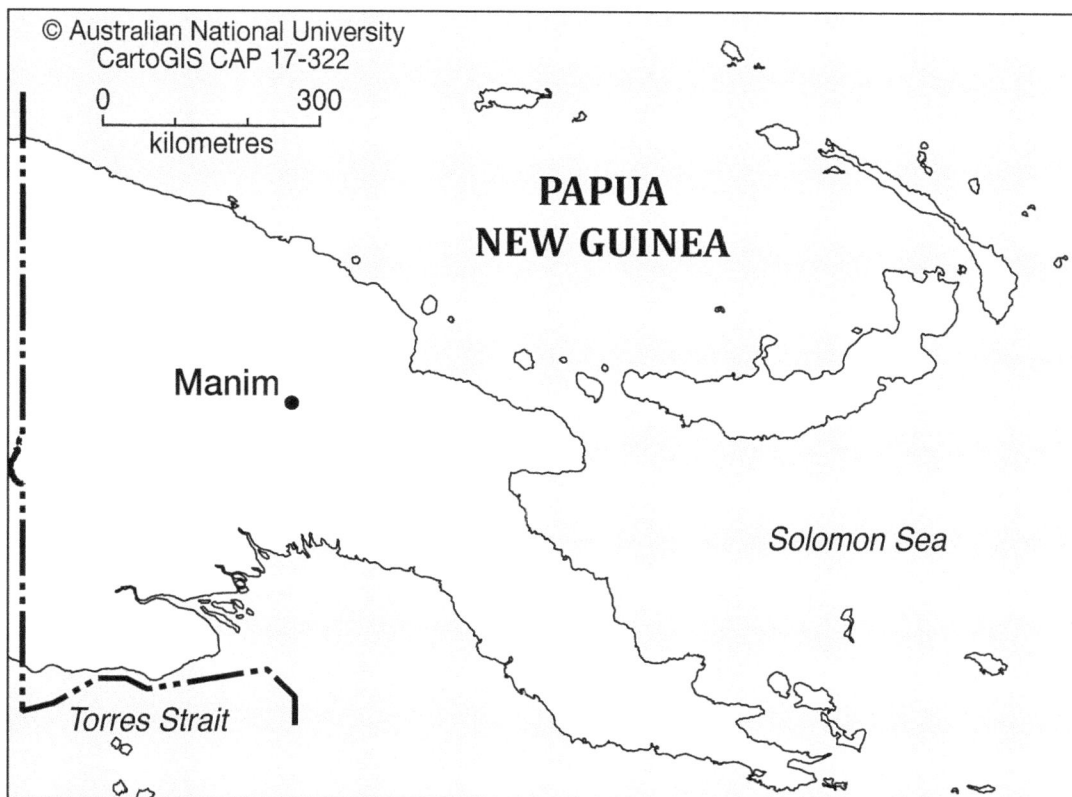

Figure 6.1. Location map of Manim rock shelter in Papua New Guinea.
Source: Tim Denham.

The Manim excavations

In the early 1970s, Ole Christensen conducted extensive archaeological and ethnobotanical investigations in the Wurup Valley near Mount Hagen, Western Highlands Province, Papua New Guinea. Tragically, he died in a car accident before completing his doctoral studies. In 1973 Christensen undertook excavations at four rock shelters along an altitudinal cline on the wall of the Wurup Valley: Manim (1770 m), Kamapuk (2050 m), Etpiti (2200 m) and Tugeri (2450 m). Only limited analyses of the archaeobotanical, archaeozoological and lithic assemblages from his archaeological excavations have occurred (Aplin 1981; Donoghue 1988; Mangi 1984) or been published (Christensen 1975; Donoghue 1989; Sutton et al. 2009).

At Manim, extensive excavations were undertaken within the rock shelter, exposing relatively deep stratigraphy (Figure 6.2; Table 6.1). Excavations were ordinarily conducted in arbitrary 10 cm levels within stratigraphic layers. Manim yielded dense lithic (Mangi 1984) and archaeobotanical (Donoghue 1988) assemblages associated with occupation during the early to mid-Holocene (Christensen 1975). These cultural deposits occurred within Layer V, which extended to depths of 'circa 250 cm below the surface at the back of the shelter to circa 340 cm below the surface outside of the dripline' (Christensen 1975:30).

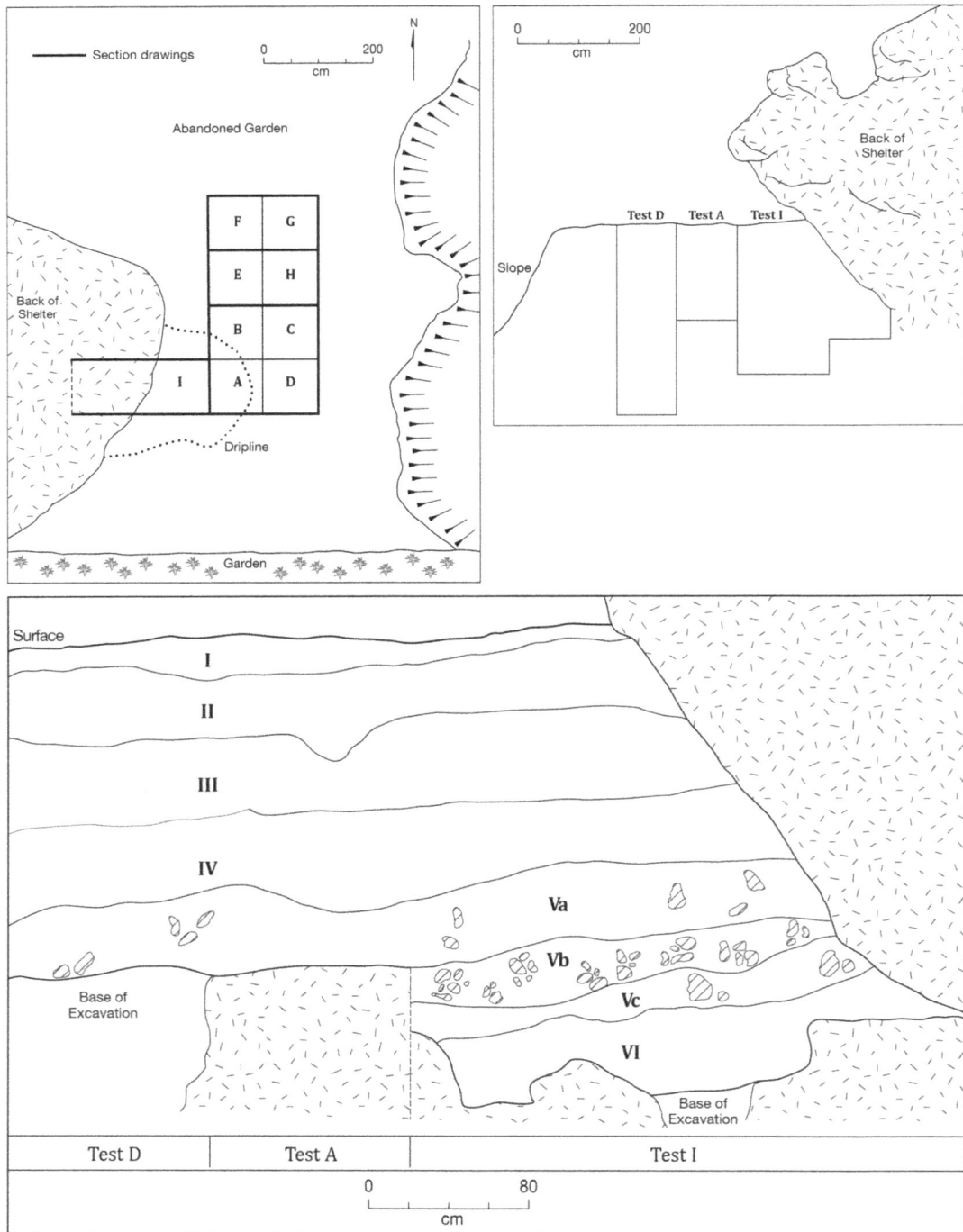

Figure 6.2. Site plan of excavations at Manim rock shelter (top left), with east–west cross-sectional view (top right), and section of south wall of Test Units D, A and I (bottom).

Source: Redrafted from Christensen field notes in Garrett (1976).

Table 6.1. Stratigraphy in Manim rock shelter (based on Christensen 1975:30, Garrett 1976:32–34 and Mangi 1984:15–17).

Layer	Levels	Description
I	1–3	Root mat (upper c. 10 cm) formed on a clay-rich sediment containing charcoal, sparse cultural material and occasional lenses of sand and clay. The clay lenses potentially delineate shallow hearths and are associated with fire-cracked rocks.
II	4–7	Dark organic sand containing charcoal, clusters of fire-cracked rock, stone flakes and fragments of cooking stones throughout.
III	8–13	Bands of sands, which vary in colour and texture, and contain sparse cultural materials.
IV	14–17	The upper portion comprises a dark grey clay containing abundant charcoal and other cultural material, such as fire-cracked rock and stone flakes. The lower portion is a yellowish sand containing sparse cultural materials.
Va	18–21	Black organic layer containing densely packed cultural materials, primarily charcoal, fire-cracked rock and lithic artefacts. Towards the base, the sediment is browner, less organic and more clay-rich, and contains fewer cultural materials.
Vb	22–24	
Vc	25–26	
VI	27–29	White sand between rocks.

Levels for Layers are provided for Unit I. Associated depths can be inferred from Figure 6.2.

Source: Author's research.

The lithic assemblage at Manim

An independent re-evaluation of the stone assemblage at Manim is not possible, given the extensive damage and losses to the lithic collection during the destruction of the Weston archaeological store as a result of the Canberra fires of 2003. Consequently, any evaluation is constrained by previously published and unpublished reports (Burton 1984; Christensen 1975; Garrett 1976; Mangi 1984). Although these documents provide ample detail, they contain inconsistencies and do not enable a complete reconstruction of the provenance for all ground stone artefacts.

There are differences in the reporting of the ground stone axe-adzes and related artefact classes at Manim. Mangi (1984:55, 90) provides a working definition for a ground axe-adze as 'characterised by a ground edge at one end "resembling those hafted and used as axes and adzes in recent times and usually exhibit signs of polishing"' (cf. Bulmer 1966:66; White 1972:6). Although it is not possible to define these artefacts as axes or adzes without knowledge of how they were hafted, Mangi (1984:90) referred to them as 'axes' for convenience. Burton (1984) also referred to them as axes, based on the presumption that except for one small wood-working adze, only axes were manufactured in quarries in the Wahgi Valley vicinity; although he notes that this ethnographic inference may not extend to archaeological samples (John Burton, pers. comm. 2016). Axe-adzes at Manim were reported as lenticular (Mangi 1984) or ovoid (Burton 1984) in cross-section.

As well as five complete ground stone axe-adzes, there were four broken axe-adzes, three 'roughouts' or blanks, and twenty-three 'axe flakes' (Mangi 1984:105–106). 'Axe roughouts' were extensively flaked on all sides and conformed in shape to an axe-adze, but lacked any grinding or polishing; namely, they may potentially be at an earlier stage of the manufacturing process prior to grinding and polishing. 'Axe flakes' were differentiated from other flakes based on the presence of striations along the polished surface (Mangi 1984:90); they were derived from breakage or reworking of ground axe-adzes.

All except one axe flake were collected from Layer V, the main period of cultural deposition at Manim; the exception derived from overlying Layer IV. Mangi (1984) undertook a tripartite subdivision of Layer V (Va, Vb and Vc). The vast majority of stone artefacts, flakes and debitage were derived from Layers Va and Vb: Layer Va yielded all whole and broken axe-adzes, two roughouts and ten axe flakes; and, Layer Vb yielded one roughout and twelve axe flakes.

Previous radiocarbon dating

In the preliminary report of the excavations, there is some confusion over the provenance and antiquity of the earliest ground axe-adzes at Manim (Table 6.2). Christensen states:

> ANU-1372 (3580 ± 80) comes from the top of the stratigraphic unit within which ground stone axe/adzes first appear. ANU-1373 (5860 ± 130) is from the lowest spit within which axe/adzes (lenticular) appear. (Christensen 1975:31)

Subsequently in the same report, the first appearance of ground stone axe-adzes is stated as being in Level 'G19, dated to 5860 ± 130 BP' (Christensen 1975:32), presumably, Level 19 in Test Unit G. There is an inconsistency because ANU-1373 is listed as being from Level 21 (Christensen 1975:Table 1) and not Level 19 as stated in the text.

In his analysis, Mangi (1984:106) states that all the earliest complete ground and polished axe-adzes come from Layer Va in Test Unit I, although specifics are only given for two from Level 21 and one from Level 20 (1984:Figures VIIa-c). Furthermore, a consideration of Christensen's field notes (transcribed in Mangi 1984:Appendix I) confirms the interpretation that the oldest axe-adzes derive from Level 21 in Test Unit I, rather than Level 19, but that they come from the top of this excavation level and could be readily assigned to Level 20.

Mangi's interpretation is corroborated by Burton (1984:227–228) who states that the earliest ground stone axe-adzes come from Level 21. Burton (1984:Figure 10.14) depicts the oldest finds, both derived from Level 21 in Test Unit I and describes them as 'two miniature axes of ovoid section made from local stone' (Figure 6.3; Burton 1984:227). Burton (1984:227) also discusses a small cutting edge fragment from a ground stone axe that is likely derived from the Tuman quarries; the provenance for this fragment (Artefact 327), which is from a provenance below ANU-1372 (3580 ± 80 BP), is given as Quadrant 2, Level 19 in Test Unit I (Burton 1984:Table 10.7).

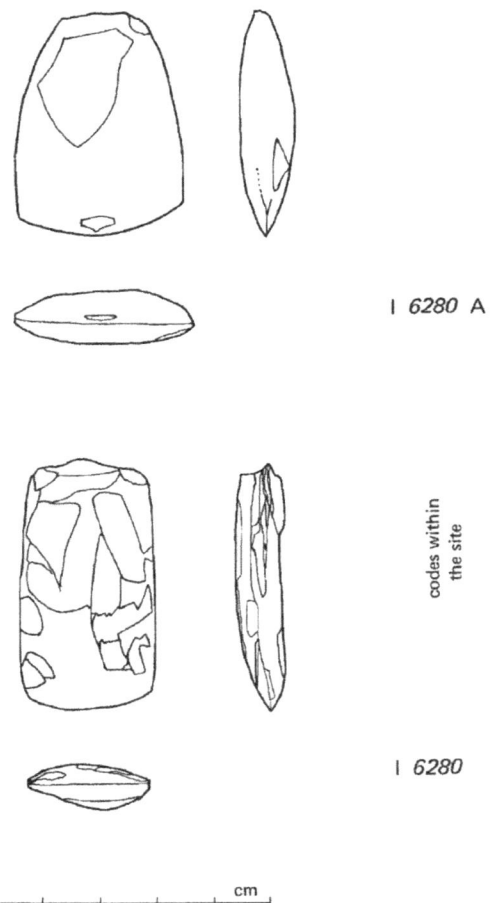

Figure 6.3. The oldest ground axe-adzes from Level 21, Quadrant 6, Test Unit I at Manim rock shelter (Burton 1984:Figure 10.14, reproduced with permission): top, artefact 6280A; bottom, artefact 6280.

Source: Burton 1984:Figure 10.14.

A review of the current literature confirms that the earliest Tuman quarry axes and the earliest ground axes at Manim derive from Levels 19 and 21 (and, conservatively from Level 20), respectively, in Test Unit I. Based on previously published data, the earliest Tuman quarry axes at Manim predate c. 4090–3690 cal BP and the earliest ground axe-adzes date to c. 7010–6400 cal BP. However, there is uncertainty over the precise antiquity of these artefacts because the radiocarbon dates that are used to date them are largely derived from Test Unit G, which was the furthest excavated from Test Unit I that contained several of the most significant ground stone artefacts.

Table 6.2. Previously reported conventional radiocarbon dates on wood charcoal for Manim.

Laboratory code	Radiocarbon age (BP)	Sample type[1]	Radiocarbon date (cal BP)	% (2 sigma)	Test Unit	Level/Quad	Layer[2]
ANU-1368	410 ± 70	Wood charcoal	538–308	95.4	F	3	II
ANU-1369	270 ± 80	Wood charcoal	504–254 225–136 115–73 34–modern	68.9 17.2 2.9 6.3	G	6	II
ANU-1370	2380 ± 110	Wood charcoal	2741–2296 2268–2156	85.3 10.1	E	11	IV
ANU-1371	2300 ± 90	Wood charcoal	2703–2630 2619–2559 2544–2110 2080–2068	5.8 3.5 85.6 0.5	E	12	IV
ANU-1372	3580 ± 80	Wood charcoal	4140–4130 4091–3686 3664–3645	0.6 93.6 1.3	H	16	Va
ANU-1373	5860 ± 130	Wood charcoal	7138–7134 7006–6396 6367–6351	0.1 94.8 0.5	G	21	Va
ANU-1375	9670 ± 220	Wood charcoal	11 804–10 401	95.4	I	26	Vb
ANU-1467[3]	9260 ± 120	Wood charcoal	10 755–10 200	95.4	G	32	Vc
ANU-1468[3]	9870 ± 610	Wood charcoal	13 010–9886 9847–9817	95.2 0.2	G	33	Vc
ANU-1376[4]	5570 ± 410	Wood charcoal	7414–7391 7372–7357 7332–5583	0.3 0.2 94.9	H	34	Vc

Most dates from Christensen (1975:30–31), except ANU-1467 and ANU-1468 from Mangi (1984:23–25). However, the radiocarbon ages for these latter two dates were incorrectly reported in Mangi (1984). Radiocarbon calibrations calculated using IntCal13 (Reimer et al. 2013) and OxCal v4.2.4 (Bronk Ramsey 2009).

Notes:

1. Sample types vary on the original submission forms and radiocarbon age reports from The Australian National University (ANU) laboratory. They include carbonised wood, charcoal, charred wood and wood; however, it has been inferred that all samples were wood charcoal.

2. Layer designations are derived from Christensen's field notes and layer-level designations as reported in Mangi (1984:Appendix I). Further, and following Mangi (1984), Layer V has been subdivided into three sub-units—Layers Va, Vb and Vc—given that these are relevant for stone artefact distributions within the profile. Further, ANU-1467, ANU-1468 and ANU-1376 are all derived from the basal levels of Layer Vc in Test Units G and I.

3. The radiocarbon ages for ANU-1467 and ANU-1468 were reversed in Mangi (1984:23–25). The original radiocarbon submission forms and original radiocarbon age reports were consulted for the present study.

4. ANU-1376 is anomalous. Mangi (1984:25) reported from the radiocarbon dating report that it was of small size, being 10 per cent of the ANU laboratory requirement for a conventional radiocarbon date at the time.

Source: Author's research.

New AMS dating strategy

A new AMS dating strategy has been devised to provide greater radiometric precision and a higher degree of association between dated materials and ground stone axe-adzes for Test Unit I. Foremost, it was decided to focus on short-lived plant products, where possible, for radiocarbon dating, primarily *Pandanus* kernel and nut fragments (pidgin: *karuka*; highland *Pandanus* spp.). These materials do not have an in-built 'old-wood effect', because they are produced annually. Individual *Pandanus* fragments were subject to AMS dating, which can provide higher precision for small organic remains than possible using conventional methods.

The lowest stone axes were collected from Quadrant 6 within Levels 20 and 21 of Layer V (Mangi's Layer Va). Due to the high density of cultural materials present, Christensen divided each arbitrary spit or level into six quadrants in Test Units E, F, G, H and I when excavating above, through and below Layer V. Here, the intention is to date materials from the same quadrant from which significant stone artefacts were recovered within Test Unit I in order to provide a higher degree of association than relying on inter-test unit and cross-site correlations.

A series of macrobotanical samples were selected for AMS dating through the whole stratigraphic column within Test Unit I to determine the reliability of the original dating program. Particular focus was placed upon the internal chronostratigraphic integrity of the main cultural deposit (Layer V, equivalent to Levels 18–26), as well as its relationship to overlying (Layer IV, Level 17) and underlying (Layer VI, Level 27) units within Quadrant 6. A series of near-continuous AMS dates through these levels was designed to derive the most accurate dates for the earliest stone axe-adzes and associated artefact classes. Individual pieces of archaeobotanical materials were selected for dating from sieved materials (as was the case with the original dating program); none had been sampled in situ from the walls or floor of the excavation.

The results of the new AMS dating program within Test Unit I are in relatively good chronostratigraphic order (Table 6.3). As noted for other cave and rock shelter sites (see Denham and Mountain 2016), there is some clustering of dates within stratigraphic units, which may be suggestive of intermixing within defined periods of occupation, as well as result from the different apparent ages of annually grown *Pandanus* kernels and nuts with respect to wood charcoal, which may have an in-built 'old-wood effect' of up to several hundred years.

The uppermost four AMS dates (Wk-22063-65 and Wk-22358) predominantly date to the last 800 years. They are not in strict chronostratigraphic order, as Wk-22358 is older than its stratigraphic position would suggest, perhaps indicating an in-built 'old-wood effect'; namely, the wood charcoal was already several hundred years old at the time it was burned, whereas Wk-22065 was younger. However, an inversion in the original wood charcoal dates between Levels 3 (ANU-1368) and 6 (ANU-1369) (Table 6.2; Christensen 1975) suggests that it is more likely that the upper six levels of the site are somewhat intermixed, probably as a result of scuffage, trampling and incidental digging during periodic visitation.

The remaining AMS dates down the profile are in relatively good stratigraphic order. The slightly younger date for *Pandanus* in Level 19 (Wk-22071) when compared to those for gymnosperm from Levels 17 and 18 (Wk-22069 and Wk-22070) may represent a slight 'old-wood effect' in the gymnosperm samples when compared to *Pandanus*, or indicate limited intermixing between Levels 17–19. The other anomaly is a wildly aberrant, ancient date on *Pandanus* in Level 25 (Wk-22076), which is suggestive of residual material being redeposited in a younger context.

The new AMS dates compare relatively favourably with the original conventional dates. There are some minor discrepancies between dates for the same numerical levels, but these are anticipated because the new and old samples were derived from different test units. Namely Level 21 in Test Unit I may not represent precisely the same period of cultural deposition as Level 21 in Test Unit G. Therefore some variation in dates for levels within major cultural strata would be anticipated across the site, especially given variations in the depth of cultural materials across the site, even if the dates for the major cultural strata are broadly consistent.

Table 6.3. New AMS dates for Manim. Radiocarbon calibrations calculated using IntCal13 (Reimer et al. 2013) and OxCal v4.2.4 (Bronk Ramsey 2009).

Laboratory code	Radiocarbon age (BP)	Sample type	Radiocarbon date (cal BP)	% (2 sigma)	Test Unit	Level/Quad	Layer
Wk-22063	108 ± 30	Charcoal	270-211 205-187 148-12	27.1 2.4 65.9	I	2	I
Wk-22064	279 ± 30	Charcoal	437-350 334-284 167-155	53.7 39.3 2.5	I	4	II
Wk-22358	857 ± 30	Charcoal	900-867 824-815 800-693	8.3 1.4 85.7	I	5	II
Wk-22065	655 ± 32	Charcoal	673-625 607-556	45.6 49.8	I	6	II
Wk-22067	2243 ± 30	Charcoal	2340-2295 2270-2155	26.6 68.8	I	10	III
Wk-22068	2634 ± 30	Charcoal	2791-2727	95.4	I	12	III
Wk-22069	3106 ± 30	Gymnosperm	3384-3235	95.4	I	17/6	IV
Wk-22070	3279 ± 30	Gymnosperm	3578-3446	95.4	I	18/6	Va
Wk-22071	3086 ± 30	*Pandanus* sp.	3371-3220	95.4	I	19/6	Va
Wk-22072	5712 ± 30	*Pandanus* sp.	6626-6587 6568-6411	5.3 90.1	I	20/6	Va
Wk-22073	6437 ± 30	*Pandanus* sp.	7426-7293	95.4	I	21/6	Va
Wk-22074	7430 ± 32	*Pandanus* sp.	8335-8184	95.4	I	22/6	Vb
Wk-22075	8229 ± 30	*Pandanus* sp.	9300-9086 9051-9034	93.7 1.7	I	24/6	Vb
Wk-22076	18 686 ± 78	*Pandanus* sp.	22 770-22 375	95.4	I	25/6	Vc
Wk-22077	9062 ± 35	*Pandanus* sp.	10 253-10 187	95.4	I	27/1	VI

Layer and Level correlations for Test Unit I are given in Table 6.1.

Source: Author's research.

The antiquity of ground stone technology at Manim

The new AMS dates provide a robust framework for interpreting the antiquity of the earliest ground stone axe-adzes at Manim. Technically, the two oldest axe-adzes at the site derive from Quadrant 6, Level 21 in Test Unit I, which yielded a date of 7430–7290 cal BP (Wk-22073). A third axe-adze was recovered from Quadrant 6, Level 20 in Test Unit I, which yielded a date of 6630–6410 cal BP (Wk-22072). Based on a consideration of Christensen's recommendation in his field notes, the stone axe-adzes can be conservatively dated to 6630–6410 cal BP, although based on a more literal reading of association within discrete quadrants and levels they date to 7430–7290 cal BP. The new chronology is broadly consistent with previous dating that suggested an antiquity of c. 7010–6400 cal BP based on a conventional date from an adjacent unit (ANU-1373).

Using the new AMS dates, associated artefact classes can be more accurately dated. Three axe roughouts were collected at Manim, from Level 17, Test Unit G and Levels 20 and 23, Test Unit I (Mangi 1984:106; Fig. VIId). Based on the original dating program, the roughout in Test Unit G predates c. 4090–3690 cal BP (ANU-1372) and the deepest in Test Unit I predates 8340–8180 cal BP (Wk-22074) and postdates c. 9300–9090 cal BP (Wk-22075).

Of the 22 axe flakes collected from Layer V (Mangi's Layers Va and Vb), 14 were derived from Test Unit I (although no specific information is available on their distribution by level). Given that Layer Vb in Test Unit I is represented by Levels 22–24 (Mangi 1984:28), at least some axe flakes predate 8340–8180 cal BP (Wk-22074) and possibly extend as far back as c. 9300–9090 cal BP (Wk-22075).

Additionally, Mangi (1984:108–109, 117) reports on the distribution of grindstones at Manim. All are located within Layer V: four in Layer Va, nine in Layer Vb, and two in Layer Vc. The dates for Layer Vb in Test Units G and I indicate that grindstone technology may date back to over 11 800–10 400 cal BP (ANU-1375). As Mangi (1984:108) speculates, can these grindstones be associated with the production of ground stone axe-adzes? Although grindstones can serve many uses, including processing of plant and animal products, they can also be used to work stone tools. If they were used for stone axe-adze grinding, there is scope for a much greater antiquity for this type of lithic industry in the Upper Waghi Valley region.

A subsidiary question concerns the antiquity of stone exploitation and stone axe manufacture at the Tuman quarries (Burton 1984). The previously reported date of a cutting edge fragment of c. 4090–3690 cal BP (ANU-1372) was derived from Level 19 in Test Unit G, some distance at the site from the find spot in Level 19/2 in Test Unit I. A more closely associated sample of *Pandanus* from Level 19/6 in Test Unit I returned a more recent calibrated date range of 3370–3220 cal BP (Wk-22071). In part, the discrepancy in ages of c. 700–500 years could be accounted for by an 'old-wood effect' in ANU-1372, although it may in part reflect discrepancies in the antiquity of levels between test units at the site.

A revised occupation chronology for Manim

The new AMS dating program at Manim, in conjunction with a re-evaluation of previous research on the lithic assemblage, suggests that the main periods of occupation reflected two different cultural orientations. The earlier and main period of occupation started before c. 9300–9090 cal BP (Wk-22075 in Level 24) and lasted until c. 6570–6410 cal BP (Wk-22072 in Level 20). The associated cultural deposit is represented by Levels 20 to 25/26 in Test Unit I, although it is reflected only in Levels 20–23 in Quadrant 6 of Test Unit I. The high rates of lithic deposition of debitage classified by Mangi (1984:Volume 2) as unaltered cores, wasted flakes and 'uncertain' (Figure 6.4), as well as the occurrence of ground stone axe-adzes and axe flakes, are suggestive of on-site stone tool reduction and manufacture. Within this period of occupation, the earliest ground stone axe-adzes conservatively date to 6630–6410 cal BP (Wk-22072, Level 20), although more literally to 7430–7290 cal BP (Wk-22073, Level 21). However, ground stone technology likely predates 9300–9030 cal BP (Wk-22075, Level 24) based on the distribution of axe flakes within Layers Va and Vb, and possibly earlier if grindstones are considered.

A later period of occupation occurs around c. 3400–3200 cal BP (Wk-22069-20071) and is represented by Levels 17–19. This occupation has much lower rates of lithic deposition and is characterised by the presence of a fragment of a Tuman quarry axe-adze. During this period, people likely visited the site less frequently, may have adventitiously reworked stone artefacts occasionally, but did not engage in more systematic on-site stone tool manufacture. Rather, they obtained axe-adzes through social networks of exchange from specific quarry sites.

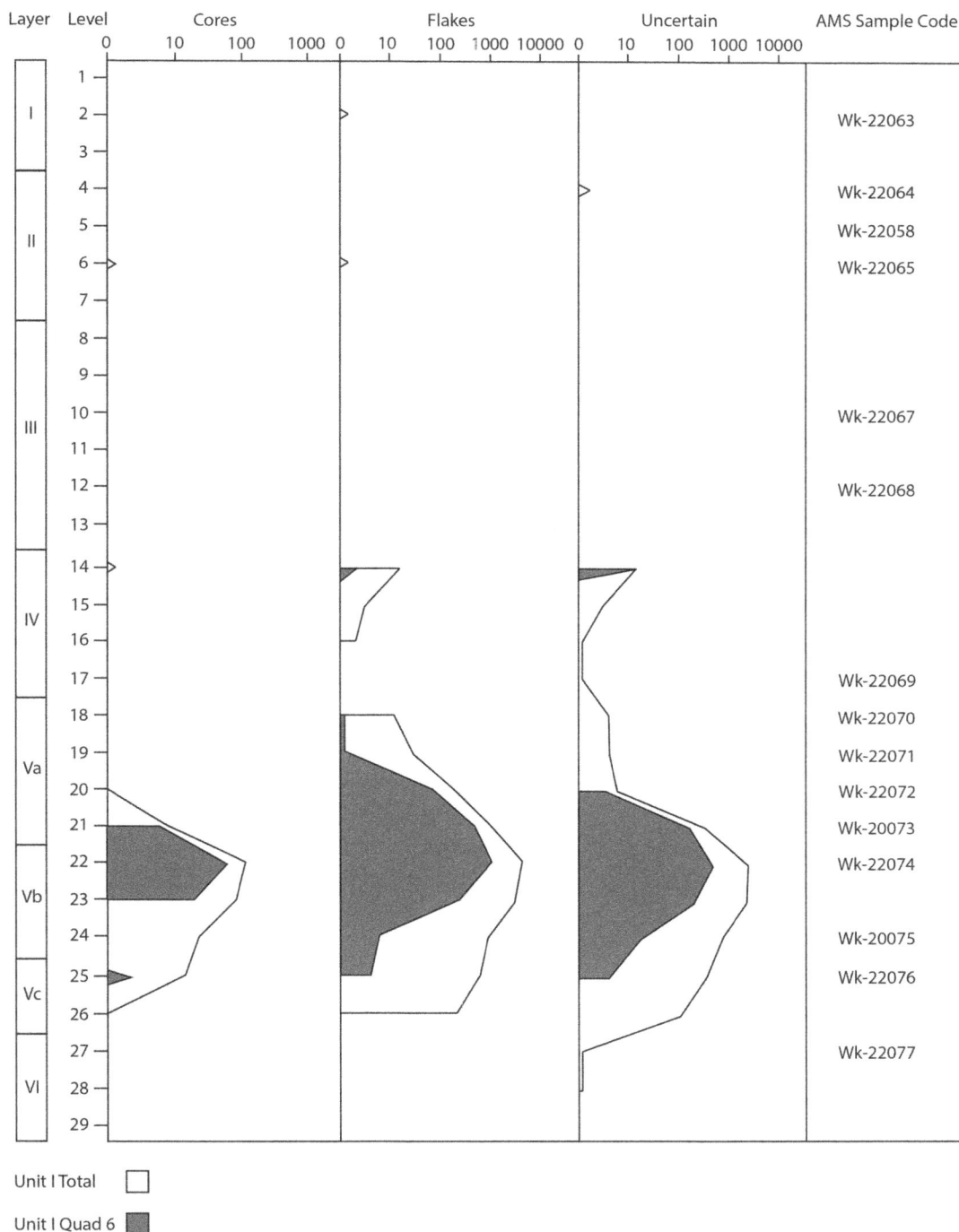

Figure 6.4. Distribution of debitage (comprising cores, flakes and 'uncertain' (as classified by Mangi 1984:vol. 2)) within Test Unit I and Quadrant 6; Test Unit I also depicted.

Note logarithmic scaling of frequencies and AMS sample provenances.

Source: Tim Denham.

Was there a highland Neolithic?

In terms of Lubbock's original meaning, the lithic assemblage at Manim does exhibit a Neolithic, namely, the occurrence of ground stone artefacts. Yet, the antiquity of edge ground artefacts on Sahul (the former land mass including Australia and New Guinea) has been claimed to date well into the Pleistocene and is seemingly coeval with initial colonisation of the continent (Geneste et al. 2012; Hiscock et al. 2016). Consequently, the advent of ground stone tools is not a significant technological marker in the region and has little salience for understanding long-term social history on Sahul, even though the Manim assemblage does shed light on the prevalence of ground stone axe-adzes in the Upper Wahgi Valley region.

As applied in Europe, East Asia and South-East Asia (e.g. Bellwood 2005), the Neolithic often encompasses a range of material cultural traits in addition to ground stone axe-adzes, such as agriculture, sedentism, pottery and so on. Consequently, it is necessary to broaden a consideration of the Neolithic to include both diachronic and synchronic lines of evidence that may be relevant to, or have been invoked in, the highlands context. Diachronic interpretations rely on archaeological, geomorphological and palaeoecological lines of evidence to document processes in the past; whereas synchronic interpretations use present-day genetic and linguistic distributions to infer processes in the past.

Diachronic lines of evidence

Even though the prevalence of ground stone axe-adzes at Manim provides a Neolithic signature of sorts, the significance of this finding to understanding social change, as opposed to agricultural history, is unclear. Ground stone axe-adzes enhanced the ability of people to fell trees. Thereby the technology contributed to the ability of people to disturb and eventually clear montane rainforest on the floor of the Upper Wahgi Valley, which was clearly manifest by 7000–6400 cal BP (Denham and Haberle 2008; Haberle et al. 2012); namely, by the time of the earliest, archaeologically verifiable, cultivation practices on the wetland margin at Kuk Swamp (Denham et al. 2003).

The agricultural chronology at Kuk Swamp, as well as at other wetland sites in the Upper Wahgi Valley and vicinity, indicates the long antiquity of cultivation practices in the highlands (Denham 2018; Golson et al. 2017). Multidisciplinary evidence of environmental manipulation, forest disturbance and plant exploitation dates to c. 10 000 cal BP on the wetland margin at Kuk, with subsequent indirect palaeoecological evidence suggestive of shifting cultivation on the valley floor from then until c. 7000 cal BP. Cultivation using mounds occurs on the wetland margin at Kuk at c. 7000–6400 cal BP, with the digging of ditches to drain cultivated plots occurring from c. 4400–4000 cal BP.

The agricultural chronology at Kuk is practice-focused; namely, it is built upon multidisciplinary evidence of cultivation practices (Denham 2009). Although archaeobotanical and palaeoecological findings indicate the range of plants present, exploited and potentially cultivated at different times, there are no clear morphotypic changes suggestive of domestication for any plant. Indeed, the domestication status of plants under cultivation in New Guinea is not always clear today (Yen 1991) and is not definitive for the determination of agriculture in the Pacific context (following Hather 1996 and Spriggs 1996). Additionally, the primary domestic animals of Pacific agriculture—pig (*Sus scrofa*) and chicken (*Gallus gallus*)—were probably introduced to the island of New Guinea within the last 3000 years and only became significant to highlands agriculture much more recently (Sutton et al. 2009). Archaeobotanical and zooarchaeological assemblages from the highlands are not comprehensive or particularly germane to debates concerning the Neolithic.

In terms of sedentism, house structures have been claimed to date to the Pleistocene at two multi-occupation sites in the highlands—Wañelek (Bulmer 1977b, 1991) and NFX (Watson and Cole 1977). The association between structural elements and radiocarbon dates, as well as the reliability of those dates, at both sites are problematic and should be discounted until more definitive archaeological evidence is forthcoming (Denham 2016; Denham and Ballard 2003). Clearer evidence for early house structures occurs from c. 4500–4000 cal BP in the highlands (Bulmer 1977b, 1991; Watson and Cole 1977); although the archaeology of open settlements may reflect, in large part, sampling biases and site preservation.

Pottery has been reported from c. 3000 cal BP contexts at two sites in the highlands: Wañelek (Gaffney et al. 2015b) and NFB (Huff 2016). Both claims are likely to be controversial, even though a coastal Lapita site with pottery dating to c. 2800 cal BP on the south coast of New Guinea is well attested (McNiven et al. 2011). Yet large parts of the highlands were aceramic at contact from the 1930s onwards and were likely always so. Consequently, pottery is marginal to long-term history in the highlands and remained so until the period of European-Australian exploration of the interior during the 20th century.

Putative signatures of the Neolithic occur at vastly different times and have greatly different significance for societies in the highlands of New Guinea. Although agriculture and ground axe-adze technology date to the early to mid-Holocene and become more prevalent from the mid-Holocene onwards, other putative Neolithic signatures are later and less important. Open settlements likely date from c. 4500–4000 cal BP, while pottery remained marginal after its introduction around c. 3000 cal BP and domesticated animals, especially pigs, only became central to highlander social life within the last few hundred years.

Synchronic lines of evidence

The evaluation of synchronic evidence is similarly problematic. Despite recent claims (Bergström et al. 2017), the degrees to which biological, linguistic and genetic markers are consilient and represent the spread of agricultural or Neolithic peoples are unclear. In the New Guinea context, as elsewhere, some conflate the Neolithic with agriculture and make broad generalisations about the past based on contemporary distributions of genes and languages.

For example, an agricultural-based expansion of Proto Trans New Guinea Phylum (pTNG) speakers has been inferred from distributions of major linguistic groups. Even though composition of the Trans New Guinea Phylum is problematic (Foley 2000; Wurm 1992), there is general agreement that approximately several hundred languages in New Guinea are highly related and can be traced to an ancient proto-form (Pawley 2000; Wurm 1975). Pawley proposed that the expansion of pTNG languages across the highlands and into the lowlands was driven by agriculture (Pawley 1998:684). Foley had similarly proposed an agriculture-driven model to account for the recent expansion of three large language groups (Enga, Chimbu, Eastern Highlands; Foley 1992). According to Pawley's model, agricultural groups were able to expand and displace or assimilate non-agricultural groups. Over time, the demic diffusion of agriculturalists was inferred to have occurred at the expense of non-agricultural populations who were marginalised to the least favourable locations, i.e. the lowlands.

Pawley's model appears to fit recent language maps of New Guinea, as well as some recent genetic evidence (Bergström et al. 2017). However, the antiquity, place of origin and dispersal of pTNG, as well as some genetic markers, are currently unknown. Thus, it is not possible to synchronise linguistic and genetic distributions either to the multidisciplinary chronology for the emergence and transformation of agricultural practices (Golson et al. 2017), or to putatively Neolithic cultural traits (such as undertaken for Proto Oceanic and Proto Austronesian; Blust 2009 and Ross 1996, respectively).

The emergence of agrarian societies

As Thomas noted (1999), the concept of the Neolithic has come to mean different things to different people who work in different contexts. The term does not constitute a stable or bounded category that has a constant, or universal, application across space and time. If the term is deployed in different ways by different people in different contexts, in what ways is it relevant to the highlands of New Guinea? Perhaps another way to consider the issue is to ask: why invoke the Neolithic? Does usage of the term shed light on the long-term history of the highlands?

The foregoing review of diachronic and synchronic lines of evidence does not reveal a Neolithic horizon for the highlands of New Guinea. Material cultural traits that are often bound up with narratives of the Neolithic occur at markedly different times—such as agriculture, sedentism, pottery and domestic animals—while others are currently absent from the archaeological record—such as mortuary practices. At present, the term Neolithic has no real meaning for the highlands and it makes more sense to shift the debate to the emergence of agrarian societies.

The emergence of agriculture in the highlands of New Guinea does not seem to represent the crossing of a major and irreversible threshold (Denham 2007, 2018). Rather, the conceptual and substantive boundaries between societies reliant on foraging and cultivation are likely to have been porous in the past in New Guinea. Early agriculture is relatively poorly defined in the archaeological record in terms of time, place and practice (Denham 2009). For most societies, cultivation and foraging formed part of the subsistence repertoire up until the recent past; namely, they were complementary rather than alternative strategies (Denham and Haberle 2008). Even though societies in the highlands have come to rely on agriculture for the majority of their food, the historical processes through which this occurred remain to be elicited.

For the New Guinea highlands, the Neolithic is a foreign concept in terms of its origins and application. Instead, the long-term history of the highlands should be considered in terms of the language and literature concerning the emergence of agrarian societies. Although much of the recent focus in the highlands has been on the emergence of early agriculture (Denham et al. 2003), attention needs to refocus on how transformations in agriculture were socially embedded (following Golson 1982; Golson and Gardner 1990; Modjeska 1982). Not only does the adoption of an agricultural innovation—whether new practice, crop or animal—need to make social sense, it also has unforeseen social consequences—whether in terms of demography, commodification of surplus and sexual division of labour. Taken together, agrarian and social changes through time led to the distinctive character of highland societies.

Concluding comments

Although stone tool assemblages do not generally reflect a clear shift to agrarian practices and lifeways, if they are taken together with wetland archaeological and palaeoecological findings they provide a regional record of human–environment interaction during the early to mid-Holocene (Denham and Haberle 2008; Golson 1982). Currently, the only regional counter-point within the highlands is the dense early to mid-Holocene occupation at Nombe (Denham and Mountain 2016; Evans and Mountain 2005), potentially supplemented by Kiowa (Gaffney et al. 2015a). However, how are these records to be read in terms of the ways people became reliant on the cultivation of food? What did this change mean for their social worlds?

At present, little is known of the emergence of agrarian societies beyond the practices and technologies of cultivation. There is almost no understanding of how the social worlds of communities changed as they reoriented the rhythms of social life around an increasing reliance on cultivated, as opposed to gathered, food. Nonetheless, people in this part of the highlands started to become increasingly reliant on cultivated food through the Holocene. The agricultural record of the Upper Wahgi Valley, as well as other valleys in the highlands, needs to be read in terms of this shift to agrarian lifeways without reference to the Neolithic.

Acknowledgements

The dating research and reanalysis was funded by an Australian Research Council Discovery grant to Denham (DP0666524). The author would like to thank: Jack Golson for permission to undertake research on the Wurup Valley material and paper archive; Nic Dolby and Alice Bedingfield for assistance with selection and identification of plant macroremains for radiocarbon dating; Duncan Wright for assistance with submission of the dates to Waikato for radiocarbon dating; Fiona Petchy for her patience and assistance with the dating of macrobotanical samples at the Radiocarbon Dating Laboratory, University of Waikato; Kay Dancey and Jenny Sheehan for drafting of Figures 6.1–6.4, with assistance of Elle Grono for Fig. 6.4; and John Burton and Rachel Wood for addressing queries. I would like to thank Mathieu Leclerc and James Flexner for the invitation to contribute to this volume and constructive comments on drafts of this paper.

References

Aplin, K. 1981. 'Kamapuk fauna: A late Holocene vertebrate faunal sequence from the Western Highlands District, Papua New Guinea with implications for palaeoecology and archaeology'. Unpublished BA (Hons) thesis, The Australian National University, Canberra.

Bellwood, P. 2005. *First farmers*. Oxford: Blackwell.

Bergström, A, SJ Oppenheimer, AJ Mentzer, K Auckland, K Robson, R Attenborough, MP Alpers, G Koki, W Pomat, P Siba, Y Xue, MS Sandhu and C Tyler-Smith. 2017. 'A Neolithic expansion, but strong genetic structure, in the independent history of New Guinea'. *Science* 6356:1160–1163. doi.org/10.1126/science.aan3842.

Blust, R. 2009. *The Austronesian languages*. Canberra: Pacific Linguistics.

Bronk Ramsey, C. 2009. 'Bayesian analysis of radiocarbon dates'. *Radiocarbon* 51:337–360. doi.org/10.1017/S0033822200033865.

Bulmer, S. 1966. 'The prehistory of the Australian New Guinea Highlands: A discussion of archaeological field survey and excavations, 1959–60'. Unpublished MA thesis, University of Auckland, Auckland.

Bulmer, S. 1975. 'Settlement and economy in prehistoric Papua New Guinea: A review of the archaeological evidence'. *Journal de la Société des Océanistes* 31:7–75. doi.org/10.3406/jso.1975.2688.

Bulmer, S. 1977a. 'Waisted blades and axes'. In *Stone tools as cultural markers: Change, evolution and complexity*, edited by RVS Wright, 40–59. Canberra: Australian Institute of Aboriginal Studies.

Bulmer, S. 1977b. 'Between the mountain and the plain: Prehistoric settlement and environment in the Kaironk Valley'. In *The Melanesian environment*, edited by JH Winslow, 61–73. Canberra: Australian National University Press.

Bulmer, S. 1991. 'Variation and change in stone tools in the highlands of Papua New Guinea: The witness of Wanelek'. In *Man and a half: Essays in Pacific anthropology and ethnobiology in honour of Ralph Bulmer*, edited by A Pawley, 470–478. Auckland: The Polynesian Society.

Bulmer, S. 2005. 'Reflections in stone: Axes and the beginnings of agriculture in the central highlands of New Guinea'. In *Papuan pasts: Cultural, linguistic and biological histories of Papuan-speaking peoples*, edited by A Pawley, R Attenborough, J Golson and R Hide, 387–450. Pacific Linguistics 572. Canberra: Pacific Linguistics, Research School of Pacific and Asian Studies, The Australian National University.

Bulmer, S and R Bulmer. 1964. 'The prehistory of the Australian New Guinea Highlands'. *American Anthropologist* 66 (4, Pt.2):39–76.

Burton, J. 1987 [orig. 1984]. *Axe makers of the Wahgi: Pre-colonial industrialists of the Papua New Guinea highlands*. Ann Arbor, Michigan: University Microfilms [citations refer to the 1984 thesis].

Childe, VG. 1925. *The dawn of European civilisation*. London: Kegan Paul.

Christensen, OA. 1975. 'Hunters and horticulturalists: A preliminary report of the 1972–4 excavations in the Manim Valley, Papua New Guinea'. *Mankind* 10 (1):24–36.

David, B and TP Denham. 2006. 'Unpacking Australian prehistory'. In *The social archaeology of Australian Indigenous societies*, edited by B David, B Barker and I McNiven, 52–71. Canberra: Aboriginal Studies Press.

Denham, TP. 2003. 'The Kuk morass: Multi-disciplinary investigations of early to mid Holocene plant exploitation at Kuk Swamp, Wahgi Valley, Papua New Guinea'. 2 volumes. Unpublished PhD thesis, The Australian National University, Canberra.

Denham, TP. 2006. 'The origins of agriculture in New Guinea: Evidence, interpretation and reflection'. In *Blackwell guide to archaeology in Oceania: Australia and the Pacific Islands*, edited by I Lilley, 160–188. Oxford: Blackwell.

Denham, TP. 2007. 'Early to mid-Holocene plant exploitation in New Guinea: Towards a contingent interpretation of agriculture'. In *Rethinking agriculture: Archaeological and ethnoarchaeological perspectives*, edited by TP Denham, J Iriarte and L Vrydaghs, 78–108. Walnut Creek: Left Coast Press.

Denham, TP. 2009. 'A practice-centred method for charting the emergence and transformation of agriculture'. *Current Anthropology* 50:661–667. doi.org/10.1086/605469.

Denham, TP. 2016. 'Revisiting the past: Sue Bulmer's contribution to the archaeology of Papua New Guinea'. *Archaeology in Oceania* 51 (S1):5–10. doi.org/10.1002/arco.5115.

Denham, TP. 2018. *Tracing early agriculture in the Highlands of New Guinea: Plot, mound and ditch*. Oxford: Routledge. doi.org/10.4324/9781351115308.

Denham, TP and C Ballard. 2003. 'Jack Golson and the investigation of prehistoric agriculture in Highland New Guinea: Recent work and future prospects'. *Archaeology in Oceania* 38:129–134. doi.org/10.1002/j.1834-4453.2003.tb00539.x.

Denham, TP and SG Haberle. 2008. 'Agricultural emergence and transformation in the Upper Wahgi valley during the Holocene: Theory, method and practice'. *The Holocene* 18:499–514. doi.org/10.1177/0959683607087936.

Denham, TP and MJ Mountain. 2016. 'Resolving some chronological problems at Nombe rock shelter in the highlands of Papua New Guinea'. *Archaeology in Oceania* 51:73–83. doi.org/10.1002/arco.5114.

Denham, TP, SG Haberle, C Lentfer, R Fullagar, J Field, M Therin, N Porch and B Winsborough. 2003. 'Origins of agriculture at Kuk Swamp in the highlands of New Guinea'. *Science* 301:189–193. doi.org/10.1126/science.1085255.

Donoghue, D. 1988. 'Pandanus and changing site use: A study from Manim Valley, Papua New Guinea'. Unpublished BA (Hons) thesis, University of Queensland, Brisbane.

Donoghue, D. 1989. 'Carbonised plant fossils'. In *Plants in Australian archaeology*, edited by W Beck, A Clarke and L Head, 90–100. Tempus 1. St Lucia: University of Queensland.

Evans, B and M-J Mountain. 2005. '*Pasin bilong tumbuna*: Archaeological evidence for early human activity in the highlands of Papua New Guinea'. In *Papuan pasts: Cultural, linguistic and biological histories of Papuan-speaking peoples*, edited by A Pawley, R Attenborough, J Golson and R Hide, 363–386. Pacific Linguistics 572. Canberra: Pacific Linguistics, Research School of Pacific and Asian Studies, The Australian National University.

Florin, SA and X Carah. 2018. 'Moving past the "Neolithic problem": The development and interaction of subsistence systems across northern Sahul'. *Quaternary International* 489:46–62. doi.org/10.1016/j.quaint.2016.12.033.

Foley, W. 1992. 'Language and identity in Papua New Guinea'. In *Human biology in Papua New Guinea: The small cosmos*, edited by RD Attenborough and MP Alpers, 136–149. Research Monographs on Human Population Biology no. 10. Oxford: Oxford University Press.

Foley, W. 2000. 'Linguistic prehistory in the Sepik-Ramu Basin'. Talk presented at the Papuan Pasts Conference, Research School of Pacific and Asian Studies, The Australian National University, Canberra.

Gaffney, D, A Ford and GR Summerhayes. 2015a. 'Crossing the Pleistocene–Holocene transition in the New Guinea highlands: Evidence from the lithic assemblage of Kiowa rockshelter'. *Journal of Anthropological Archaeology* 39:223–246. doi.org/10.1016/j.jaa.2015.04.006.

Gaffney, D, GR Summerhayes, A Ford, J Scott, TP Denham, J Field and WR Dickinson. 2015b. 'Earliest pottery on New Guinea mainland reveals Austronesian influences in highland environments 3000 years ago'. *PLoS ONE* 10 (9):e0134497. doi.org/10.1371/journal.pone.0134497.

Garrett, A. 1976. 'Hunters and horticulturalists: Site reports of excavations in the Manim Valley, Papua New Guinea'. Unpublished manuscript on file with author.

Geneste, J-M, B David, H Plisson, J-J Delannoy and F Petchey. 2012. 'The origins of ground-edge axes: New findings from Nawarla Gabarnmang, Arnhem Land (Australia) and global implications for the evolution of fully modern humans'. *Cambridge Archaeological Journal* 22:1–17. doi.org/10.1017/S0959774312000017.

Golson, J. 1982. 'The Ipomoean revolution revisited: Society and sweet potato in the upper Wahgi Valley'. In *Inequality in New Guinea Highland societies*, edited by A Strathern, 109–136. Cambridge: Cambridge University Press.

Golson, J. 2001. 'New Guinea, Australia and the Sahul connection'. In *Histories of old ages: Essays in honour of Rhys Jones*, edited by A Anderson, I Lilley and S O'Connor, 185–210. Canberra: Pandanus Books, The Australian National University.

Golson, J. 2005. 'The middle reaches of New Guinea history'. In *Papuan pasts: Cultural, linguistic and biological histories of Papuan-speaking peoples*, edited by A Pawley, R Attenborough, J Golson and R Hide, 451–492. Pacific Linguistics 572. Canberra: Pacific Linguistics, Research School of Pacific and Asian Studies, The Australian National University.

Golson, J and D Gardner. 1990. 'Agriculture and sociopolitical organization in New Guinea Highlands prehistory'. *Annual Review of Anthropology* 19:395–417. doi.org/10.1146/annurev.an.19.100190.002143.

Golson, J, TP Denham, PJ Hughes, P Swadling and J Muke (eds). 2017. *Ten thousand years of cultivation at Kuk Swamp in the Highlands of Papua New Guinea.* Terra Australis 46. Canberra: ANU Press. doi.org/10.22459/TA46.07.2017.

Haberle, SG, C Lentfer, S O'Donnell and TP Denham. 2012. 'The palaeoenvironments of Kuk Swamp from the beginnings of agriculture in the highlands of Papua New Guinea'. *Quaternary International* 249:129–139. doi.org/10.1016/j.quaint.2011.07.048.

Hather, JG. 1996. 'The origins of tropical vegeculture: Zingiberaceae, Araceae and Dioscoreaceae in Southeast Asia'. In *The origins and spread of agriculture and pastoralism in Eurasia*, edited by DR Harris, 538–550. London: University College London Press.

Hiscock, P, S O'Connor, J Balme and T Maloney. 2016. 'World's earliest ground-edge axe production coincides with human colonisation of Australia'. *Australian Archaeology* 82:2–11. doi.org/10.1080/03122417.2016.1164379.

Hodder, I. 1990. *The domestication of Europe*. Oxford: Blackwell.

Huff, J. 2016. 'Revisiting NFB: Ceramic technology in the eastern highlands of Papua New Guinea at 3200 calBP'. *Archaeology in Oceania* 51 (S1):84–90. doi.org/10.1002/arco.5109.

Lubbock, J. 1865. *Pre-historic times*. London: Williams and Norgate. doi.org/10.5962/bhl.title.50856.

Mangi, J. 1984. 'Manim 2: 10 years BP: A prehistory of Manim rockshelter, Western Highlands Province, Papua New Guinea'. Unpublished B Litt thesis, 2 vols, The Australian National University, Canberra.

McNiven, IJ, B David, T Richards, K Aplin, B Asmussen, J Mialanes, M Leavesley, P Faulkner and S Ulm. 2011. 'New direction in human colonisation of the Pacific: Lapita settlement of south coast New Guinea'. *Australian Archaeology* 72:1–6. doi.org/10.1080/03122417.2011.11690525.

Modjeska, CM. 1982. 'Production and inequality: Perspectives from central New Guinea In *Inequality in New Guinea Highland societies*, edited by A Strathern, 50–108. Cambridge: Cambridge University Press.

Mountain, MJ. 1991. 'Highland New Guinea hunter-gatherers: The evidence of Nombe Rockshelter, Simbu, with emphasis on the Pleistocene'. Unpublished PhD thesis, The Australian National University, Canberra.

Pawley, A. 1998. 'The Trans New Guinea Phylum hypothesis: A reassessment'. In *Perspectives on the Bird's Head of Irian Jaya, Indonesia*, edited by J Miedema, C Odé and RAC Dam, 665–690. Amsterdam and Atlanta: Editions Rodopi.

Pawley, A. 2000. 'The Trans New Guinea Phylum: Recent research and its implications'. Talk presented at the Papuan Pasts Conference, Research School of Pacific and Asian Studies, The Australian National University, Canberra.

Reimer, PJ, E Bard, A Bayliss, J Beck, PG Blackwell, C Bronk Ramsey, PM Grootes, T Guilderson, H Haflidason, I Hajdas, C Hattž, TJ Heaton, DL Hoffmann, A Hogg, KA Hughen, KF Kaiser, B Kromer, SW Manning, M Niu, RW Reimer, DA Richards, EM Scott, JR Southon, RA Staff, CSM Turney and J van der Plicht. 2013. 'IntCal13 and Marine13 radiocarbon age calibration curves 0–50,000 years cal BP'. *Radiocarbon* 55:1869–1887. doi.org/10.2458/azu_js_rc.55.16947.

Ross, M. 1996. 'Reconstructing food plant terms and associated terminologies in Proto Oceanic'. In *Oceanic studies: Proceedings of the first international conference on Oceanic linguistics*, edited by J Lynch and F Pat, 163–221. Pacific Linguistics Series C-133. Canberra: Research School of Pacific and Asian Studies, The Australian National University.

Spriggs, M. 1996. 'Early agriculture and what went before in Island Melanesia: Continuity or intrusion?' In *The origins and spread of agriculture and pastoralism in Eurasia*, edited by DR Harris, 524–537. London: University College London Press.

Sutton, A, MJ Mountain, K Aplin, S Bulmer and TP Denham. 2009. 'Archaeozoological records for the highlands of New Guinea: A review of current evidence'. *Australian Archaeology* 69:41–58. doi.org/10.1080/03122417.2009.11681900.

Thomas, J. 1999. *Understanding the Neolithic*. London: Routledge.

Trigger, B. 2003. *A history of archaeological thought*. Cambridge: Cambridge University Press.

Watson, VD and JD Cole. 1977. *Prehistory of the Eastern Highlands of New Guinea*. Seattle: University of Washington Press.

White, JP. 1967. '*Taim bilong bipo*: Investigations towards a prehistory of the Papua New Guinea Highlands'. Unpublished PhD thesis, The Australian National University, Canberra.

White, JP. 1972. *Ol Tumbuna: Archaeological excavations in the Eastern Central Highlands, Papua New Guinea*. Terra Australis 2. Canberra: Department of Prehistory, Research School of Pacific Studies, The Australian National University.

White, JP, KAW Crook and BP Ruxton. 1970. 'Kosipe: A late Pleistocene site in the Papuan Highlands'. *Proceedings of the Prehistoric Society* 36:152–170. doi.org/10.1017/S0079497X00013128.

Wurm, SA (ed.). 1975. *New Guinea area languages and language study. Volume 1: Papuan languages and the New Guinea linguistic scene*. Canberra: Department of Linguistics, Research School of Pacific and Asian Studies, The Australian National University.

Wurm, SA. 1992. 'Linguistic prehistory in the New Guinea area'. In *Human biology in Papua New Guinea: The small cosmos*, RD Attenborough and MP Alpers, 25–35. Research Monographs on Human Population Biology no. 10. Oxford: Oxford University Press.

Yen, DE. 1991. 'Domestication: The lessons from New Guinea'. In *Man and a half: Essays in Pacific anthropology and ethnobiology in honour of Ralph Bulmer*, edited by A Pawley, 558–569. Auckland: The Polynesian Society.

Exchange and contacts

7

Axes of entanglement in the New Georgia group, Solomon Islands

Tim Thomas

Regional exchange networks of great variety and complexity are among the most studied phenomena in archaeological and ethnographic accounts of Island Melanesia. Malinowski's (1922) pioneering ethnography of the *kula* system of southern Papua New Guinea produced an enduring image of exchange as foundational to Melanesian social life, and subsequent ethnographic efforts dedicated to elucidating the role of exchange in political structures, gender relations, ritual and symbolism (Leach and Leach 1983; Strathern 1988), have made lasting contributions to social theory. Archaeologists, for their part, have focused on identifying the range and pattern of exchange networks—from the expansive material transfers of the Lapita cultural complex (Kirch 1988; Summerhayes 2000) to the development of smaller but more intensive networks of later periods (Allen 1984).

However, despite a common interest in these networks, archaeological and ethnographic accounts of the region remain distinct both in terms of approach and in what they take exchange phenomena to mean. Archaeological accounts tend to be resolutely materialist, tracking distributions of objects as a signal of interaction and mobility, for reasons that are, at root, culture historical. Because the archaeological data of exchange are artefact finds, archaeologists tend to explain exchange via object properties, as the redistribution of valued material. In contrast, ethnographic work in the region is comparatively idealist, seeing exchange as the definition and manipulation of social relations via the symbolism of exchange media. Where archaeologists find reasons for exchange in the properties of objects, ethnographers find reasons in the meaning of relations.

This contrast of 'objects' versus 'relations' focused approaches to exchange maps straightforwardly onto a theoretical distinction between commodity and gift economies. In Marx's (1976:164–165) classic definition of commodity fetishism, value created during relations of production comes to be seen as a socio-natural property of the thing itself. In such systems, value is established by comparing objects, and ultimately even relations between people are objectified and patterned after relations between objects (Lukács 1971). Conversely, gift economies create lasting chains of obligations between persons, such that exchange objects are valued only insofar as they make manifest or embody relations. If people and things assume the social form of objects in a commodity economy, then in a gift economy they assume the social form of persons (Gregory 1982:41; Mauss 1990). Accordingly, when archaeologists and ethnographers explain exchange in different ways they also imply different kinds of economy.

Understanding the source of this difference is helped by considering exceptions. These tend to occur only when data and interest overlap—archaeologists working on museum collections and the recent past, for example, have sometimes taken relational approaches (Flexner 2016;

Gosden 2004; McNiven 2013; Torrence and Clarke 2013). Generally, the more our data consist solely of objects (i.e. the longer the time before present), the more likely we are to rely on materialist explanations. One reason for this is that Western ontologies consider meaningful relations to be an immaterial product of human cognition—the work of living minds—and consequently inaccessible when the people are gone. Ethnographic idealism is the flip side of the same coin: when the people are still present, artefacts are considered superfluous to the discovery of meaning, rendered 'merely illustrations' (Strathern 1990:171). This suggests that our apparently data-driven division in explanatory frames is actually the product of an underlying limit to the common way we think about subjects and objects.

The way we explain exchange is a token of this conceptual limit, and this has been an important focus in attempts to transcend it. The distinction between gift and commodity economies, for example, is emblematic of deeper conceptual differences in the way subjects, objects and relations are conceived. Strathern (1988) points out that whereas Western commodity systems are reliant upon a conception of individuals and objects as autonomous categories ontologically prior to, and conceptually separate from, their relations, Melanesian gift economies consider relations to be ontologically prior to any objects or persons that might emerge from them. People (and things) in the latter view are consequently not individuals at all, but rather composite sites of relations, and are thus 'dividual'. Broadening the implications of gift economies in this way, Strathern develops a Melanesian model of sociality in which the primary concern of social life is not how to create lasting relations between persons and other entities, but rather how to create distinct persons and things out of pre-existing relations. In this sense the model can be taken as comparable to other recent critiques of modernist assumptions and Enlightenment-era dualisms (e.g. subject–object, mind–body, culture–nature). Latour's (1993) actor–network theory (ANT) is a well-known example, arguing for a symmetrical anthropology in which people and things are linked as equivalent 'actants' in network arrangements, and that it is this relationality that produces the effects, discoveries, objects and distinctions of our cultural concern.

In archaeology, Ian Hodder's recent development of entanglement theory (2012) is inspired by these insights and deploys them to interrogate long-term patterns of human–thing relations via archaeological data. Hodder argues that humans and things co-constitute each other in increasingly complex networks of relations; however, his approach is an attempt to bridge the gap between purely relational and materialist, object-oriented models. Finding that Latour and Strathern overemphasise relations at the expense of an understanding of how material entities produce real effects and constraints that last beyond their current connections, Hodder builds hierarchical or asymmetrical relationships into his model (Hodder 2014:22–25). His key focus is on 'entrapment', a process by which people and things become dependent on each other in ever-increasing entanglements that have both positive and negative consequences. Disentanglement, or the separation of people and things from their constituting relations, is thought to be temporary and ultimately impossible beyond local occurrences.

Hodder's approach then, raises the prospect of integrating archaeological and ethnographic insights in Melanesia, of balancing the material and relational. But in doing so it comes with some problems. Like other accounts developed in reaction to Western models of object autonomy, Hodder spends most of his time mapping out the complex networks of relationships underlying forms we take for granted. Latour does the same, and has recently satirised his own tendency to repeatedly focus on the 'surprise' of finding that ANT analysis reveals that the objects and domains we take to be distinct are 'actually' composed of heterogeneous networks (Latour 2013:35). Surely if reality is relational we should be more surprised that objects are claimed to exist and endure? However satisfying it is to undermine taken-for-granted objects by showing that they are relationally constituted, it still leaves the challenge of defining how they are made to appear autonomous at all.

Early ANT provided a way of conceptualising this as 'punctualisation'—a simplification or encapsulation of network parts to make actants that exist in relation to others, and thus form larger-scale networks (Law 1992:384–385). And despite being usually taken as purely relational, Strathern's (1988) account of Melanesian sociality makes a similar argument by showing, for example, how collective events create images of group unity by encompassing their many internal relations, or how a gift exchange creates an oppositional pairing of persons occluding the many relations of production underlying the gift. In later work Strathern (1996) refers to these objectification processes as 'cutting the network'—offering the parallel example of patents, which create property objects by encompassing and eclipsing the network of relations that led to the discovery (prior studies, chains of research results etc.). The wider point is that social life involves an endless movement between relational entanglement and objectification. Far from disentanglement being of minor temporary importance, it is often the very focus of relations.

In the following case study I attempt to show how the circulation and use of a single class of artefacts can act as the fulcrum point for processes of both entanglement and network cutting— that is, the production of relations and the production of objects with definite properties. Furthermore, these processes can be seen to operate at various scales relevant to the scope of both ethnographic and archaeological enquiry.

Entanglement in New Georgia

Archaeological research in the New Georgia group of the Solomon Islands has identified a late period cultural sequence documenting the establishment of a coastal polity in the Roviana region after 400 BP (Sheppard and Walter 2006), with parallel changes on other islands throughout the group slightly later (Thomas 2009, 2014). This sequence is marked particularly by changes in the occurrence, layout and density of settlement sites and ritual monuments. Prior to 400 BP, dispersed monumental shrines and settlements occurred on isolated ridgelines in the interior of islands, but these were subsequently abandoned in favour of sprawling composite villages on the coast, featuring numerous shrines of diverse function in close association with house platforms, wharves and fortified areas (Sheppard et al. 2000; Walter and Sheppard 2000). By the mid-1800s these communities had come into sustained contact with European whalers, traders and naval ships, and lasting historical records and early ethnographies attest to expansive regional relationships spanning most of the western Solomons (Bennett 1987; Hocart 1922; McKinnon 1975).

These changes reflect a late period shift in political and social focus towards seaborne trade networks and expanding cycles of headhunting raids—success in these becoming increasingly seen as primary indices of chiefly and tribal efficacy. Tribal groupings formed around lineages of successful warrior chiefs (*bangara*) whose ability to manipulate regional alliance and trade relationships helped fund collective raids against neighbouring islands. Successful headhunting was taken to be ancestral sanction made manifest—a state of being *mana*, or efficacious, promising that ancestral spirits would join descendants in all endeavours and the tribe would prosper. Note that, in the languages of New Georgia, *mana* is not a substantive noun indicating some spiritual substance, but rather refers to a relational state of spiritual cooperation. Shrines, housing ancestral skulls and shell valuables, were the focal point of ancestral propitiation and maintenance of that cooperation. By controlling access to shrines, leaders controlled the ritual life of the community and, by extension, other realms of ritually dependent practice (Sheppard and Walter 2006; Thomas 2014).

McKinnon (1975) and Zelenietz (1979) both argue that new economic opportunities offered by recently arrived European traders fuelled an expansion of headhunting during the 19th century. McKinnon focuses on the introduction of iron tools, particularly the 'tomahawk' or axe head, which became a staple item of early trade and a key weapon used in headhunting raids. Iron axes are common finds on shrines in New Georgia, indicating their complete integration into local practice (Thomas et al. 2001:553; Walter et al. 2004). McKinnon (1975) argues that they increased productivity, affording more time away from primary food production and, as weapons, were superior to indigenous equivalents. Leaders in key locations courted European favour, and monopolised access to trade goods in order to achieve military dominance over lesser-equipped rivals. Having achieved dominance, well-connected leaders were able to supply more of the resources (hawksbill turtle shell, or 'tortoiseshell') that Europeans wanted, and could parlay this against acquiring more European things and more military power. In other words, exogenous technology disrupted political equilibrium by freeing up time to spend on more effective violence and domination, leading to a society spiralling out of control—until pacification by British colonial powers in the 1890s.

McKinnon's (1975) account is an early attempt to approach the social effects of people–thing entanglement, and like Hodder (2012) depicts this as a process of entrapment leading to ever-increasing cycles of dependence. But it is also clear in subsequent research that McKinnon gets many of the ethnographic details wrong (Aswani 2000; Dureau 2000). The timeline, too, is challenged by the archaeological demonstration of much earlier indicators of intensive headhunting (Sheppard et al. 2000), although raiding certainly expanded in range in the latter half of the 19th century. Moreover, such accounts reflect a kind of instrumental 'substantivism' (Feenberg 1991:7–8) in which taken-for-granted properties of iron have explanatory agency. Although it is obvious that the advent of European trade introduced new things and networks of trade, and thus new social possibilities for action, it is not clear that it was only the properties of objects that motivated Solomon Islanders' negotiations of these changes.

It is worth reflecting on the fact that shrines are the primary depositional context of iron axes in New Georgia. This is not, in itself, an indication that axes made of iron in particular were special items of high value or mystery. There is no detectable pattern of association between iron axes and types of shrine for example, and stone axes are found deposited on older shrines in exactly the same way, indicating a seamless integration of materials (Thomas 2004:328–335). Axes were interred along with the crania and other belongings of the dead during rituals of enshrinement (Walter et al. 2004). As such, they occur alongside local products (shell valuables, tools) as well as other materials of European origin (willow pattern ceramics and stoneware, parts of firearms, metal cookware, pipe stems, hoop iron). This conforms to the 'indigenous appropriation' of European things described by Thomas (1991)—new forms were subsumed into existing categories. Placed on shrines at the end-point of a transcultural biography, such artefacts had become fully absorbed into the habitus of life in 19th-century New Georgia. They belonged on shrines as much as the bones of their local owners, because, by the late 1800s, a person was a product of relations that extended beyond New Georgia.

In the following I take another look at the changing political economy of axes in New Georgia, starting with an account of the status of axes in local conception and practice.

Clubs (axes) appear

According to contemporary observations, iron axes were ubiquitous by the 1860s (Shineberg 1971). Hocart, on Simbo in 1908, describes them as follows:

> The so-called tomahawk is by the natives termed *manja*, like the aboriginal club it has displaced. It is made with Harrison's No. 2 iron blade set upon a handle 90 cm. long, with a section like that of a convex lens. It is broadest below the axe head, where it is curved with the convex side towards the blade. The extremity is pointed to be stuck in the earth, for the owner will never lay it down flat while he is squatting, but always keeps it planted head up, and when one of us used to lay his tomahawk down it was always set upright again. This is doubtless founded in caution, for it is sooner snatched into the right position; besides that, it is easier to keep in sight. Rapidity also accounts for keeping the edge of the blade upward when shouldering it. (Hocart 1931:301)

These conventions of orientation might also be explained by the social status of axes, as being more than inanimate objects. Axe handles were heavily ornamented with carvings and shell inlay, using motifs reserved for the embodiment of spiritual potency. As with other inlaid artefacts, such as war canoes, these motifs are abstract depictions of spirits occurring in long chains or lineages (see Thomas 2013). Handles were sometimes carved with predatory figures, so that the blade emerges from the mouth of a crocodile and/or frigate bird (Figure 7.1). Items decorated in this way appeared as manifestations of a violent ancestral efficacy— an immanent spirit in particular form. Axes thus had attributes of personhood, and accordingly were treated as if they had a proper orientation, an appropriate 'posture'.

Figure 7.1. Hafted trade axe, 19th century, Roviana Lagoon.

Source: Photo by Hughes Dubois (Waite and Conru 2008:Figure 78), used with permission.

This can be clearly seen in the ceremonial treatment of axes during preparatory ceremonies of headhunting and in those conducted after successful return. Hocart (1931) recorded these ceremonies at chiefly shrines called *inatungu*. Prior to a raid, warriors would gather at the shrine and make offerings of shell valuables and burnt food to the spirits in a ceremony known as *votu manja* 'clubs/axes appear' or 'bring out the clubs/axes', chanting: 'This is the club, thou the inatunu. Grant me an enemy to slay, and let me club … be efficacious you spirits. Grant a victim' (Hocart 1931:308). These ceremonies effectively called forth the efficacy of those dead warrior chiefs who had achieved success in their own lifetimes, enlisting this in contemporary practice. The weapons embodied the presence of these potent spirits on a raid.

In the event of a warrior successfully capturing an enemy head, the entire community would gather to make parcelled offerings of shell rings, puddings and pigs, lacing these along the handle of the weapon while the person who wielded it sat out of sight, as described here again by Hocart:

> Minju [the successful warrior] set up his club [tomahawk] and retired to the house at the back. One man blew the conch. When it sounded the women lined up, Mali, the wife of Kundaite [the chief], first. They squatted down till the conch had blown four times. When it ceased, a man went up first and laid before the tomahawk a basket of food, including the head and shoulders of a pig. The women followed. Mali took out the tomahawk, laid a ring down, and stuck the tomahawk through it; the other women laid down each a pudding crowned with a ring. Then men followed with the same. When the list was exhausted Minju and Mali came up. Mali pulled out the

tomahawk, but so that her ring remained hanging upon it. She then passed a stem of *piro* through the ring, applying it to the handle of the tomahawk. She took the rings from each pudding and slipped them up the tomahawk and *piro*. Seizing the ends of the *piro* in one hand, she then drew out the tomahawk, tied up the ends of the *piro* and carried it off. (Hocart 1931:316)

The first ring laid down and threaded along the handle of the axe by Mali was the *singe inatungu* or sacred ring of the shrine, and it was used to gather up those rings offered on top of puddings by the community. All except the sacred ring were given to the successful warrior as compensation for securing a victim. However, the warrior later gave the rings to the attendant of the *inatungu* shrine who had conducted the initial 'clubs appear' ceremony, because they were ultimately owed to the spirits of that shrine in recognition of the true source of success: the ancestors (Hocart 1931:316; Thomas 2004:272–274).

The performance of the ceremony of return then, acknowledges the relational nature of agency in New Georgia—a warrior was only successful as such due to his axe, which was only efficacious because of the ancestral spirits it embodies, whose own success when alive also depended on similar relations with previous ancestral spirits, and so on. Importantly however, at each stage in this chain encompassment occurs. When threaded with the *singe inatungu* ring and community offerings, the axe presented a composite image of successful action arising out of collaboration between a warrior and propitiated spirits—as the focal point of the ceremony it was an agent, an object eclipsing its relations. When the warrior received the rings he similarly eclipsed the axe and the spirits. And when the warrior gave the rings back to the *inatungu* shrine, the chiefly lineage, and tribe itself, encompassed his success.

The latter encompassment is made possible by the fact that the *inatungu* shrine was the seat of local tribal identity. In Roviana *inatungu* is the nominalised form of *atungu*, the respectful term for the 'sitting' or 'high chief', and in nearby Marovo the *inatungu* is the apical founding spirit of the chiefly lineage, and thus the source of all tribal agency (Hviding 1996:125). Indeed, it was chiefs who organised headhunting raids and so initiated the 'clubs appear' ceremony. The community was totally implicated in these projects because it was only through lateral patron–client relations with tribal members that chiefs could act in the manner befitting a leader. The community was involved from the start in preparing feasts and gathering resources for a raid.

Axes used in headhunting were clearly entangled with the definition of persons and internal relations in the performance of tribal agency. In managing raids, chiefs also used axes to manage the limits of tribal boundaries. Headhunting itself encompassed internal relations in opposition to a realm of asocial violence—it cut a much wider potential network. In Roviana oral histories archetypal episodes of violence conducted by chiefs are those that result in the fissioning of tribes. Tae-Bangara (c. 1750–1780) for example, is remembered as a ruthless and eager warrior, who, through success in warfare, established the zenith of Roviana political dominance. But, his ruthlessness extended to killing rival kinsmen, and he was eventually murdered by the warriors of his brother Odikana who then left to form the Saikile District. The sons of Tae-Bangara (Qutu, Gove, Raro) again fought amongst themselves and created further splits in the Roviana polity, with Raro and Gove establishing the Munda District (Aswani 2000:50–51). Rather than integrating competing tribes, surrounding islands like Tetepare and southern Rendova were depopulated by raiding. Chiefs of the late 19th century modelled themselves on the exploits of these ancestors—Nona of Kalikoqu, Lepe of Kindu, and most famously, Ingava of Sisiata, are renowned as rulers who demonstrated the supremacy of Roviana tribes by conducting increasingly large-scale and frequent raids on Choiseul and Santa Isabel (see also Chapter 9 this volume). Somerville famously recorded (or exaggerated) that on one occasion Ingava:

> went away on a headhunting expedition to Ysabel Island … He took twenty tomako (war canoes) containing about five hundred men, and two good-sized English built boats, containing between three and four hundred rifles, and nine thousand rounds of ammunition. (Somerville 1897:399)

It was raids like these, and their impingement on the safety and dealings of European residents, that ultimately drew the British Government to establish a protectorate and enforce peace.

This tension between raiding and its internal versus external consequences reflects the dual role of chiefs as managers of war and managers of peace and alliance. Ingava, for example, is remembered as 'a very good bangara, for he never fought a Munda man' (Hocart n.d.[a]:20), and seems to have occasionally brokered peace between warring factions (Hocart 1931:305). Such chiefs spanned an oppositional crux in Roviana sociality—they managed boundaries by defining relations in terms of enemies and friends, outsiders and insiders, foreigners and kin. On the one hand a chief's role as the entrepreneurial head of a cognatic descent group tended to accumulate followers, alliances and relationships, but on the other, leadership in headhunting established difference. Tae-Bangara and his sons are remembered as 'great' because they successfully differentiated currently recognised tribes through violent endeavour—they managed descent group integrity by making enemies of kin who threatened to diffuse that integrity. If cognatic kinship, exogamous marriage and ceremonial life could result in potentially boundless relations, then warfare was a particularly effective way of creating difference and managing those boundaries (Scheffler 1965).

So, if axes were personified, then the effect of their use in headhunting was to objectify persons. Taking heads was an extreme form of alienation in that it denied people their personhood, turning them into objects: trophy heads. In killing enemies, warriors destroyed the efficacy of another group: by defeating the ancestral potency of their rivals; by abducting heads so that they could not be enshrined; and by creating malevolent spirits filled with rage at their improper death (Dureau 2000). Defeat in these terms was tantamount to social erasure—objectifying enemies was not so much a matter of encapsulating a set of relations, but rather denying these existed at all. Indeed, even captives were 'really supposed to be dead' (Hocart 1931:306) because they were alienated from their relations and origins. When raids returned with captives, ceremonies were staged to explicitly erase their prior social connections to people and place—the *inatungu* spirit of other places was ritually removed and replaced with the *inatungu* of the new locale (Hocart 1931:313) in order to facilitate the refiguring of the captive as kin (McDougall 2000:104). Heads, in contrast, simply became object indices of successful raiding. The hair and ears of the victim were burned to feed the *inatungu* (Hocart 1931:314) rendering the head void of any personal content. Hung in the rafters of the *paele* men's house, heads were considered *pinera*—things taken by force, without compensation. Consequently, the effect of headhunting was to offset or enframe sociality—it did not present one tribe as the most potent amongst many other (enemy) tribes; it claimed potency, personhood and relational sociality as the sole province of the victors and their allies.

According to my argument then, axes were entangled in crucial practices facilitating the definition of persons and objects out of fields of relations. Axes made agency visible in certain ways by helping eclipse or cut these relations at different scales. But axes were also relationally produced, and not only as vehicles of spiritual potency—they also had to be acquired through trade.

Acquiring axes

As noted in Hocart's account, axes on Simbo were subsumed under the category of 'club' or *manja*. Prior to iron axes, *manja* were paddle-shaped and made of heavy wood (Hocart 1931:301). In Roviana however, the wooden club was known as *vedara*, whilst axes were generically called *maho*. The long-handled stone-headed battle axe was *karamaho*. Very few of these stone axes have appeared in publications, but the most common was a 'waisted blade' axe with a lenticular cross-section, made from a large flake of volcanic rock. Specimens of this type are present in museum collections (some taken from shrines) and are known from sites like Panaivili (Reeve 1989:57) and elsewhere in Roviana (Felgate 2003:410), Rendova and Tetepare (Thomas 2009). Specimens of a second variety—a polished axe with an oval cross-section, made from a very fine-grained light-grey or greenish rock—have been recorded on Nusa Roviana (Nagaoka 2011:129; Thomas 2004:296) and at Panaivili (Felgate 2003:409). Miller (1979:152–155) has summarised the axe and adze collections in the Solomon Islands National Museum, finding that the majority of the New Georgian specimens are of the lenticular cross-section form (64 per cent vs 27 per cent oval cross-section), while those from Choiseul and Isabel are mainly the oval variety (65 per cent). Specimens of large flanged axes with side lugs and bosses have been found on Simbo but conform to the style of 'ceremonial' axes from the Bougainville-Choiseul area (Specht 1979).

Although no geological sourcing studies have been carried out beyond description of hand specimens (Felgate 2003:407–411), an argument can be made that most of the stone axes found in the Roviana region, and probably Simbo too, were specialist products acquired through trade partnerships. The oval cross-section axes described above were not only more common in Isabel and Choiseul but there are no known local sources of the fine-grained grey stone (possibly metamorphosed sedimentary rock, found in Isabel, Choiseul and Guadalcanal (Coulson 1985:639–641)). The lenticular cross-section axes may have been manufactured in the New Georgia archipelago given that they are made from coarse volcanics and are the most common variety. However, such axes were probably a specialist product made by people with good access to suitable stone. In Roviana, locally manufactured adzes are all *Tridacna* shell, reflecting a lack of quality stone. Oral traditions hint that specific rock types were imported— Roviana people are held to have traded shell rings for 'greenstone' from Gizo and 'blackstone' from Rendova (Dureau 1994:56). Again, this suggests that quality stone was rare in Roviana, and access to axes was dependent on relations with other groups. The axes described above as being stylistically close to those from Bougainville are further evidence that axes were being imported (Miller 1979:53).

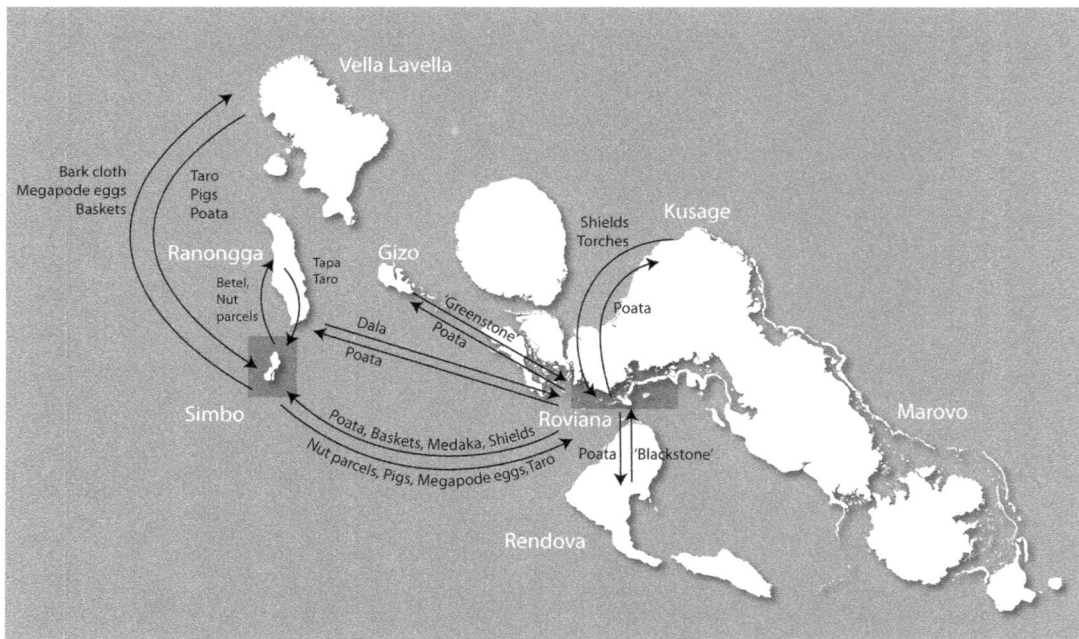

Figure 7.2. Some Simbo and Roviana trade partnerships recorded in western New Georgia.

Further connections occurred with Marovo, and as far afield as the Shortland Islands, Santa Isabel, Choiseul and the Central Solomons.

Source: Based on Hurford 2017:Map 3.4.

Inter-group trade relations in New Georgia were focused on oppositional pairings of regionally produced items (Figure 7.2). For example, the Kusage region of north New Georgia was the renowned producer of wicker war shields (*lave*) and these were traded to Roviana in exchange for shell valuables. Simbo people acquired their shields from Roviana in exchange for packages of nuts, amongst other items (Hocart 1931:301). Such trade relationships were called *baere* and were established by the mutual exchange of shell rings between chiefs, which served to foster a categorisation of people from each party as being 'like brothers'—something that came with a whole series of moral imperatives (Thomas 2004:284–290). *Baere* partnerships served to encompass the internal relations of a tribe and its products in opposition to a paired equivalent party, and reframed trade between these entities as familial sharing (see McDougall 2004:204–212). Trade was therefore the exact opposite of headhunting—where the latter denied relations outside the tribe, the former modelled relations with other tribes as a larger-scale version of internal (sibling) relations.

The suggestion that axes had always been an item acquired through trade relations in Roviana and Simbo is important because it reminds us that the replacement of stone varieties with iron had social as well as material implications. When whalers and traders first brought iron axes to New Georgia they predominantly interacted with people on Simbo (McKinnon 1975). Although relatively isolated, with poor natural resources, Simbo had a deep harbour and a group of people with a reputation for being relatively friendly. As noted, many weapons were traditionally imported to Simbo from neighbouring islands: spears and bows came from the Shortland Islands, and shields came from Kusage via Roviana (Hocart 1931:301). Europeans slotted neatly into this pattern, representing a reasonably predictable opportunity to link into axe trading networks. And, according to the accounts of Andrew Cheyne in 1844 (Shineberg 1971), this is exactly what Simbo people did: they began taking iron axes to Roviana in exchange for hawksbill turtle shell. This was then traded back to Europeans for more axes—European traders were giving one axe head in return for as little as 1.5–3 pounds of 'tortoiseshell' (Shineberg 1971:305). Quite quickly both Roviana and Simbo had a plentiful supply of iron axes, and stone was abandoned.

This alignment of iron axe trade networks was part of a lasting alliance between Simbo and Roviana. It must also have severed relations with trade partners who had previously supplied stone axes: particularly those from further afield in Choiseul or Isabel. People from Roviana were still going to these latter places—not to acquire axes, but to acquire heads with their axes. And, on the way was Vaghena in Manning Straits, an important hawksbill nesting ground.

> The people of Roviana used to go to Manning Straits to fish or catch turtle; sometimes they went headhunting besides … Since the advent of traders they eat the flesh and sell the shell; they bring a few home alive. The way it began was that they once [took] some shell to Eddystone and the people there told them to keep it for the Europeans. (Hocart n.d.(b):1)

There was clearly some symmetry to this network of relations. The European production of axes was balanced against their demand for tortoiseshell, and the Roviana production of tortoiseshell was balanced against their demand for axes. The objects were caused by each other: Cheyne, for example, hired a Chinese blacksmith and shipped bars of iron for the sole purpose of making axes for New Georgia—although later traders relied on Sheffield edge tool manufacturers like Harrison & Sons. The fact that headhunting and hawksbill harvesting journeys were combined reinforces this symmetry, and highlights the entanglement of axes in the crux between creating and cutting relations.

Long-distance headhunting raids to Choiseul and Isabel increased between the 1870s and 1890s (Bennett 1987; Jackson 1978). Perhaps not coincidentally, this was also the time when European traders became resident: they married Roviana women and acquired land for permanent trade stores. I think it likely that this gradually turned iron axes (and other trade goods) into a 'local' item—they were acquired from people who had become relatives, or, at the very least, were resident *baere*. The part of axes that established bonds between people (their acquisition through friendly trade) was internalised, and at the same time, the violent relationship-severing quality of axes was amplified, in that it could now be applied to a greater number of outsiders. In terms of indigenous relations, the result was the production of a New Georgian enclave, whose partnerships extended towards Australia and Europe.

Changes in alliances at this time are reflected in oral traditions. Prior to the rule of a chief named Pequ (perhaps in the 1860s), the people of Roviana are said to have mostly raided Isabel. However, during Pequ's reign, the people of Choiseul became a target because a war party from there had killed his sister. Hocart's informants declared that Ingava, the successor to Pequ, only ever fought in Choiseul, while other chiefs simply added that island to Isabel as a valid locale for raids. At the same time that distant groups were becoming legitimate targets, local enemies became friends: 'In the olden days they also used to catch heads in Vella Lavella' (Hocart n.d.(c):1) but this was stopped after a peace exchange:

> The *mbangara* of Roviana all went over to Vella Lavella and gave 6 to 10 shell rings to each *mbangara*. The *mbangara* of Vella Lavella came to Roviana with shell rings. After that Roviana, Eddystone, Vella Lavella, etc. did not fight with one another any longer but only against Ysabel and Choiseul. Mbitia gave rings to *mbangara* of Eddystone, Ganongga and Lunggu, but there was no fighting with them. Penggu [Pequ] would not fight them because they were like 'two brothers'. (Hocart n.d.(c):2)

It would be an exaggeration to claim that this shift in alliances and partnerships was solely a result of European residence. But it is clear that the confluence of events was such that alliances beyond the New Georgia region were no longer necessary. Choiseul could be attacked with regularity because there was no common sociality with them left to share; all partnerships were dissolved.

Conclusion

Trade axes had their origins in complex arrangements of relations involving social and material dimensions, and we could certainly follow these much further than I have done here: through trade supply routes to Europe, and the Sheffield iron industries, or other aspects of the colonial world system for example (Orser 2009). But however entangled axes were, the effect of their use in New Georgia was to cut this network, to create distinctions by individuating actors. The *votu manja* ceremony elicited efficacious axes out of a chain of relations—they were a composite thing, 'brought out' or 'made to appear'. Used successfully, they elicited a warrior who encompassed the agency of the axe and spirits. A chief claimed the efficacy of his ancestors and warriors through headhunting, and managed the relational boundaries of the tribe. Enemies were demarcated, but so were allied groups defined through oppositional trade—the composite one of a pair, 'like brothers'.

People in New Georgia clearly recognised agency as relational, and the individuations described did not completely elide their origins, as can be seen by the flows of shell rings and food offerings back through successive levels of encompassment in ceremonial contexts. Indeed, it was exactly because relational entanglement was considered to be a kind of primordial background state that acts of network cutting and encompassment were so necessary—it was the only way people and things could be seen to have properties and effects of their own.

In this sense, differentiation was a prevailing concern in New Georgian social practice— whilst artefacts like axes existed as manifestations of power gathered from chains of relations, they were used in the service of setting limits to those who could claim that power as their own. Chiefdoms in the region consequently did not seek to expand or integrate, but rather to differentiate—surrounding landscapes were depopulated rather than colonised. Even when regional alliances operated, these maintained distinction via reciprocal exchanges that established equivalent pairings.

Entanglement always needs its opposite then. Axes provide an edge where two perspectives meet—they are composed from relations, but they produce objects. We can certainly emphasise one of these perspectives over the other, but in fact social life always involves movement between relational entanglement and objectification, and the circumstantial character of this gives action and historical change its particular structure. As such, even small-scale ethnographic observables permeate larger-scale and longer-term structures amenable to archaeological analysis.

References

Allen, J. 1984. 'Pots and poor princes: A multidimensional approach to the study of pottery trading in Coastal Papua'. In *The many dimensions of pottery: Ceramics in archaeology and anthropology*, edited by S van der Leew and A Pritchard, 407–463. Amsterdam: Institute of Prae- and Protohistory.

Aswani, S. 2000. 'Changing identities: The ethnohistory of Roviana predatory head-hunting'. *Journal of the Polynesian Society* 109 (1):39–70.

Bennett, JA. 1987. *Wealth of the Solomons: A history of a Pacific archipelago, 1800–1978*. Honolulu: University of Hawai'i Press.

Coulson, F. 1985. 'Solomon Islands'. In *The ocean basins and margins, Vol 7A*, edited by A Nairn, F Stehli and S Uyeda, 607–682. New York: Plenum Press. doi.org/10.1007/978-1-4613-2351-8_13.

Dureau, C. 1994. 'Mixed blessings: Christianity and history in women's lives on Simbo, western Solomon Islands'. PhD thesis, Macquarie University, Sydney.

Dureau, C. 2000. 'Skulls, mana and causality'. *Journal of the Polynesian Society* 109 (1):71–97.

Feenberg, A. 1991. *Critical theory of technology*. New York: Oxford University Press.

Felgate, M. 2003. 'Reading Lapita in Near Oceania: Intertidal and shallow water pottery scatters, Roviana Lagoon, New Georgia, Solomon Islands'. PhD thesis, University of Auckland, Auckland.

Flexner, JL. 2016. 'Ethnology collections as supplements and records: What museums contribute to historical archaeology of the New Hebrides (Vanuatu)'. *World Archaeology* 48 (2):196–209. doi.org/10.1080/00438243.2016.1195769.

Gosden, C. 2004. *Archaeology and colonialism: Cultural contact from 5000 BC to the present*. Cambridge: Cambridge University Press.

Gregory, C. 1982. *Gifts and commodities*. London: Academic Press.

Hocart, AM. 1922. 'The cult of the dead in Eddystone of the Solomons'. *Journal of the Royal Anthropological Institute of Great Britain and Ireland* 52:71–117, 259–305. doi.org/10.2307/2843738.

Hocart, AM. 1931. 'Warfare in Eddystone of the Solomon Islands'. *Journal of the Royal Anthropological Institute of Great Britain and Ireland* 61:301–324. doi.org/10.2307/2843922.

Hocart, AM. n.d.(a). 'Chieftainship'. Unpublished manuscript. In Hocart papers, Alexander Turnbull Library, Wellington. MS-Papers-0060.

Hocart, AM. n.d.(b). 'Manning sts. & turtle fishing' (Handwritten notes, Roviana). Unpublished manuscript. In Hocart papers, Alexander Turnbull Library, Wellington. MS-Papers-0060.

Hocart, AM. n.d.(c). 'Warfare' (Handwritten notes, Roviana). Unpublished manuscript. In Hocart papers, Alexander Turnbull Library, Wellington. MS-Papers-0060.

Hodder, I. 2012. *Entangled: An archaeology of the relationships between humans and things*. Malden: Wiley-Blackwell. doi.org/10.1002/9781118241912.

Hodder, I. 2014. 'The entanglements of humans and things: A long-term view'. *New Literary History* 45 (1):19–36. doi.org/10.1353/nlh.2014.0005.

Hurford, J. 2017. 'Houses, shrines and the social landscape: A study of architecture on Tetepare, Solomon Islands'. MA thesis, University of Otago, Dunedin.

Hviding, E. 1996. *Guardians of Marovo Lagoon: Practice, place and politics in maritime Melanesia*. Pacific Islands Monograph Series 14. Honolulu: University of Hawai'i Press.

Jackson, KB. 1978. 'Tie hokara, tie vaka: Black man, white man. A study of the New Georgia group to 1925'. PhD thesis, The Australia National University, Canberra.

Kirch, PV. 1988. 'Long-distance exchange and island colonization: The Lapita case'. *Norwegian Archaeological Review* 21:103–117. doi.org/10.1080/00293652.1988.9965475.

Latour, B. 1993. *We have never been modern*. Cambridge, Massachusetts: Harvard University Press.

Latour, B. 2013. *An inquiry into modes of existence: An anthropology of the moderns*. Translated by Catherine Porter. Cambridge, Massachusetts: Harvard University Press.

Law, J. 1992. 'Notes on the theory of the actor-network: Ordering, strategy, and heterogeneity'. *Systems Practice* 5 (4):379–393. doi.org/10.1007/BF01059830.

Leach, J and E Leach. 1983. *The Kula: New perspectives on Massim exchange*. Cambridge: Cambridge University Press.

Lukács, G. 1971. 'History and class consciousness: Studies in Marxist dialectics'. Cambridge, Massachusetts: MIT Press.

Malinowski, B. 1922. *Argonauts of the western Pacific: An account of native enterprise and adventure in the archipelagos of Melanesian New Guinea*. London: Routledge. doi.org/10.4324/9781315014463.

Marx, K. 1976. *Capital: A critique of political economy*. London: Penguin Books Limited.

Mauss, M. 1990. *The gift: The form and reason for exchange in archaic societies*. London: W.W Norton.

McDougall, D. 2000. 'Paths of pinauzu: Captivity and social reproductions in Ranongga'. *Journal of the Polynesian Society* 109 (1):99–113.

McDougall, D. 2004. 'The shifting ground of moral community: Christianity, property and place in Ranongga (Solomon Islands)'. PhD thesis, University of Chicago, Chicago.

McKinnon, JM. 1975. 'Tomahawks, turtles and traders: A reconstruction in the circular causation of warfare in the New Georgia Group'. *Oceania* 45 (4):290–307. doi.org/10.1002/j.1834-4461.1975.tb01872.x.

McNiven, IJ. 2013. 'Between the living and the dead: Relational ontologies and the ritual dimensions of dugong hunting across Torres Strait'. In *Relational archaeologies: Humans, animals, things*, edited by C Watts, 97–116. London: Routledge.

Miller, D. 1979. *National sites survey summary report*. Honiara: Solomon Islands National Museum.

Nagaoka, T. 2011. 'Late prehistoric-early history houses and settlement space on Nusa Roviana, New Georgia Group, Solomon Islands'. PhD thesis, University of Auckland, Auckland.

Orser, CE. 2009. 'World-systems theory, networks, and modern-world archaeology'. In *International handbook of historical archaeology*, edited by D Gaimster and T Majewski, 253–268. New York: Springer. doi.org/10.1007/978-0-387-72071-5_14.

Reeve, R. 1989. 'Recent work on the prehistory of the western Solomons, Melanesia'. *Bulletin of the Indo-Pacific Prehistory Association* 9:46–67.

Scheffler, HW. 1965. *Choiseul Island social structure*. Berkeley: University of California Press.

Sheppard, PJ and R Walter. 2006. 'A revised model of Solomon Islands culture history'. *Journal of the Polynesian Society* 116:47–76.

Sheppard, PJ, R Walter and T Nagaoka. 2000. 'The archaeology of head-hunting in Roviana Lagoon, New Georgia, Solomon Islands'. *Journal of the Polynesian Society* 109 (1):4–38.

Shineberg, D. 1971. *The trading voyages of Andrew Cheyne, 1841–44*. Honolulu: University of Hawai'i Press.

Somerville, BT. 1897. 'Ethnographical notes in New Georgia, Solomon Islands'. *Journal of the Royal Anthropological Institute of Great Britain and Ireland* 26:357–413.

Specht, J. 1979. 'Axe heads and zoomorphs in the Solomon Islands'. In *Birds of a feather: Osteological and archaeological papers from the South Pacific in honour of R.J. Scarlett*, edited by A Anderson, 247–263. Oxford: British Archaeological Reports.

Strathern, M. 1988. *The gender of the gift*. Berkeley: University of California Press.

Strathern, M. 1990. 'Artifacts of history: Events and the interpretation of images'. In *Culture and history in the Pacific*, edited by J Siikala, 25–44. Helsinki: Finnish Anthropological Society.

Strathern, M. 1996. 'Cutting the network'. *The Journal of the Royal Anthropological Institute* 2 (3):517–535. doi.org/10.2307/3034901.

Summerhayes, G. 2000. *Lapita interaction*. Terra Australis 15. Canberra: Department of Archaeology and Natural History and Centre for Archaeological Research, The Australian National University.

Thomas, N. 1991. *Entangled objects: Exchange, material culture and colonialism in the Pacific*. Cambridge, Massachusetts: Harvard University Press.

Thomas, T. 2004. 'Things of Roviana: Material culture, personhood and agency in nineteenth century Solomon Islands'. PhD thesis, University of Otago, Dunedin.

Thomas, T. 2009. 'Communities of practice in the archaeology of New Georgia, Rendova and Tetepare'. In *Lapita: Ancestors and descendants*, edited by PJ Sheppard, T Thomas and G Summerhayes, 119–145. NZAA Monograph 28. Auckland: New Zealand Archaeological Association.

Thomas, T. 2013. 'Sensory efficacy in the material culture of New Georgia, Solomon Islands'. In *Melanesia: Art and encounter*, edited by L Bolton, N Thomas, E Bonshek, J Adams and B Burt, 199–208. London: British Museum Press.

Thomas, T. 2014. 'Shrines in the landscape of New Georgia'. In *Monuments and people in the Pacific*, edited by H Martinsson-Wallin and T Thomas, 47–76. Studies in Global Archaeology 20. Uppsala: Department of Archaeology and Ancient History, Uppsala University.

Thomas, T, P Sheppard, and R Walter. 2001. 'Landscape, violence and social bodies: Ritualized architecture in a Solomon Islands society'. *The Journal of the Royal Anthropological Institute* 7 (3):545–572. doi.org/10.1111/1467-9655.00077.

Torrence, R and A Clarke. 2013. 'Creative colonialism: Locating indigenous strategies in ethnographic museum collections'. In *Reassembling the collection: Ethnographic museums and indigenous agency,* edited by R Harrison, S Byrne and A Clarke, 171–195. Santa Fe: School for Advanced Research Press.

Waite, D and K Conru. 2008. *Solomon Islands art: The Conru collection*. Milan: Five Continents Editions.

Walter, R and P Sheppard. 2000. 'Nusa Roviana: The archaeology of a Melanesian chiefdom'. *Journal of Field Archaeology* 27 (3):295–318. doi.org/10.1179/jfa.2000.27.3.295.

Walter, R, T Thomas and P Sheppard. 2004. 'Cult assemblages and ritual practice in Roviana Lagoon, Solomon Islands'. *World Archaeology* 36 (1):142–157. doi.org/10.1080/0043824042000192614.

Zelenietz, M. 1979. 'The end of head hunting in New Georgia'. In *The pacification of Melanesia*, edited by M Rodman and M Cooper, 91–108. Ann Arbor: University of Michigan Press.

8

Four hundred years of niche construction in the western Solomon Islands

Peter Sheppard

Introduction

In a recent issue of *Current Anthropology* (Fuentes and Wiessner 2016), dedicated to how anthropology might bridge or reintegrate across the evolutionary/scientific and constructivist or humanistic approaches which seem to divide us, the editors offer the extended evolution synthesis (EES) and niche construction theory (NCT; Laland et al. 2014) as a way forward. Fuentes states that 'humans construct ecological, technical and cultural niches that influence the structure of evolutionary landscapes' and argues:

> A contemporary evolutionary approach has to treat what humans do and experience as a complex system that has specific histories, has inherited ecologies and institutions, and includes a myriad of categories of action and perception as they relate to the interactions between individuals, groups, and the communities in which they exist. (Fuentes 2016:S14–S15)

This would appear to mirror, albeit coming from the opposite side of the 'divide', the move by Hodder (2012), to mesh consideration of materiality, actor-network theory and notions of entanglement with evolutionary theory. Both approaches would appear to be highlighting the importance of historical contingency, which underlies both biological evolutionary theory and culture history. For those interested in proximate explanations of the archaeological record either approach could be methodologically useful, although both can lead into highly detailed explanatory narratives. This leaves one with the question as to how such a narrative differs from a traditional detailed culture history. In the following I will briefly sketch out an historical narrative 'explaining' or describing, within the terms of the EES-NCT framework proposed by Fuentes (2016), the culture history of the western Solomon Islands and consider to what extent it led me to enrich my understanding of the archaeological and historical record. In particular I will focus on how the situation-specific developments in Roviana Lagoon have altered the cultural environment or niche to which Roviana and neighbouring societies have had to respond or adapt. A combination of an inherited set of geographical and environmental features of the lagoon and inherited Austronesian cultural schemata have led to the development of a cultural niche employing headhunting, which has created a powerful selective force. Neighbouring societies have either adopted this cultural form or have fallen victim to it, dramatically changing regional demography and culture as seen in language distribution. Ultimately these forces come into conflict with, and succumb to, expanding global capitalism.

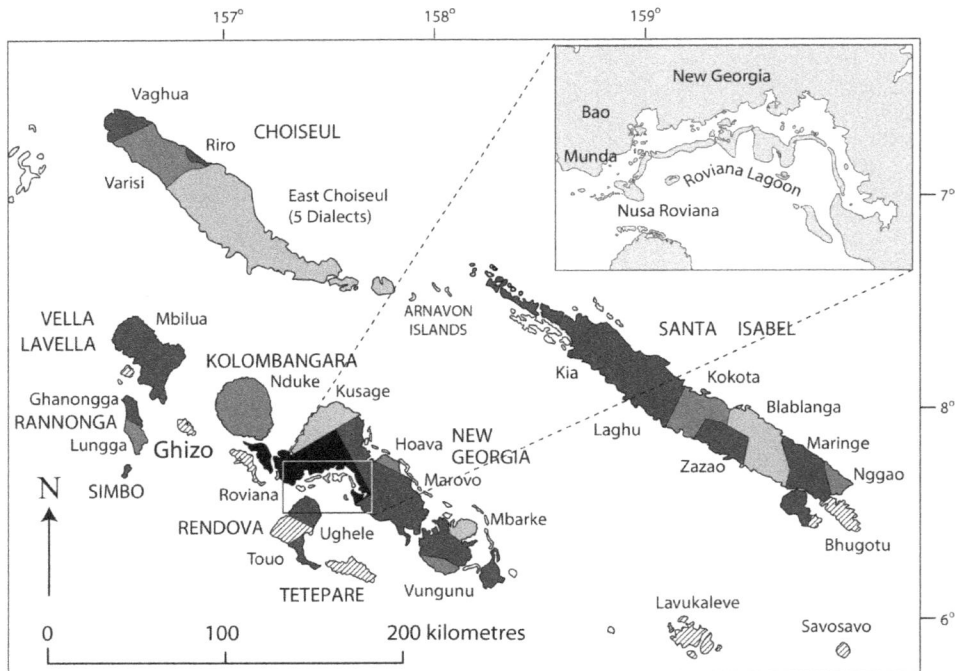

Figure 8.1. The western Solomon Islands and its languages.
Source: Peter Sheppard.

The western Solomons

In the 19th century, the western Solomons (Figure 8.1) was an area of considerable linguistic diversity; yet it had an overarching cultural tradition or community of practice (Thomas 2009) centred on a political economy sharing systems of exchange, religion and authority. A total of 24 Austronesian and four Non-Austronesian (NAN East Papuan) languages are found within a distance of 425 km along the chain of islands which make up the region, with Roviana forming the largest language group (Lewis et al. 2016). Crossing these linguistic boundaries, both Austronesian and NAN, was much commonality in material culture. In the 19th century European traders noted the importance of particular forms of shell rings which served as means of exchange in commodity transactions as well as means of social exchange and symbolic marking of many types (Aswani and Sheppard 2003). Headhunting, both for heads and captives, was endemic and large war canoes (*tomoko* in Roviana), holding up to 30 men, were found throughout the region (Woodford 1909). Ancestral skull shrines, which, although varying somewhat in form throughout the region (Figure 8.2), shared very similar components and functions. Together these items were key components of a distinctive western Solomon culture complex. How then did this complex form in the context of the underlying cultural diversity signalled by language? An EES perspective would suggest the pattern seen in the western Solomons involves a complex history of evolutionary forces generating both cultural diversity and homogeneity, within a specific physical ecology or geographical setting (i.e. arrangement of islands and lagoons, soil types, raw material distributions, etc.) which itself frames patterns of interaction into which different evolutionary lineages can contribute novel cultural variation at different times. As these histories of interaction are worked out, the cultural environment may change and the selective environment or niche in which variety generating or reducing interaction takes place will vary. I argue that this has taken place in the western Solomons, with early variety generating forces overtaken in the last 400 years by forces selecting for cultural conformity.

Figure 8.2. Roviana ancestral skull shrine.
Source: Reverend George Brown 1899, courtesy Auckland Methodist Archives.

Inherited ecologies: Regional geography and resources

At the centre of the western Solomons is the large Roviana Lagoon, extending 40 km along the south-west coast of New Georgia. In addition to being central, and closely networked to neighbouring islands (Sheppard and Walter 2008), Roviana is rich in natural resources of high productivity as attested by the high modern population density and number of villages. It is the most densely populated area in the western Solomons outside of the provincial capital Ghizo. The resources of the lagoons are rich (Aswani 1997) and the region must rank amongst the most productive in the western Solomons. The lagoons are enclosed by upraised barrier reefs and the interiors of many of these contain rich dark garden soils. Their chemistry confirms they are capable of supporting highly productive intensive horticulture (Furusawa and Ohtsuka 2009) unlike mainland soils. The large villages, except that along the Munda shore, are located on the barrier islands at the passages between islands. In summary, Roviana would appear to be a most, if not *the* most, advantageous area for human settlement in the western Solomons.

Two material resources become important in western Solomons' history: fossil giant clam (*Tridacna*) shell and shell of hawksbill turtles. Fossil *Tridacna* is found in the upraised reefs of the barrier islands. This shell was used to make shell money and valuables (Aswani and Sheppard 2003). Despite Roviana being described as a 'mint', it is not clear if Roviana or any other area is especially favoured in this resource. Early accounts such as that of Ribbe (1903:292) and others (Richards and Roga 2004; Welsch 1998) indicate *Tridacna* is found throughout the tectonically active western Solomons. Hawksbill shell, called tortoiseshell by early Western traders, was traditionally used to make decorative body ornaments in the western Solomons. Turtles are found throughout the Solomons and were commonly hunted. The largest nesting site in the South-West Pacific is on the Arnavon Islands in the strait between Choiseul and Santa Isabel (Hamilton et al. 2015), 100 km north-west of Roviana. In the late 19th century this area became the major source of 'tortoise' shell in the western Solomons (Bennett 1985).

Inherited cultural schema: Categories of action and perception

The western Solomons was probably initially settled in the Late Pleistocene (Wickler 2001) by a low density foraging or wild food producing population speaking a NAN (Dunn et al. 2005) language, which over time diversified in place (Ross 2010). By the late 19th century only two NAN-speaking groups remained in the western Solomons: a small group on the south-eastern coast of Rendova (Touo) and speakers of Mbilua on Vella Lavella.

Today most people in the region speak related Austronesian languages forming part of the North-West Solomonic family (Ross 1988), which extends north into the Bismarck Archipelago. It is difficult to determine when Austronesians moved from the Bismarcks into the Solomons. Presumably it is marked by the spread of the Lapita cultural complex associated with the appearance, in the Bismarcks c. 3500 cal BP, of domesticates, fully developed food production (Spriggs 1997:61) and new technologies including ceramics. In the western Solomons, late Lapita sites with ceramics similar to those found in New Ireland (Garling 2003) appear from c. 2600 cal BP (Sheppard and Walter 2006). This movement finds support in the linguistic evidence, which shows Proto North-West Solomonic most closely related to the languages of south New Ireland and moving into the western Solomons after it diverged from Proto Oceanic (Ross 2010).

These new people, or new Austronesian cultural tradition, would presumably have replaced the previous foraging lifeway in a short period of time, given new enhanced food production capability. Once established, Proto North-West Solomonic broke up over the following millennia into the many languages of the western Solomons. Linguistics indicates very complicated sets of local histories leading to the extreme diversity seen today (Ross 2010:265). In a few locations, the NAN language survived, although speakers must have rapidly adopted much of this new cultural formation. For example, on the relatively large island of Vella Lavella, where NAN is exclusive, the presence of late Lapita sites like those found in Roviana (Sheppard et al. 2010), suggests either a failed settlement by Austronesian speakers or the adoption of the presumed Austronesian late Lapita lifeway but not the language.

Austronesian language and tradition involved not just a new foodway but also the introduction of new cultural schema or systems (Shore 1996) of core cultural values and meanings common to much of the Austronesian world (Fox 1995; Reuter 2006; Scaglion 1996). Study of terms and meanings in language is the only effective approach to tracing the history of terms and creating hypotheses regarding meaning (Pawley and Ross 2006). However, reflexes of Austronesian terms may be polysemous or have multiple meanings or senses which can seem in English to be more or less related (Pawley 2005). Thus when we see considerable coherence within a term, even across a large number of languages related at some time depth, what we are seeing is inheritance of a semantic field providing opportunities to select or elaborate meanings within new contexts. Given this caveat, and in the absence of any detailed reconstructions for North-West Solomonic, I would suggest the following as some key semantic fields related to core cultural schema at the Proto Oceanic level, which would have been part of the North-West Solomonic cultural inheritance.

Austronesian societies emphasise notions of precedence (Vischer 2009) and order found both in histories of movement and place, and in genealogy (Fox 1997). Into this are set both bilateral and lineal systems of social relationships with what Fox (1995) calls apical demotion as a means to develop hierarchy by promoting lineages seen to be closer to apical ancestors. Semantic fields of hierarchy have been constructed for Proto Oceanic by Pawley (1982) who identified terms for 'chief' and the firstborn son of the chief which were subsequently revised by Lichtenberk (1986) who proposed terms for 'big, great person' and oldest child. Underlying and animating these terms and relationships are the values of *mana* and *tabu* which can be reconstructed back to Proto Oceanic (Kirch and Green 2001:239). As Keesing (1985) and Burt (1988) report, these terms reflect complex fields of meaning. Keesing (1985:203) describes the Proto Oceanic term *mana* as a:

stative verb, with meanings of 'be efficacious, be true, be realized, be potent,' and the implication that such efficacy and potency was a result of blessings or protection or potentiation by ancestral or other spirits.

In a similar vein the term *tabu* refers to a field of meanings which, according to Keesing (1985:204), has as its basic Proto Oceanic meaning the relational concept of 'off limits' and is used to structure relations of people to people and people to things. Burt (1988:75) notes that:

> Ultimately *abu* in Kwara'ae appears to be a way of dealing with power, of controlling not just the spiritual and reproductive powers of men and women but also the political power to which these powers contributed.

Both terms then are fundamental terms expressing and structuring agency (Keesing 1985:204) in the Proto Oceanic social world, which included both the living and ancestors; thus extending relationships of agency to the ancestors. Ultimately through these inherited terms we see the potential for expressing differential access to power and the development of hierarchy in Austronesian societies like Roviana.

Another inherited structuring principle, which is important historically in the Solomons and presumably has ancient roots, is the distinction between coast and bush. In particular the distinction made between people of the interior and those of the coast (Miller 1980; Roe 2000). This relates in part to the importance of topogenies and origin stories in Austronesian societies (Fox 1997) that are often told in terms of movements from the interior to the coast, even, as Miller (1980) points out, on very small islands like Simbo where the distances can be less than a kilometre. These topogenies, or sequences of named places, map people onto the landscape and like genealogies define groups, yet at the same time appear to reflect a real tension over coastal access and resources. Where interior populations are found today, in islands like Malaita, the coast/bush dichotomy has historically been very important, with significant trade in resources between the regions (Roe 2000). Modern populations in the western Solomons are essentially coastal; however, some of their 19th-century ancestors lived in the bush and thus for them even recent history is one of movement to the coast to take advantage of opportunities found there; something which may have been going on for millennia.

Evolution of the Roviana chiefdom

Following the late Lapita tradition, which is estimated to last until c. 2000 BP, the archaeological record in the western Solomons is blank until 800 BP when dated inland sites appear (Sheppard and Walter 2009). In Roviana, the Bao Period, beginning by at least 1200 CE, is marked by the appearance of isolated 'shrines' on the ridges to the back of the coastal flats on the mainland. These shrines consist of earthen platforms faced with basalt slabs. Often there is a small depression or stone-lined box set into the platform at one end (Figure 8.3). Adjacent to the platform is commonly found one or more large flat 'table' stones supported on a set of cobbles. Excavation in and around these sites shows they are completely clean of cultural material and there is no evidence of associated occupation. Most notable is the absence of any hearth or surface ovens (*oputu*). Shrines of this form are also found in a few locations on the barrier islands of Roviana Lagoon where they are marked by the presence of large (150 kg+) basalt slabs transported from the interior of New Georgia. The oldest, dated c. 1200 CE, is 2 km into the hills of the Bao area to the back of Munda. This shrine and region is considered to be a Roviana origin location, associated in oral tradition with the chief Ididubanara who traditionally moved down to the lagoon sometime in the early 17th century, based on genealogy (Aswani 2000; Hall 1964; Nagaoka 1999). Accordingly, a shrine site (Site 79) on the barrier island of Nusa Roviana containing abundant basalt construction is associated in oral tradition with Ididubanara; using radiocarbon, it dates to after the mid-14th century (Sheppard et al. 2000).

Figure 8.3. Early Bao Period shrine in Roviana.
Source: Peter Sheppard.

In the late 16th or early 17th century, we see the sudden appearance of a new type of shrine associated with historic Roviana, common on the barrier islands in or near settlements. At their simplest, these are small platforms made of coral cobbles; often a number of small platforms are aggregated together and surrounded with an enclosure. Small cists on these platforms are generally made of sheet coral and typically contain human skulls, shell rings and other shell artefacts, or in historic sites, metal and glass objects. The ground around these platforms is densely covered with shell and animal bone, which are the remains of food offerings. An oven (*oputu*) composed of basalt cobbles is always nearby. Photographs of Roviana shrines usually show a wooden superstructure such as a post supporting a box containing skulls (Figure 8.2) and it may be that the current sheet coral boxes on the platforms are constructions enclosing skulls after the original wooden structures rotted. Unlike the earlier faced shrines, isolated away from evidence of residential occupation, these later forms are usually found in close proximity to house platforms and within village contexts. The distribution on the barrier island of Nusa Roviana, which is traditionally considered to be the focal point of the Roviana chiefdom, is a good example.

Nusa Roviana is located in the centre of Roviana. Unlike the other islands, it has a high, steep-sided narrow central ridge, providing a good defensive feature looking out over approaches to the lagoon. The island is densely carpeted with the remains of continuous settlement covering the coastal flats around the ridge (Sheppard et al. 2000; Sheppard et al. 2002; Walter and Sheppard 2001). The ridge itself contains a large fortified complex which extends along the ridgetop for 700 m. The fortification consists of three major (up to 3 m high) stone and earth walls and a deep rock cut ditch at the southern end. These cut across the ridge and enclose a series of nine named shrines. Sequences of narrow terraces descend the steep slopes to the east and west. Dates on shell from under the walls indicates construction beginning after 1500 CE (Sheppard et al. 2000).

Figure 8.4. The Roviana chief (H)Ingava wearing a *bakiha rapoto* and *hokata* (arm-rings), both forms of *poata*.

Source: Edge-Partington 1907.

How should we interpret this dramatic change which correlates with the establishment of the Roviana chiefdom as it was known in the 19th century? Oral history relates that the inland people from Bao, under Ididubanara, moved to the coast to more easily procure the fossil *Tridacna* needed to manufacture shell rings. Ididubanara fought with the people who lived on Nusa Roviana and the islands, chasing them from the lagoon, thus establishing Roviana with a base on Nusa Roviana (Aswani and Sheppard 2003). Subsequent oral tradition recounts what Fox (1995) might describe as apical demotion, when chiefs (*banara*) within a particular lineage became *mateana* (meteor, or used to translate 'angel' in English (Waterhouse 1949:73)), and at the location of a shrine (Zare) in the Nusa Roviana hillfort ascended to heaven or descended into the earth. These individuals founded the main chiefly lineage of Roviana two generations after Ididubanara (Aswani 2000).

Status in Roviana is signalled by a chest ornament known as *bakiha rapoto* which consists of a decorated *bakiha* or high-value shell ring made from fossil *Tridacna* (Figure 8.4). In 1908, Hocart reported these rings were made from fossil *Tridacna* that was the food waste of *tamasa* (gods or spirit-beings; Hocart n.d.(b)), giving them an association with ancestral spirits. They were used to inaugurate chiefs as children and placed under their skulls when they were finally placed in the ancestral skull shrine. These rings not only had powerful ritual and symbolic associations, they were also the most valuable of a hierarchy of shell valuables known as *poata*. *Poata* could be exchanged to mark social relationships and occasions (e.g. marriage, peace settlements, rewarding warriors, etc.) but also used to pay for any kind of commodity (e.g. canoes or taro), services or knowledge such as magical spells (Aswani and Sheppard 2003; Thomas 1991). These *poata* made possible a regionally networked economy in commodities (e.g. purchase of food for feasts, etc. (Sheppard and Walter 2013)). Chiefs were ultimately powerful and able to command respect if they had access to enough *poata* to make feasts, cover the cost of social exchanges of their people, build canoe houses and large 30-man war canoes, and reward warriors after a successful headhunting expedition (Hocart 1931, n.d.(a)).

Headhunting (see also Chapter 7 this volume) was central to Roviana culture and political economy. Chiefs mounted very large headhunting raids involving, on occasion (in 1893, for example), as many as 500 men, large numbers of rifles and 22 war canoes (*tomoko*) (Somerville 1897). Chiefs funded the construction of *tomoko* at a cost of the equivalent of 1 *poata* per rib (i.e. 11 *poata* or 5500 copra in 1908 (Hocart n.d.(b)). Following a successful headhunt warriors were rewarded with a feast and *poata* and the heads were hung in the rafters of the chief's canoe house. Early traders describe raids returning large numbers of heads with 93 reported from a raid in 1844 (Shineberg 1971:62). This activity underwrote the power of chiefs, as the skulls were a materialised display of chiefly *mana* or efficacy provided by the ancestors, as were the living captives (McDougall 2000) who provided the means for ritual sacrifice (Hocart 1931) and labour for such things as shell valuable production.

By the 19th century Roviana society had evolved, drawing on inherited Austronesian cultural schema, into a powerful hierarchical chiefly society established in an optimal location both in terms of food resources and geographical centrality. Through respect for ancestors and the *mana* they could bestow, apical demotion which privileged certain lineages, the elaboration of headhunting as a means of demonstrating ancestral blessing and *mana*, and the development of a shell valuable economy which provided a mechanism for running both a social exchange economy and a trade in commodities, Roviana developed a society with strong power differentials. This required continual predatory expansion in order to obtain heads and captives, thus profoundly altering the cultural environment or niche impacting neighbouring societies.

But what were the drivers for this evolution? The shrine record suggests an abrupt change which correlates with oral tradition of movement from the interior (Aswani and Sheppard 2003). However, some of the elements of the headhunting complex such as the *tomoko* and the shell valuable tradition existed outside of Roviana at about this time. The Spanish on Santa Isabel in 1568 CE described what can only be *tomoko*. 'Their canoes are very well made and very light ... shaped like a crescent, the largest holding about thirty persons' (Amherst and Thomson 1901:109). They also observed leaders on Isabel wearing white chest ornaments made of 'white alabaster', probably fossil *Tridacna*. Developments at this time in Roviana were thus not simply local innovations but pulled on older regional traditions of material culture. The changes in Roviana itself appear, however, to be fundamentally the result of competition between bush and coastal groups for rich coastal resources in what was an optimal location. Defence of this location required the creation of a hill fort on a very well situated and uniquely defensible ridge on Nusa Roviana. These developments, specific to Roviana, would, I suggest, promote changes toward hierarchical social organisation crafted out of the cultural schemata or traditions outlined above.

Expansion of the predatory Roviana-type headhunting culture and niche

Roviana society depended on headhunting and raiding for captives. It was almost by definition expansionist, altering the niche or cultural environment of the region. By the end of the 19th century, populations of the New Georgia group (New Georgia, Rendova, Simbo, Rannonga, Vella Lavella, Kolombangara) had adopted the fundamental aspects of the headhunting complex (Woodford 1888) and the political organisation or at least the ability to organise which it supported. This certainly included the material manifestations of the *bakiha* and other shell valuables, skull shrines, *tomoko* war canoes and canoe houses as shown in 19th-century photographs. There is clear evidence, from oral traditions and archaeological research, of the adoption of the shrine and shell valuable complex probably within the 18th century. The extent to which all of these developed together in a 'peer polity' (Renfrew 1986) type of interactive entanglement is not clear; however, the Roviana development had clearly altered the regional cultural niche.

Oral tradition

Oral tradition collected by the missionary George Carter indicates an important history of fighting between Roviana and Vella Lavella.

> During the time when Tungahanika was *mbangara* in Roviana Kokorapa there occurred a great fight at Roviana Island [Nusa Roviana]. Over 1000 men from Mbilua [southern Vella Lavella] came up and attacked Roviana Island. … When the Mbilua raiding party arrived, the Roviana people were on the top of the hill (Carter 1963—Anonymous).

> When a man called Kopele became chief at Mbilua he made peace between Roviana and Mbilua. He gave a native money [*bakiha*] to the people of Roviana for peace. This money is called 'thousand peace', and it is still kept by Inoro of Ilangana (Carter 1963—Talasasa).

The Roviana genealogical charts collected by Hocart would place Tungahanika c. 1800 CE (Schneider 1996:Figure 7).

Archaeological research

Archaeological research on Vella Lavella demonstrates dense settlement in the interior hills (McKenzie 2007; Sheppard and Walter 2014; Sheppard et al. 2010). Skull shrines with shell valuables are found along the tops of the first ridges and are the named shrines to which modern people living on the coast affiliate. In most respects, these shrines and their contents are identical to the late period shrines in Roviana. Most date within the last several hundred years while the earliest dates are late 17th century, making them younger than the oldest late period shrines in Roviana.

The coastal flats of Vella were not inhabited during the 19th century for fear of attack, although canoe houses were maintained from which headhunting expeditions were conducted in *tomoko* (McKinnon 1972). At the time, the islands between Roviana and Vella Lavella were depopulated by headhunting (McKinnon 1972:64) and most of Kolombangara was depopulated to the extent that much of it, like Ghizo, was claimed by the colonial government as waste land.

Research by Thomas on Rendova and Tetepare to the south and east of Roviana provides a story similar to that from Vella Lavella. In the NAN Touo region of southern Rendova, the sequence of early simple shrines without any human remains, shell valuables or ovens followed by shrines containing all of those is, according to Thomas (2009), almost identical to that in Roviana, with the exception that the late period shrines date no earlier than 1700 CE. On the island of Tetepare, just to the east of Rendova, Thomas reports a similar sequence. As in the area to the west of Roviana, the population of Tetepare was unable to survive the raiding of the 19th century and is today the largest uninhabited island in the Pacific (Thomas 2009:136).

Nineteenth century and entanglement with the Western capitalist economy

The 19th century saw new elements enter the evolutionary landscape of the western Solomons. These interacted with the established structure to first intensify it and then radically transform and replace it. Roviana's optimal central location, sheltered anchorage and the patronage of powerful Roviana chiefs made Munda, by 1875, the focus of European trade in the western Solomons (Woodford 1888). By 1886 there were six traders stationed there, on small islands off the coast of Munda.

By 1886 traders were dealing in a variety of goods including iron, tobacco, long-handled axes and Snider rifles which they exchanged for turtle shell and copra. Turtle shell was especially sought as it was compact and fetched a good price in Sydney. In 1851 Lewis Truscott secured more than a thousand pounds of turtle shell from New Georgia, and in 1874 the trader Fergusson delivered to Sydney 1700 pounds of turtle shell accumulated by the Rendova chiefs (Bennett 1985:46, 57). Turtle shell provided a good return and by 1886, three turtle shells were exchanged for a Snider rifle at Munda. By the late 1880s these were the only items which would get them 'payable quantities' of turtle shell and copra (Bennett 1985:90; McKinnon 1975:303).

In the mid-1800s turtles were common in the waters of New Georgia but the demands of trade meant that by the 1890s turtles were very scarce and had to be hunted outside of New Georgia (Bennett 1985:94; Somerville 1897:369). If turtle hunting within Roviana Lagoon could be an individual or family activity, hunting expeditions into other areas required the manpower and protection provided by chiefs (Woodford 1890). This mapped well onto the headhunting economy and combined head/turtle expeditions provided heads/captives and evidence of chiefly *mana* as well as the returns from the shell, including shell rings purchased from traders. These resources were then used to finance ever greater expeditions, which with the new iron axes and rifles had an increasing impact on the populations of the western Solomons (McKinnon 1975).

The following describes an expedition to hunt turtles in the Arnavon nesting sites between Choiseul and Santa Isabel as told by Gemu a Roviana chief:

> One day, only a few years ago [prior to 1906], a large party came over from Roviana on a turtle hunting expedition … and found the Lauru [Choiseul] men poaching on our hunting grounds. … They were all killed … Hiqava [Ingava], Vonge and Miabule [chiefs of Roviana] took part and killed many men. We took two hundred heads back to Munda. (Carter 1981:6)

People in Choiseul and Isabel retreated first to defensive positions in the interior and ultimately along the islands to the west or east away from Roviana. In Santa Isabel this is known amongst the Cheke Holo people as the time of 'flight from death' when there were often not enough people left alive to bury the dead (White 1991:89). Woodford reported in 1888 that Santa Isabel and Choiseul were nearly depopulated (Woodford 1888:375, 1890:154, 205). As can be seen in Figure 8.1 this created the present language distribution, creating a compression of languages at the far ends of the islands and a low-density population speaking one language in the impacted areas closest to Roviana.

Imposition of the colonial economy

While the intensified Roviana chiefly economy was effective in providing turtle shell to traders, the associated violence had an adverse effect on overall trade, in particular trade in copra, which depended on safe family level production in coastal locations and a benign trading environment. A change in the relations of production and shift of authority into the Western capitalist economy was needed—if Western trade was to flourish. This required suppression of the traditional Roviana political economy. During his visit to Roviana in 1880 the Methodist missionary George Brown stayed with the local traders and reported their view:

> The traders were unanimous in their desire that the British Government should stop this wholesale murder, and were equally unanimous in their opinion that the presence of a small ship of war during the headhunting season, the punishment of a few ring leaders, and the confiscation of all canoes captured whilst engaged in a raid would soon stop the horrible business. (Brown 1909:342)

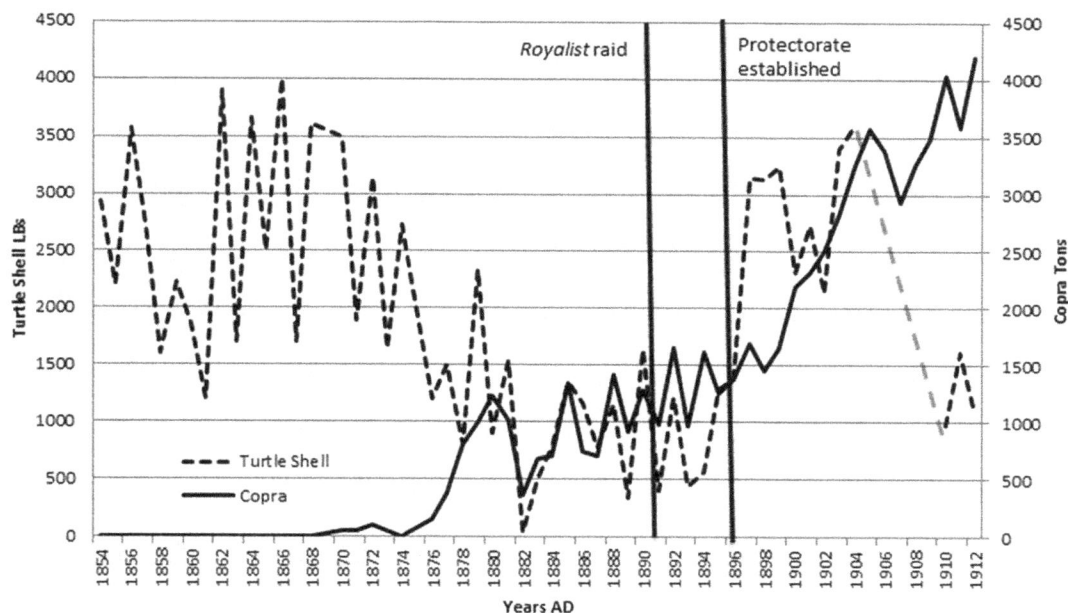

Figure 8.5. Export of copra and turtle shell from the Solomons in the 19th and early 20th centuries.

Data up to 1896 is on goods landed at Sydney from Bennett (1985:Appendix 4) and subsequently from the Annual Reports of the Solomon Islands Protectorate.

Source: Peter Sheppard.

In September 1891 the British warship *Royalist* arrived at Roviana and sent a party of marines to investigate the murder of a local trader. When the demands to deliver the guilty parties were not met the British proceeded, over two days, to burn all the villages on Nusa Roviana and in Munda. Captain Davis estimated he destroyed 400 houses, 150 canoes and 1000 heads (Davis 1892:11).

By 1900 headhunting appears to have virtually ceased (Carter 1963:6, 9). Figure 8.5 shows the collapse in the turtle shell trade—most of which probably came from the western Solomons—and its replacement by copra at the end of the 19th century after the establishment of the colonial economy. This created a new set of relations of production, based primarily on family-level production, which although still ultimately tied to chiefly adjudication of land use rights, was not connected to the headhunting economy.

The end of headhunting was enforced by the British but it also seems to have collapsed under the weight of its destructive impact on the region. That, along with European diseases and the creation of an environment antithetical to family-level trade in copra, saw the end of the headhunting economy (Zelenietz 1979). Chiefly *mana* now had to be sought through associations with traders and, within a decade, entanglement with a new cultural niche created by the Christian Church.

Concluding comments: Evolution, niche construction and history

As noted by Laland and O'Brien (2010) there is a risk for NCT explanations in archaeology to become 'just-so stories', or 'just' detailed culture histories. However, as they also note, if NCT helps us construct or think about and approach our data in a new way then that has to be useful. To that end, I think an NCT consideration of western Solomon history does help focus our attention on some overlooked aspects and highlights areas where data is needed.

This version of history can be critiqued as very Roviana-centric; however, by the late 19th century Roviana was viewed by the British as the centre of the 'problem' and the key to securing colonial control—a view shared by the Methodists who made their regional base in Munda in 1902 (Goldie 1914). But more fundamentally the Roviana environment and its geography provided special features which made it what might be called an evolutionary hotspot. Not all geographical locations are equal (Sheppard and Walter 2008) and its central location, sheltered lagoon and very productive natural environment attracted population and potentially competition, along with interaction, to Roviana throughout its history. This created a feedback loop, through the ongoing development of the niche created by this growing population. Much of this could potentially be quantified and assessed against other areas in the western Solomons.

Beyond their geographical inheritance, the Roviana had an Austronesian inheritance providing a set of core values and ideology that created the basis for the development of hierarchy and socio-political control. The form this took was broadly Austronesian but in its details unique to the western Solomons. Elsewhere in the Oceanic Austronesian world, hierarchy correlates with economic intensification and/or control of prestige exchange (Friedman 1982). In Roviana there is no evidence of local agricultural intensification such as enhanced taro irrigation; instead there existed a networked regional economy where commodification and exchange, founded on an elaborate system of shell valuables, provided the basis for the support of hierarchy through trade (Aswani and Sheppard 2003; Sheppard and Walter 2013). Even in the dangerous environment created by headhunting, chiefly feasting could depend on transport of food by canoe from outside the language area (Hocart 1931). Roviana chiefs sought to obtain and ultimately intensify the harvest of human skulls—not taro. How one explains in evolutionary terms the selection of skulls as the tokens for a maximisation logic is unclear; however, in the Austronesian world *mana* or efficacy ultimately derives from humans, who are most fundamentally materialised by skulls, making them a highly valued symbol, seemingly with high selective value.

I argue that, in Roviana, the appearance of late period skull shrines, fortifications and headhunting are all related and appear after 1600 CE. Explanation for this sudden development in simple evolutionary terms (e.g. perhaps as energy sinks or costly signalling (Boone 1998)) is not obvious. Roviana people explain this development as the result of conflict between bush and coastal people and the desire for the bush chief Ididubanara to obtain the resources of the coast, as exemplified by his desire for shell valuables. Once established, the predatory nature of the Roviana chieftainship rapidly altered the cultural environment or niche in which surrounding societies functioned, resulting in the spread of the headhunting complex and associated culture. This was most probably initially confined to the New Georgia group, with some regional reassortment of population in the early 19th century.

The entanglement with the niche provided by the world economy in the 19th century created new economic drivers as chiefs linked—through the trade in turtle shell—their political economies to that of the traders attracted to the advantages provided by the dominant regional power. The hunting of turtle shell oriented the chiefs toward Choiseul and Santa Isabel, and the intensification of the headhunting complex—provided by new technologies, new sources of finance, increasing numbers of captive labourers and more effective weapons—had a devastating effect on the cultural geography of the region, resulting in the linguistic and demographic distribution seen today. Ultimately this came into conflict both with the colonial trading economy, which needed peaceful, family-level production of copra, and the power behind this new economy. The shift of power from chiefs to the new colonial government and the associated prohibition of the core features of the Roviana political economy and associated ideology effectively destroyed the foundations of 19th-century Roviana society (Rivers 1922). As related to Hocart shortly after the end of headhunting: 'Now the chiefs stop nothing' (Hocart n.d.(a)). Roviana society, and that of its neighbours, now entered into a new creative process of cultural niche construction, creating a colonial economy where the chiefs and people engaged with, and created societies entangled with, capitalism and the ideology of Christianity. Whether an evolutionary logic can be seen in the working out of these entanglements of colonialism is an interesting question.

References

Amherst, Lord, of Hackney and B Thomson. 1901. *The discovery of the Solomon Islands by Alvaro de Mendana in 1568.* Vols 1 and 2. London: Hakluyt Society.

Aswani, S. 1997. 'Customary sea tenure and artisanal fishing in the Roviana and Vonavona Lagoons, Solomon Islands: The evolutionary ecology of marine resource utilization'. Unpublished PhD thesis, University of Hawai'i, Honolulu.

Aswani, S. 2000. 'Changing identities: The ethnohistory of Roviana predatory headhunting'. *Journal of the Polynesian Society* 109 (1):39–70.

Aswani, S and P Sheppard. 2003. 'The archaeology and ethnohistory of exchange in precolonial and colonial Roviana: Gifts, commodities and inalienable possessions'. *Current Anthropology.* 44:S51–S78. doi.org/10.1086/377667.

Bennett, J. 1985. *Wealth of the Solomons: A history of a Pacific archipelago, 1800–1978.* Honolulu: University of Hawai'i Press.

Boone, J. 1998. 'The evolution of magnanimity'. *Human Nature* 9 (1):1–21. doi.org/10.1007/s12110–998–1009–y.

Brown, G. 1899. *Burial Place Rubiana.* George Brown Photographer, Courtesy of the Auckland Methodist Archives, Auckland.

Brown G. 1909. *George Brown, D.D.: Pioneer-missionary and explorer.* London: Hodder and Stoughton.

Burt, B. 1988. 'Ábu'a 'i Kwara'ae: The meaning of tabu in a Solomon Islands society'. *Mankind* 18 (2):74–89.

Carter, G. 1963. 'Tunahanika'. Translation from Anonymous. In George Carter Papers. Archives University of Auckland, Auckland.

Carter, G. 1981. *Ti–è varanè: Stories about people of courage from Solomon Islands.* Rabaul: Unichurch.

Davis CE. 1892. *Australian Station, Solomon Islands, 1891: Correspondence respecting Outrages by Natives on British Subjects and other matters, which have been under inquiry during the Year 1891, being continuation of reports of cases dealt with in former years, together with other cases which have since arisen.* Sydney: Government Printer.

Dunn, M, A Terrill, G Reesink, R Foley and S Levinson. 2005. 'Structural phylogenetics and the reconstruction of ancient language history'. *Science.* 309 (23):2072–2075. doi.org/10.1126/science.1114615.

Edge-Partington, T. 1907. 'Ingava, chief of Rubiana, Solomon Islands: Died 1906'. *Man* 7:22–23. doi.org/10.2307/2788122.

Fox, J. 1995. 'Austronesian societies and their transformations'. In *The Austronesians*, edited by P Bellwood, J Fox and D Tryon, 214–228. Canberra: The Australian National University.

Fox, J. 1997. 'Place and landscape in comparative Austronesian perspective'. In *The poetic power of place: Comparative perspectives on Austronesian ideas of locality*, edited by J Fox, 1–21. Canberra: Research School of Pacific and Asian Studies, The Australian National University.

Friedman, J. 1982. 'Catastrophe and continuity in social evolution'. In *Theory and explanation in archaeology: The Southampton conference*, edited by C Renfrew, M Rowlands and B Segraves, 175–196. New York: Academic Press.

Fuentes, A. 2016. 'The extended evolutionary synthesis, ethnography, and the human niche: Toward an integrated anthropology'. *Current Anthropology* 57 (S13):S13–S26. doi.org/10.1086/685684.

Fuentes, A and P Wiessner. 2016. 'Reintegrating anthropology: From inside out: An introduction to supplement 13'. *Current Anthropology* 57 (S13):S3–S12. doi.org/10.1086/685694.

Furusawa, T and R Ohtsuka. 2009. 'The role of barrier islands in subsistence of the inhabitants of Roviana Lagoon, Solomon Islands'. *Human Ecology* 37 (5):629–642. doi.org/10.1007/s10745-009-9266-x.

Garling, S. 2003. 'Tanga takes to the stage: Another model "Transitional" site? New evidence and a contribution to the "incised and applied relief tradition" in New Ireland'. In *Pacific archaeology: Assessments and prospects*, edited by C Sand, 213–233. Nouméa: Service des Musées et du Patrimoine.

Goldie, J. 1914. 'The Solomon Islands'. In *A century in the Pacific*, edited by J Colwell, 561–585. Sydney: William H. Beale.

Hall, A. 1964. 'Customs and culture from Kazukuru: Folklore obtained after the discovery of the shrine at Bao'. *Oceania* 35:127–135. doi.org/10.1002/j.1834-4461.1964.tb00839.x.

Hamilton, R, T Bird, C Gereniu, J Pita, P Ramohia, R Walter, C Goerlich and C Limpus. 2015. 'Solomon Islands largest hawksbill turtle rookery shows signs of recovery after 150 years of excessive exploitation'. *PLoS ONE* 10 (4):e0121435. doi.org/10.1371/journal.pone.0121435.

Hocart, AM. 1931. 'Warfare in Eddystone of the Solomon Islands'. *Journal of the Royal Anthropological Institute of Great Britain and Ireland* 61:301–324. doi.org/10.2307/2843922.

Hocart, AM. n.d.(a). 'Chieftainship'. Unpublished manuscript. In Hocart papers, Alexander Turnbull Library, Wellington. MS-Papers-0060.

Hocart, AM. n.d.(b). 'Trade and money'. Unpublished manuscript. In Hocart papers, Alexander Turnbull Library, Wellington. MS-Papers-0060.

Hodder, I. 2012. *Entangled: An archaeology of the relationships between humans and things*. Malden, MA: Wiley-Blackwell. doi.org/10.1002/9781118241912.

Keesing, R. 1985. 'Conventional metaphors and anthropological metaphysics: The problematic of cultural translation'. *Journal of Anthropological Research* 41 (2):201–217. doi.org/10.1086/jar.41.2.3630416.

Kirch PV and RC Green. 2001. *Hawaiki, Ancestral Polynesia: An essay in historical anthropology*. Cambridge: Cambridge University Press.

Laland, KN and MJ O'Brien. 2010. 'Niche construction theory and archaeology'. *Journal of Archaeological Method and Theory* 17(4):303–322.

Laland K, T Uller, M Feldman, K Sterelny, GB Müller, A Moczek, E Jablonka, J Odling-Smee, GA Wray, HE Hoekstra, DJ Futuyma, RE Lenski, TF Mackay, D Schluter and JE Strassmann. 2014. 'Does evolutionary theory need a rethink?' *Nature* 514 (7521):161. doi.org/10.1038/514161a.

Lewis, M, G Simons and C Fennig (eds). 2016. *Ethnologue: Languages of the world, nineteenth edition*. Dallas, Texas: SIL International.

Lichtenberk, F. 1986. 'Leadership in Proto-Oceanic society: Linguistic evidence'. *Journal of the Polynesian Society* 95:341–356.

McDougall, D. 2000. 'Paths of pinauzu: Captivity and social reproduction in Ranongga'. *Journal of the Polynesian Society* 109 (1):99–114.

McKenzie, A. 2007. 'Ancestral skull shrines: Material dialogues of social interaction in the western Solomon Islands'. Unpublished MA thesis, University of Auckland, Auckland.

McKinnon, J. 1972. 'Bilua changes: Culture contact and its consequences, a study of the Bilua of Vella Lavella in the British Solomon Islands'. Unpublished PhD thesis, Victoria University, Wellington.

McKinnon, J. 1975. 'Tomahawks, turtles and traders: A reconstruction in the circular causation of warfare in the New Georgia group'. *Oceania* 45 (4):290–307. doi.org/10.1002/j.1834-4461.1975.tb01872.x.

Miller, D. 1980. 'Settlement and diversity in the Solomon Islands'. *Man* 15:451–466. doi.org/10.2307/2801344.

Nagaoka, T. 1999. 'Hope pukerane: A study of religious sites in Roviana, New Georgia, Solomon Islands'. Unpublished MA thesis, University of Auckland, Auckland.

Pawley, A. 1982. 'Rubbishman, commoner, big-man, chief? Evidence for hereditary chieftainship in Proto-Oceanic'. In *Oceanic studies: Essays in honour of Aarne A. Koskinen*, edited by J Siikala, 33–52. Helsinki: Finnish Anthropological Society.

Pawley, A. 2005. 'The meaning(s) of Proto Oceanic Panua'. In *A polymath anthropologist: Essays in honour of Ann Chowning*, edited by C Gross, H Lyons and D Counts, 211–223. Auckland: University of Auckland.

Pawley, A and M Ross. 2006. 'The prehistory of Oceanic languages: A current view'. In *The Austronesians: Historical and comparative perspectives,* edited by P Bellwood, J Fox and D Tryon, 43–80. Canberra: ANU E Press.

Renfrew, C. 1986. 'Introduction: Peer polity interaction and socio-political change'. In *Peer polity interaction and socio-political change*, edited by C Renfrew and J Cherry, 1–18. Cambridge: Cambridge University Press.

Reuter, TA. 2006. 'Land and territory in the Austronesian world'. In *Sharing the Earth, carving up the land: Territorial categories and institutions in the Austronesian world*, edited by T Reuter, 11–38. Canberra: ANU E Press.

Ribbe, C. 1903. *Zwei jahre unter den Kannibalen der Salomo-Inseln.* Dresden: Beyer.

Richards, R and K Roga. 2004. 'Barava: Land title deeds in fossil shell from the western Solomon Islands'. *Tuhinga: Records of the museum of New Zealand Te Papa Tongarewa* 15:17–26.

Rivers, W. 1922. *Essays on the depopulation of Melanesia.* Cambridge: Cambridge University Press.

Roe, D. 2000. 'Maritime, coastal and inland societies in Island Melanesia: The bush-saltwater divide in Solomon Islands and Vanuatu'. In *East of Wallace's Line: Studies of past and present maritime cultures of the Indo-Pacific region*, edited by S O'Connor and P Veth, 197–222A. Rotterdam: A. Balkema.

Ross, M. 1988. *Proto Oceanic and the Austronesian languages of western Melanesia.* Canberra: Pacific Linguistics.

Ross, M. 2010. 'Lexical history in the Northwest Solomonic languages: Evidence for two waves of Oceanic settlement in Bougainville and the northwest Solomons'. In *A journey through Austronesian and Papuan linguistic and cultural space: Papers in honour of Andrew Pawley,* edited by J Bowden, NP Himmelmann and M Ross, 245–270. Canberra: Pacific Linguistics.

Scaglion, R. 1996. 'Chiefly models in Papua New Guinea'. *The Contemporary Pacific* 8 (1):1–31.

Schneider, G. 1996. 'Land dispute and tradition in Munda, Roviana Lagoon, New Georgia, Solomon Islands from headhunting to the quest for the control of land'. Unpublished PhD thesis, University of Cambridge, Cambridge.

Sheppard, P, S Aswani, R Walter and T Nagaoka. 2002. 'Cultural sediment: The nature of a cultural landscape in Roviana Lagoon'. In *Pacific landscapes: Archaeological approaches*, edited by T Ladefoged and M Graves, 35–61. Bearsville, California: Easter Island Foundation Press.

Sheppard, P and R Walter. 2006. 'A revised model of Solomon Islands culture history'. *Journal of the Polynesian Society* 115:47–76.

Sheppard, P and R Walter. 2008. 'The sea is not land: Comments on the archaeology of islands in the western Solomons'. In *Comparative island archaeologies,* edited by J Connolly and M Campbell, 167–178. Oxford: BAR International Series.

Sheppard, P and R Walter. 2009. 'Inter-tidal late Lapita sites and geotectonics in the western Solomons'. In *Lapita: Ancestors and descendants*, edited by P Sheppard, T Thomas and G Summerhayes, 73–100. Auckland: New Zealand Archaeological Association.

Sheppard, P and R Walter. 2013. 'Diversity and networked interdependence in the western Solomons'. In *Pacific archaeology: Documenting the past 50,000 years, papers from the 2011 Lapita Pacific archaeology conference*, edited by G Summerhayes and B Hallie, 138–147. Dunedin: University of Otago Studies in Archaeology.

Sheppard, P and R Walter. 2014. 'Shell valuables and history in Roviana and Vella Lavella'. In *The things we value: Culture and history in the Solomon Islands*, edited by B Burt and L Bolton, 32–45. London: Sean Kingston Publishing.

Sheppard, P, R Walter and T Nagaoka. 2000. 'The archaeology of head-hunting in Roviana Lagoon, New Georgia, Solomon Islands'. *Journal of the Polynesian Society* 109 (1):9–37.

Sheppard, P, R Walter and K Roga. 2010. 'Friends, relatives, and enemies: The archaeology and history of interaction among Austronesian and NAN speakers in the western Solomons'. In *A journey through Austronesian and Papuan linguistic and cultural space: Papers in honour of Andrew Pawley*, edited by J Bowden, N Himmelmann and M Ross, 95–112. Canberra: Pacific Linguistics Press.

Shineberg, D. 1971. *The trading voyages of Andrew Cheyne, 1841–1844*. Canberra: The Australian National University.

Shore, B. 1996. *Culture in mind: Cognition, culture and the problem of meaning*. Oxford: Oxford University Press.

Somerville, B. 1897. 'Ethnographical notes in New Georgia, Solomon Islands'. *Journal of the Royal Anthropological Institute of Great Britain and Ireland* 26 (4):357–413.

Spriggs, M. 1997. *The island Melanesians*. Oxford: Blackwell.

Thomas, N. 1991. *Entangled objects: Exchange, material culture and colonialism in the Pacific*. Cambridge, Massachusetts: Harvard University Press.

Thomas, T. 2009. 'Communities of practice in the archaeological record of New Georgia, Rendova and Tetepare'. In *Lapita: Ancestors and descendants*, edited by P Sheppard, T Thomas and G Summerhayes, 119–145. NZAA Monograph 28. Auckland: New Zealand Archaeological Association.

Vischer, MP. 2009. *Precedence: Social differentiation in the Austronesian world*. Canberra: ANU E Press. doi.org/10.22459/P.05.2009.

Walter, R and P Sheppard. 2001. 'Nusa Roviana: The archaeology of a Melanesian chiefdom'. *Journal of Field Archaeology* 27 (3):295–318. doi.org/10.1179/jfa.2000.27.3.295.

Waterhouse, J. 1949. *A Roviana and English dictionary, with English-Roviana index and list of natural history objects and appendix of old customs, revised and enlarged by L M Jones*. Sydney: Epworth Printing and Publishing House.

Welsch, R. 1998. *An American anthropologist in Melanesia: A.B. Lewis and the Joseph N. Field South Pacific expedition, 1909–1913*. Honolulu: University of Hawai'i Press.

White, G. 1991. *Identity through history: Living stories in a Solomon Islands society*. Cambridge: Cambridge University Press. doi.org/10.1017/CBO9780511621895.

Wickler, S. 2001. *The prehistory of Buka: A stepping stone island in the northern Solomons*. Canberra: Department of Archaeology and Natural History and Centre for Archaeological Research, The Australian National University.

Woodford, CM. 1888. 'Exploration of the Solomon Islands'. *Proceedings of the Royal Geographical Society* 10:351–376.

Woodford, C. 1890. *A naturalist among the head-hunters*. London: George Phillip and Son.

Woodford, C. 1909. 'The canoes of the British Solomon Islands'. *Journal Royal Anthropological. Institute* 9:505–516. doi.org/10.2307/2843216.

Zelenietz, M. 1979. 'The end of head hunting in New Georgia'. In *The pacification of Melanesia*, edited by M Rodman and M Cooper, 91–108. Ann Arbor: University of Michigan Press.

9

Sustenance and sustainability: Food remains and contact sites in Vanuatu

James Flexner, Edson Willie and Mark Horrocks

Introduction

Food is intimately linked to notions of cultural identity and belonging (Twiss 2007, 2015). For Melanesian Islanders, *aelan kaekae* (island food; Figure 9.1) is a ubiquitous part of everyday experience. Tubers, especially yams and taro, tree crops such as breadfruit and coconut, bananas, tropical fruits, fish and shellfish are heavily showcased on Islander plates, along with ritually important pigs on special occasions. Foods are traditionally cooked over open wood fires, or in earth ovens, which are necessary for making the well-loved delicacy of *lap lap* (a kind of starchy pudding). Increasingly in the modern era, these foods are supplemented with imported rice, noodles, and tinned meats and fish (e.g. Errington et al. 2013:83–101; Gewertz and Errington 2010). There is a longer history of colonial exchanges of foods in Melanesia, which we examine here using recent examples from mission sites and surrounding areas in southern Vanuatu. The 'mixing' of Melanesian and introduced ingredients in Islander meals can be seen as reflective of an ongoing process of successful negotiations of colonialism and modernity while also maintaining an overarching sense of *kastom*, or tradition (e.g. Flexner 2016a).

The idea that particular dishes or ingredients represent the 'pure' form of authentic cuisine is philosophically untenable in regards to the colonial period (see Flexner 2017). It also is likely not realistic for any period of human history, as any notion of culinary purity ignores the reality that people have been exchanging, transforming and remixing ingredients and recipes for millennia. On the other hand, it is also inappropriate to ignore the political reality that culinary exchanges did not (and do not) always occur on equal terms. Further, there are certain traditional culinary practices that are integral to local cultural and ecological sustainability in many cases, and we should not ignore neocolonial processes that might damage these practices. Food exists at a complex nexus between global and local forces, which has real ramifications for cultural practices, identities and ecologies as they change through time (Paolisso 2007; Tarble 2008; Wilk 1999).

Figure 9.1. A typical Melanesian spread. Note the addition of white rice and instant noodles to the traditional yams, fish, bananas and fruit.

Source: James Flexner.

Appropriation, at least in regards to food, has been a part of human society for millennia. *Food appropriation* describes the exchange of ingredients, recipes, technologies of preparation or general ideas about cuisine. Food appropriation does not necessarily reflect inherently unequal social or political relationships. In contrast, *culinary imperialism* represents a more specific case of food appropriation based on the existence of unequal power relations in economic, political, racial or other terms (Flexner 2015). Culinary imperialism can occur where a dominant group's cuisine spreads into the cultures of colonised or subaltern peoples. It can also involve the dominant group taking the ingredients or recipes of a subaltern group, and repurposing or recasting the appropriated cuisine in elite terms and for elite purposes.

To explore this distinction, we turn to a series of case studies from the historical archaeology of mission sites in southern Vanuatu. Using data from a sample of excavated mission sites and Melanesian villages, we explore the role that food played during a series of initial cross-cultural encounters with Presbyterian missionaries on the islands of Tanna and Erromango in the mid-1800s. As we will see, the relationship between food appropriation and culinary imperialism is not a simple either-or distinction. Rather, it is a nested relationship: cross-cultural interactions often resulted in food appropriation, and some of those interactions were structured by colonial inequalities. Further, the exchange of foods in mission interactions, and other interactions with foreigners, were part of a broader pattern of integration of foreign objects and concepts (including the foreign god of Christian missionaries, see Flexner 2016a), which were then subsumed into Melanesian *kastom*.

Early southern Vanuatu mission encounters

The history of mission encounters in southern Vanuatu is a complex one, involving dramatic martyrdoms, heroic efforts by Samoan teachers (themselves only recent converts to Christianity), significant cultural misunderstandings, the creation of friendships, entanglement in local political struggles in the region, catastrophic setbacks and eventually the establishment of large, elaborate mission complexes that won large numbers of converts (Adams 1984; Flexner 2016a; Miller 1978, 1981). Here we focus on early Presbyterian mission sites inhabited from 1856 to 1862. During this time missionaries were able to establish footholds on Tanna and Erromango, but were unable to have a dominant influence among Tannese and Erromangan people. The mission sites that date to this time period saw minimal investment in infrastructure, and were temporary in nature. On both Tanna and Erromango, missionaries were either killed or driven off in 1861–62, often in response to major epidemics for which the evangelists were held responsible (Adams 1984:143–145; Gordon 1863:184–203; Patterson 1864:494–498).

One of the common threads of these encounters is material exchange, which mediated the relationships between Melanesians and Presbyterian missionaries. European-derived material culture both provided a sense of identity for the missionaries themselves, and was intended to serve as 'curiosities' to draw Melanesians into the sphere of missionary influence (Flexner and Ball 2016). In contrast, introduced items in surrounding Melanesian villages were remarkably uncommon, despite what mission-era documents suggest about the importance of material exchange to the work of conversion (Flexner et al. 2016). Another line of evidence that presents a clearer picture of the Melanesian contribution to mission exchanges is the ethnographic collections of Islander 'curiosities' that were integrated into mission houses in the field (e.g. Smith 2005:273), and eventually filtered into museum collections around the world (Flexner 2016b).

Returning to food, it is clear that ingredients, recipes and traditions were also exchanged during interactions between missionaries and Melanesian Islanders. Missionaries were, to some extent, dependent upon local garden surpluses for survival. HA Robertson, missionary on Erromango from 1872, describes the local cuisine at length and with great appreciation. The local diet consisted of tubers, particularly taro and yams, bananas, breadfruit, various fruits, fish and shellfish. Further, certain recipes were described as particularly delicious, such as *neoki*, a starchy pudding of yam or papaya, prawns and coconut (Robertson 1902:376–381). On the other side, bread was an essential element of missionary cuisine. Making bread was part of the everyday routine around the mission house, a connection to old European baking traditions (e.g. Patterson 1864:452; Watt 1896:81). But for Christian missionaries, bread was more than just a form of sustenance. The symbolic element of bread cannot be ignored for its iconographic centrality to Christianity (e.g. Patterson 1864:151, 158), allowing missionaries to remember the Last Supper with each meal as they prayed over their food. Again, these meals likely featured both European and Melanesian dishes (e.g. Watt 1896:84).

The sites

Faunal and plant microfossil data from four sites, two from Erromango and two from Tanna (Figure 9.2), reflect the archaeological residues of these kinds of culinary exchanges in the New Hebrides. The sampled sites include one early mission site from each island, and one nearby site of indigenous Melanesian occupation. These sites were test excavated, and 100 per cent of the recovered faunal assemblage was analysed. Bulk sediment samples were collected during excavation, and plant microfossils were identified from a selection of these.

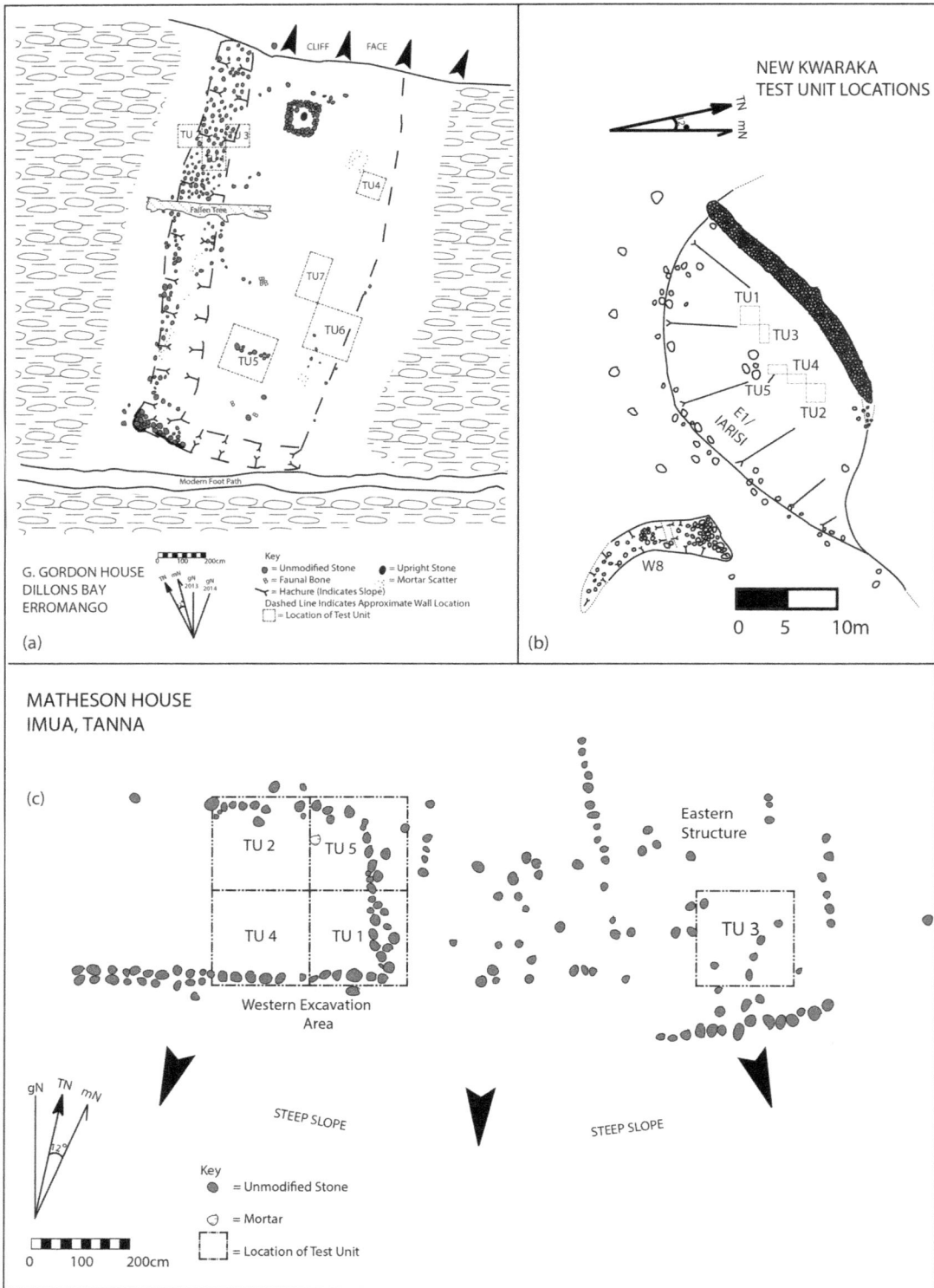

Figure 9.2. Plan maps of excavated areas: (a) G. Gordon House, Dillon's Bay, Erromango; (b) 'New Kwaraka', Kwamera area, Tanna; (c) Imua Mission House, Kwamera area, Tanna.

Source: James Flexner.

Undam

The site of Undam is located in an area that continues to be actively gardened near the Williams River, Dillon's Bay, Erromango. After local discovery of indigenous pottery, a single test pit was excavated in the area, which yielded shells, charcoal and fire-cracked rock. One of the sediment samples from this test pit, taken from 10–20 cm below the surface, was analysed. This deposit is undated, though the test pit did not contain any introduced material. While it is likely the stratigraphy has been disturbed by recent planting activity, we believe the faunal and plant microfossil signatures (discussed below) would be representative of a longer history of Melanesian landscape management and subsistence patterns. Undam is on the opposite bank and upriver from the later mission site occupied by the Gordons at Dillon's Bay.

G. Gordon House

G. Gordon House was inhabited by Canadian missionaries George and Ellen Gordon from 1856 to 1861 (Gordon 1863; Robertson 1902). The house is located high on a cliff overlooking the Williams River in Dillon's Bay, and was somewhat remote from the primary villages in the area at the time it was occupied. We excavated a series of test units across this site (Figure 9.2a), which gave us a sample of material culture and allowed us to generally understand that this was a relatively small, simple lime mortar house built with minimal imported materials. We recovered a modest assemblage of European artefacts, including iron nails, bottle glass, transfer-printed whiteware and a single sherd of Chinese porcelain from this site. Our plant microfossil samples come from the occupation and abandonment layers of the house in TU5 and TU6. The site was abandoned in 1861 after the Gordons were killed by local warriors, and the presence of a high percentage of burned glass artefacts in the assemblage suggests that their house was burned shortly thereafter (see Flexner 2016a:26–36 for a more detailed account).

New Kwaraka

The Melanesian village site from Tanna is associated with a significant local oral tradition (Flexner et al. 2016). Yeni Iarisi, the chief of the village of Kwaraka in the 1850s, travelled to neighbouring Aneityum, where he saw the work of John Geddie, resident missionary on the island from 1848, and recently converted Aneityumese teachers. Liking what he saw, Iarisi decided to bring the Gospel to Tanna, returning to arrange for the settlement of teachers and conversion of his village. This caused tensions in the community, and Iarisi moved with a small group of followers to a site across the river from the main village at a place called Anuikaraka (current social memories term the site 'New Kwaraka').

Following from the oral tradition, we excavated five 2x2 m and 1x2 m test units inside the stone enclosure remembered as the site of New Kwaraka. The site yielded very little in the way of imported material culture (a single pipe bowl fragment is the one likely 19th-century artefact), though we did recover large quantities of charcoal and shell. The plant microfossil samples come from the most likely occupation layers of TU1, TU2 and TU3 (Figure 9.2b).

In addition, we excavated a 1x6 m trench across a conical mound down the hill. These excavations yielded no European material, and radiocarbon dates indicate that the mound was constructed sometime between the late-1600s and mid-1700s, which predates European contact in the region. The mound contained large shells, pig bone and red ochre, and these artefacts suggest some kind of ritual activity in the area. Plant microfossil samples were taken from the stone construction fill of the mound, and the underlying layer, which we interpret as the original ground surface from before the mound was constructed.

Imua

The mission site at Imua (a local orthography of 'Samoa' in honour of the original missionary teachers in the area) was inhabited by Canadian missionaries John and Mary Matheson from 1861 to 1862. The Mathesons had initially settled near Kwamera, south Tanna, in 1858, but they left Tanna in 1860 due to illness, travelling to Aneityum (Mary Matheson was John Geddie's niece) and Erromango, where they almost certainly stayed at the Gordons' house (Adams 1984; Patterson 1864). Upon returning to Tanna, the Mathesons built a wattle and mortar house on a hill overlooking the main harbour where the air was thought to be 'healthier'. Unfortunately, their fortunes were not much better than the Gordons' and they had to flee in February 1862. Excavation of the site revealed a dense abandonment deposit containing a remarkable assemblage of artefacts, including a matched set of transfer-printed ceramics with pastoral motifs (Flexner and Ball 2016). Essentially, as they fled, the Mathesons appear to have left most of the domestic material culture in place. Plant microfossil samples from Imua came from the abandonment layer in each of the five excavated 2x2 m units (Figure 9.2c).

Faunal analysis results

Local shellfish were a prominent feature of colonial diets in the New Hebrides. Faunal data from the four excavated sites reflects regular use of shellfish as an ingredient in the diets of both missionaries and Melanesians (Table 9.1). Missionaries appear to have been almost entirely reliant on local seafood as their primary source of protein. Presumably this could have been supplemented occasionally by salted beef or pork, which would not necessarily leave an archaeological trace. We believe salted meat would have been a rare element of missionary diet, as the mission supply ships did not visit often during the 1860s.

Table 9.1. Faunal remains (number of identified specimens and weight) from Vanuatu mission sites.

Taxon	G. Gordon House Count	Weight (g)	Imua Mission Count	Weight (g)	New Kwaraka Count	Weight (g)	Undam Count	Weight (g)	Totals Total (Count)	Total (Weight)
Arcidae			19	14.33					19	14.33
Arciidae	1	1.3							1	1.3
Cerithiidae	2	1.31	140	15.21					142	16.52
Conidae	2	2.49	18	11.36			1	11.31	21	25.16
Conus			28	23.62					28	23.62
Cowrie			3	2.49					3	2.49
Crustacean			1	0.005					1	0.005
Cymattidae			10	4.11					10	4.11
Cypraea			24	17.88	3	8.93			27	26.81
Gafrarium			49	26.09					49	26.09
Limpet			33	3.555					33	3.555
Muricidae	1	0.13	2	1					3	1.13
Nerita			28	8.405					28	8.405
Nerita sp.	1	0.4							1	0.4
Olividae			1	0.2					1	0.2
Ostreidae			9	6.81					9	6.81
Polymesoda			13	3.4					13	3.4
Pulmonadae			10	3.39					10	3.39
Strombidae			4	0.83					4	0.83
Sus scrofa					12	15.385			12	15.385
Sus(?)					34	30.98			34	30.98
Terebra							3	0.04	3	0.04
Tridachna sp.	1	0.71							1	0.71

Taxon	G. Gordon House Count	G. Gordon House Weight (g)	Imua Mission Count	Imua Mission Weight (g)	New Kwaraka Count	New Kwaraka Weight (g)	Undam Count	Undam Weight (g)	Totals Total (Count)	Totals Total (Weight)
Triton			59	35.69					59	35.69
Trochidae	2	2.13	36	29.89					38	32.02
Turbo	1	10.96	20	23.08	97	110.455			118	144.495
Turbo sp.	2	0.68							2	0.68
Unidentified	12	1.65	68	26.5	3	2.28	10	3.97	93	34.4
Sum of column	**25**	**21.76**	**575**	**257.845**	**149**	**168.03**	**14**	**15.32**	**763**	**462.955**

Source: Authors' data.

The shell assemblages of the mission sites appear to be slightly richer, though there might be some issues with preservation and sample size, particularly for the site of Undam, which is represented by a single test pit. Major taxa represented include:

- **Undam**: *Terebra, Conidae*;
- **Imua**: *Turbo, Trochidae, Triton, Nerita, Gafrarium, Cypraea, Conidae, Cerithiidae, Arcidae*;
- **New Kwaraka**: *Turbo, Cypraea*;
- **G. Gordon House**: *Turbo, Trochidae, Tridacna, Nerita, Muricidae, Conidae, Cerithiidae, Arcidae*.

It is notable that the richness of European artefacts at Imua was much higher than at G. Gordon House, but the two shell assemblages are comparable. The lower diversity of the shell assemblages at New Kwaraka may be a reflection of poor preservation conditions at the site.

Marine resources including fish, shellfish and crustaceans were probably obtained as gifts or via material exchanges, since missionaries would probably not have had the right to collect resources from the reefs and beaches of Tanna or Erromango. There was some unidentified crustacean shell from Imua, further evidence for reliance on marine sources.

The other significant finding from faunal analysis is the presence of pig in large concentration at TU6 in New Kwaraka. The mound from which these bones come also contained large shells and red ochre, and has been interpreted as a ritual feature. On both Tanna and Erromango, pigs were important in ceremonial exchanges (Spriggs 1986; Spriggs and Wickler 1989). In the early days, it would have been nearly impossible for the missionaries to be able to obtain such a prestige food except on rare occasions, though we note that there is some unidentified mammal bone from Imua, which could be pig, or possibly sheep or goat. Pig is present on later mission sites, such as HA Robertson's house in Dillon's Bay, Erromango (Flexner 2016a:55–57), which may be a reflection of shifting power dynamics as increasing numbers of Melanesian people converted to Christianity.

Plant microfossils

Sediment samples were analysed for the recovery of pollen, phytoliths and starch grains (Horrocks 2005). Results from plant microfossil analysis likewise indicate that the missionaries relied heavily on local communities for food. Microscopic charcoal, pollen and phytolith evidence from the four excavated sites (Figures 9.3 and 9.4) reflects the landscapes shaped by ground clearing for traditional Melanesian shifting agriculture, which surrounded the mission sites. The typical suite of Oceanic tree crops, especially banana (*Musa* sp.) coconut (*Cocos nucifera*) and screwpine (*Pandanus* sp.) are particularly prominent in the pollen and phytolith assemblages. However, it is interesting to note that screwpine pollen was relatively rare from the Erromango sites. One of the Imua samples yielded a starch grain of cf. lesser yam (*Dioscorea esculenta*) (starch type 2, Figure 9.4). *Nuk*, as the tuber is known in the local Nafe language, would have been a common ingredient on missionary and Melanesian tables alike.

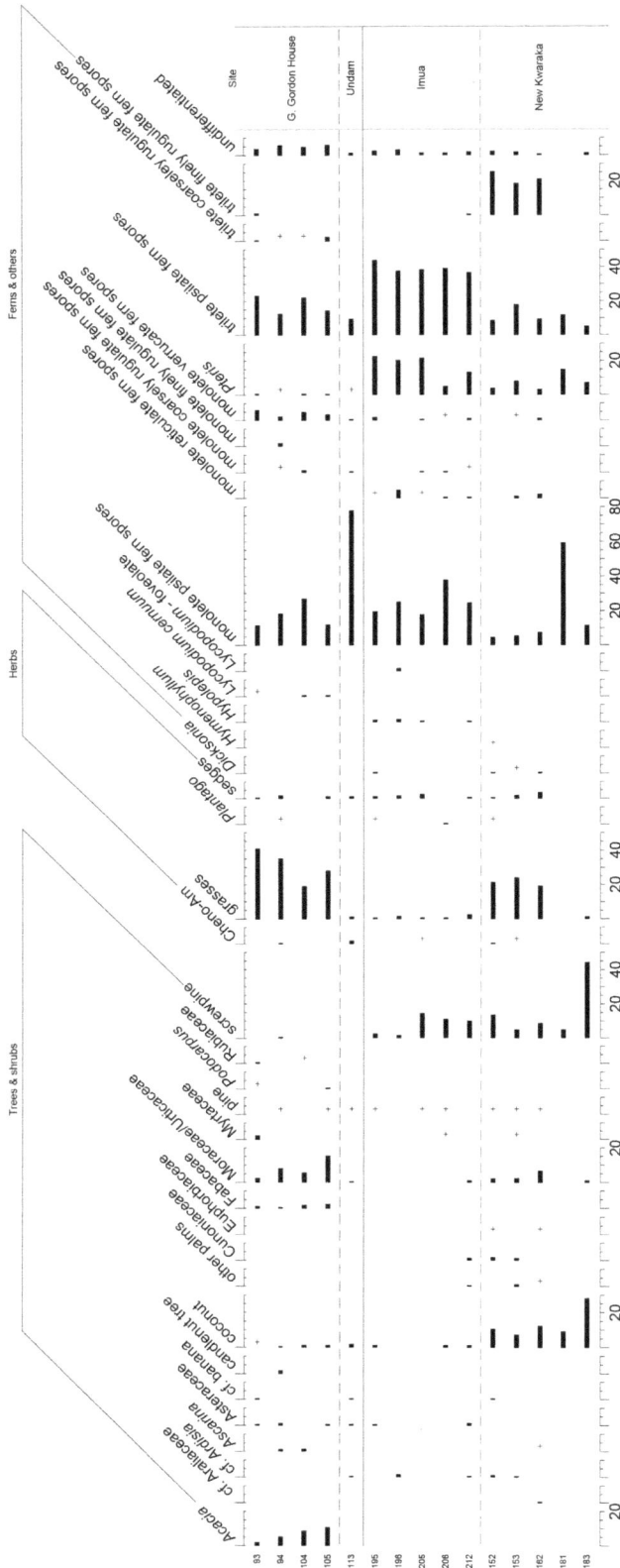

Figure 9.3. Pollen percentage diagram from G. Gordon House and Undam, Erromango Island, and Imua and New Kwaraka, Tanna Island (+ = found after count).

Source: Mark Horrocks.

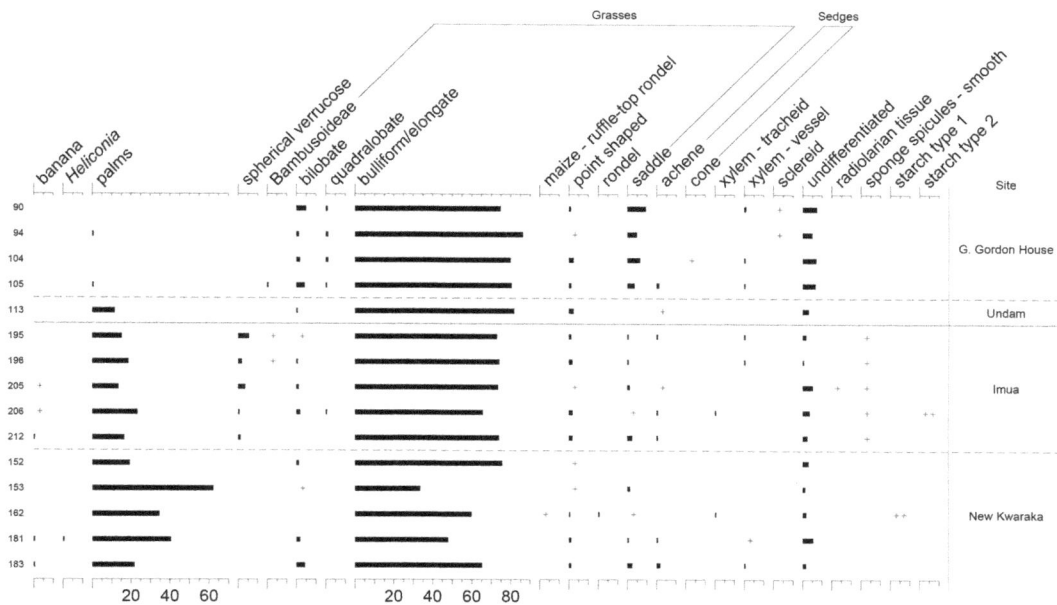

Figure 9.4. Phytolith percentage and starch diagram from G. Gordon House and Undam, Erromango Island, and Imua and New Kwaraka, Tanna Island (+ = found after count, ++ = present).

Source: Mark Horrocks.

At New Kwaraka, there was starch identified most likely from sweet potato (*Ipomoea batatas*) or giant taro (*Alocasia macrorrhizos*), starch grains of which can be difficult to differentiate (starch type 1, Figure 9.4). Either of these two species would have been common in the local suite of domesticates. Among the New Kwaraka phytoliths was a *Heliconia* leaf phytolith from the pre-contact TU6 samples. *Heliconia indica* leaf is still used as a food wrapping today, and has been found in human dental calculus from ancient burials elsewhere in Vanuatu (Horrocks et al. 2014). There is a long history of using leaves to wrap foods that are going to be cooked in the Oceanic earth oven, which continues today. However, it is worth noting that *Heliconia* remains rare in Pacific archaeological contexts, and considering the diversity of the genus in the Americas, further study is needed to understand the history of this plant in pre-Columbian as well as colonial exchanges in the region. Intriguingly, New Kwaraka also yielded phytoliths of cf. maize (*Zea mays*) from the contact-era deposits. Thus there also appears to be some degree of a Tannese 'early adoption' of new cultivars brought to the New Hebrides by outsiders, possibly missionaries or early traders. In this case, maize, which is originally a Central American cultigen (Piperno and Flannery 2001), was added to the already rich suite of starchy plant crops grown by Melanesian gardeners.

Historical archaeology perspectives on appropriation, imperialism and sustainability

Archaeological evidence from contact-era sites on Tanna and Erromango, both mission houses and Melanesian villages, reflects patterns of continuity and change in the plant and animal foods that characterised the diets of foreign missionaries and indigenous people. Food was often the first thing exchanged with European visitors in the Pacific, and this was the case in Vanuatu (e.g. Beaglehole 1969:501–502). Island cuisine, based on an abundance of root crops, starchy puddings, greens, coconut cream and seafood, is an integral part of Pacific peoples' identities and ways of life. It is clear that in the case of the mission sites, missionaries not only integrated island foods into their own tables, but they were in fact reliant on Melanesian foods, particularly on seafood as a protein source. While the plant microfossils are not necessarily direct evidence of food consumption on mission sites, as they might have been carried by wind or washed into the sediment by rain, they do represent the kinds of plant crops that were present in the landscape during the mid-1800s. On the other hand, the documentary evidence (described above) does represent the extent to which local cuisine was present on missionary tables.

At the same time, Pacific Islanders were also great adapters of introduced crops. The rapid spread of sweet potato throughout much of the Pacific before European contact (e.g. Barber 2012), and into the New Guinea highlands after contact (e.g. Bourke 2009), provides one salient example. The presence of maize in the contact-era deposits at New Kwaraka provides another, and considering the link to oral traditions, it is possible that along with the Gospel, Iarisi brought new crops to south Tanna. Yet not all introduced crops are widely adopted, and maize remains a relatively minor cultigen in contemporary gardens in Vanuatu.

After the 1870s, there was a shift in the power balance of the Vanuatu missions. Missionaries were able to dominate the religious beliefs of rapidly declining Melanesian populations, and at the same time to draw on increasingly efficient global trade networks. Yet evidence from these later missions shows that Melanesian foods continued to be the main portion of the diet, a pattern that continues today in Vanuatu, though this is changing rapidly. Instant noodles, tinned meat and fish, and rice increasingly feature on island tables, a reflection of the ability of mass-produced global food commodities to colonise local diets. This is a worrisome development for Islander health, environments and cultures, though indigenous ni-Vanuatu are making efforts to sustain traditional cuisine. A 'slow food' and 'local food' movement has grown in the last few years, particularly as the Vanuatu Cultural Centre works to promote local foods in island communities. The first Slow Food Festival, held on Tanna in August, 2016 (Guiomar 2016), is a reflection of this positive trend.

In early colonial exchanges, Melanesian people generally had the opportunity to choose which ingredients to adopt from foreigners. Missionaries were dependent on local people, who provided the only source of fresh food, since missionaries would not have had rights to garden plots sufficient to sustain themselves, nor would they have been permitted to gather marine resources. Returning to the concepts introduced above, these exchanges appear to be primarily about food appropriation. It is only really in the post–World War II era that some forms of culinary imperialism are evident in Vanuatu, primarily in relation to the ubiquity of rice, biscuits, instant noodles and tinned fish and meat, and again it is interesting to see resistance to these interloper ingredients.

Food of course is about much more than calories and nutrients. It is also wrapped up in senses of identity and personhood. Food can be symbolically or ritually loaded, as with pigs who are typically only sacrificed on special occasions, or the large ceremonial yams grown on Tanna and Erromango (one such yam observed by missionary George Turner in 1842 was over 1.5 m long and weighed over 22 kg; Turner 1861:87). If Melanesian personhood and material culture are 'partible' in nature (Gosden 2004:35–39; Strathern 1990), then food is the ultimate partible medium for exchange, as it lends itself so well to being divided and shared. As Lindstrom (2013:263) notes in relation to the experiences of missionary Agnes Watt: 'The Tannese when describing mutual personhood talk in terms of shared blood, shared name, shared place and shared spirit.' To this list we might add shared food as an essential element of Islander practice and belief.

Acknowledgements

We would like to thank the people of Tanna and Erromango who were our hosts and in many cases partners in this research. The overall project was funded by an Australian Research Council DECRA (Discovery Early Career Researcher Award) Fellowship (DE130101703) hosted at The Australian National University.

References

Adams, R. 1984. *In the land of strangers: A century of European contact with Tanna, 1774–1874.* Canberra: The Australian National University.

Barber, I. 2012. 'A fast yam to Polynesia: New thinking on the problem of the American sweet potato in Oceania'. *Rapa Nui Journal* 26 (1):31–42.

Beaglehole, JC (ed.). 1969. *The journals of Captain James Cook on his voyages of discovery: The voyage of the* Resolution *and* Adventure *1772–1775*. Cambridge: The Hakluyt Society.

Bourke, RM. 2009. 'History of agriculture in Papua New Guinea'. In *Food and agriculture in Papua New Guinea*, edited by RM Bourke and T Harwood, 10–26. Canberra: ANU E Press. doi.org/10.22459/FAPNG.08.2009.

Errington, F, D Gewertz and T Fujikara. 2013. *The noodle narratives: The global rise of an industrial food into the twenty-first century.* Berkeley: University of California Press.

Flexner, JL. 2015. 'Food appropriation and culinary imperialism'. In *Archaeology of food: An encyclopedia*, edited by KC Metheny and MC Beaudry, 201–203. Lanham, MD: Rowman and Littlefield.

Flexner, JL. 2016a. *An archaeology of early Christianity in Vanuatu: Kastom and religious change on Tanna and Erromango, 1839–1920*. Terra Australis 44. Canberra: ANU Press. doi.org/10.22459/TA44.12.2016.

Flexner, JL. 2016b. 'Ethnology collections as supplements and records: What museums contribute to historical archaeology of the New Hebrides (Vanuatu)'. *World Archaeology* 48 (2):196–209. doi.org/10.1080/00438243.2016.1195769.

Flexner, JL. 2017. 'Reform and purification in the historical archaeology of the South Pacific, 1840–1900'. *International Journal of Historical Archaeology* 21 (4):827–847. doi.org/10.1007/s10761-017-0398-1.

Flexner, JL and AC Ball. 2016. 'Sherds of paradise: Domestic archaeology and ceramic artefacts from a Protestant mission in the South Pacific'. *European Journal of Archaeology* 19 (4):728–754. doi.org/10.1080/14619571.2016.1147319.

Flexner, JL, E Willie, AZ Lorey, H Alderson, R Williams and S Ieru. 2016. 'Iarisi's domain: Historical archaeology of a Melanesian village, Tanna Island, Vanuatu'. *Journal of Island and Coastal Archaeology* 11 (1):26–49. doi.org/10.1080/15564894.2015.1052865.

Gewertz, D and F Errington. 2010. *Cheap meat: Flap food nations in the Pacific Islands.* Berkeley: University of California Press.

Gordon, J (ed.). 1863. *The last martyrs of Eromanga, being a memoir of the Rev. George N. Gordon, and Ellen Catherine Powell, his wife.* Halifax: MacNab and Shafer.

Gosden, C. 2004. *Archaeology and colonialism: Cultural contact from 5000 BC to the present.* Cambridge: Cambridge University Press.

Guiomar, O. 2016. 'Tanna hosts Vanuatu's first "slow foods" festival—big success'. *Asia Pacific Report*, 31 August. asiapacificreport.nz/2016/08/31/tanna-hosts-vanuatus-first-slow-foods-festival-big-success/.

Horrocks, M. 2005. 'A combined procedure for recovering phytoliths and starch residues from soils, sedimentary deposits and similar materials'. *Journal of Archaeological Science* 32:1169–1175. doi.org/10.1016/j.jas.2005.02.014.

Horrocks, M, MK Nieuwoldt, R Kinaston, H Buckley and S Bedford. 2014. 'Microfossil and Fourier Transform InfraRed analyses of Lapita and post-Lapita human dental calculus from Vanuatu, Southwest Pacific'. *Journal of the Royal Society of New Zealand* 44:17–33. doi.org/10.1080/03036758.2013.842177.

Lindstrom, L. 2013. 'Agnes C. P. Watt and Melanesian personhood'. *Journal of Pacific History* 48 (3):243–266. doi.org/10.1080/00223344.2013.832020.

Miller, JG. 1978. *Live: A history of church planting in the New Hebrides, Book I: A history of church planting in the New Hebrides to 1880.* Sydney: Committees on Christian Education and Overseas Missions, General Assembly of the Presbyterian Church of Australia.

Miller, JG. 1981. *Live: A history of church planting in the New Hebrides, Book II: The growth of the Church to 1880.* Sydney: Committees on Christian Education and Overseas Missions, General Assembly of the Presbyterian Church of Australia.

Paolisso, M. 2007. 'Taste the traditions: Crabs, crab cakes, and the Chesapeake Bay blue crab fishery'. *American Anthropologist* 109 (4):654–665. doi.org/10.1525/aa.2007.109.4.654.

Patterson, G. (ed.). 1864. *Memoirs of the Rev. S. F. Johnston, the Rev. J. W. Matheson, and Mrs. Mary Johnston Matheson, missionaries on Tanna, with selections from their diaries and correspondence, and notices of the New Hebrides, their inhabitants, and mission work among them.* Philadelphia: W.S. & A. Martien.

Piperno, DR and KV Flannery. 2001. 'The earliest archaeological maize (*Zea mays* L.) from highland Mexico: New accelerator mass spectrometry dates and their implications'. *Proceedings of the National Academy of Sciences* 98 (4):2101–2103. doi.org/10.1073/pnas.98.4.2101.

Robertson, HA. 1902. *Erromanga: The martyr isle.* Toronto: The Westminster Company.

Smith, AM. 2005. '"Curios" from a strange land: The Oceania collections of the Reverend Joseph Annand'. In *Canadian missionaries, indigenous peoples: Representing religion at home and abroad*, edited by AJ Austin and JS Scott, 262–278. Toronto: University of Toronto Press.

Spriggs, M. 1986. 'Landscape, land use, and political transformation in southern Melanesia'. In *Island societies: Archaeological approaches to evolution and transformation*, edited by PV Kirch, 6–19. Cambridge: Cambridge University Press.

Spriggs, M and S Wickler. 1989. 'Archaeological research on Erromango: Recent data on southern Melanesian prehistory'. *Bulletin of the Indo-Pacific Prehistory Association* 9:68–91. doi.org/10.7152/bippa.v9i0.11283.

Strathern, M. 1990. *The gender of the gift: Problems with women and problems with society in Melanesia.* Berkeley: University of California Press.

Tarble, K. 2008. 'Coffee, tea, or chicha? Commensality and culinary practice in the Middle Orinoco following colonial contact'. In *Desencuentros culturales: Una mirada desde la cultura material de las América*, edited by AR Martinez, 53–71. Barcelona: Universidad Pampeu Fabra.

Turner, G. 1861. *Nineteen years in Polynesia: Missionary life, travels, and researches in the islands of the Pacific.* London: John Snow.

Twiss, KC. 2007. 'We are what we eat'. In *The archaeology of food and identity*, edited by KC Twiss, 1–15. Carbondale: Southern Illinois University Press.

Twiss, KC. 2015. 'Food and identity'. In *Archaeology of food: An encyclopedia*, edited by KC Metheny and MC Beaudry, 189–190. Lanham, MD: Rowman and Littlefield.

Watt, ACP. 1896. *Twenty-five years' mission life on Tanna, New Hebrides*. Paisley: J. and R. Parlane.

Wilk, R. 1999. '"Real Belizean food": Building local identity in the transnational Caribbean'. *American Anthropologist* 101 (2):244–255. doi.org/10.1525/aa.1999.101.2.244.

Practices

10

From gathering to discard and beyond: Ethnoarchaeological studies on shellfishing practices in the Solomon Islands

Annette Oertle and Katherine Szabó

Introduction

Shell-bearing archaeological sites in tropical island environments are subject to various environmental and human influences, which affect how a site forms and transforms over time. The immense range of species diversity in the tropical Indo-Pacific marine province means that marine subsistence practices may vary between different environmental zones and groups of people. Shellfish are an important coastal resource that is relatively low cost to gather and process. Island Melanesia is rich in zones of mangrove forest, intertidal rocky shore, sandy beaches and reefs, all of which support certain species of shellfish that can be used for food or raw materials for artefact production.

The practice of shellfishing is complex in nature with a huge range of shell species and a variety of gathering practices based on habitat, location, time of day and individual human behaviours. Additionally, cooking techniques and discard patterns can also vary from one site to another. Varying processing methods and discard patterns affect the preservation of shell and the formation of a site (Claassen 1998). Overall, it can be difficult to truly understand the various levels of behaviour that led to the incorporation of shell into the archaeological context (*sensu* Schiffer 1972). Ethnoarchaeology, which consists of undertaking fieldwork as a participant observer and documenting the way the archaeological record is formed in specific human groups (Davidson 1988), is one of the tools used by archaeologists to piece together information about shell gathering, processing and disposal methods. This chapter will detail such an ethnoarchaeological approach for studying shell material in the tropical Indo-West Pacific. Such data can provide the information needed to make inferences about the systemic context from which the shell material originally came.

Firstly, we will outline key ethnographic and ethnoarchaeological studies on shellfishing in the Pacific and discuss issues of linking modern human behaviour to archaeological material. Ethnoarchaeological fieldwork on the island of Malaita in the Solomon Islands, undertaken to record traditional shellfish gathering, processing and discard practices, will then be detailed. Comparing the data acquired with previous studies in Island Melanesia shows some similarities in gathering behaviours; however, new data on processing and discard show the importance of considering these steps as part of the story and how specific behaviours impact shell preservation and site formation. Previous ethnographic studies in the Indo-Pacific primarily focus on gathering practices (Meehan 1982; Thomas 2002) and the role of women and children (Bird and Bird 2000; Jones 2009). Although processing and discard practices have been considered, they have not formed the focus of any particular study. This study aims to fill this void by understanding each step, from the systemic environment from which the shells are collected to the archaeological context into which they are introduced (Figure 10.1).

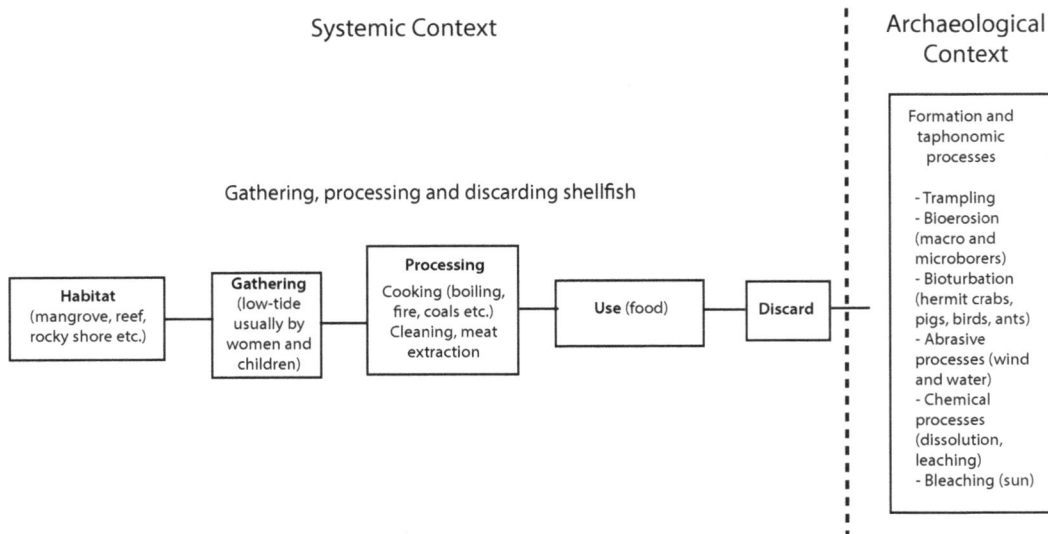

Figure 10.1. Systemic to archaeological context of shellfishing (after Schiffer 1972).
Source: Annette Oertle.

Ethnoarchaeology as a link between past and present

In the Indo-Pacific, ethnographic shellfishing studies have primarily been undertaken in the more recent past, as is clear from Waselkov's (1987) in-depth survey on ethnographic shellfishing. Focused ethnographic and ethnoarchaeological studies on shellfishing are few and tend to focus on particular aspects of shellfishing practices (Bird and Bird 2000; Carter 2014; Malm 2009; Meehan 1982; Swadling and Chowning 1981; Thomas 2002). These recent ethnographic studies provide valuable data on modern behaviours in these regions, but the lack of information on the behaviours associated with processing and disposing of shellfish is something that needs to be addressed to maximise their usefulness for archaeology. Inferences about past human behaviours based purely on ethnographic studies can be questionable even with the inclusion of each pre-depositional stage (see Wylie 1985), and especially when the practices of one cultural group in the present are seen as sufficient to interpret those of an unrelated (or even related) group in the past.

O'Connell (1995) highlights the complexity of archaeological interpretations based upon ethnoarchaeological research on faunal remains. Interpretations about site structure and faunal remains need to take into account the unpredictability of behaviour. For example, the transport of body parts can vary situationally, and various agents can cause similar patterns of damage on bone (O'Connell 1995). Consideration of seasonality is also an important factor, as certain species may be collected during particular seasons and specific habitats targeted based upon tidal range (Jimenez et al. 2011); for example, the active collection of reef resources during spring tides (de Boer et al. 2002). Continuity of behaviours and assumptions regarding the scale of site formation are the primary issues faced when dealing with ethnoarchaeological research. Faulkner (2006:11) highlights the problems with using ethnographic data from distinct areas to interpret a range of archaeological data in Australian archaeology. This introduces a simplistic and limiting view of human–environment interactions, reiterating the main issue of using ethnography to interpret archaeological data: it tends to assume continuity between the recorded ethnographic present and behaviours in the past (Faulkner 2006:11). Nevertheless, ethnoarchaeology can provide insights into how various external factors may impact human behaviours. 'Ethnoarchaeological studies have greatly increased our sensitivity to the diverse environmental and cultural factors that can affect or determine the nature of the static archaeological remains that we recover' (Sinopoli 1991:177).

Ethnoarchaeology can also be a component of the 'slow science' approach to archaeology where a greater focus on ethics, social engagement and critical reflections on power relations are made (Cunningham and MacEachern 2016). We approach ethnoarchaeology as a 'research strategy framed within different theoretical structures' (Politis 2016:705) through the use of an array of methods and recording techniques. Although there has been much in the way of specialised literature and debate around the use of ethnographic analogy and ethnoarchaeology within archaeological interpretation (David and Kramer 2001; Gould and Watson 1982; O'Connell 1995; Politis 2016), space precludes full engagement with these issues here. We nevertheless acknowledge that present behaviours may diverge from past ones for a wide variety of reasons incorporating both cultural and environmental factors. With regards to method, this (to us) reinforces the need to develop independent physical proxies which can clearly link certain behaviours to particular physical manifestations; whether in the past or present. In terms of shellfishing, these physical markers are primarily found in the processing and discard phases. The following section discusses these phases as part of the overall stages of shellfishing whilst also outlining the recurring themes recorded from ethnographic studies on Indo-Pacific shellfishing practices.

Shellfishing in the Indo-Pacific

Recurring themes

Numerous ethnographical studies have recorded modern shellfishing practices around the world, each focusing on certain aspects, such as exploitation pressure (see de Boer et al. 2000; Hockey et al. 1988); site formation definitions (see Bailey 1993; Balme 1995; Bird et al. 2002); species selection (see Attenbrow 1992; Balme 1995; Carter 2014; Catterall and Poiner 1987; Hardy et al. 2016; Meehan 1982); gathering time and catch size (see de Boer et al. 2002; Voorhies and Martínez-Tagüeña 2016); behavioural ecology (see Macintosh et al. 2002; Thomas 2002); cooking techniques (see Aldeias et al. 2016); and gender roles (see Attenbrow 1992; Bird and Bird 2000; Jones 2009; Malm 2009). In Oceania, the initial ethnoarchaeological studies on modern fishing (see Kirch 1976; Kirch and Yen 1982) showed the importance and potential of ethnoarchaeology, however these early studies did not record substantive and quantitative data on labour and time or the consequent yield (Ono 2010). Over time, however, the methods of recording quantitative shellfish yields have improved (e.g. Thomas 2002) and some more recent studies have produced wide-ranging datasets. Betty Meehan's (1982, 1988) work in northern Australia, for example, is one of the most comprehensive ethnographic studies of shellfishing in the world and is frequently cited by other archaeologists. It covers gathering and processing practices of the Anbarra people, along with some basic discard practices that are primarily dependent on the location and size of camps.

The role of men, women and children in exploiting marine resources represents a recurring theme of study in the region. In Oceania, gathering shellfish is an activity usually done by groups of women and children (Bird and Bird 1997, 2000; Bird et al. 2004; Jones 2009; Malm 2009; Meehan 1982), but men also go shellfishing on occasion (Malm 2009; Meehan 1982; Katherine Szabó, pers. obs. Langalanga Lagoon 2016). Similarly, women go fishing from time to time, even if it is an activity usually done by men. Nevertheless, in the Solomon Islands women dominate the shellfishing niche (Kruijssen et al. 2015). These issues are important since differing foraging strategies between children and adults can affect how a shell midden will appear in the archaeological record (Bird and Bird 2000). Such influence was documented by Attenbrow (1992), who used Meehan's observation of targeting extra species for variety as well as the children's role in collecting multiple species of varying sizes as a way to help distinguish between shell bed and shell midden sites in New South Wales.

Another recurring pattern in shellfishing studies is the range of particular shell species targeted in the Indo-Pacific region. Large, high-return shell taxa like *Tridacna*, *Anadara* and *Polymesoda* appear to have been preferred across a range of study sites and geographic areas (Bird et al. 2004; Carter 2014; Meehan 1982; Swadling and Chowning 1981:159; Thomas 2002:200). *Marcia hiantina* (formerly *Tapes hiantina*) was actively preferred by the Anbarra people compared to other species of shell (Meehan 1982). This gathering strategy focused on a single species is a conscious part of Anbarra behaviour (Meehan 1982:71). In contrast, at the Natunuku site in Viti Levu, Fiji, a suite of species were primary targets, with secondary and incidental species being collected when encountered (Szabó 2001). The tailored behaviours associated with species selection are an important aspect to consider in ethnoarchaeological studies, especially in terms of how they can impact upon the archaeological record.

Stages of shellfishing

The initial stage of shellfishing is *gathering* and has been a focus in all ethnographic studies in this region (e.g. Bird and Bird 1997, 2000; Bird et al. 2004; Carter 2014; Malm 2009; Meehan 1982; Swadling and Chowning 1981; Thomas 2002). Comparison of prehistoric and modern fishing practices are perceived as problematic (Ono 2010). Nowadays the time and labour component of gathering shells is still predominantly accomplished by hand. However, the use of modern knives would impact processing techniques and time, and metal pots and stoves would facilitate boiling and steaming. Motorised boats may also reduce the time taken to reach inshore and coral reef environments, but intertidal shellfish gathering is still constrained by the limited period of low tide during the day, which is dependent on seasonal and monthly cycles.

The second stage of *processing* shells can either be done in the field or the shellfish can be taken to be cleaned or cooked elsewhere (camp, home). Field processing can be dependent on the size of the catch as well as the species of shell, with large shells such as *Tridacna* and *Lambis* sometimes being recorded as processed at the point of collection (Bird et al. 2004; Meehan 1982; Thomas 2002). As Bird et al. (2002:467) state, 'field processing contributes to systematic and archaeologically detectable variability in shell middens', with the absence of evidence for large shellfish not necessarily signifying that they were not targeted and consumed. The shells that are transported back home to be processed are either boiled or roasted on fires (Bird et al. 2004; Meehan 1982). Meehan (1982:87–99) observes a number of different methods of cleaning and cooking shells, varying in terms of hearth constructions, heating methods and camp locations.

The final stage of shellfishing is *discarding* and has had little focus yet in ethnoarchaeological studies. Actual discard practices have only been explored briefly by studies undertaken by Beck (2007), Beck and Hill (2004), Bird et al. (2004) and Meehan (1982). Meehan (1982) separates the location of discard sites into dinnertime camps, home bases and processing sites. These site definitions have been reused by a number of archaeologists (Bailey 1993; Balme 1995; Bird et al. 2002; Ceci 1984; Clarke 1994; O'Connor and Veth 1993; Ulm 2006), but in doing so, uniformity of shellfish deposition and the behaviours underpinning these processes has been broadly assumed to be spatially, geographically and culturally consistent. Part of ethnoarchaeological research on Malaita, Solomon Islands, reported in this chapter was developed to test whether the depositional behaviours and resulting site types reported by Meehan could be transposed into other cultural and geographical contexts.

Theoretical approaches

When considering overall patterns of shellfish collection, different theoretical frameworks can be used to interpret foraging behaviours. Work by Frank Thomas (2002) in the Kiribati Islands, for example, focused on foraging behaviours through the lens of central place foraging and prey choice foraging models. Based on these models, it is argued that decisions about shellfish culling and transport can be predicted through prey attributes within a cost/benefit framework (Thomas 2002:182).

Research in the Torres Strait focused on the shellfish gathering and processing practices of the Meriam people and paired these ethnographic observations with central place foraging theory (Bird and Bird 1997, 2000; Bird et al. 2002, 2004). Bird and Bird (1997:53) found that midden sites varied depending on resource processing characteristics and foraging range. Their research among the Meriam aimed to understand the factors that influence subsistence behaviour rather than assume them as analogous to those of the past (Bird and Bird 1997:54). They highlighted that the variability in modern Meriam shell deposition is patterned in predictable ways due to subsistence decisions, which are anticipated by central place foraging models (Bird and Bird 1997:54).

Ethnoarchaeological fieldwork in the Solomon Islands

The main aim of our ethnoarchaeological fieldwork in the Solomon Islands was to observe and record the progression of shellfishing subsistence (from gathering, to processing and final discard) in a region with differing landscapes and culture than previous ethnographic studies in northern Australia (Meehan 1982), the Torres Strait (Bird and Bird 1997, 2000) and western Kiribati (Thomas 2002). By observing the entire progression of shellfishing (Figure 10.2), we hoped to pinpoint and identify any behaviour that left physical markers on the shell material, which could then be linked to similar traces on archaeological shell. This study highlights the specific stages where certain physical markers may manifest.

Fieldwork was undertaken on the island of Malaita, at Langalanga Lagoon (south-west) and Lau Lagoon (north-east). Both of these lagoons are dotted with artificial islands that have been deliberately built up using limestone, shell and coral blocks. Langalanga is a sheltered and calm lagoon with natural outer islands and a barrier reef protecting the inner natural and artificial islands, and coastline (Figure 10.3). Lau Lagoon is generally shallower, but larger, with prevalent easterly winds coming in from the Pacific Ocean. At Langalanga Lagoon it was necessary to canoe over to a larger island at the edge of the reef to go shellfishing, whereas at Lau Lagoon you only needed to follow the ocean retreating at low tide. At Lau, it was also possible to walk to some of the closer artificial islands when the tide was low enough. Mangrove habitats can be found on larger islands or along the coastline at both lagoons, including some deliberately planted plots in Langalanga Lagoon. Although each lagoon has its geographic singularities, both have a range of mangrove, rocky shore and reef environments that are abundant in shellfish.

Gathering

Processing (cooking)

Discard

Processing (removing meat)

Figure 10.2. Photos of the shellfishing stages from gathering, processing and discard.
Source: Annette Oertle and Katherine Szabó.

Langalanga Lagoon, western side of Malaita

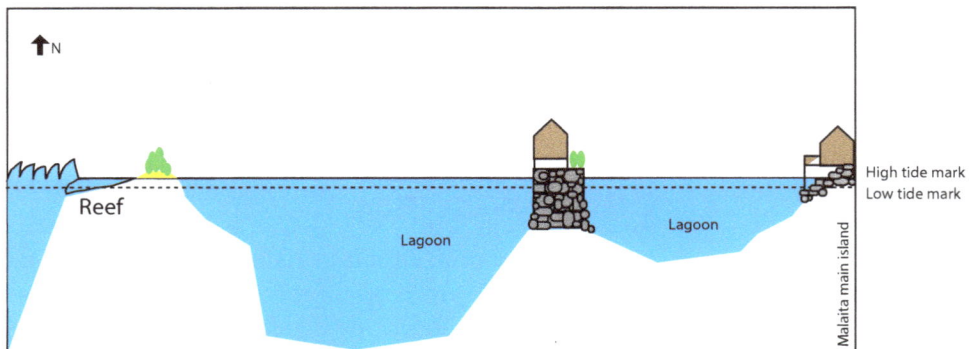

Lau Lagoon, eastern side of Malaita

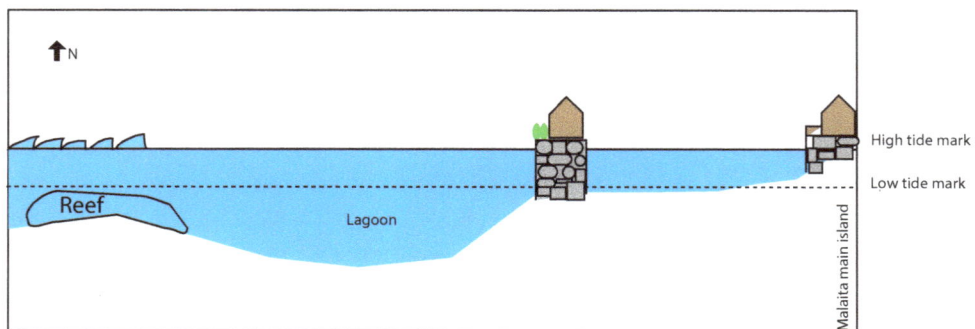

Figure 10.3. Langalanga and Lau lagoons, geography and environmental differences.
Source: Annette Oertle.

Gathering

Shellfish gathering occurred during low tide at both lagoons. Mangrove and intertidal reef habitats were targeted as they were both close to villages and contained diverse and rich shellfish populations. Behaviours regarding shellfish gathering in the Solomon Islands tended to be comparable to other studies. More explicitly, collecting shellfish was a practice generally undertaken by women and children, although men were observed on occasion to be subsistence-gathering as well as collecting shellfish for sale. Both bivalves and gastropods were collected and taken home. A range of shell species was targeted, with size being variable but focused on adult shells. As other studies have mentioned (see Meehan 1982; Swadling and Chowning 1981), children usually gathered *Atactodea striata* in the high-water mark beach grit due to the ease of sifting their fingers through the sand to find handfuls of this small bivalve close to the surface. When going out to gather shellfish in Langalanga, the number of accompanying gatherers (women and/or children) was primarily based on how many people could fit into a dugout canoe, whereas at Lau Lagoon the number of women and children going out to gather was less restricted due to the ease of access.

The method of gathering shells was consistent at both lagoons: shells were picked up by hand and placed in a bag or bucket (e.g. plastic, fabric or woven). None of the targeted shells needed a tool to pry from a rock (for example, limpet species). Instead, shells were easily picked up from the sand/mud or gently plucked from a rock. A stick or other pointed implement was usually used when digging out *Anadara antiquata* from the mud, as the shell is covered in fine bristles which can become embedded in fingers (Florence Kabi, Lau Lagoon, pers. comm. 2016). These shells are positioned in the substrate with their hinge facing upwards and can be visible through a small hole/depression in the substrate. On the reef flats gastropods were easily spotted during low tide, hiding in pools of water or in between rocks. Loose rocks were pushed over to reveal various gastropods like *Nerita* spp. and *Thais* spp. hiding in the shade. Other major taxa targeted for collection are summarised in Table 10.1.

Table 10.1. Species collected from lagoons, Malaita, Solomon Islands.

Gastropods	Bivalves
Lambis lambis	*Anadara antiquata*
Trochus/Tectus spp.	*Gafrarium tumidum*
Turbo spp.	*Gafrarium pectinatum*
Drupa spp.	*Geloina expansa*
Thais spp.	*Periglypta* spp.
Nerita spp.	*Chama* spp.
Cypraea/Monetaria spp.	*Atactodea striata*
Conidae spp.	*Ostreidae*
Polinices/Natica spp.	
Haliotis spp.	

Source: Authors' summary.

Processing

The processing stage of shellfishing included cleaning and cooking, which was accomplished through separation and boiling. Roasting was occasionally done for certain taxa of shell such as *Turbo* spp., however the primary method of cooking shellfish was by boiling. Whether this is a recent method of cooking due to the introduction of metal pots is unclear as there is no archaeological evidence of prehistoric or historic ceramic use on Malaita (Sheppard and Walter 2006:52). Once the catch was taken back home, the shells were separated out into bivalves and gastropods. Some bivalves were kept in freshwater for a short period to clean out the sand from their digestive tracts. All the shellfish were cooked before eating with bivalves boiled in one pot and gastropods in another. This was due to the greater time it took to cook the gastropods. The bivalves were cooked when the valves opened (5–10 minutes), whilst the gastropods took 15–20 minutes to cook. Individual shell cooking time was also dependent on the species and size. We observed no on-site processing of shellfish.

After cooking, gastropods had to be cleaned and the guts removed before eating, whereas bivalves could be eaten straight away. To remove the meat from *Turbo* spp., the shell was given a light tap on a hard surface then, with a sharp flick of the wrist, the entire animal and operculum came away. No tool was required. With other gastropods with opercula (such as *Nerita* spp.), a small twig or plant stem was used to remove the opercula and pry the meat out. The meat from some gastropod shells, like *Lambis* spp., could not be easily removed so the shells had to be broken to get inside (Figure 10.4). This breakage was focused on the dorsal area of the body whorl and actioned by holding the shell in hand and striking with a rock. Breakage was also necessary for *Cypraea* and *Conus* shells. These consistent breakage patterns can be linked to fragmented archaeological shell material based on shell species, location of breakage and the shape of the broken edge and thus assist in identifying processing techniques archaeologically. This is particularly useful to indicate whether shell breakage patterns reveal meat extraction or artefact production.

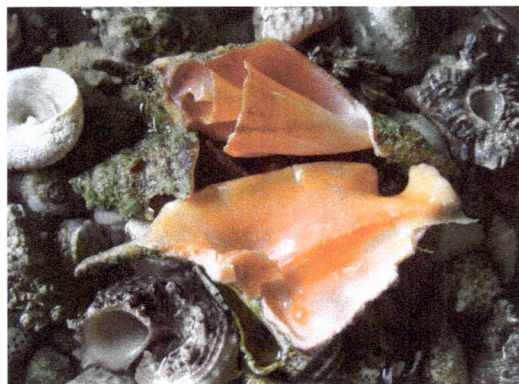

Figure 10.4. Breakage patterns on *Lambis lambis* from processing.

Source: Annette Oertle.

Discard

The final stage of shellfishing is the disposal of the leftover shell material. Once discarded, the shell moves into the archaeological context. The shell refuse was kept together in a pot or bucket once the meat was removed. Any remaining entrails or non-calcareous opercula were fed to the chickens or pigs. At Langalanga the smaller shell pieces were used as infill for the artificial islands. This has stratigraphic implications for the anthropogenic islands themselves as the fragments trickle through the wide interstices between coral blocks.

Modern refuse was located away from buildings and out of the way of high traffic areas. Such areas included vegetated corners, edges of garden beds, corners of piers, into the lagoon and in the edges of mangrove stands. Shell discard was also left in the open and only covered or disturbed by more shell discard, falling leaf litter or incoming tides. Shell concentrations were discrete and scattered around various houses and gardens. The majority of shell concentrations were from single discard events. Concentrations located in mangrove beds, on piers or thrown into the lagoon were dispersed or covered in mud relatively quickly. Shell concentrations located in garden beds or near vegetation were relatively undisturbed environmentally but human or animal agents were the main vectors of disturbance. Terrestrial hermit crabs were also movers of discarded gastropods, leaving their old shell behind (see Szabó 2012). This was seen on numerous nightly wanderings where recently discarded gastropods had been quickly occupied by hermit crabs and were wandering around the gardens.

Discussion

Modern shellfishing behaviours highlight the roles of women and children in gathering shellfish. They have specific knowledge of the habitat and know the methods for finding different species. This is also seen in the various ways to clean and cook shell. The stages of processing and discard provide the greatest potential for physical markers on shell material and therefore for obtaining a better understanding of archaeological site formation and transformation. Cooking methods such as roasting can provide physical and chemical markers which can remain through to the archaeological record. It is well understood that heating of bone or rock will affect the microstructure and biochemistry of the material, but understanding of the response of shell to heating, on the other hand, is poor. A handful of recent studies (Aldeias et al. 2016; Milano et al. 2016) will complement burning experiments undertaken during fieldwork in the Solomon Islands to attempt to better understand these changes.

In terms of discard, the locations of midden deposits are very discrete with a low possibility of in situ preservation considering Indo-Pacific environmental factors. Large-scale environmental events are common in the Indo-Pacific (such as earthquakes, tsunamis and cyclones) and have a significant impact on human behaviour, resource availability, as well as archaeological site locations and preservation. Solomon Islanders have witnessed first-hand the effects of modern sea-level rise with a number of islands now gone or impacted by shoreline recession (Albert et al. 2016). First-hand accounts from people living in Langalanga and Lau lagoons mention a number of small islands, both natural and artificial, which have slowly decreased in size or been destroyed by cyclones. Residents have also noted changes in mangrove and reef zones due to sea-level rise. Smaller-scale environmental changes such as increased wave action, sediment build-up, bioturbation and bioerosion also influence the preservation of archaeological shell material. The separation of shell refuse (smaller shells for infill dropped into the gaps between coral blocks on artificial islands and shoreline extensions) and the differing locations where they are discarded minimises the likelihood of site preservation. If it had been done in the past, this form of shell discard as island infill would cause serious issues for archaeologists due to the constant addition, movement and removal of sand, shells and rock involved in the creation and life cycle of an artificial island. All contextual information about the discard of a shell would be impossible to know. Using discarded shell material as infill for island building in the Solomon Islands may also be a contributing factor in the minimal number of preserved coastal archaeological sites recorded for this region.

It is also important to remember that not all archaeological shell material in a site is likely to be food refuse. Malaita is the only remaining hub of shell money production in the Solomon Islands (Guo 2006) and fragmented or broken shell representing industrial debris from shell money production may be found in archaeological sites. Another possible concentration of fragmented gastropods may be formed as refuse from hermit crab extraction. This was observed in Langalanga Lagoon where every afternoon a woman would gather hermit crabs in the mangroves next to her house. She would then take them back to a rocky outcrop at the edge of the mangroves to smash them open, remove the hermit crabs and then use them as bait for fishing. The broken shells were left there, just above the high tide mark. Heavy rains or higher than normal waves would most likely wash them away.

Conclusion

The issues involved in projecting modern human behaviours onto past societies are well recognised, but we can attempt to disentangle it by using a combination of scientific methods. Every aspect of shellfishing needs to be understood to minimise assumptions and strengthen inferences based on archaeological material. It is thus necessary to consider the varying nature of shellfishing in terms of variability in prey choice, field processing and transportation, but it is also essential to assess how these factors affect site formation. Ethnoarchaeology must also concentrate on discard and formation processes (Davidson 1988:29) as they provide a connection between the systemic and the archaeological record. If we can understand more of the life history behind an archaeological object, we can piece together the past with greater clarity. It is also important not to overlook the variability of human behaviour. A model that has great explanatory power in one location may not translate so well to others and the distinct differences in shell discard between Meehan's iconic Anbarra studies and those noted for Malaita serve to demonstrate this.

The short amount of time spent observing modern shellfishing practices at two different lagoons on Malaita, Solomon Islands has highlighted the need to follow and record the progression of shellfish gathering, processing and discard. The specific methods of processing shell can leave physical markers on shell material, whilst the distribution of shell discard and an understanding of the environmental impacts on site preservation in this tropical island region provide a valuable background in understanding how an archaeological site would form and transform over time.

Acknowledgements

Annette Oertle is a recipient of a National Geographic Young Explorers Grant (9854–16) and Katherine Szabó is a recipient of an Australian Research Council Future Fellowship (FT140100504), which funded fieldwork in the Solomon Islands.

Thanks to the Solomon Island National Museum, in particular Tony Heorake and Edna Belo who provided valuable assistance. This study was not possible without the assistance of Serah Kei and Philemon Bulu at Langalanga Lagoon and Florence Kabi at Lau Lagoon. We wish to thank the two anonymous reviewers as well as the editors. This research was conducted under a Solomon Islands Research Permit sponsored by the National Museum of the Solomon Islands and University of Wollongong Human Research Ethics approvals HE16/230 and HE16/228.

References

Albert, S, JX Leon, AR Grinham, JA Church, BR Gibbes and C Woodroffe. 2016. 'Interactions between sea-level rise and wave exposure on reef island dynamics in the Solomon Islands'. *Environmental Research Letters* 11:1–9. doi.org/10.1088/1748-9326/11/5/054011.

Aldeias, V, S Gur-Arich, R Maria, P Monteiro and P Cura. 2016. 'Shell we cook it? An experimental approach to the microarchaeological record of shellfish roasting'. *Archaeological and Anthropological Sciences* 1–19.

Attenbrow, V. 1992. 'Shell bed or shell midden'. *Australian Archaeology* 34:3–21. doi.org/10.1080/03122 417.1992.11681447.

Bailey, G. 1993. 'Shell mounds in 1972 and 1992: Reflections on recent controversies at Ballina and Weipa'. *Australian Archaeology* 37:1–18. doi.org/10.1080/03122417.1993.11681491.

Balme, J. 1995. '30,000 years of fishery in western New South Wales'. *Archaeology in Oceania* 30 (1):1–21. doi.org/10.1002/j.1834-4453.1995.tb00324.x.

Beck, ME. 2007. 'Midden formation and intrasite chemical patterning in Kalinga, Philippines'. *Geoarchaeology: An International Journal* 22 (4):453–475. doi.org/10.1002/gea.20161.

Beck, ME and ME Hill Jr. 2004. 'Rubbish, relatives and residence: The family use of middens'. *Journal of Archaeological Method and Theory* 11 (3):297–333. doi.org/10.1023/B:JARM.0000047316.02424.7c.

Bird, DW and RB Bird. 2000. 'The ethnoarchaeology of juvenile foragers: Shellfishing strategies among Meriam children'. *Journal of Anthropological Archaeology* 19:461–476. doi.org/10.1006/jaar.2000.0367.

Bird, DW and RLB Bird. 1997. 'Contemporary shellfish gathering strategies among the Meriam of the Torres Strait Islands, Australia: Testing predictions of central place foraging model'. *Journal of Archaeological Science* 24:9–63.

Bird, DW, RB Bird and JL Richardson. 2004. 'Meriam ethnoarchaeology: Shellfishing and shellmiddens'. *Memoirs of the Queensland Museum, Culture* 3 (1):183–197.

Bird, DW, JL Richardson, PM Veth and AJ Barham. 2002. 'Explaining shellfish variability in middens on the Meriam Islands, Torres Strait, Australia'. *Journal of Archaeological Science* 29:457–469. doi.org/10.1006/jasc.2001.0734.

Carter, M. 2014. 'Subsistence shell fishing in NW Santa Isabel, Solomon Islands: Ethnoarchaeology and the identification of two *Polymesoda* (Solander 1786) species'. *Ethnoarchaeology* 6(1):40–60. doi.org/10.1179/1944289013Z.00000000013.

Catterall, CP and IR Poiner. 1987. 'The potential impact of human gathering on shellfish populations, with reference to some NE Australian intertidal flats'. *OIKOS* 50(1):114–122. doi.org/10.2307/3565407.

Ceci, L. 1984. 'Shell midden deposits as coastal resources'. *World Archaeology* 16 (1):62–74. doi.org/10.1080/00438243.1984.9979916.

Claassen, C. 1998. *Shells*. Cambridge: Cambridge University Press.

Clarke, AN. 1994. 'Winds of change: An archaeology of contact in the Groote Eylandt archipelago, Northern Australia'. Unpublished PhD thesis, The Australian National University, Canberra.

Cunningham, JJ and S MacEachern. 2016. 'Ethnoarchaeology as slow science'. *World Archaeology* 48 (5):628–641. doi.org/10.1080/00438243.2016.1260046.

David, N and C Kramer. 2001. *Ethnoarchaeology in action*. Cambridge: Cambridge University Press. doi.org/10.1017/CBO9781316036488.

Davidson, I. 1988. 'The naming of parts: Ethnography and the interpretation of Australian prehistory'. In *Archaeology with ethnography: An Australian perspective*, edited by B Meehan and R Jones, 17–32. Canberra: Department of Prehistory, Research School of Pacific Studies, The Australian National University.

de Boer, WF, AF Blijdenstein and F Longamane. 2002. 'Prey choice and habitat use of people exploiting intertidal resources'. *Environmental Conservation* 29 (2):238–252. doi.org/10.1017/S0376892902000140.

de Boer, WF, T Pereira and A Guissamulo. 2000. 'Comparing recent and abandoned shell middens to detect the impact of human exploitation on the intertidal ecosystem'. *Aquatic Ecology* 34:287–297. doi.org/10.1023/A:1009957409421.

Faulkner, P. 2006. 'The ebb and flow: An archaeological investigation of late Holocene economic variability on the coastal margin of Blue Mud Bay, Northern Australia'. Unpublished PhD thesis, The Australian National University, Canberra.

Gould, RA and PJ Watson. 1982. 'A dialogue on the meaning and use of analogy in ethnoarchaeological reasoning'. *Journal of Anthropological Archaeology* 1:355–381. doi.org/10.1016/0278-4165(82)90002-2.

Guo, PY. 2006. 'From currency to agency: Shell money in contemporary Langalanga, Solomon Islands'. *Asia-Pacific Forum* 31:17–38.

Hardy, K, A Camara, R Piqué, E Dioh, M Guéye, HD Diadhiou, M Faye, H Diaw and M Carre. 2016. 'Shellfishing and shell midden construction in the Saloum Delta, Senegal'. *Journal of Anthropological Archaeology* 41:19–32. doi.org/10.1016/j.jaa.2015.11.001.

Hockey, PAR, AL Bosman and WR Siegfried. 1988. 'Patterns and correlates of shellfish exploitation by costal people in Transkei: An enigma of protein production'. *Journal of Applied Ecology* 25 (1):353–363. doi.org/10.2307/2403631.

Jimenez, H, P Dumas, M Léopold and J Ferraris. 2011. 'Invertebrate harvesting on tropical urban areas: Trends and impact on natural populations (New Caledonia, South Pacific)'. *Fisheries Research.* 108 (1):195–204. doi.org/10.1016/j.fishres.2010.12.021.

Jones, S. 2009. *Food and gender in Fiji: Ethnoarchaeological explorations.* Lanham, Maryland: Lexington Books.

Kirch, PV. 1976. 'Ethno-archaeological investigations in Futuna and Uvea (Western Polynesia): A preliminary report'. *Journal of the Polynesian Society* 85:27–69.

Kirch, PV and DE Yen. 1982. *Tikopia: The prehistory and ecology of a Polynesian outlier.* B.P. Bishop Museum Bulletin 238. Honolulu: Bishop Museum.

Kruijssen, F, J Albert, M Morgan, D Boso, F Siota, S Sibiti and A Schwarz. 2015. 'Livelihoods, markets and gender in Solomon Islands: Case studies from Western and Isabel Provinces'. *SPC Women in Fisheries Information Bulletin* 26:24–36.

Macintosh, DJ, EC Ashton and V Tansakul. 2002. 'Utilisation and knowledge of biodiversity in the Ranong Biosphere Reserve, Thailand'. *ITCZM Monograph* 7:1–30.

Malm, T. 2009. 'Women of the coral gardens: The significance of marine gathering in Tonga'. *SPC Traditional Marine Resource Management and Knowledge Information Bulletin* 25:2–15.

Meehan, B. 1982. *Shell bed to shell midden.* Canberra: Australian Institute of Aboriginal Studies.

Meehan, B. 1988. 'The "Dinnertime Camp"'. In *Archaeology with ethnography: An Australian perspective*, edited by B Meehan and R Jones, 171–181. Canberra: Department of Prehistory, Research School of Pacific Studies, The Australian National University.

Milano, S, AL Prendergast and BR Schöne. 2016. 'Effects of cooking on mollusk shell structure and chemistry: Implications for archaeology and paleoenvironmental reconstruction'. *Journal of Archaeological Science: Reports* 7:14–26. doi.org/10.1016/j.jasrep.2016.03.045.

O'Connell, JF. 1995. 'Ethnoarchaeology needs a general theory of behavior'. *Journal of Archaeological Research* 3:205–255. doi.org/10.1007/BF02231450.

O'Connor, S and P Veth. 1993. 'Where the desert meets the sea: A preliminary report of the archaeology of the southern Kimberley coast'. *Australian Archaeology* 37:25–34. doi.org/10.1080/03122417.1993.11681493.

Ono, R. 2010. 'Ethno-archaeology and early Austronesian fishing strategies in near-shore environments'. *Journal of the Polynesian Society* 119:269–314.

Politis, GG. 2016. 'The role and place of ethnoarchaeology in current archaeological debate'. *World Archaeology*. 48 (5):705–709. doi.org/10.1080/00438243.2016.1230516.

Schiffer, MB. 1972. 'Archaeological context and systemic context'. *American Antiquity* 37 (2):156–165. doi.org/10.2307/278203.

Sheppard, PJ and R Walter. 2006. 'A revised model of Solomon Islands culture history'. *Journal of the Polynesian Society* 115:47–76.

Sinopoli, CM. 1991. 'Seeking the past through the present: Recent ethnoarchaeological research in South Asia'. *Asian Perspectives* 30 (2):177–192.

Swadling, P and A Chowning. 1981. 'Shellfish gathering at Nukalau Island, West New Britain Province, Papua New Guinea'. *Journal de la Société des océanistes* 72–73 (37):159–167. doi.org/10.3406/jso.1981.3057.

Szabó, K. 2001. 'The reef, the beach and the rocks: An environmental analysis of mollusc remains from Natunuku, Viti Levu, Fiji'. In *The archaeology of Lapita dispersal in Oceania: Papers from the Fourth Lapita Conference, June 2000, Canberra, Australia,* edited by GR Clark, AJ Anderson and T Vunidilo, 159–166. Terra Australis 17. Canberra: Pandanus Books.

Szabó, K. 2012. 'Terrestrial hermit crabs (Anomura: Coenobitidae) as taphonomic agents in circum-tropical coastal sites'. *Journal of Archaeological Science* 39:931–941. doi.org/10.1016/j.jas.2011.10.028.

Thomas, FR. 2002. 'An evaluation of central-place foraging among mollusk gatherers in Western Kiribati, Micronesia: Linking behavioural ecology with ethnoarchaeology'. *World Archaeology* 34 (1):182–208. doi.org/10.1080/00438240220134313.

Ulm, S. 2006. *Coastal themes: An archaeology of the southern Curtis Coast, Queensland.* Terra Australis 24. Canberra: ANU E Press. doi.org/10.26530/OAPEN_458881.

Voorhies, B and N Martínez-Tagüeña. 2016. 'Clamming up: Ethnoarchaeological study of a Costa Rican artisanal clam fishery'. *The Journal of Island and Coastal Archaeology* 13:43–65. doi.org/10.1080/15564894.2016.1262483.

Waselkov, GA. 1987. 'Shellfish gathering and shell midden archaeology'. *Advances in Archaeological Method and Theory* 10:93–210. doi.org/10.1016/B978-0-12-003110-8.50006-2.

Wylie, A. 1985. 'The reaction against analogy'. *Advances in Archaeological Method and Theory* 8:63–111. doi.org/10.1016/B978-0-12-003108-5.50008-7.

11

Mummification of the human body as a vector of social link: The case of Faténaoué (New Caledonia)

Frédérique Valentin and Christophe Sand

Introduction

This chapter details mummified bodies that were seated in braided baskets and displayed at the opening of a small rock shelter, on top of a karstic peak dominating an old village situated in the Faténaoué Valley (Témala-Voh, New Caledonia). These bodies call attention to a characteristic of Kanak, and more generally Melanesian, societies: the need for an extended physical connection with ancestors. This trait is exemplified by the burial practices of Ndani (Irian Jaya, Indonesia), Buang and Anga (Papua New Guinea) societies in the present day (Beckett and Nelson 2015; Vial 1936), as well as in the societies of the Torres Strait during the 19th century (Pretty 1969). Over the nearly 3000 years of its prehistoric and traditional Kanak history, the New Caledonia archipelago has seen the development of an exceptional diversity of burial traditions (Sand et al. 2003, 2008). While archaeological studies can identify differences between time periods, there is also clear regional variability in burial practices, body treatments and status-dependent mortuary rituals between contemporaneous communities and chiefdoms (Valentin and Sand 2001, 2008).

In this chapter, the term 'mummification' is defined as the treatment of a corpse aiming at preventing decomposition of soft tissues of the body. Thus a 'mummy' corresponds to human remains with preserved soft tissues (Aufderheide 2003). We will describe the techniques and successive operations leading to the preparation and conservation of mummies in the Kanak society of Témala by using oral history, ethnohistorical written records, archaeological and bioarchaeological data gained from fieldwork undertaken in 2001 at the site of Faténaoué and an examination of photographs of the site dating back to the beginning of the 20th century. This will allow us to highlight the particular vision of the ancestor within this society and to explore its role and place in the context of the New Caledonian micro-regional sociocultural systems.

Written ethnohistorical reports and oral history concerning mummification

Three first-hand written reports depict the practice of mummification of the human body in New Caledonia. At the end of the 1860s, Patouillet witnesses the smoking of the corpse of a chief in a house in Wagap (Patouillet 1873:170–172). Glaumont, who lived in New Caledonia at the end of the 19th century, records the use of mummification for the chiefs in the Belep Islands and in the central chain of Grande Terre. He describes in detail the process. It occurs in a house and comprises perforations of the skin to introduce preservative plant products, desiccation of the body, clothing and make-up of the face (Glaumont 1888:128). Vincent, who stayed in the Houailou region during the 1890s, mentions the contracted position of the smoked body and indicates that the treatment, practised in a house, used to be exclusively for chiefs, but was applied to people of lesser status at the end of the 19th century in the Touho region (Vincent 1895:53).

Other ethnohistorical reports demonstrate the existence of mummies in New Caledonia and the Loyalty Islands. Vieillard, Deplanche and Bourgarel, who stayed in New Caledonia between 1855 and 1867, mention mummified bodies in open air settings, deposited on the ground or in trees, sometimes in 'a kind of coffin', in the Canala region (Bourgarel 1866:414; Vieillard and Deplanche 1863:63). In 1869, Bonnafont (1871:236–237) mentions uncorrupted bodies wrapped in mats and deposited for several years at the surface of caves and rock shelters in the Loyalty Islands. Father Lambert (1901:285), who lived in New Caledonia during the second half of the 19th century, has observed parts of human bodies with desiccated skin in caves of Isle of Pines. Similar observations were made by Sarasin at the beginning of the 20th century in caves and rock shelters in the north of Grande Terre (Sarasin 1929 [2009:235]; Sarasin and Roux 1917:96), and on Maré and Lifou in the Loyalty Islands (Sarasin and Roux 1917:244, 246, 274, Figure 144). Sarasin has illustrated a mummy placed in a vegetal basket in a crouched position, knees against shoulders, about 70 cm high, and described it as a 'dry mummy with the skin hard and parchment-like' (Sarasin 1929 [2009, plate 16, Figure 4:233]). This particular mummy seems to be the same one illustrated later by Nevermann (1942:48).

In addition to the written records, oral histories about the north of Grande Terre describe the process of mummification of the human body and the transport of the mummy to its resting place. According to Leenhardt (1947:110–112), the Faténaoué people, who speak languages related to the Poapoâ and Poai (Hienghène) languages and are associated to the Hoot ma Waap customary area, used to travel for several days to transport their dead to a secret place; and smoke the body and make small openings in the body using vegetal spines to remove the bodily fluids. Kasarhérou (1986:3) reports also that the Faténaoué people used to smoke the bodies before transport to the resting place with wooden poles of about 2 m long, using a technique similar to that used to smoke fish and meat. More specifically, an oral history collected by Gony in 2001 in the Gomen region (*fwai* language) (Valentin and Gony 2016:14–17) describes two distinct processes to smoke a body in function of the social status of the dead. The process for elites is complicated and performed in several different locations. It includes massaging the body with vegetal oils or leaves; draining of bodily fluids by making small openings in the body; contraction of the body; its smoking (sometimes wrapped in a vegetal envelope); and the use of two vegetal baskets. One is of simple shape and used to transport the mummy to its resting place, as illustrated on engraved bamboos (Dellenbach and Lobsiger 1939:338). The second, made at the resting place, is referred to as an 'armchair', in which the body was seated. The process ends with the placement of the mummy in a secret place, an isolated cavity at altitude. In the Paicî-Camuhi customary area (immediately adjacent to the south of Hoot ma Waap area), the desiccated body is placed and conserved on a net stretched between posts near the top of the central post in the chiefly house (Boulay 1990:103).

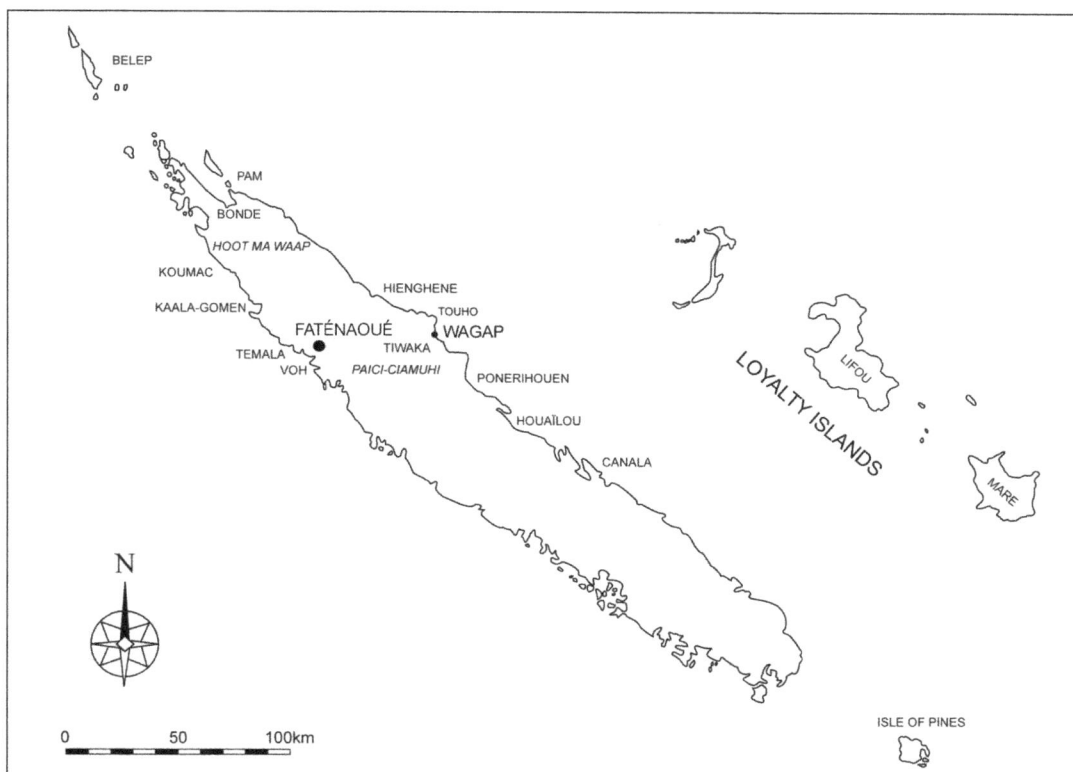

Figure 11.1. Map of New Caledonia with the location of the different sites mentioned in the text.
Source: Institute of Archaeology of New Caledonia and the Pacific.

Bioarchaeological study of the Faténaoué mummies

The Faténaoué site is located in the Témala-Voh region, in the north-western part of Grande Terre, New Caledonia, bordering the Paicî-Camuhi customary area to the south (Figure 11.1). The cavity sheltering the mummies is located in the central chain, at an elevation of more than 500 m above an old Kanak hamlet and about 12 km in straight line from the mouth of the Témala River, on top of a peak associated to the Mount Tenda Formation (624 m) dominating the Faténaoué Valley.

The site of Faténaoué and the mummies were probably visited by Europeans since the beginning of the French colonisation of Grande Terre in the mid-19th century. A written report describes a visit to the site in December 1938 (Leenhardt 1947) and published photographs have been taken since the 1930s (Brou 1970, 1977; Larsen and Larsen 1960; Leenhardt 1947). We have been able to assemble a series of 10 sets of photographs housed in the New Caledonian Archives at the New Caledonian Museum and in private collections. The photographs were taken over a period of about 70 years, from the middle of the 1930s to the beginning of the 2000s. The photographs of Ernest Lauchlan Sinclair (ANC 139Fi) (Figure 11.2) and E Perkins, the latter being published in 1942 in *National Geographic* (de Chetelat 1942), are the earliest of the lot. These photographs provide unexpected and complementary data to perform dynamic bioarchaeological analysis of the mummies. Archaeologists studying a site generally observe only the last state of a long succession of transformative actions, particularly in open air sites. Our bioarchaeological field study of the Faténaoué mummies was conducted in 2001, at the request of the North Province of New Caledonia, in agreement with the traditional Kanak landowners. No human remains were displaced/moved while our field observations were undertaken, with the exception of the sampling of soft tissues and bone fragments, as reported in Sand et al. (2016).

In 2001, two mummies were visible at the entrance of a cavity of limited size (4.6 m x 4.6 m, and not more than 1.0 m high) opening on a small platform 4.4 m long, located on top of a limestone peak of limited accessibility. Facing the valley, the two bodies were seated, upper and lower limbs flexed, knees against the chest, in a position held by a winding rope as indicated by the constrained position of the shoulders (projecting forwards) and the accumulation of ropes at the feet of both individuals (Figure 11.3). Each body was in a basket, with a third basket behind them and a low stone wall protecting them at the front. The two individuals are adult and rather old, as arthritis lesions were observed at the joints of the skeletons. The northernmost one is male and the sex of the other (in central position) is unknown. This second individual is better preserved and died between 1888 and 1916, as revealed by the colorimetric analysis of a bone fragment (post mortem delay 99 +/- 14 years, Jean-Noël Vignal, IRCGN, Rosny-sous-Bois, France, pers. comm. 2002). An oral history associated with the site and naming the deceased (Mae Kahouta from Faténaoué and his wife from Hienghène), confirms this early 20th-century date (Kasarhérou 1986). The death of these individuals therefore occurred after the first installation of European settlers in the region, following the opening of the settlements of Koné in 1880, Pouembout in 1883 and Voh a few years later (Merle 1995; Saussol 1979).

The two individuals could have been from the same biological group. They display similar morphological features. Particularly, both are very tall, exceeding 1.8 m in height, which is a distinctive trait of the men of the Baco region as noticed by the ethnologist Sarasin at the beginning of the 20th century (Sarasin 1916–1917:86). Ancient mitochondrial DNA extracted from bone samples taken from the two individuals show that both do not possess the 9-bp deletion identifying haplogroup B, an Asian-derived lineage found at high frequencies in Polynesian populations (Matisoo-Smith 2016). It also revealed that one of them (the second individual) belongs to the haplogroup Q (Q1), a haplogroup already identified in New Caledonia (Q2) and frequent in several forms in north Melanesia (Friedlaender et al. 2007). Isotopic data measured in bone collagen extracted from fragments sampled from the two individuals indicate that they had a diet relying mainly on vegetal food items, in combination with a few marine products such as shellfish and algae (Herrscher and Valentin 2016).

In 2001, the two bodies were partially skeletonised and displayed comparable distributions of preserved soft tissues. The northernmost body is represented by skeletal elements partially maintained in articulation by desiccated soft tissues surrounding the joints and covering the chest. Remains of ligaments, muscles and skin of brown dark colour are extremely dry, lacking fat and displaying a homogenous and fibrous aspect. The second individual is comprised of skeletal elements in articulation, largely covered by brown, homogenous, fibrous and extremely dry soft tissues, lacking fat. Notably, the skull is covered by remains of soft tissues which present two different layers (skin and muscle) in the neck region. Moreover, the tissues covering the chest are folded, due to the early retraction of the layers underlying the skin, which is a particular feature of desiccated and mummified bodies (Aufderheide and Rodriguez-Martin 1998). No body part was ablated from the bodies, the thoraces were not opened and the necks were not disarticulated on purpose. The bones are unburned and the mummies are characterised by extreme dryness and the loss of lipid in soft tissues. Hair and nails are absent as observed not only in 2001 but also in the earlier photographs. These features suggest in both cases a desiccation perhaps by sun and/or low heat and smoke exposure, as shown by un-flexed extremities of the bodies (implying no contraction of muscles at the extremities) and no explosion of the brain cases (Symes et al. 2008). An early loss of epidermis is also suggested, as hair and nails (elements associated with the epidermis that are absent here) take longer to disintegrate than other soft tissues in natural conditions of decomposition; in this respect, the Faténaoué mummies recall the smoked bodies from the Aseki region in Papua New Guinea (Beckett and Nelson 2015).

Figure 11.2. View of the Faténaoué mummies at the beginning of the 1930s (courtesy Archives de la Nouvelle-Calédonie—Fonds Ernest Lauchlan Sinclair—139Fi).

Source: Ernest Lauchlan Sinclair.

Figure 11.3. The mummies of Faténaoué as they were during the 2001 archaeo-anthropological study.

Source: Christophe Sand.

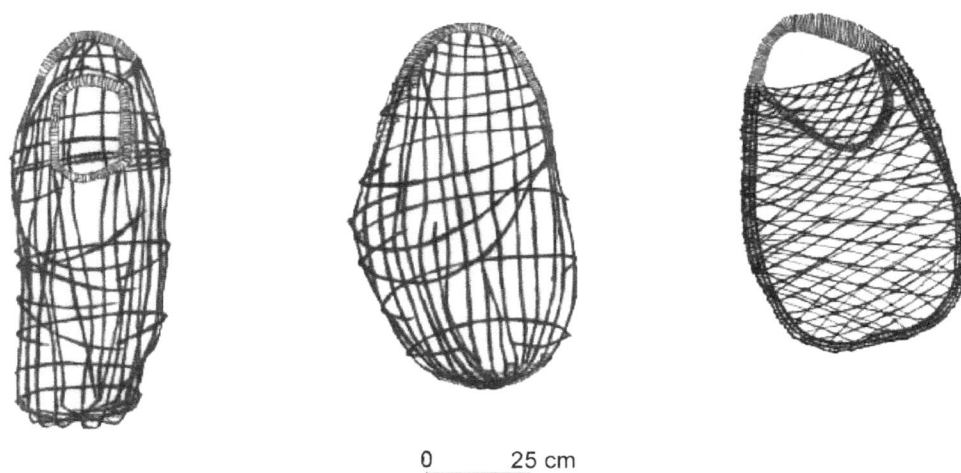

0   25 cm

Figure 11.4. The form of the three baskets still visible in the Faténaoué burial shelter.
Source: Christophe Sand.

As mentioned earlier, the Faténaoué mummies are enclosed in baskets. The baskets can be associated with the net style as defined by Balfet (1952), which is comprised of three elements: a net, a frame and a rope used to tie the net to the frame. The frame consists of an assemblage of stems of a vine (*Smilax* sp.), while the netting and rope are made of coconut fibres (*Coco nucifera*). The three baskets are of different forms, with variation in the shape of the frame and the presence of handles or openings (Figure 11.4) adorned with shell in at least one case, as testified by Leenhardt's 1938 photographs. Other vegetal elements such as a small vegetal bundle placed between the skull and the knee of the northernmost individual and a wooden pole can be seen on the early photographs. While altered from their original state, these materials do not seem to have been exposed to fire or smoke.

The human remains of at least five individuals, some charred, were scattered at the feet of the two Faténaoué mummies along with various grave goods (Figure 11.3). This assemblage comprises only dry bones among which the cranial extremity is under-represented. It includes both male and female individuals according to the morphology of the coxal bone (Bruzek 2002), all of whom appearing to be relatively old. Our analysis of the photographs (Figure 11.2) indicates that more skeletal elements, especially skulls and bones with desiccated soft tissues still attached, were originally present in the rock shelter. This demonstrates that these scattered bones are what is left from the degradation of at least nine to perhaps 11 other mummies, also placed in baskets. At least three other baskets were identified on the early photographs.

Discussion

Potential purpose for mummification

Overall, the bioarchaeological features of the Faténaoué mummies reflect a sequence of actions practised over time and in several distinct locations that reflects the particular vision of the ancestor within this Kanak society from the north of Grande Terre. This sequence conforms in several ways with first-hand written reports and oral history related to the site and other areas of north Grande Terre. The inferred removal of the epidermis can be associated with the massage of the body mentioned in the oral tradition. The flexion of the corpse, knees against chest, is also reported in the oral history and the written records. It was probably done a short time after death on a still-supple body. Combined with verticality, the contracted position encourages desiccation and the elimination of decomposition fluids. At Faténaoué, the position was maintained with ropes constraining shoulders and torso, a detail not mentioned in oral histories and written records but documented from other funerary contexts in the north of Grande Terre (Sarasin 1929 [2009]). The desiccation of the bodies at Faténaoué appears to result from the sun and/or low heat and smoke exposure, in agreement with oral histories and written records. No traces of covering clothing or of make-up were identified at Faténaoué, but the bodies were adorned as shell bracelets were seen by Leenhardt in 1938 (Leenhardt 1947). Finally, the mummies were transported to the Faténaoué rock shelter already mummified. Wooden poles were observed at the site, which could have been associated with the transport of the mummies. The large number of mummies that once existed in the site relative to the small size and configuration of the shelter, as well as the absence of absorbing material and combustion remains (except some charred bones) also support this view. However, this does not exclude other activities at the site, like basket-making as mentioned in oral traditions. The baskets in which the mummies rest do not seem particularly adapted for transport but rather conceived for display. Some of them have a square or rectangular shell-adorned opening placed in front of the face of the mummy.

Comparisons with other mummies from Oceania highlight the uniqueness of the Faténaoué mummies. If the removal of epidermis observed at Faténaoué is a frequent practice in mummification processes of Oceanian populations (Beckett and Nelson 2015; Pretty and Calder 1998), other features appear specific to New Caledonia: no body part was removed from the bodies, the thoraces were not opened, the necks were not disarticulated on purpose and there is no apparent effort to re-establish a living human appearance, as documented, for example, for Torres Straits mummies (Bonney and Clegg 2011; Flower 1879; Pretty and Calder 1998) or funerary mannequins of Malekula, Vanuatu (Speiser 1923 [1996]). The use of basket containers at Faténaoué also differs from the stretchers used to present mummies in the Torres Strait during the 19th century (Pretty 1969) and the armchairs used today in the Anga societies of Papua New Guinea (Beckett and Nelson 2015).

The purpose of making mummies may also be different at Faténaoué. Cases of temporarily preserving the physical living appearance of the dead, and the abandonment, inhumation or cremation of the prepared body subsequent to funerary ceremonies, are reported for Australia and the Torres Strait Islands (Bonney and Clegg 2011; Pretty and Calder 1998). In Polynesian societies (except perhaps in New Zealand, where mummies were placed in rock shelters; Orchiston 1971; Simmons 1967), the preservation or mummification of the body was also a component of the funerary system, as it appears it had, in some instances, an intermediate function in a complex sequence of activities surrounding the physical remains of the dead (Aufderheide 2003; Handy 1927; Linton 1925; Maureille and Sellier 1996).

Considering the staging observed at Faténaoué, we think that the purpose of the mummification of human bodies in the Faténaoué society was probably to obtain long-lasting media to ensure extended networks of social relationships for future generations. At first glance, the Faténaoué living/dead relationship suggests avoidance. Ropes hamper the bodies, baskets enclose them and the mummies are placed in an isolated and secret location, apart from the dwelling areas, thus establishing a distance from the living and the present. The physical remains of the dead could have inspired fear or respect. As elsewhere in Melanesia, fear is an emotion mentioned in the New Caledonian ethnographic literature (Leenhardt 1930 [1980]:217), and regulations related to prohibition (taboo) limit close physical living/dead interactions to selected members of the society (Leenhardt 1947; Sarasin 1929 [2009]). However, three aspects support our hypothesis of the establishment of a dead/living social link not only to 'contemplate the landscape and address his blessing' (Leenhardt 1947:111) but for future mediations. The Faténaoué mummies were placed at an elevated location dominating the settlement, faces turned towards the living

(Leenhardt 1947:111). The relation between the face, the eyes and the opening in the basket confers to the mummy a form of 'beingness', a being possessing the faculty of perception and communication despite the fact its living human appearance was not re-established. Finally, the mummies were apparently produced to be durable, to resist time and potentially to be active, even at distance, for a duration exceeding the time of those who made them.

Place in the regional Kanak sociocultural system

The New Caledonian practice of mummification of the dead appears to be localised mainly in the northern part of Grande Terre. More precisely, it appears to overlap the Hoot ma Waap customary area, which is also characterised by a particular mask tradition (Guiart 1987), with an extension to the south in the Paicî-Camuhi area. The practice was witnessed during the 19th century in the regions of Wagap (Patouillet 1873:170–172), Touho (Vincent 1895:53), and Belep (Glaumont 1888), and mummies were seen not only in the Faténaoué Valley but also in the Khongo Valley (Routhier 1957), and in caves in the Koumac region (Sand and Bolé 2012; Sarasin 1929 [2009]). The practice does not seem present with the same intensity in other New Caledonian regions, confirming Leenhardt's hypothesis of a custom of the north of Grande Terre that becomes rare south of Ponérihouen (Leenhardt 1930 [1980:217]), except maybe in the Canala region (Yves-Béalo Gony, pers. comm. 2013). By contrast, the mummies observed in the Loyalty Islands appear to be the result of a natural mummification process (Bonnafont 1871). In caves on Lifou Island, still supple and fat bodies with nails and hair, dating to the beginning of Christian conversion era, are extended, wrapped in mats and placed in wooden containers (Sand et al. 1995; Valentin and Bolé 2001). Written sources also mention that body embalming was not part of the funerary practice on Lifou Island (Hadfield 1920).

The Faténaoué mummies do not appear to express a short-lived mortuary phenomenon but rather a multigenerational practice associated with a particular group and developed over a long period in the extended sociocultural region of northern Grande Terre. Available chronological information from direct dating on bone and oral history naming the deceased indicate that the practice, still active at the turn of the 20th century, ceased only after European colonisation. The variation in the level of degradation of mummies and baskets and the number of mummified individuals suggest that the practice was carried out earlier and most probably predated the 19th century (Sand et al. 2016).

The intensity of the practice of mummification in the Voh-Témala region, with mummies in the Khongo Valley (Routhier 1957), and at least nine to 11 mummies on top of Faténaoué peak and others in cavities towards the base of the same peak (Kasarhérou 1986), might result from a twofold sociopolitical phenomenon: an identity affirmation at a border zone and an indigenisation process, developed by newcomers in the region as episodes of friction occurred. During the first half of the 19th century, Paicî populations expanded from the east coast to the Voh-Témala region, leading to conflicts between local settlers and Kanak foreigners from the south-east (cf. Bensa 2000). During the second half of the 19th century, changes in the Faténaoué chiefdom related to the European colonisation of the region occurred, as recorded by the ethnographer J Guiart (1987:90–92):

> Le clan des maîtres du sol à Hwatenewe [Faténaoué] aurait été à l'origine dit: Pwaduya ma Bwanehot. Il aurait été par la suite remplacé par les Pwacili Hmaè [clan composite], originaires de Koné. (The clan of the masters of the ground at Hwatenewe [Faténaoué] was possibly originally named: Pwaduya ma Bwanehot. It appears it subsequently got replaced by the Pwacili Hmaè [a composite clan], originating from Koné.)

The chief Hmaè Kahouta of Faténaoué belonged to this Pwacili Hmaè clan and was one of the last Kanak mummified in the Voh-Témala region and his body was transported to the top of the karstic peak.

Figure 11.5. Alignment of skulls in a Kanak funerary outcrop (courtesy Archives du Musée Néo-Calédonien).
Source: Origin unknown: image from Archives du Musée Néo-Calédonien.

Conclusion

To conclude, the practice of mummification and the form of relation between mummies and survivors described here do not appear to be a phenomenon introduced from outside New Caledonia. Several facets of the treatment are fully inscribed in the mortuary system built by traditional Kanak societies during the second millennium CE, particularly in the north of Grande Terre (Valentin and Sand 2001, 2008). Notably, inhumations are set apart from the living space, placed at its edge, as for example at Pwanitio, in the Tiwaka Valley (Sand 1997), or in remote and rocky areas inappropriate for cultivation, or in the forest (Saussol 1990:24). The treatment of the skulls is an aspect reflecting the final stage of another complex mortuary process: they were exposed, aligned and the face turned outside, on or behind a low wall, protected by a canoe or at the opening of a rocky outcrop in several regions of Grande Terre (Bourgarel 1865; Leenhardt 1930 [1980]; Sarasin and Roux 1917; Vieillard and Deplanche 1863 [2001]) (Figure 11.5).

Mummification of the human body and mummies from a localised area, overlapping the Hoot ma Waap and the Paicî-Camuhi customary areas of New Caledonia, are therefore elements of a cultural package related to the traditional Kanak complex (Sand et al. 2003, 2008). It is the identity and/or social marker of a particular group that required the inscription of the deceased's name in the genealogical memory and its integration in the legitimation of claims to land at a time where groups' reconfiguration was at play (Saussol 1979).

Acknowledgements

We would like to thank the Dounehote family for allowing us access to the Faténaoué burial shelter in 2001 and for permitting us to collect samples for scientific analysis on the mummies. The administrative permit was delivered by the President of the Northern Province to the (then) Department of Archaeology of New Caledonia. The study was fulfilled through funding accorded by the Northern Province and the CNRS UMR 7041. We would also like to thank the Archives of New Caledonia, the Museum of New Caledonia and the Viale family for giving us access to archival data related to the Faténaoué mummies.

References

Aufderheide, AC. 2003. *The scientific study of mummies*. Cambridge: Cambridge University Press.

Aufderheide, AC and C Rodriguez-Martin. 1998. *Cambridge encyclopedia of human paleopathology.* Cambridge: Cambridge University Press.

Balfet, H. 1952. 'La vannerie: Essai de classification'. *L'Anthropologie* 56:259–280.

Beckett, RG and AJ Nelson. 2015. 'Mummy restoration project among the Anga of Papua New Guinea'. *Anatomical Record* 298:1013–1025. doi.org/10.1002/ar.23139.

Bensa, A. 2000. 'Le chef kanak. Les modèles et l'histoire'. In *En pays kanak,* edited by A Bensa and I Leblic. Paris: Editions de la Maison des sciences de l'homme. doi.org/10.4000/books. editionsmsh.2771.

Bonnafont. 1871. 'Des sépultures aux îles Loyalty'. *Bulletins de la Société d'Anthropologie de Paris* 6 (6):236–240. doi.org/10.3406/bmsap.1871.4465.

Bonney, H and M Clegg. 2011. 'Heads as memorials and status symbols: The collection and use of skulls in the Torres Strait Islands'. In *The bioarchaeology of the human head: Decapitation, deformation and decoration*, edited by M Bonogofsky. Gainsville, FL: University Press of Florida. doi.org/10.5744/ florida/9780813035567.003.0002.

Boulay, R. 1990. *La maison kanak.* Marseille: Editions Parenthèses.

Bourgarel, A. 1865. *Notes ethnographiques sur la Nouvelle-Calédonie et dépendances.* Paris.

Bourgarel, A. 1866. 'Des races de l'Océanie française, de celles de la Nouvelle-Calédonie en particulier, deuxième partie: Caractères extérieurs, mœurs et coutumes des Néo-Calédoniens'. *Mémoires de la Société d'Anthropologie de Paris* II:375–416.

Brou, B. 1970. *Mémento d'histoire de la Nouvelle-Calédonie, Préhistoire et protohistoire, antiquité et moyen âge.* Nouméa: Société Calédonienne d'Editions.

Brou, B. 1977. *Préhistoire et société traditionnelle de la Nouvelle-Calédonie.* Publications de la Société d'Etudes Historiques de Nouvelle-Calédonie 16. Nouméa: Société d'Etudes Historiques de Nouvelle-Calédonie.

Bruzek, J. 2002. 'A method for visual determination of sex, using the human hipbone'. *American Journal of Physical Anthropology* 117:157–168. doi.org/10.1002/ajpa.10012.

de Chetelat, E. 1942. 'War awakened New Caledonia'. *The National Geographic Magazine* 82 (1):31–55.

Dellenbach, M and G Lobsiger. 1939. 'Quelques scènes de la vie sociale, religieuse et matérielle des Néo-Calédoniens, gravées sur bambous'. *Archives suisses d'Anthropologie générale* 8 (3–4):336–350.

Flower, WH. 1879. 'Illustrations of the mode of preserving the dead in Darnley Island and in South Australia'. *The Journal of the Anthropological Institute of Great Britain and Ireland* 8:389–395. doi.org/10.2307/2841081.

Friedlaender, JS, FR Friedlaender, JA Hodgson, M Stoltz, G Koki, G Horvat, S Zhadanov, TG Schurr and DA Merriwether. 2007. 'Melanesian mtDNA Complexity'. *PLoSOne* 2:e248. doi.org/10.1371/journal.pone.0000248.

Glaumont, G. 1888. 'Usage, mœurs et coutumes des Néo-Calédoniens'. *Revue d'Ethnographie* 7:73–141.

Guiart, J. 1987. *Mythologie du masque en Nouvelle-Calédonie.* Publication de la Société des Océanistes 18. Paris: La Société des Océanistes.

Hadfield, E. 1920. *Among the natives of the Loyalty group.* London: Macmillan.

Handy, ESC. 1927. *Polynesian religions.* B.P. Museum Bulletin 79. Honolulu: Bishop Museum.

Herrscher, E and F Valentin. 2016. 'Analyses isotopiques et comportements alimentaires des défunts de Faténaoué'. In *Les momies de Faténaoué/Hwatenewe (Voh, Province Nord). Etude archéologique et anthropologique d'un site funéraire kanak ancien,* edited by C Sand, F Valentin and B Gony, 85–91. Arkaeologia Pacifika 3. Nouméa: Institut d'archéologie de la Nouvelle-Calédonie et du Pacifique.

Kasarhérou, E. 1986. 'Compte-rendu de la mission effectuée à Tieta du 7 au 14 avril 1986'. Unpublished manuscript. Service des Musées et du Patrimoine de la Nouvelle-Calédonie, Nouméa.

Lambert, (le Père). 1901. *Mœurs et superstitions des Néo-Calédoniens.* Paris: Maisonneuve.

Larsen, M and H Larsen. 1960. *La cyprée d'or, expédition Nouvelle-Calédonie.* Neuchâtel: A la Braconnière.

Leenhardt, M. 1930 [1980]. *Notes d'ethnologie Néo-Calédonienne.* Travaux et mémoires de l'Institut d'ethnologie 8. Paris: Institut d'Ethnologie.

Leenhardt, M. 1947. 'Sépultures Néo-Calédoniennes'. *Journal de la Société des Océanistes* 3:110–112. doi.org/10.3406/jso.1947.1570.

Linton, R. 1925. *Archaeology of the Marquesas Islands.* B.P. Bishop Museum Bulletin 23. Honolulu: Bishop Museum. Reprint 1971, New York: Kraus Reprint Co.

Matisoo-Smith, E. 2016. 'Analyse de l'ADN ancien et affinités génétiques des défunts de Faténaoué'. In *Les momies de Faténaoué/Hwatenewe (Voh, Province Nord). Etude archéologique et anthropologique d'un site funéraire kanak ancien,* edited by C Sand, F Valentin and B Gony, 75–83. Arkaeologia Pacifika 3. Nouméa: Institut d'archéologie de la Nouvelle-Calédonie et du Pacifique.

Maureille, B and P Sellier. 1996. 'Dislocation en ordre paradoxal, momification, décomposition: observations et hypothèses'. *Bulletins et Mémoires de la Société d'Anthropologie de Paris* 8 (3–4):313–327. doi.org/10.3406/bmsap.1996.2451.

Merle, I. 1995. *Expériences coloniales. La Nouvelle-Calédonie (1853–1920).* Paris: Belin.

Nevermann, H. 1942. *Kulis und Kanaken, Forscherfahrten auf Neukaledonien und in den Neuen Hebriden.* Braunschweig: G. Wenzel und Sohn.

Orchiston, DW. 1971. 'Maori mummification in protohistoric New Zealand'. *Anthropos* 66 (5/6):753–766.

Patouillet, J. 1873. *Trois ans en Nouvelle-Calédonie.* Paris: E. Dentu.

Pretty, GL. 1969. 'The Macleay Museum: Mummy from the Torres Straits: A postscript to Elliot Smith and the diffusion controversy'. *Man* 4 (1):24–43. doi.org/10.2307/2799262.

Pretty, GL and A Calder. 1998. 'Mummification in Australia and Melanesia'. In *Mummies, disease and ancient cultures*, edited by TA Cockburn, E Cockburn and TA Reyman, 289–307. Cambridge: Cambridge University Press. doi.org/10.1017/CBO9781139878340.017.

Routhier, P. 1957. Carte géologique de la Nouvelle-Calédonie et notice explicative. Feuille n°3 Voh-Hienghène 1/100 000e. Paris: Ministère de la France d'Outre-mer, ORSTOM (Office de la recherche scientifique et technique outre-mer).

Sand, C. 1997. 'Variété de l'habitat ancien en Nouvelle-Calédonie: Étude de cas sur des vestiges archéologiques du Centre-Nord de la Grande Terre'. *Journal de la Société des Océanistes* 104 (1):39–66. doi.org/10.3406/jso.1997.2012.

Sand, C and J Bolé. 2012. 'Visite de deux sites de sépultures dans le domaine de Karst de la Commune de Koumac (Province Nord)'. Unpublished report. Nouméa: Institut d'archéologie de la Nouvelle-Calédonie et du Pacifique.

Sand, C, J Bolé and A Ouetcho. 1995. *Contribution à la reconstitution de la préhistoire des îles Loyauté, premiers résultats des fouilles archéologiques de 1994–1995, Lifou, Maré, Ouvéa*. Les Cahiers de l'Archéologie en Nouvelle-Calédonie 5. Nouméa: Institut d'archéologie de la Nouvelle-Calédonie et du Pacifique.

Sand, C, J Bolé and A Ouetcho. 2003. 'Prehistory and its perception in a Melanesian Archipelago: The New Caledonia example'. *Antiquity* 77 (297):505–519. doi.org/10.1017/S0003598X00092565.

Sand, C, J Bolé, A Ouetcho and D Baret. 2008. *Parcours archéologique. Deux décennies de recherches du Département Archéologie de Nouvelle-Calédonie (1991–2007)*. Les Cahiers de l'Archéologie en Nouvelle-Calédonie 17. Nouméa: Institut d'archéologie de la Nouvelle-Calédonie et du Pacifique.

Sand, C, F Valentin and B Gony (eds). 2016. *Les momies de Faténaoué/Hwatenewe (Voh, Province Nord). Etude archéologique et anthropologique d'un site funéraire kanak ancien*. Arkaeologia Pacifika 3. Nouméa: Institut d'archéologie de la Nouvelle-Calédonie et du Pacifique.

Sarasin, F. 1916–1917. 'Etude anthropologique sur les Néo-Calédoniens et les Loyaltiens. Première partie: Les caractères extérieurs'. *Archives Suisses d'Anthropologie générale* 2 (1–2):83–103.

Sarasin, F. 1929 [2009]. *Ethnographie des Kanak de Nouvelle-Calédonie et des Îles Loyauté (1911–1912)*. Paris: Ibis Press.

Sarasin, F and J Roux. 1917. *La Nouvelle-Calédonie et les Iles Loyalty*. Bâle: Georg & co.

Saussol, A. 1979. *L'Héritage. Essai sur le problème foncier mélanésien en Nouvelle-Calédonie*. Paris: Société des Océanistes. doi.org/10.4000/books.sdo.563.

Saussol, A. 1990. 'Le pays kanak'. In *La maison kanak*, edited by R Boulay, 21–30. Marseille: Editions Parenthèses.

Simmons, DR. 1967. 'A note on the lake Hauroko burial'. *Journal of the Polynesian Society* 76 (3):257, 367–368.

Speiser, F. 1923 [1996]. *Ethnology of Vanuatu. An early twentieth century study*. Bathurst: Crawford House Press.

Symes, SA, CW Rainwater, EN Chapman, DR Gipson and AL Piper. 2008. 'Patterned thermal destruction of human remains in forensic setting'. In *The analysis of burned human remains*, edited by CW Schmidt and SA Symes, 15–54. London: Academic Press. doi.org/10.1016/B978-012372510-3.50004-6.

Valentin, F and J Bolé. 2001. 'Etude expérimentale de sépultures sur sites sans prélèvement des ossements. Résultats préliminaires des analyses paléobiologiques et des pratiques funéraires des sites de Nonimé, Mucaweng et Hnajoisisi à Lifou (Iles Loyauté)'. Unpublished internal report. Nouméa: Département Archéologie du Service des Musées et du Patrimoine de Nouvelle-Calédonie.

Valentin, F and B Gony. 2016. 'La pratique de la momification en Nouvelle-Calédonie, informations ethno-historiques et données de traditions orales'. In *Les momies de Faténaoué/Hwatenewe (Voh, Province Nord). Etude archéologique et anthropologique d'un site funéraire kanak ancien*, edited by C Sand, F Valentin and B Gony, 11–21. Arkaeologia Pacifika 3. Nouméa: Institut d'archéologie de la Nouvelle-Calédonie et du Pacifique.

Valentin, F and C Sand. 2001. 'Inhumations préhistoriques en Nouvelle-Calédonie'. *Journal de la Société des Océanistes* 113 (2):27–41. doi.org/10.4000/jso.1579.

Valentin, F and C Sand. 2008. 'Prehistoric burials from New Caledonia'. *Journal of Austronesian Studies* 2 (1):1–30.

Vial, LG. 1936. 'Disposal of the dead among the Buang'. *Oceania* 7 (1):64–68. doi.org/10.1002/j.1834-4461.1936.tb00378.x.

Vieillard, E and E Deplanche. 1863 [2001]. *Essai sur la Nouvelle-Calédonie.* Paris: Challamel. Réédition Paris: L'Harmattan.

Vincent, JBM. 1895. *Les Canaques de la Nouvelle-Calédonie, esquisse ethnographique.* Paris: Challamel.

12

Organic residue analysis and the role of Lapita pottery

Mathieu Leclerc, Karine Taché, Stuart Bedford and Matthew Spriggs

The social practices related to food preparation and consumption are known to reveal important aspects of any culture, as resources are usually consumed not only for their taste and nutritional value but also for the significance they hold in specific contexts (Twiss 2012). Organic residue analysis represents a useful way to identify specific foods and relate them directly to artefacts. In contexts where containers are thought to bear a special value, directly identifying the content of pottery through organic residue analysis has the potential to highlight the status of different food resources within the community.

Such is the case with Lapita pottery, associated with the first human presence in Remote Oceania about 3000 years ago. Given the widespread sharing of intricate decorative motifs, highly organised designs and remarkable vessel forms across Vanuatu, New Caledonia, Fiji, Samoa and Tonga, archaeologists generally believe that the people who manufactured and used decorated Lapita pots attributed great cultural significance to their iconography (Chiu 2007; Mead 1975; Sand and Bedford 2010; Siorat 1990). Current models assume that the symbolic significance of these vessels was more important than their economic value. It has been suggested that dentate-stamped Lapita ceramics were used to promote, signal and convey information about the social status and power of Lapita communities, notably in the contexts of special events and/or ceremonies, such as funerals or feasts for example (Best 2002; Chiu 2007; Spriggs 2003; Terrell and Welsch 1997). The archaeological record shows that generally Lapita occupations have been relatively short-lived (200 years maximum) and quickly followed by the emergence of distinctive regional decorative styles, perhaps signalling the decreased significance of Lapita pottery following the disintegration of a shared cultural system.

If largely accepted, the idea that dentate-stamped Lapita pottery was involved in special symbolic/ceremonial activities rather than prosaic domestic cooking is largely based on indirect contextual evidence. Our ongoing project is testing this hypothesis using organic data *directly* acquired from the vessels and reflecting their use. As a first step, the authors have recently analysed lipid residues absorbed within the walls of Lapita pottery from the cemetery site of Teouma in Vanuatu, in an effort to yield direct evidence of the food(s) associated with these decorated vessels (Leclerc et al. 2018). Besides confirming that food was indeed placed in the vessels, the homogenous lipid profiles and carbon isotopic values obtained in this pilot study suggests that similar food types or mixtures were placed in these vessels, potentially supporting their use for specialised functions. At this stage it is still premature to identify exactly which food(s) are associated with decorated Lapita pottery, but additional analyses of archaeological material and food items are currently being undertaken to shed further light on this question. Ultimately, by identifying the content of Lapita pottery, we wish to better understand the social value of various food items.

This chapter aims to develop a few core concepts that are essential in order to reach this level of interpretation. The theoretical framework on which these interpretations will be based and more specifically the concept of highly valued food will be introduced. The implications of this framework and the relevance of organic residue analysis as opposed to other approaches to understand 3000-year-old behaviours will also be debated. Lastly, a review of the food items most likely to be found in Lapita pottery will be presented based on archaeological and environmental data.

On the social role of highly valued food

It has long been emphasised by anthropological studies that food acts as a social indicator in addition to its obvious nutritional values (Appadurai 1981; Ashley et al. 2004; Gumerman 1997; Mintz and Du Bois 2002). Because food is inherently interwoven with social habits and social structure (Atalay and Hastorf 2006; Bourdieu 1990), it represents a unique medium to convey social information about the status of consumers (Danforth 1999; Lévi-Strauss 1965). Food is not only a passive conveyer of messages but also contributes actively to the construction of the social structure (Ashley et al. 2004; Bourdieu 1998; Mintz 1996). Generally, it does so by carrying two contrasting types of social information: food can be used to homogenise a group and reinforce social bonds and/or to differentiate subgroups and establish social statuses (Appadurai 1981; Dietler 1996; van der Veen 2003). Both agendas can be promoted by the consumption of highly valued foods in special contexts and/or specific locations, either public or private (Curet and Pestle 2010; van der Veen 2003:406). For example, it is well established that religious rituals and feasts represent exceptional occasions and often involve the communal consumption of highly valued foods as a social display of power. These occasions also contribute in a particularly significant way in defining, strengthening and/or distinguishing social groups (Dietler 1996; Dietler and Hayden 2012; Hayden 2012; Wiessner 2012). In many societies, special events involving the communal and all-inclusive consumption of food are held to promote the unity of a group, in contrast with other feasts or rituals where access to certain types of foodstuffs is restricted (Hayden 2012; van der Veen 2003). In the latter case, exotic and/or foreign foods are often used as markers of social detachment (van der Veen 2003:415).

Highly valued food is a concept related to the culturally defined differentiation between staple food items and luxuries—that is, food with extra social value. This differentiation is based on several interrelated factors of varying importance depending on the situation, including the rarity, difficulty of preparation and acquisition (labour investment), exoticism, succulence and semiotic weight of the food (Appadurai 1986; Berry 1994; Curet and Pestle 2010; Dietler and Hayden 2012; Hayden 1996). On other occasions, quantity rather than qualitative traits appear to be more significant in revealing value, as reported for example by the ethnographic studies of De Garine (1976), Goody (1982) and Leach (2003) in African and East Polynesian communities where vast quantities of 'normal' food are used in ritual/feasting contexts.

Highly valued food items are thus specific to particular cultural contexts, and the status of any food item may also vary diachronically (van der Veen 2003:409–410). As a result, the criteria listed above do not always indicate high social value, as illustrated for instance by MacLean and Insoll's (2003) demonstration that exotic goods do not necessarily equate to luxury goods. Nevertheless, examples of exotic and scarce food items attributed high social value are numerous in the literature (see Ervynck et al. 2003) and several archaeologists have successfully reconstructed the value of food types based on their differential distribution and the presence of clear material correlates for feasting practices (e.g. Emery 2003; Kirch and O'Day 2003; LeFebvre and DeFrance 2014).

For more recent time periods, other sources of data can be used to reconstruct the value of specific food items. In Polynesia, for example, certain foodstuffs are known to have been highly valued based on ethnohistorical and linguistic data (Kirch 2012; Kirch and O'Day 2003). In some cases, such information can be verified through independent lines of evidence. One isotopic study of human skeletons, for example, confirmed that fat and meaty food were highly valued amongst Polynesian groups in the recent past (around 750 to 300 BP) (Kinaston et al. 2013).

In the case of 3000-year-old Lapita pottery from Teouma, however, information about high-status food contained in proto-historic reports should not be adopted uncritically since it cannot be assumed that particular species kept the same symbolic roles over time. On one hand, ethnoarchaeological studies yield interesting data attesting to long-term continuity in human–things relational systems and allowing for inspiring archaeological hypotheses and models through analogical inferences (Hamon 2016). However, it is rather naïve to suppose systematic persistence in behaviours over millennia, as similarities in material culture do not necessarily equate with diachronic continuity, particularly when comparing social groups separated by such long periods of time There are several examples of presumed ancestral traditions changing significantly through time (e.g. Cunningham and MacEachern 2016; Sillar and Ramón Joffré 2016) and even some cases where the social value of food items is known to have shifted from one extreme to the other, as in the case of oyster or deer in Europe (Grant 2002:20–22; van der Veen 2003:409–410 for other examples). Overall, 'it is far too easy to assume that the values assigned to particular foodstuffs in the past were the same as they are today' (Grant 2002:22). In Melanesia, several ethnoarchaeological studies have addressed the cultural importance of specific ingredients in a more recent past (e.g. Miles 1997; Wiessner 2012). While certainly relevant, the information provided by these sources should be considered with caution: 'That many practices … look like ancient forms should not lead us to assume that they are in some way survivals from an ancient past' (Cunningham and MacEachern 2016:636).

In sum, we argue that ethnoarchaeological analogies are not sufficient to provide convincing interpretations on the use of Lapita pots dating back about 3000 BP. In Vanuatu, for example, the often assumed particular social status of pigs during early human occupation is solely based on excavations from much more recent sites (400 BP; Garanger 1972), as well as reports from the 16th-century Spanish navigator Quiros and contemporary *kastom*. To presume that pigs had a special status 3000 years ago based on its social importance in the last centuries appears as a weak inference. The absence of full circle tusks in Lapita sites could also be taken as counter-evidence for the high status of pigs in ancient times, considering that tusked boars now represent social, political and economic capital in northern Vanuatu (Rodman 1996). It is true that pigs were part of a selective cultural complex and carried over long distances as they were introduced into the new territories colonised by Lapita peoples, but so were chicken, rats and a range of plant species. The other introduced species, animal and vegetal, could have equally been considered socially valuable. In light of this reasoning, we argue that every foodstuff available at the time of the Teouma cemetery could have had special value and potentially been placed in decorated Lapita pottery.

Organic residue analysis of Lapita pottery

In Melanesia, the archaeological study of food and resource exploitation is generally conducted through the prism of optimal foraging theory and behavioural ecology (e.g. Denham and Barton 2006; Hawkins 2015). While these approaches have some evident benefits, they provide little information about the cultural perception and social value of food items in human groups some 3000 years ago. Data from zooarchaeological assemblages and isotope studies have revealed that

Lapita groups had a mixed diet composed of marine and terrestrial resources (e.g. Hawkins 2015; Kinaston, Buckley et al. 2014; Valentin et al. 2010), but they can hardly be used to examine the Lapita mindset regarding food. On the other hand, results from the organic residue analysis of Lapita and post-Lapita pottery will allow a better understanding of eating/serving habits and the social value of the food by directly relating food items to specific vessels.

The first wave of organic residue analysis on decorated Lapita vessels from Teouma supports the idea that these vessels were meant to hold a specific type of food (or mixture of food), tentatively supporting their specialised function (Leclerc et al. 2018). Indeed, lipid residues extracted from the decorated vessels were strikingly similar, which suggests that similar types of food were placed in every dentate-stamped container analysed. Specific food types were exclusively selected to be put in Lapita pottery, and it is plausible these particular foods held a particular cultural status. The homogeneity of molecular and isotopic values across all samples, despite variation in the forms and/or decorative motifs of the containers analysed, also contradicts any hypothesis that specific types of food could have been associated with specific forms of vessels. Interestingly, to date organic residue analysis strongly suggests that marine foods were not processed in Lapita pottery but the results do not allow us yet to distinguish between plants, non-ruminant animals and/or freshwater resources as the main components of the residues. Ongoing and future analyses will provide more information and precision regarding the food content of Lapita pottery, but in the meantime it is relevant to assess the archaeological and environmental context of these food types and on what grounds they may have been imbued with special or high social value.

Lapita foods and vessels

The scholarship on Lapita diet reveals that a generalist subsistence strategy combining marine and terrestrial broad-spectrum foraging, hunting and the cultivation of native and introduced plant species (so-called 'transported landscapes') characterises Lapita settlements (e.g. Crowther 2009; Hawkins 2015; Horrocks et al. 2014; Kinaston, Buckley et al. 2014; Valentin et al. 2010). It has also been confirmed directly by Leclerc et al. (2018), and indirectly by Crowther (2006, 2009) as well as Horrocks and Bedford (2005), that food was placed in Lapita decorated vessels. Whether the vessels were used to cook, prepare or serve the foods is however still uncertain, even if some technological features of decorated Lapita pottery suggest they are ill-designed for cooking (Ambrose 1997).

Freshwater resources

Keeping in mind that Teouma represents a colonising site and that raw materials used to manufacture some of the vessels have been traced back to New Caledonia, it is safe to assume that during their trip, the population that eventually settled on Efate and used Teouma as a cemetery must have been more accustomed to marine resources compared to freshwater species. To this day, very little research has been done on freshwater shellfish exploited by Lapita populations (cf. Szabó 2009) and remains from freshwater fish species are yet to be recovered from Lapita assemblages (Rintaro Ono, pers. comm. 2017). As opposed to the commonly available marine resources, the relative novelty, exoticism and rarity of the freshwater resources available on Efate must have been noticed by Lapita occupants. These traits correspond to some of the criteria usually associated with high-status food, as mentioned before. Consequently, it is plausible that freshwater resources were placed in decorated Lapita vessels and used in non-secular contexts at the cemetery.

Non-ruminant terrestrial animals

Zooarchaeological remains recovered from various Lapita sites, including Teouma, confirm that terrestrial animal species were exploited by the occupants (Hawkins 2015; Kirch 2017; Sand 2010; Summerhayes et al. 2010). In fact, some of the animal populations were heavily impacted by human predation, to the point of extinction for species such as the tortoise, the crocodile and some bird species (Hawkins et al. 2016; Mead et al. 2002; Worthy et al. 2015). The idea, based on optimal foraging models, is that these abundant large animals were targeted first by Lapita newcomers because they represented prime, easy-to-catch preys providing vital amounts of calories and protein that greatly helped them settling in. Fruit bats (*Pteropodidae*) also represent a terrestrial species known to have been heavily exploited by Lapita communities (Bedford 2006; Kirch and Yen 1982; Worthy and Clark 2009). In addition to these native species, a number of domesticated and commensal animals (pigs, chicken, rats, but probably not dogs) were introduced into Remote Oceania by Lapita settlers (Anderson 2009; Hawkins 2015; Matisoo-Smith et al. 1998; Storey et al. 2008). The prime importance of these native and non-native terrestrial animals for the survival of the group during the earlier phase of occupation would have been acknowledged by Lapita peoples. It is plausible that such primary reliance raised the social status of these foods, thereby leading to their placement in highly decorated vessels and involvement in burial practices.

Plant resources

Considering that Teouma represents a colonising site (Bedford et al. 2010), it is argued that C3 plants were scarce during the early phase of Lapita occupation at Teouma. A number of C3 endemic plant species suitable for consumption were present in the archipelago when Lapita groups first arrived, although how rich the environment was is still a matter of debate (cf. Green 1991; Lebot and Sam in press; McClatchey 2012). It is generally argued that the bulk of edible plant resources at the time were limited to leafy vegetables, palms (including coconut, given that it was found in pre-human levels dated to 5000 BP on Aneityum—Spriggs 1984) and some tree crops such as *Inocarpus fagifer*, *Canarium* and *Barringtonia* (Walter and Sam 2002). With regards to newly introduced crops such as taro, yam and banana, it is safe to assume that their quantity must have been limited in the early stage of Lapita occupation, since time was required before the cultivation of introduced plant species thrived enough to make horticulture a viable and steady alternative to hunting and gathering. Overall, these conditions are in accordance with data obtained from faunal analysis and bulk isotopic studies of human bones, which indicate that plant resources, introduced or endemic, were not a major part of the diet in the early phase of the occupation.

Native C3 plants were most certainly less available than marine resources. Considering the significant quantity of marine remains recovered not only at Teouma but also on a majority of Lapita sites and the importance of maritime subsistence activity amongst Lapita people (Bedford 2006; Davidson et al. 2002; Kirch 1997:197–203; Szabó 2001), it is safe to assume that such resources were ubiquitous and commonly consumed at the time of Lapita occupations (Kinaston, Bedford et al. 2014; Kinaston, Buckley et al. 2014; Valentin et al. 2010).

The amount of work and effort necessary for the successful exploitation of plant resources would have been significant, especially for introduced crops. Consequently, the cost of acquisition would have been quite high for such foods. It has been demonstrated that these crops were introduced in Vanuatu as 'vegetative propagules', which are 'highly sensitive to salt sprays and drought' (Lebot and Sam in press). This implies that a considerable amount of care would have been required to protect these crops during the risky canoe trips over long distances. Lebot and Sam also highlight that the successful establishment of gardens by Lapita people colonising a new land was most likely the object of great and delicate attention. Moreover, it shows an intention to keep these crops available for the group, wherever they would establish themselves next. This demonstrates that these crops represented something worthwhile, to be preserved despite the effort, and regardless of whether this importance was based on a nutritional or cultural basis (or both).

During the first stages of occupation, the availability of these introduced resources must have been somewhat limited given the finite number of shoots introduced and the time required before gardens could be established. Months or years would have passed before the first occupants would have been able to collect the first harvests, and perhaps a decade before getting sufficient stock to supply a small community (Addison 2008; Lebot and Sam in press). Thereby, it is safe to claim that in the early days of settlement, introduced plant resources (such as taro, yam and banana) were labour-intensive to produce and relatively scarce. Overall, introduced plant species in Lapita communities fit many of the criteria associated with highly valued food. While this cannot be taken as a proof of the proposed scenario, the fact that starchy plants, including introduced species such as yam and taro, are nowadays very common in the diet of populations across Oceania (Pollock 1992; Walter and Lebot 2007) is consistent with the emulation process undergone by high-value and prestigious items, which typically become mainstream over time through a trickle-down effect (Grant 2002:20–22; van der Veen 2003:409–410).

Conclusions

Lapita people had access to a variety of food resources, several of which could have been placed in dentate-stamped vessels and possibly been highly valued. Relying solely on ethnohistorical sources to determine which resources could have been placed in Lapita pottery is not a reliable approach. Alternatively, organic residue analysis provides a means to look at research questions about Lapita foods and foodways from a refreshing perspective, potentially gaining new insights into the perceptions these people had of their food through its potential to identify the food content of decorated Lapita pottery. An initial pilot study suggests that specific foods were selected to be placed in Lapita pots, possibly confirming their specialised use. While molecular and isotopic values have allowed us to rule out marine resources as the content of the analysed samples, it is yet impossible to distinguish between plants, non-ruminant animals and/or freshwater resources as the main contributors of the residues. Here we demonstrated that all three could have been highly valued food. We are still at the dawn of our inquiry of Lapita foods and foodways using organic residues of dentate-stamped pottery, but it is clear from this chapter that interesting ideas can and have already been brought up. The outcomes are expanding our understanding of the Lapita mindset in regards to food beyond what has been possible so far.

Overall, the discussion presented in this chapter serves as a promising foundation on which upcoming results will build upon to provide new insights on Lapita people's cultural perceptions of food, and their use of decorated vessels in general. Ongoing and future analysis of archaeological ceramics and modern fats and oils will refine our interpretations and provide data that will allow us to address even broader research questions, such as comparing the content of plain and decorated ceramics, or testing whether the specialised use of Lapita pottery detected in our pilot also prevailed at other Lapita sites across Remote Oceania.

Acknowledgements

Thanks to the Asia-Pacific Innovation Program for an Early Career Development Award that allowed Mathieu Leclerc to attend a workshop on organic residue analysis at Queens College, City University of New York, in February 2018 where fruitful discussions in relation to the paper were had. Thanks to Janine Billadello, Aida Romera and Evan Mann for assistance with laboratory work.

References

Addison, D. 2008. 'The changing role of irrigated Colocasia esculenta (taro) on Nuku Hiva, Marquesas Islands: From an essential element of colonization to an important risk-reduction strategy'. *Asian Perspectives* 47 (1):139–155. doi.org/10.1353/asi.2008.0008.

Ambrose, W. 1997. 'Contradictions in Lapita pottery, a composite clone'. *Antiquity* 71:525–538. doi.org/10.1017/S0003598X00085306.

Anderson, AJ. 2009. 'The rat and the octopus: Initial human colonization and the prehistoric introduction of domestic animals to Remote Oceania'. *Biological Invasions* 11 (7):1503–1519. doi.org/10.1007/s10530-008-9403-2.

Appadurai, A. 1981. 'Gastro-politics in Hindu South Asia'. *American Ethnologist* 8:494–511. doi.org/10.1525/ae.1981.8.3.02a00050.

Appadurai, A. 1986. 'Introduction: Commodities and the politics of value'. In *The social life of things: Commodities in cultural perspective*, edited by A Appadurai, 3–63. Cambridge: Cambridge University Press. doi.org/10.1017/CBO9780511819582.003.

Ashley, B, J Hollows, S Jones and B Taylor. 2004. *Food and cultural studies*. London: Routledge. doi.org/10.4324/9780203646915.

Atalay, S and CA Hastorf. 2006. 'Food, meals, and daily activities: Food *habitus* at Neolithic Çatalhöyük'. *American Antiquity* 71 (2):283–319. doi.org/10.2307/40035906.

Bedford, S. 2006. *Pieces of the Vanuatu puzzle. Archaeology of the north, south and centre*. Terra Australis 23. Canberra: ANU E Press. doi.org/10.22459/pvp.02.2007.

Bedford, S, M Spriggs, HR Buckley, F Valentin, R Regenvanu and M Abong. 2010. 'A cemetery of first settlement: The site of Teouma, South Efate, Vanuatu / Un cimetière de premier peuplement: Le site de Teouma, au sud d'Efaté, au Vanuatu'. In *Lapita: Ancêtres Océaniens/Oceanic ancestors*, edited by C Sand and S Bedford, 140–161. Paris: Musée du Quai Branly and Somogy Éditions d'Art.

Berry, CJ. 1994. *The idea of luxury: A conceptual and historical investigation*. Cambridge: Cambridge University Press. doi.org/10.1017/CBO9780511558368.

Best, S. 2002. *Lapita: A view from the east*. NZAA Monograph 24. Auckland: New Zealand Archaeological Association.

Bourdieu, P. 1990. *The logic of practice*. Cambridge: Polity Press.

Bourdieu, P. 1998. *Practical reason*. Palo Alto: Stanford University Press.

Chiu, S. 2007. 'Detailed analysis of Lapita face motifs: Case studies from Reef/Santa Cruz Lapita sites and New Caledonia Lapita site 13A'. In *Oceanic explorations: Lapita and Western Pacific settlement*, edited by S Bedford, C Sand and SP Connaughton, 241–264. Terra Australis 26. Canberra: ANU E Press. doi.org/10.26530/oapen_459398.

Crowther, A. 2006. 'Taro processing and early Lapita pottery'. In *Ancient starch research*, edited by R Torrence and H Barton, 188. Walnut Creek: Left Coast Press.

Crowther, A. 2009. 'Investigating Lapita subsistence and pottery use through microscopic residues on ceramics: Methodological issues, feasibility and potential'. Unpublished PhD thesis, University of Queensland, Brisbane.

Cunningham, JJ and S MacEachern. 2016. 'Ethnoarchaeology as slow science'. *World Archaeology* 48 (5):628–641. doi.org/10.1080/00438243.2016.1260046.

Curet, AL and WJ Pestle. 2010. 'Identifying high-status foods in the archaeological record'. *Journal of Anthropological Archaeology* 29:413–431. doi.org/10.1016/j.jaa.2010.08.003.

Danforth, ME. 1999. 'Nutrition and politics in prehistory'. *Annual Review of Anthropology* 28:1–25. doi.org/10.1146/annurev.anthro.28.1.1.

Davidson, J, BF Leach and C Sand. 2002. 'Three thousand years of fishing in New Caledonia and the Loyalty Islands'. In *Fifty years in the field: Essays in honour and celebration of R Shutler Jr's archaeological career*, edited by S Bedford, C Sand and DV Burley, 153–164. Auckland: New Zealand Archaeological Association.

De Garine, IL. 1976. 'Food, tradition and prestige'. In *Food, man, and society*, edited by DN Walcher, N Kretchmer and HL Barnett, 150–173. New York: Plenum. doi.org/10.1007/978-1-4684-2298-6_10.

Denham, T and H Barton. 2006. 'The emergence of agriculture in New Guinea—A model of continuity from pre-existing foraging practices'. In *Behavioral ecology and the transition to agriculture*, edited by DJ Kennett and B Winterhalder, 237–264. Berkeley: University of California Press.

Dietler, M. 1996. 'Feasts and commensal politics in the political economy: Food, power and status in prehistoric Europe'. In *Food and the status quest: An interdisciplinary perspective*, edited by P Wiessner and W Schiefenhovel, 87–125. Providence: Berghahn.

Dietler, M and B Hayden. 2012. 'Digesting the feast: Good to eat, good to drink, good to think'. In *Feasts: Archaeological and ethnographic perspectives on food, politics, and power*, edited by M Dietler and B Hayden, 1–20. Tuscaloosa: University Alabama Press.

Emery, KF. 2003. 'The noble beast: Status and differential access to animals in the Maya world'. *World Archaeology* 34 (3):498–515. doi.org/10.1080/0043824021000026477.

Ervynck, A, W Van Neer, H Hüster-Plogmann and J Schibler. 2003. 'Beyond affluence: The zooarchaeology of luxury'. *World Archaeology* 34 (3):428–441. doi.org/10.1080/0043824021000026431.

Garanger, J. 1972. *Archéologie des Nouvelles-Hébrides: Contribution à la connaissance des îles du Centre.* Publications de la Société des Océanistes 30. Paris: Société des Océanistes, Musée de l'Homme. doi.org/10.4000/books.sdo.859.

Goody, J. 1982. *Cooking, cuisine and class: A study in comparative sociology*. Cambridge: Cambridge University Press. doi.org/10.1017/CBO9780511607745.

Grant, A. 2002. 'Food, status and social hierarchy'. In *Consuming passions and patterns of consumption*, edited by P Miracle and N Milner, 17–24. Cambridge: McDonald Institute for Archaeological Research.

Green, RC. 1991. 'Near and Remote Oceania—Disestablishing "Melanesia" in culture history'. In *Man and a half: Essays in Pacific anthropology and ethnobiology in honour of Ralph Bulmer*, edited by A Pawley, 491–502. Auckland: The Polynesian Society.

Gumerman, G. 1997. 'Food and complex societies'. *Journal of Archaeological Method and Theory* 4 (2):105–139. doi.org/10.1007/BF02428056.

Hamon, C. 2016. 'Debates in ethnoarchaeology today: A new crisis of identity or the expression of a vibrant research strategy?' *World Archaeology* 48 (5):700–704. doi.org/10.1080/00438243.2016. 1234409.

Hawkins, S. 2015. 'Human behavioural ecology, anthropogenic impact and subsistence change at the Teouma Lapita site, central Vanuatu, 3000–2500 BP'. Unpublished PhD thesis, The Australian National University, Canberra.

Hawkins, S, TH Worthy, S Bedford, M Spriggs, G Clark, G Irwin, S Best and P Kirch. 2016. 'Ancient tortoise hunting in the southwest Pacific'. *Nature: Scientific Reports* 6 (38317). doi.org/10.1038/srep38317.

Hayden, B. 1996. 'Feasting in prehistoric and traditional societies'. In *Food and the status quest: An interdisciplinary perspective*, edited by P Wiessner and W Schiefenhovel, 127–147. Providence: Berghahn.

Hayden, B. 2012. 'Fabulous feasts: A prolegomenon to the importance of feasting'. In *Feasts: Archaeological and ethnographic perspectives on food, politics and power*, edited by M Dietler and B Hayden, 23–64. Tuscaloosa: University of Alabama Press.

Horrocks, M and S Bedford. 2005. 'Microfossil analysis of Lapita deposits in Vanuatu reveals introduced Araceae (aroids)'. *Archaeology in Oceania* 39:67–74. doi.org/10.1002/j.1834-4453.2005.tb00587.x.

Horrocks, M, MK Nieuwoudt, R Kinaston, HR Buckley and S Bedford. 2014. 'Microfossil and Fourier Transform InfraRed analyses of Lapita and post-Lapita human dental calculus from Vanuatu, Southwest Pacific'. *Journal of the Royal Society of New Zealand* 44 (1):17–33. doi.org/10.1080/03036758.2013.84 2177.

Kinaston, R, S Bedford, M Richards, S Hawkins, A Gray, K Jaouen, F Valentin and HR Buckley. 2014. 'Diet and human mobility from the Lapita to the early historic period on Uripiv Island, Northeast Malakula, Vanuatu'. *PLoS ONE* 9 (8):e104071. doi.org/10.1371/journal.pone.0104071.

Kinaston, RL, HR Buckley and A Gray. 2013. 'Diet and social status on Taumako, a Polynesian outlier in the southeastern Solomon Islands'. *American Journal of Physical Anthropology* 151:589–603. doi.org/10.1002/ajpa.22314.

Kinaston, R, HR Buckley, F Valentin, S Bedford, M Spriggs, S Hawkins and E Herrscher. 2014. 'Lapita diet in Remote Oceania: New stable isotope evidence from the 3000-year-old Teouma Site, Efate Island, Vanuatu'. *PLoS ONE* 9 (3):e90376. doi.org/10.1371/journal.pone.0090376.

Kirch, PV. 1997. *The Lapita peoples: Ancestors of the Oceanic world*. Cambridge, Massachusetts: Blackwell.

Kirch, PV. 2012. 'Polynesian feasting in ethnohistoric, ethnographic, and archaeological contexts'. In *Feasts: Archaeological and ethnographic perspectives on food, politics, and power*, edited by M Dietler and B Hayden, 168–184. Tuscaloosa: University Alabama Press.

Kirch, PV. 2017. *On the road of the winds: An archaeological history of the Pacific Islands before European contact*. Revised and expanded edition. Berkeley: University of California Press. doi.org/10.1002/arco.5168.

Kirch, PV and SJ O'Day. 2003. 'New archaeological insights into food and status: A case study from pre-contact Hawaii'. *World Archaeology* 34 (3):484–497. doi.org/10.1080/0043824021000026468.

Kirch, PV and DE Yen. 1982. *Tikopia: The prehistory and ecology of a Polynesian outlier*. B.P. Bishop Museum Bulletin 238. Honolulu: Bishop Museum.

Leach, H. 2003. 'Did East Polynesians have a concept of luxury foods?' *World Archaeology* 34 (3):442–457. doi.org/10.1080/0043824021000026440.

Lebot, V and C Sam. in press. 'Green desert or "all you can eat"? How diverse and edible was the flora of Vanuatu before human introductions?' In *Debating Lapita: Distribution, chronology, society and subsistence*, edited by S Bedford and M Spriggs. Canberra: ANU Press.

Leclerc, M, K Taché, S Bedford, M Spriggs, A Lucquin and OE Craig. 2018. 'The use of Lapita pottery: Results from the first analysis of lipid residues'. *Journal of Archaeological Science: Reports* 17:712–722. doi.org/10.1016/j.jasrep.2017.12.019.

LeFebvre, MJ and SD DeFrance. 2014. 'Guinea pigs in the Pre-Columbian West Indies'. *Journal of Island & Coastal Archaeology* 9:16–44. doi.org/10.1080/15564894.2013.861545.

Lévi-Strauss, C. 1965. 'The culinary triangle'. *Partisan Review* 33:586–595.

MacLean, R and T Insoll. 2003. 'Archaeology, luxury and the exotic: The examples of Islamic Gao (Mali) and Bahrain'. *World Archaeology* 34 (3):558–570. doi.org/10.1080/0043824021000026512.

Matisoo-Smith, E, RM Roberts, GJ Irwin, JS Allen, D Penny and DM Lambert. 1998. 'Patterns of prehistoric human mobility revealed by mitochondrial DNA from the Pacific rat'. *Proceedings from the National Academy of Sciences* 95:15145–115150.

McClatchey, WC. 2012. 'Wild food plants of Remote Oceania'. *Acta Societatis Botanicorum Poloniae* 81:371–380. doi.org/10.5586/asbp.2012.034.

Mead, JI, DW Steadman, SH Bedford, CJ Bell and M Spriggs. 2002. 'New extinct Mekosuchine crocodile from Vanuatu, South Pacific'. *Copeia* 3:632–641. doi.org/10.1643/0045-8511(2002)002 [0632:NEMCFV]2.0.CO;2.

Mead, SM. 1975. 'The decorative system of the Lapita potters of Sigatoka, Fiji'. In *The Lapita style of Fiji and its associations*, edited by SM Mead, L Birks, H Birks and E Shaw, 19–43. Polynesian Society Memoir 38. Wellington: The Polynesian Society.

Miles, WFS. 1997. 'Pigs, politics and social change in Vanuatu'. *Society and Animals* 5 (2):155–167. doi.org/10.1163/156853097X00051.

Mintz, SW. 1996. *Tasting food, tasting freedom*. Boston: Beacon Press.

Mintz, SW and CM Du Bois. 2002. 'The anthropology of food and eating'. *Annual review of Anthropology* 31:99–119. doi.org/10.1146/annurev.anthro.32.032702.131011.

Pollock, NJ. 1992. *These roots remain: Food habits in islands of the Central and Eastern Pacific since Western contact*. Honolulu: University of Hawai'i Press.

Rodman, W. 1996. 'Pigs in paradise'. In *Arts of Vanuatu*, edited by J Bonnemaison, 158–168. Honolulu: University of Hawai'i Press.

Sand, C. 2010. *Lapita calédonien. Archéologie d'un premier peuplement insulaire océanien*. Paris: Société des Océanistes. doi.org/10.4000/books.sdo.1128.

Sand, C and S Bedford. 2010. *Lapita: Ancêtres Océaniens/Oceanic ancestors*. Paris: Musée du Quai Branly and Somogy Éditions d'Art.

Sillar, B and G Ramón Joffré. 2016. 'Using the present to interpret the past: The role of ethnographic studies in Andean archaeology'. *World Archaeology* 48 (5):656–673. doi.org/10.1080/00438243. 2016.1211033.

Siorat, J-P. 1990. 'A technological analysis of Lapita pottery decoration'. In *Lapita design, form and composition: Proceedings of the Lapita design workshop, Canberra, Australia*, edited by M Spriggs, 59–82. Canberra: Department of Prehistory, Research School of Pacific and Asian Studies, The Australian National University.

Spriggs, M. 1984. 'Early coconut remains from the South Pacific'. *Journal of the Polynesian Society* 93:71–76.

Spriggs, M. 2003. 'Post-Lapita evolutions in Island Melanesia'. In *Pacific Archaeology: Assessments and prospects, Proceedings of the International Conference for the 50th anniversary of the first Lapita excavation, Koné-Nouméa 2002*, edited by C Sand, 205–212. Les Cahiers de l'Archéologie en Nouvelle-Calédonie 15. Nouméa: Département Archéologie, Service des Musées et du Patrimoine de Nouvelle-Calédonie. doi.org/10.4000/books.editionsmsh.2801.

Storey, AA, T Ladefoged and EA Matisoo-Smith. 2008. 'Counting your chickens: Density and distribution of chicken remains in archaeological sites of Oceania'. *International Journal of Osteoarchaeology* 18:240–261. doi.org/10.1002/oa.947.

Summerhayes, GR, E Matisoo-Smith, H Mandui, J Allen, J Specht, N Hogg and S McPherson. 2010. 'Tamuarawai (EQS): An early Lapita site on Emirau, New Ireland, PNG'. *Journal of Pacific Archaeology* 1 (1):62–75.

Szabó, K. 2001. 'The reef, the beach, and the rocks: An environmental analysis of mollusc remains from Natunuku, Viti Levu, Fiji'. In *The archaeology of Lapita dispersal in Oceania: Papers from the Fourth Lapita Conference, June 2000, Canberra, Australia*, edited by G Clark, AJ Anderson and T Vunidilo, 159–166. Terra Australis 17. Canberra: Pandanus Books.

Szabó, K. 2009. 'Molluscan remains from Fiji'. In *The early prehistory of Fiji*, edited by G Clark and AJ Anderson, 183–211. Canberra: ANU E Press. doi.org/10.22459/TA31.12.2009.08.

Terrell, JE, and RL Welsch. 1997. 'Lapita and the temporal geography of prehistory'. *Antiquity* 71:548–572. doi.org/10.1017/S0003598X0008532X.

Twiss, K. 2012. 'The archaeology of food and social diversity'. *Journal of Archaeological Research* 20 (4):357–395. doi.org/10.1007/s10814-012-9058-5.

Valentin, F, HR Buckley, E Herrscher, R Kinaston, S Bedford, M Spriggs, S Hawkins and K Neal. 2010. 'Lapita subsistence strategies and food consumption patterns in the community of Teouma (Efate, Vanuatu)'. *Journal of Archaeological Science* 37 (8):1820–1829. doi.org/10.1016/j.jas.2010.01.039.

van der Veen, M. 2003. 'When is food a luxury?' *World Archaeology* 34 (3):405–427. doi.org/10.1080/0043824021000026422.

Walter, A and V Lebot. 2007. *Gardens of Oceania*. ACIAR Monograph no. 122. Canberra: Australian Centre for International Agricultural Research.

Walter, A and C Sam. 2002. *Fruits of Oceania*. Translated by P Ferrar. ACIAR Monograph no. 85. Canberra: Australian Centre for International Agricultural Research. Originally published as *Fruits d'Océanie*, Marseille: IRD Éditions.

Wiessner, P. 2012. 'Of feasting and value: Enga feasts in a historical perspective (Papua New Guinea)'. In *Feasts: Archaeological and ethnographic perspectives on food, politics, and power*, edited by M Dietler and B Hayden, 115–143. Tuscaloosa: University Alabama Press. doi.org/10.1525/aa.2002.104.4.1236.

Worthy, TH and GC Clark. 2009. 'Bird, mammal and reptile remains'. In *The early prehistory of Fiji*, edited by GC Clark and AJ Anderson, 231–258. Terra Australis 31. Canberra: ANU E Press. doi.org/10.22459/TA31.12.2009.10.

Worthy, TH, S Hawkins, S Bedford and M Spriggs. 2015. 'Avifauna from the Teouma Lapita site, Efate Island, Vanuatu, including a new genus and species of megapode'. *Pacific Science* 69 (2):205–254. doi.org/10.2984/69.2.6.

13

Technological process in pre-colonial Melanesia

Dylan Gaffney

Technology is a process. As a process, it materialises knowledge, identity and society. In this essay, I introduce the concept of technological process, which draws on the tenets of process archaeology and the anthropology of technology in describing materials and people as dynamic, mutually constitutive lines of flow. These lines are best codified as a *chaîne opératoire* (operational sequence), which allows us to tease apart socially meaningful, diachronic variation and change. How technological process, as a narrative device and interpretive concept, can be uniquely applied to the pre-colonial past in Melanesia is explored through the production and exchange of red-slipped pottery around Madang in the recent pre-colonial past. Common themes in this research, and other case studies from the area, draw attention to unique aspects of the technological process in north-east New Guinea, which involves growth, personification, magic and ritual. This has implications for how we understand technology in deeper archaeological time.

Introduction

In anthropology, theoretical shifts are re-emerging that conceptualise technical action as a central process in the co-construction of knowledge, identity and society (Dobres 2000; Ingold 2016; Wellner et al. 2015; see originally Mauss 1934). Similarly, in the subfield of archaeology, material culture research has become increasingly interested in the entanglements and interactions between people and non-human things, examining, for instance, how technical activities like production and exchange shape substantial aspects of people's cognitive and social ontologies (Gosden 2008; Malafouris 2010). These shifts are influenced by post-structuralism, which sees people and things as mutually constitutive processes or *flows*. Gosden and Malafouris' (2015) recent article most succinctly advocates for this, presenting a synthetic 'process archaeology' as one dialectic between *flow* and *form*. *Flow* being the permanent state of change experienced by people and things, and *form* being ephemeral. From the perspective of process archaeology, the emphasis then shifts away from artefacts, people and environments as static and synchronic *forms* and re-conceptualises these things as dynamic and diachronic lines of *flow*, constantly undergoing making and remaking, binding together and unravelling, always in processes of becoming. These processes underlie all people, materials and technologies. It is timely, then, to investigate the technology of pre-colonial Melanesia—especially aspects of production and exchange, which have been so central to developing theoretical models in the discipline—with these new ideas in mind.

This essay presents 'technological process' as a useful narrative and interpretive concept to re-conceptualise how we approach the complexities of materiality and the lived experience in the human past. This builds upon the *chaîne opératoire* as a methodological device to link higher order process theory with micro anthropological/archaeological observations. By forming these links, we can (1) more easily delineate past social groups and communities of practice, and (2) enliven our narratives of pre-colonial technology and society. The approach is illustrated through the production and exchange of red-slipped pottery around Madang in the ethnographic present, the colonial period and the recent archaeological past. I later find commonalities in my own research with other case studies from north-east New Guinea, including the manufacture of *garamut* drums on the Rai Coast and the process of *lalong* canoe building in Astrolabe Bay. I speculate that making *things* in pre-colonial Melanesia was intertwined and inseparable from making ritual, magic, language and reciprocal relationships. It is through the technological process that both non-human things and people were grown and initiated into networks of active interrelationships. I suggest that thinking about technology in this way can be useful in understanding the broader social context of material culture in Melanesia's deeper archaeological past.

Technology as process

Technology is a generative learning practice, which moulds the parameters of human thought, movement and action (Minar & Crown 2001); it produces embodied knowledge (Inoue 2006; Jørgensen 2013). Central to technical knowledge acquisition is the concurrent interplay of conscious intentionality, embodied knowledge and materials (Lemonnier 1986). It is through this continuous dynamism, tension and energy transfer between mind, body and matter that people internalise and create meaning, constituting their social world (Gosden 1994; Keller and Keller 1996).

Tim Ingold has produced a substantial body of work that builds upon these ideas. He sees this knowledge acquisition as process; as a transformative correspondence between maker and material (Ingold 2013). Materials are malleable and move in response to action upon them, and according to the nature of their own properties (Ingold 2012). In this way, the maker or user is guided in the technological process *with* the material, arriving at different temporary forms together. This is contrastive to what Ingold labels the hylomorphic model, which perceives people imposing form or mental templates on inert raw substances to create different types of finished products. Rather, materials are never finished, but continue to undergo change throughout their life history.

By Ingold's reckoning, materials and consciousness can then be seen as progressing along life-lines. The 'artefacts' and 'objects' we examine as archaeologists are simply temporary stoppages or 'blobs' along these lines (Ingold 2015:3). If we want to get at the meaningful technological processes along which people and materials have travelled, and which have shaped their social and cognitive ontologies, we must then turn our analytical lens 90 degrees, from horizontal snapshots of blob-jects, to drawing out vertical linear processes. As these lines correspond and become bound up with others they become entangled, which results in mutative networks of interrelations with nodes of connectivity constantly undergoing strengthening and severance (Knappett 2011; Thomas this volume).

Gosden and Malafouris (2015) draw together these trends in anthropology and advocate for a process ontology, through which people, social groups and materials create modes of becoming. They advance three theoretical postulates for applying such a process ontology to a successful 'process archaeology': (1) reality is best understood as modes of becoming rather than states of being; (2) people, objects and things are always in flux; (3) human becoming is understood as transformations between energy and matter. If we think about technology from a process archaeology perspective, technology is not inert and lifeless, but represents distinct lines of flux. It is every process of human action *with* matter that produces, creates, distributes, uses, destroys or in some other way affects the world.

Although Gosden and Malafouris present the higher order theoretical postulates of process archaeology, they are yet to delve into the middle-range linking devices that will allow us to tie these ideas to archaeological material culture. However, Carl Knappett (2005), exploring similar modes of becoming on Bronze Age Crete, has stressed the need for such methodological innovations and advocates for the *chaîne opératoire* approach to describe technology not as concrete and object-centric, focused on temporary *form*, but rather, as a study of techniques, examining the *flow* of technological process.

For analytical purposes the *chaîne opératoire* can be subdivided into phases of procurement, production, distribution, consumption, alteration, re-use and discard (Figure 13.1). Within these phases, a 'technical element' is the smallest analytical unit of study, formed by the interplay between a gesture, an intention, and matter (modified from Lemonnier 1992:31). As technical elements are repeated, through habitual material engagement, the boundaries between gesture, intentionality and matter become blurred, generating embodied knowledge (cf. Malafouris 2008). 'Technical syntax' is a sequence of technical elements in order. The culturally specific arrangements of extended syntaxes, from procurement to discard, compose the *chaîne opératoire*, regulated by broader social and technological conventions. These distinctions are important because technical elements are more fluid in terms of sharing, and are often passed horizontally within or between groups, while syntaxes are more conservative and are likely to be passed from parent to child, teacher to pupil (Apel 2008). For instance, in potting technology, because decorative elements or minor technical variations are less reliant on extended syntaxes, they are more readily shared across social boundaries than vessel forming techniques (Arnold 1985; Mayor 2005). Thus, individual elements may be widely distributed, while syntaxes are usually diagnostic of production groups (Roux and Courty 2005).

By using the *chaîne opératoire*, we are able to look at the in-between of raw materials and 'finished' objects, assembling what Gosden and Malafouris (2015) describe as the 'chronoarchitecture' of action. We then move away from blob-based, classic typological approaches and towards line-based, process methods for material culture analysis, which can more effectively identify social groups working within broader communities of practice, and allow us to flesh out our archaeological narratives.

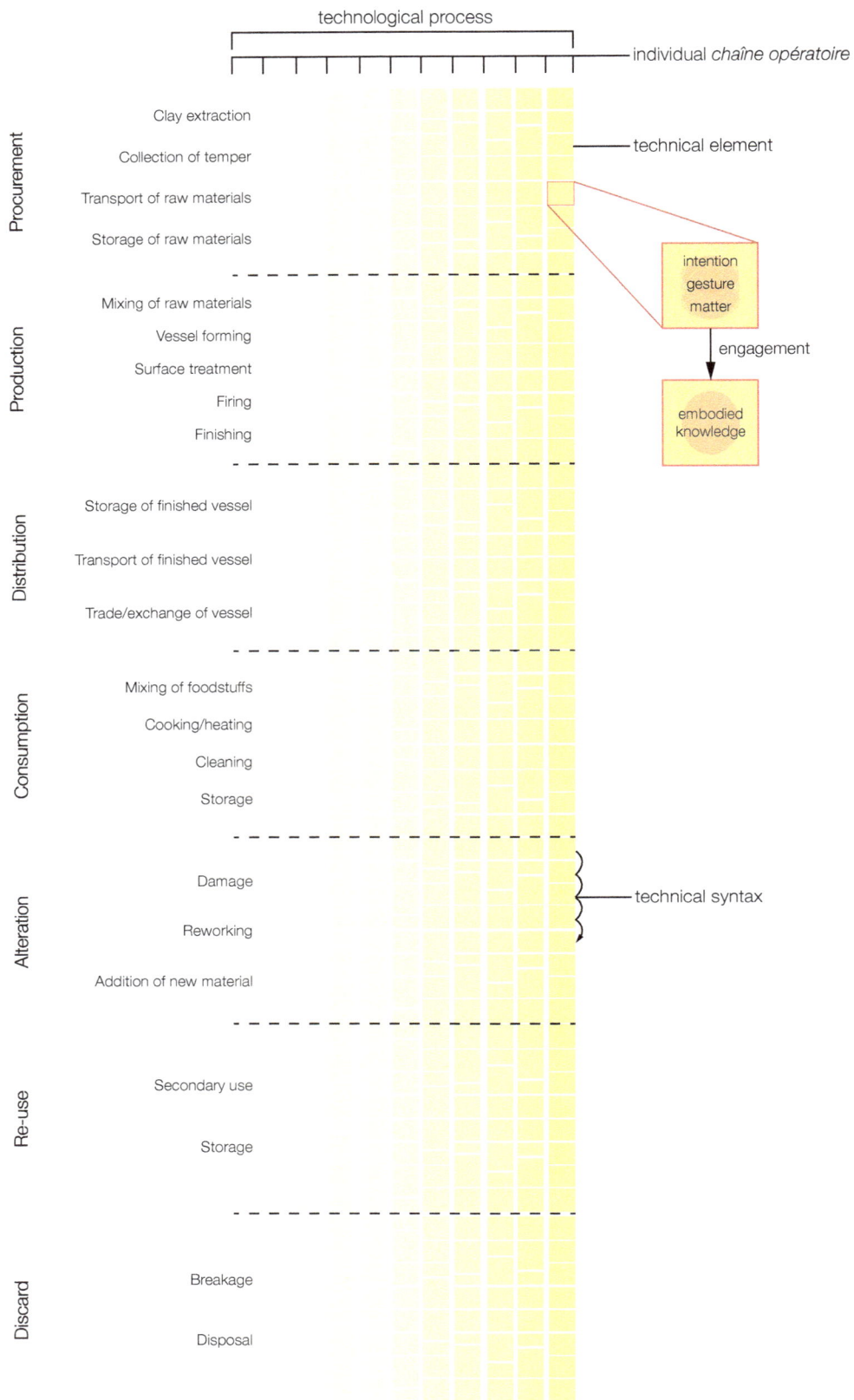

Figure 13.1. Analytical terminology of a ceramic *chaîne opératoire*.
Source: Dylan Gaffney.

Technological process on the north-east coast of New Guinea

To illustrate how the concept of technological process can be instructive for understanding pre-colonial Melanesian societies, I now turn to pottery-making around the north-east coast of New Guinea. The north-east coast stretches from the mouth of the Sepik in the north to the Markham in the south, and is characterised by uplifted coral, active volcanic islands and tropical coastal plains flanked by steep mountain ranges. It is an important area as it was likely host to early human groups as they passed along the coast into the Pacific 50 000 years ago (Groube et al. 1986), and has subsequently been used as a conduit into the Bismarck Archipelago and the Central Highlands (Gaffney, Summerhayes et al. 2015; Gaffney et al. 2016; Gaffney et al. in press). More recently it has seen increasingly specialised modes of production and exchange leading up to ethnographic contact in the 1870s (Lilley 2017). This involved a number of middlemen trading groups, marginally situated relative to material resources, but at the heart of coastal and inter-island exchange networks (Harding 1967; Hogbin 1947; Sahlins 1974:262–276). One of these trading groups was the Bel (Bilbil and Gedaged) speaking group around Madang, who speak an Austronesian language derived from Proto North New Guinea (Ross 1988). They are organised into nested segmentary groups who operate in cooperative social and material networks around the north-east coast, and were once the hub of the extensive Madang exchange system, using sea-going canoes to distribute their pottery over hundreds of kilometres to the north and east in return for subsistence crops, practical objects and valuables. This exchange network was severely disrupted during the Pacific War when occupying forces destroyed many of the canoes, but pottery-making, known as *vai*, continues into the present.

Ceramic *chaînes opératoires* will illustrate how this specific technological process initiated a broader social world of growth, personification, magic and ritual. This process is examined over different temporal ranges, with each study moving us back deeper through time: (1) the synchronic potting cycle observed ethnographically; (2) the more extended evidence of technological and social change identified ethnohistorically, during the contact and colonial periods; and (3) the more diachronic changes observed archaeologically over the last millennium before present.

Modern pottery production and exchange around Madang

At Bilbil and Yabob villages around Madang, many women produce brilliant, red-slipped, paddle and anvil pottery used as cooking vessels and water containers (Gaffney 2016; Gaffney and Summerhayes 2017).[1] A number of social conventions still govern pottery-making. Only women at Bilbil or Yabob may produce pottery in this manner, so if a woman moves from her natal potting village to a different, non-potting marital village, she will be prohibited from production of ceramics and the sharing of technical knowledge. This convention is called the *vou* and is a form of magic that can be likened to intellectual copyright amongst the Bel groups. Transgression of the *vou* can result in violent retribution.

---

1   Pottery-making has since ceased at Yabob Village and only continues at Bilbil. These villages comprise the Bilbil language speakers to the south of modern Madang town.

Today, the potters dig for suitable clay around yam and sweet potato gardens, and collect sand temper from the mainland beaches and river mouths. They carry *bilum* (string bags) laden with these raw materials back to their houses, where the clay is treated and stored in large balls for use. When required, bits of these clay balls will be broken off and blended with the sand temper—forming a mixture called the *isol*. The correct *isol* is essential to the mechanical durability of the pot as it moves through the production process. It is not prescribed by a set recipe or ratio, but is *figured out* by the feel in the potter's hands: the mix that does not stick to the hand and can be rolled easily is preferred as it reduces resistance to the potter's movements. The potter then begins to bring the pot into its primordial form, creating a rim preform. This involves the potter pressing her thumb into a ball of *isol* and throwing it in a circular fashion with her hands, resembling a wheel-throwing technique to form the pot's 'mouth'. This technique is unique to Madang, along with potters around Tumleo on the Sepik Coast, and around eastern Indonesia, which has led some researchers to suggest they derive from a common technological tradition (Pétrequin and Pétrequin 1999). At a later stage, more *isol* is added to the base of the mouth preform and the body begins to take form, using hand moulding at first, later shifting to a variety of specialised paddles and anvils. For most of the potters who have grown up learning these techniques, potting is 'not hard' and procedural body habit seems to coalesce with the material, working itself into new forms with ease as the potter's hands move in response to the wetted *isol* mix.

There are four recognisable shapes produced in repeated *chaînes opératoires*. The *bodi* is a small cooking pot with an everted rim, and an exemplar *chaîne opératoire* is presented in Figure 13.2. The *magob* is a similar cooking pot with incurving rim, the *tangeng* a larger pot used for feasts, and the *you-bodi* a single or multi-spouted water container. However, these 'finished' vessel types are in no way finished. After a preliminary firing stage, vessels can be refashioned and reworked into other forms. Moreover, if an in-use *bodi* is broken, it can be modified around the rim to produce a *magob*. Damaged vessels can also become *su*, and act as supports for fresh pots during cooking. Fragments of these *su* can later be used as lids to retain heat when cooking. And more inventively, damaged *su* can act as flowerpots around the gardens. In the 21st century, the conventional pottery forms have also been actively modified to appeal to Western tourist markets. These modifications include miniaturisation, body perforations and the addition of non-functional spouts.

Lastly, a red slip, called *main*, is applied to the 'skin' of the pot prior to firing. Once fired, the slip hardens from a dull orange to a bright red and the vessel is considered to have become as a young man, just like the young men emerge from the fires of initiation decorated with red paint.

The pots do not become socially inert at the end of the production process, nor does technology, as a mode of engagement between people and things, cease to acquire or create meaning during distribution, use and discard (Sellet 1993; Sillar and Tite 2000). The pottery users, around Madang and elsewhere, engage and create meaningful embodied knowledge during cooking or while storing the pot in such a way that it will not break. As fully initiated pots, the Bilbil and Yabob vessels actively help to generate revenue for the villages, or establish important reciprocal relationships through bride price.

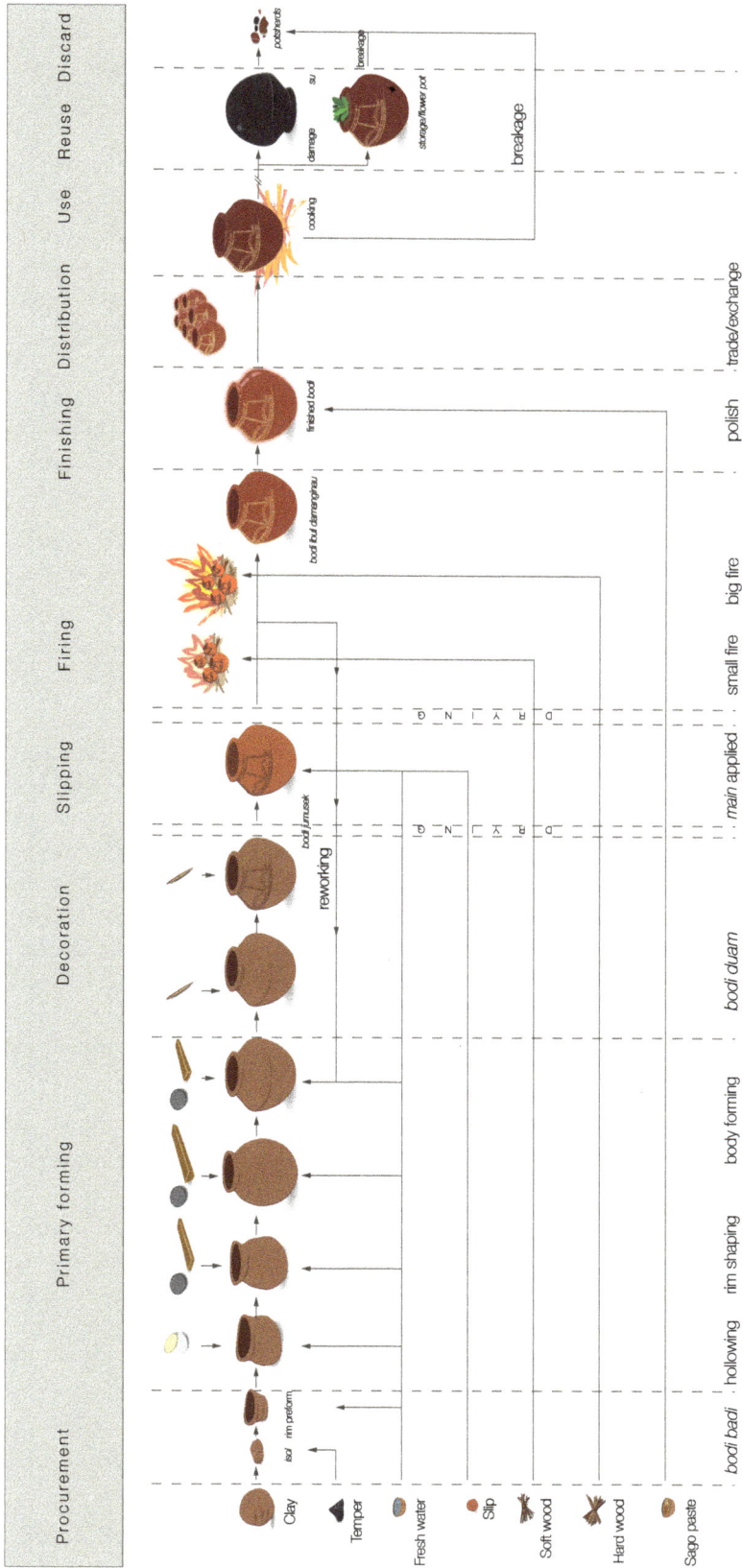

Figure 13.2. A modern *chaîne opératoire* of a Madang-style *bodi*.

Source: Dylan Gaffney.

Colonial-period pottery around Madang

This modern pottery-making is a conscious attempt to maintain *kastom* in the face of the 21st century, as women increasingly find work in town centres rather than in villages. This is interlinked with reinvigorating and relearning *sing sing* dances, canoe making, and other pre-colonial technological processes to assert local identity (Suwa 2005). It is important to note that these ethnographic *chaînes opératoires* are simply the most recent analogues in long technological lines, which have been reworked during colonial disruptions and encounters in the late 19th and early 20th centuries (see Spriggs 2008). Many technological processes, especially relating to ancestor and spirit worship, initiation rituals and magic-making, were forcibly prevented by the Lutheran Church, and German and Australian administrators (Mennis 2006:138). I have elsewhere used ethnohistorical information to outline the interplay between ceramic *chaînes opératoires* and this time of dramatic social flux around Bilbil and Yabob (Gaffney 2018). This not only stretches out the technological process—from a synchronic ethnographic snapshot to longer diachronic flows—but also examines the archaeologically intangible aspects of pottery-making, which were once key to production and exchange.

During the colonial period, the Bilbil and Yabob were forcibly moved from offshore islands onto the mainland, and a number of pottery centres seem to have disappeared. This movement changed the dynamics of raw material procurement as potters could then access materials without having to maintain land use rights with different coastal peoples. This also led to shifts in sand temper selection, as potters chose mainland volcanic sands over calcareous sands from the offshore uplifted islands, although clay sources remained the same.

An examination of Madang-style pots in Australasian museums[2] and ethnographic accounts (Kakubayashi 1978; Maahs 1949; May and Tuckson 2000:195–196; Mennis 2006; Miklouho-Maclay 1975; Smith 1967; Werner 1911) shows that despite these forcible relocations, procurement shifts, prohibitions on *kastom* and even the attempted introduction of European-style wheel throwing in the 1960s, the technology of the *vai* has remained relatively invariant (Figure 13.3). The only minor modification to forming has been the addition of a carination, formed during paddling, which may have been innovated during World War II while Bel potters were displaced around the north-east coast. Alongside invariance to the 'traditional' ceramic *chaînes opératoires*, the Bilbil and Yabob have been highly innovative in developing complimentary 'tourist' pottery, which shows how technological processes can either mutate or persist in the face of changing consumers and social upheaval (Gaffney 2018).

Despite formal consistency in 'traditional' pottery, the ethnohistorical literature demonstrates that pottery-making did not operate on its own, and was inexorably intertwined with other technological processes such as magic-making. Oral traditions suggest that the clay, temper and slip procurement, along with the collection of firing materials, water and sago paste for polishing, likely required an active knowledge of magic and the local spirit world (Mennis 1980b:24; see also Aufinger 1942; Hannemann 1944; May and Tuckson 2000; Mennis 2006, 2011, 2014). Bel magic revolved around animism and ancestor worship. This invoked the strength of the *tibud* (nature spirits) and the *meziab* (ancestral spirits) in everyday routine. *Tibud* were spirits that inhabited the natural realm: every tree, each point of land, the sea and animals. Developing a familiarity with technological processes required one to learn the *tibud* for different objects and places, and to negotiate these supernatural agents in daily life. The *meziab* were spirits of the ancestors, compiled into a singular social unit with the authority to protect and punish.

---

2   These museums include (1) The Macleay Museum, University of Sydney; (2) Australian Museum; (3) Auckland War Memorial Museum.

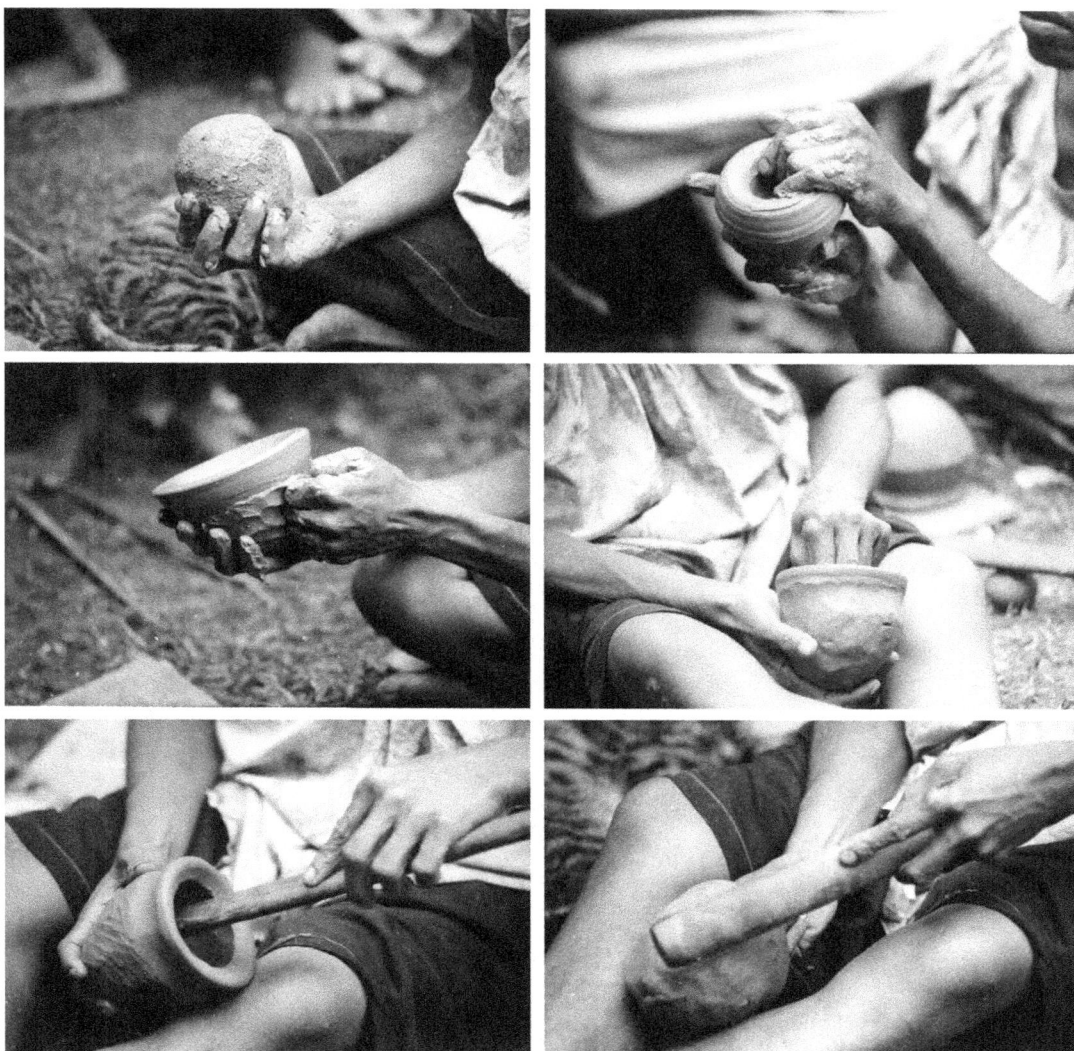

Figure 13.3. Photographs of Yabob pottery-making in 1968 taken by Robin Hide.

(1) a ball of *isol* mix; (2) spinning the rim preform; (3) adding more *isol* to the rim preform; (4) beginning to hand mould the vessel body; (5) beginning to paddle the body; (6) paddling the exterior of the *bodi*. The process is identical to the *chaîne opératoire* recorded in 2014–15 by Gaffney.

Source: Robin Hide, used with permission.

One instance of this is in the anvil stones used by Bel potters in the mid-20th century, which were passed down from mother to daughter, teacher to student (Smith 1967). These anvils contained magical properties necessary for driving out *tibud* from the raw clay. The source of these stones on the Rai Coast was perhaps the home of positive ancestral *meziab* (Tuckson 1966). As such, magic was an integral tool in the pottery production chain.

Pre-colonial pottery around Madang

Bilbil and Yabob pottery-making extends back into the pre-colonial period around 650 years, when the first Bel-speaking migrants moved to the north-east coast (Gaffney et al. 2018), and perhaps before that when Bel-speaking groups lived somewhere around the Bismarck Sea (Lilley 1986; Mennis 2006). Because we know technological knowledge must be experienced to be acquired, and technical syntaxes require extended learning procedures, we can assume that the groups who produced archaeological 'Madang-style' potteries were related to those who make pots today. Especially if the *vou* was used to control which groups could pot, as it was in the 19th to 21st centuries. These archaeological ceramics closely resemble modern and colonial period Bilbil and Yabob pots, and previous researchers have correctly assumed they were made following an unbroken technological process (Allen 1971; Egloff 1975; Lilley 1986).

We can now stretch this technological process back deeper into the archaeological past using assemblages of Madang-style pottery excavated from Nunguri site (TP1) on Bilbil Island, dating from about 550 years before present through to ethnographic contact (Gaffney et al. 2018). I have elsewhere analysed these ceramics to identify the *chaînes opératoires*: the nature of raw material procurement, production techniques, decorating, finishing, use and discard (Gaffney 2016). Here, I highlight some important aspects of this research as they pertain to the diachronic nature of technological process and how this corresponds with broader society.

Geochemical analyses show that a variety of sand tempers from black, white and calcareous beach sands were mixed with locally available clays to produce *isol* (Gaffney 2016:288–302). These clays chemically overlap with the mainland sources used by Bilbil potters today, although some may be closer to those from the modern Yabob area (Gaffney 2016:396). The variation in tempers probably indicates that a number of production groups collected clays from a shared resource zone.

Analyses of the potsherds' forms and manufacturing marks—residual traces from the movements of the potter with the *isol*—indicates that each production group made pots in similar ways, following five distinct forming sequences. However, there was substantial gestural variation within each sequence and a large degree of morphological freedom in how the individual pots took form (Gaffney 2016:415). In the past, people may have been able to identify the pots of specific craftswomen, as they can today. Despite this variation, these five extended technical syntaxes were repeated over time through shared learning frameworks. They are illustrated in Figure 13.4 and show how a variety of *isol* mixtures could facilitate the production of each form. These forms were globular and included: (1) an everted rimmed cooking pot; (2) an everted rimmed cooking pot with external bevelling; (3) an everted rimmed cooking pot with internal bevelling; (4) an incurving pot probably used for cooking; and (5) an inverted and collared rimmed pot for water storage. Many of these forms may have been modified during or after production and it is likely that broken pots were used as *su* to support in-use cooking vessels. Innovations were made to some technical elements and short syntaxes, such as the addition of a bevelling stage to the inner rim in the last 300 years, but the basic roughing out, rim-preforming, paddling and anvilling, have remained relatively invariant over the centuries.

Decorations were also interchangeable within each raw material and forming sequence, and between production groups, despite following set structural rules (Gaffney 2016:337–394). I posit that these pre-colonial production groups were operating within a closely related community of practice. Within this community of practice, there was considerable mobility, translocation of potters and transfer of ideas, horizontally and vertically, which maintained technical variability within the community but prevented divergent threads clearly emerging in different production groups. This would account for substantial variation in form, materials and decoration, but conformity of five common production sequences diagnostic of the Madang-style.

Despite this variation, the application of red slip was an integral and invariant procedure throughout the archaeological deposit. This suggests that connotations with the red paint of initiates may extend deeper back into the pre-colonial past. Both people and pots became active participants in maintaining trade friendships along the coast. This may have implications for archaeologically intangible technologies along the north-east coast and for how magic and ritual were used to bind ceramic production processes together in the deeper past.

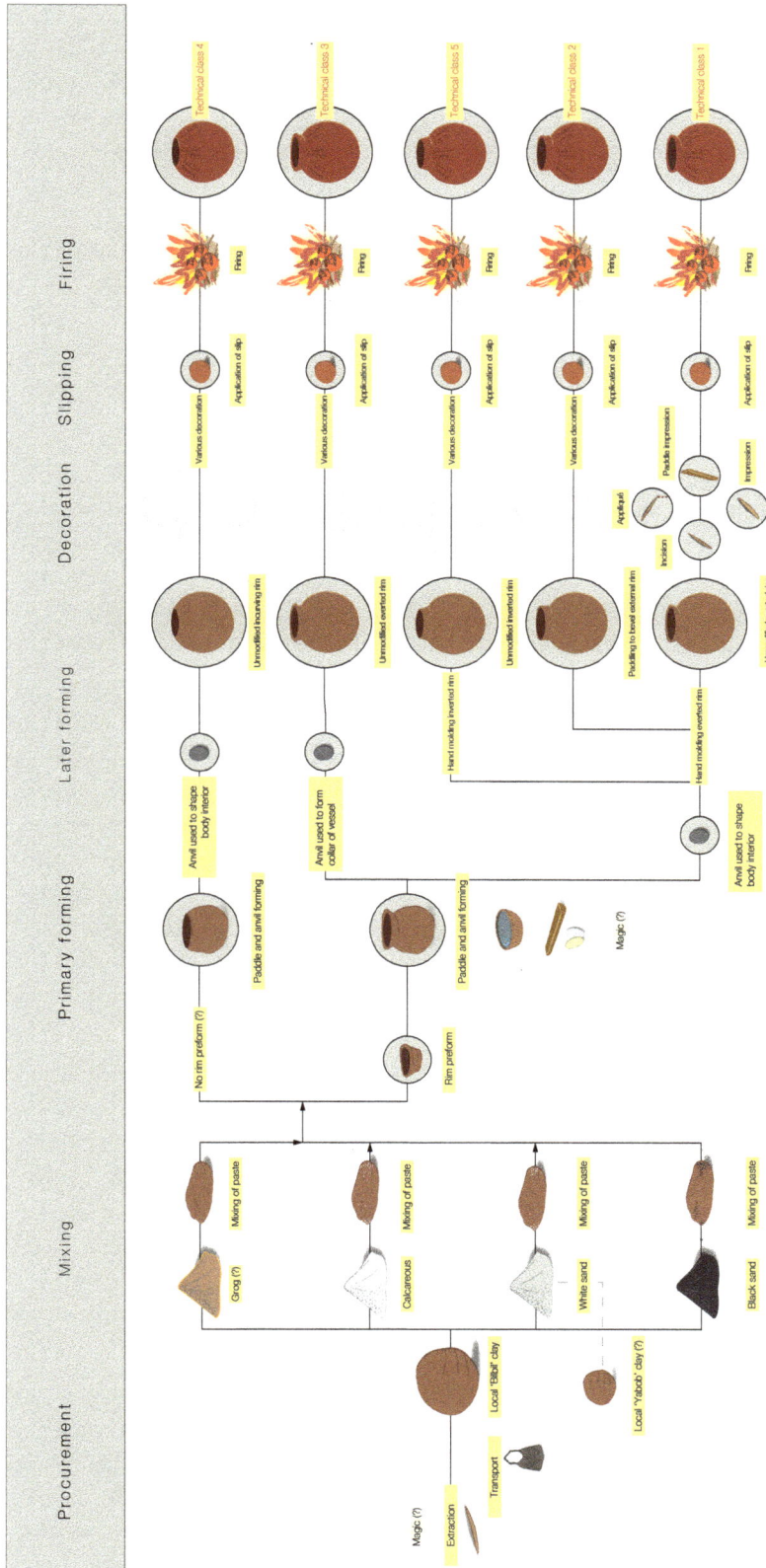

Figure 13.4. Five archaeological *chaînes opératoires* represented on Bilbil Island in the archaeological past.

Source: Dylan Gaffney.

Lastly, decorations on archaeological ceramics are dissimilar to 20th century examples. I have elsewhere suggested that appliqué and incised decorations on potsherds from the pre-colonial period would have been further allusions to scarification and tattooing rituals commonly associated with initiation around the north-east coast (Gaffney 2016:411). Just as the skin of the initiate is incised and heals over in rounded swellings, so too do the pots become incised and produce rounded nubbins around their shoulders. It is worth stating that this is not so far-fetched. Many scarification designs amongst Sepik groups are identical to those produced on historical pottery and wooden bowls (see designs in Schechter 2011; Terrell 2011), while the correlations between pottery decoration and tattooing have long been cited (Kirch 1997:131). We here see the mutual growth of initiate and material culture.

Discussion

Having outlined this technological process from the ethnographic present and back into the archaeological past, I now pick out several themes—growth, personification, magic and ritual—which appear to be integral to this technological process. These themes echo other studies from around Melanesia. The most obvious, classic analogy to this is in Malinowski's (1922) description of the Kula network in the Massim, whereby *mwali* and *soulava* shell valuables are seen as active, named participants as they build and reinforce social relations during production and exchange.

In north-east New Guinea itself, James Leach's (2002) ethnographic study of *garamut* drums among the Nekgini speakers of the Rai Coast also shows how technological processes personify active agents. *Garamut* are said to have the voice of a man and, when first created, appear in the village wearing the clothes of a young initiated male. Building on Gell's (1998) description of objects with agency, Leach (2002) calls into question the classificatory schema that separate objects from the processes that bring them to life, and records the *chaîne opératoire* of the drums as they are born, initiated and later even killed (Leach 2015). The very act of *garamut* production brings forth not only the object itself, but a social world of interrelations, producing reciprocal relationships between people and their kin, growing socially efficacious 'men': both in the form of drums and initiated males (Leach 2002). Both forms, brought forth by technological processes, take on the appearance of a man.

The *garamut* production process also involves a deeper understanding of the local spirit word. Firstly, the tree is felled, which involves inciting bush spirits and invoking myth while the axe is swung. Next, the trunk is hollowed. The trunk is marked and cut, which clears the way for spirits to come in the form of birds to 'peck away the inside of the wood' and 'peel off the bark'. Thirdly, decoration is applied. The dangerous spirits are removed by shooting a bird and throwing it from the trunk into the bush. These spirits are then replaced with water spirits, who transform the musical voice of the drums. This signals that the drums are nearing completion, which is accompanied by ritual play activities that transfer the nurturing relationship between men and wives to men and their kinsfolk (Leach 2002).

In a similar example, Mary Mennis (1980a, 2011) has recorded the *chaîne opératoire* of *lalong* (trading canoe) production and use around Madang, based on oral traditions and knowledge from Bel elders who helped their fathers build canoes in the colonial period. To produce these canoes, bush material was collected with the help of the inland people, maintaining crucial, sometimes fragile, reciprocal friendships with these groups. Like on the Rai Coast, and amongst the Bilbil and Yabob potters, magic formed central technological components in these processes of production. All initiated Bel men would use some degree of magic in their everyday routine and the knowledge of how to produce magic was entangled with the technical knowledge of canoe building. Certain Bel groups speaking the Gedaged language were said to possess the knowledge to make specific magic; the Bilbil speakers, however, could not hull canoes because they did not possess the magic with which to carry it out. This magic was the *vou*, and this form of intellectual copyright amongst the Bel has strong affinities to other groups around the north-east coast (see Leach 2002).

Associated with this magic and belief was a secret language used in every stage of canoe building: from sharpening axes, to the hulling of logs, attaching the storage compartment, and putting on the sail (Hannemann 1944:5; Mennis 1980b:24). For instance, the Bel would pray to the *tibud* inside a tree before cutting it down to use for canoe production. Aufinger (1942) described two types of secret language used by the Bel: one of metaphor and innuendo; and another of magic words—some borrowed from other languages, others invented—with which people would speak in order to exclude the uninitiated from conversation. The latter was originally created so that sailors could speak freely while on the canoe. Evil water *tibud* were familiar with Bel languages and would listen in on conversations. This could prove detrimental to the trading trip.

Ceremonial displays were also necessary for the trade voyage to commence. Upon departure, the 'father' of the canoe would swim out with the canoe and fight it with a branch. The young men would stand on the platform, decorated with feathers and *mal* (loincloths), while the leader would stand in the cabin, drumming the *vongu* drum, speaking magic, and blowing on the conch shell (Mennis 1980b:44). In this context, canoes must be seen as intertwined with the broader social processes of belief, ritual and magic. Without specific magic being enacted and specific ceremonies taking place, the canoe could not take form and be initiated into the social world where, by completing trading voyages, it would reinforce trade friendships, and maintain the movement of materials along the coast (Mennis 2011:11).

Through processes of regular routine action—learning the art of canoe building and sailing— often beginning from a young age (Mennis 1980b:17), men generated and reshaped their bodily knowledge. Pushing the *lalong* out to sea, tethering the sails and understanding the winds and the stars were all part of this technological process, making knowledge and know-how at the interface of bodies, techniques and materials (following Lemmonier 1992). This process also involved learning the magic to negotiate local *tibud* at different points of land and in the water around them. While on trade voyages in the recent pre-colonial period, along with reciting secret words to evade the water *tibud,* men would throw heated potsherds into the waves to quell them (Mennis 1980b:44). It was at this point that two technological processes—pottery and canoes— wove together integrally.

These comparisons hint at a particularly Melanesian way of making objects, which become affective, personified, material actors in an almost literal sense, through technological processes of production and exchange. Emergent from these studies are distinct technological commonalities, featuring processes of growth that involve correspondence with materials, gestures and intentionality, but also magic, spirits, ritual and language. Without these delicately balanced, highly contingent ingredients, many such *chaînes opératoires* could simply not be enacted.

In much the same way as tree crops and tubers are grown in mutually informed, generative processes (Barton and Denham 2018), so too it seems are human and non-human actors grown, many of which survive for us to analyse as artefacts, albeit often in a fragmentary form. This again touches on a particularly Melanesian way of making. It involves growth and initiation into the social world in a very real sense, and results in non-human things that can take on the affectiveness of human actors. It is through technological process—the production of the *garamut* drum, the sailing of the *lalong,* the firing and exchange of *bodi* pots—that a world of social relations is simultaneously grown. And not only do these things grow such relations, but they also take on the physical forms of their human counterparts such as the voice and ears of the drum, the mouth and skin of the pot.

These things are grown into complex worlds of extant but constantly mutating networks (Knappett 2005), where they become bound up between all the other growing and living things (Ingold 2015). These emergent affectivenesses come forth into a world of interrelations involving the correspondence of materials with other materials, people with people, people with materials (Knappett 2007). For instance, in Madang, pots, canoes and magic were bound together during the process of voyaging: sailors would calm the waves and any malignant *tibud* with heated potsherds (Mennis 1980b:44).

Although bringing forth pots was a way of initiating affective things into the world, these regular activities served also to produce female potters, creating specialised knowledge and identities within the production group, and along the north-east coast. Just as the Nekgini create drums, the Gedaged hulled canoes and the Bilbil produce pots, they also create elements of difference. These groups create unique technical knowledge—interwoven with historically contingent and group-specific magic, ritual and spirits—which sets them apart as different from other nearby groups, who produce other specialist products or who focus on root agriculture or fishing. Thus, the regular engagement between people and materials in specific and specialised ways simultaneously produced social boundaries (Stark 1998). These boundaries can be thought of as asymmetries in the networks of technological processes linking people and materials. They can be useful for delimiting specific social groupings or broader communities of practice, where people share ways of doing and making things (Sassaman and Rudolphi 2001). It is therefore within these social boundaries that individual and community identities are continually (re)made and played out. In this way identity is not a static entity but rather part of the process that is always in flux—always being made and remade.

The north-east coast of New Guinea can be seen as a broad community of practice, which shared modes of doing and making. We can identify different social groups by their production processes, or perhaps variations within these processes, but all of these groups were part of the broader mutative network of understanding. All used similar tools of initiation and magic to grow their products, and all understood the value of this magic, especially as it pertained to cultural property rights, and the maintenance of prestige, power and production.

Conclusion

In proposing their process archaeology, Gosden and Malafouris (2015) stress that archaeologists tend to trivialise the very processes that energise and give meaning to the materials that we study. Certainly in Melanesian archaeology, we often remove objects from their human creators so they can be more easily analysed. However, in studying technology as process one can conceive the material and social as being irreducibly linked.

The approach presented in this essay advocates for following the *chaîne opératoire* in order to describe technical and social life in pre-colonial Melanesia—going beyond the artefact as an inert object, and untangling the specific technological processes that bring these materials to life on the human scale. Similar approaches are beginning to be taken up in many studies of Melanesian material culture (see Coupaye 2009, 2016; Ford 2012, 2017; Gaffney 2016, 2018; Gaffney and Summerhayes 2018; Gaffney, Ford et al. 2015; Lagarde and Sand 2013; Leclerc 2016; Pétrequin and Pétrequin 1999, 2006; Szabó 2004). In presenting the case of pottery-making around Madang, tracing this technological process back through time and drawing comparisons with other technological processes on the north-east coast, we see there are commonalities in how groups in this part of Melanesia bring forth material actors, materialise meaning and grow social relationships. Melanesian archaeology is well suited to investigate these processes and contribute to the wider theoretical discourse in anthropology.

So, where do we go from here? Can we track these processes back deeper through time based on commonalities in *chaînes opératoires*? Did Lapita ceramics come into being, acting as affective material actors in solidifying crucial production and exchange relationships between groups, involving magic, intellectual property rights and ritual performance? The red slip of Madang-style ceramics seems to be the last living descendant in New Guinea from Lapita slipping techniques. Does this imply that, along with dentate stamping representing tattooing, red-slipped Lapita vessels symbolised the paints of initiation? Certainly the Lapita face motifs are an obvious indicator that these pots may have been personified in some way, perhaps as ancestor figures (Kirch 2017:96). Further back in time, did technical syntaxes such as the production and exchange of ornate obsidian stemmed artefacts in the mid-Holocene (e.g. Torrence et al. 2009), or even the cutting and grubbing activities associated with waisted tools in the Pleistocene (e.g. Ford 2017), rely on magic words and ritual performance? These questions are purely speculative, and this essay has not tried to tackle them here. But by posing these questions we can begin to enliven many of the archaeological narratives we produce for understanding the human past in Melanesia, examining the fascinating in-between of the technological process.

Acknowledgements

Thanks to James Flexner, Jessie Hurford, Mathieu Leclerc, Glenn Summerhayes, Richard Walter and one anonymous reviewer for providing comments on the draft manuscript. I am grateful to Robin Hide for permission to reproduce his photographs of Yabob pottery-making.

References

Allen, J. 1971. 'A pottery collection from the Madang District T.P.N.G.'. *Records of the Papua New Guinea Museum* 1 (2):1–5.

Apel, J. 2008. 'Knowledge, know-how and raw material—the production of Late Neolithic flint daggers in Scandinavia'. *Journal of Archaeological Method and Theory* 15 (1):91–111. doi.org/10.1007/s10816-007-9044-2.

Arnold, DE. 1985. *Ceramic theory and cultural process*. Cambridge: Cambridge University Press.

Aufinger, PA. 1942. 'Die Geheimsprachen auf den kleinen Inseln bei Madang in Neuguinea'. *Anthropos* 37/40 (4–6):629–646.

Barton, H and T Denham. 2018. 'Vegecultures and the social–biological transformations of plants and people'. *Quaternary International* 489:17–25. doi.org/10.1016/j.quaint.2016.06.031.

Coupaye, L. 2009. 'Ways of enchanting: Chaînes opératoires and yam cultivation in Nyamikum village, Maprik, Papua New Guinea'. *Journal of Material Culture* 14 (4):433–458. doi.org/10.1177/1359183509345945.

Coupaye, L. 2016. 'Yams as vernacular methodology? Approaching vital processes through technical processes'. In *Des êtres vivants et des artefacts*, edited by P Pitrou, L Coupaye and F Provost. Paris: Les actes de colloques du musée du quai Branly Jacques Chirac.

Dobres, MA. 2000. *Technology and social agency: Outlining a practice framework for archaeology*. Oxford: Wiley-Blackwell.

Egloff, BJ. 1975. 'Archaeological investigations in the coastal Madang area and on Eloaue Island of the St. Matthias Group'. *Papua New Guinea Museum and Art Gallery Records* 5:15–31.

Ford, A. 2012. 'Learning the lithic landscape in the Ivane Valley, Papua New Guinea: Modelling colonisation and occupation using lithic sources and stone tool technology'. Unpublished PhD thesis, University of Otago, Dunedin.

Ford, A. 2017. 'Late Pleistocene lithic technology in the Ivane valley: A view from the rainforest'. *Quaternary International* 448:31–43. doi.org/10.1016/j.quaint.2016.05.030.

Gaffney, D. 2016. 'Materialising ancestral Madang: Aspects of pre-colonial production and exchange on the northeast coast of New Guinea'. Unpublished MA thesis, University of Otago, Dunedin.

Gaffney, D. 2018. 'Maintenance and mutability amongst specialist potters on the northeast coast of New Guinea'. *Cambridge Archaeological Journal* 28 (2):181–204. doi.org/10.1017/S0959774317000737.

Gaffney, D, A Ford and G Summerhayes. 2015. 'Crossing the Pleistocene–Holocene transition in the New Guinea Highlands: Evidence from the lithic assemblage of Kiowa rockshelter'. *Journal of Anthropological Archaeology* 39:223–246. doi.org/10.1016/j.jaa.2015.04.006.

Gaffney, D, A Ford and GR Summerhayes. 2016. 'Sue Bulmer's legacy in highland New Guinea: A re-examination of the Bulmer Collection and future directions'. *Archaeology in Oceania* 51 (S1):23–32. doi.org/10.1002/arco.5111.

Gaffney, D and GR Summerhayes. 2017. 'An archaeology of Madang, Papua New Guinea'. University of Otago Working Papers in Archaeology 5. Department of Anthropology and Archaeology, University of Otago, Dunedin.

Gaffney, D and GR Summerhayes. 2018. 'Coastal mobility and lithic supply lines in northeast New Guinea'. *Archaeological and Anthropological Sciences*. doi.org/10.1007/s12520-018-0713-8.

Gaffney, D, GR Summerhayes, A Ford, JM Scott, T Denham, J Field and WR Dickinson. 2015. 'Earliest pottery on New Guinea mainland reveals Austronesian influences in highland environments 3000 years ago'. *PloS one* 10 (9):e0134497. doi.org/10.1371/journal.pone.0134497.

Gaffney, D, GR Summerhayes and M Mennis. in press. 'A Lapita presence on Arop/Long Island, Vitiaz Strait, Papua New Guinea?' In *Debating Lapita: Distribution, chronology, society and subsistence*, edited by S Bedford and M Spriggs. Canberra: ANU Press.

Gaffney, D, GR Summerhayes, M Mennis, T Beni, A Cook, J Field, G Jacobsen, F Allen, H Buckley and H Mandui. 2018. 'Archaeological investigations into the origins of Bel trading groups around the Madang coast, northeast New Guinea'. *Journal of Island and Coastal Archaeology* 13 (4):501–530. doi.org/10.1080/15564894.2017.1315349.

Gell, A. 1998. *Art and agency: An anthropological theory*. Oxford: Clarendon Press.

Gosden, C. 1994. *Social being and time*. Oxford: Basil Blackwell.

Gosden, C. 2008. 'Social ontologies'. *Philosophical Transactions of the Royal Society B: Biological Sciences* 363 (1499):2003–2010. doi.org/10.1098/rstb.2008.0013.

Gosden, C and L Malafouris. 2015. 'Process archaeology (P-Arch)'. *World Archaeology* 47 (5):701–717. doi.org/10.1080/00438243.2015.1078741.

Groube, L, J Chappell, J Muke and D Price. 1986. 'A 40,000 year-old human occupation site at Huon Peninsula, Papua New Guinea'. *Nature* 324:453–455. doi.org/10.1038/324453a0.

Hannemann, EF. 1944. *Village life and social change in Madang society*. Columbus, Ohio: Board of Foreign Missions, American Lutheran Church.

Harding, TG. 1967. *Voyagers of the Vitiaz Strait: A study of a New Guinea trade system*. Seattle: University of Washington Press.

Hogbin, HI. 1947. 'Native trade around the Huon Gulf, north-eastern New Guinea'. *Journal of the Polynesian Society* 56 (3):242–55.

Ingold, T. 2012. 'Toward an ecology of materials'. *Annual Review of Anthropology* 41:427–442. doi.org/10.1146/annurev-anthro-081309-145920.

Ingold, T. 2013. *Making: Anthropology, archaeology, art and architecture*. London: Routledge. doi.org/10.4324/9780203559055.

Ingold, T. 2015. *The life of lines*. London: Routledge. doi.org/10.4324/9781315727240.

Ingold, T. 2016. 'Introduction: The perception of the user-producer'. In *Design and anthropology*, edited by W Gunn and J Donovan, 19–34. New York: Ashgate Publishing.

Inoue, S. 2006. 'Embodied habitus'. *Theory, Culture & Society* 23 (2–3):229–231. doi.org/10.1177/026327640602300248.

Jørgensen, LB. 2013. 'Introduction to Part II: Technology as practice'. In *Embodied knowledge: Perspectives on belief and technology*, edited by ML Sørensen and K Rebay-Salisbury, 91–94. Oxford: Oxbow.

Kakubayashi, F. 1978. ニューギニア・マダン周辺の土器作りとその経済的機能の研究. 民族學 研究 [A study on the pottery-making and its economic function around Madang, Papua New Guinea]. *Minzokugaku-kenkyu: The Japanese Journal of Ethnology* 43 (2):138–155.

Keller, CM and JD Keller. 1996. *Cognition and tool use: The blacksmith at work*. Cambridge: Cambridge University Press.

Kirch, PV. 1997. *The Lapita peoples: Ancestors of the Oceanic world*. Oxford: Blackwell.

Kirch, PV. 2017. *On the road of the winds: An archaeological history of the Pacific Islands before European contact*. 2nd edn. Oakland: University of California Press.

Knappett, C. 2005. *Thinking through material culture: An interdisciplinary perspective*. Philadelphia: University of Pennsylvania Press. doi.org/10.9783/9780812202496.

Knappett, C. 2007. 'Materials with materiality?' *Archaeological Dialogues* 14 (01):20–23. doi.org/10.1017/S1380203807002140.

Knappett, C. 2011. *An archaeology of interaction: Network perspectives on material culture and society*. Oxford: Oxford University Press. doi.org/10.1093/acprof:osobl/9780199215454.001.0001.

Lagarde, L and C Sand. 2013. 'Simple technique, elaborate tools: Lapita flaked stone tools in New Caledonia'. In *Pacific archaeology: Documenting the past 50,000 years. Papers from the 2011 Lapita Pacific Archaeology Conference*, edited by GR Summerhayes and H Buckley. University of Otago Studies in Archaeology, no. 25. Dunedin: Department of Anthropology and Archaeology, University of Otago.

Leach, J. 2002. 'Drum and voice: Aesthetics and social process on the Rai Coast of Papua New Guinea'. *Journal of the Royal Anthropological Institute* 8 (4):713–734. doi.org/10.1111/1467-9655.00130.

Leach, J. 2015. 'The death of a drum: objects, persons, and changing social form on the Rai Coast of Papua New Guinea'. *Journal of the Royal Anthropological Institute* 21 (3):620–640. doi.org/10.1111/1467-9655.12253.

Leclerc, M. 2016. 'Investigating the raw materials used for Lapita and post-Lapita pottery manufacturing: A chemical characterisation of ceramic collections from Vanuatu'. Unpublished PhD thesis, The Australian National University, Canberra.

Lemonnier, P. 1986. 'The study of material culture today: Toward an anthropology of technical systems'. *Journal of Anthropological Archaeology* 5 (2):147–186. doi.org/10.1016/0278-4165(86)90012-7.

Lemonnier, P. 1992. *Elements for an anthropology of technology*. Ann Arbor, Michigan: Museum of Anthropology, University of Michigan.

Lilley, I. 1986. 'Prehistoric exchange in the Vitiaz Strait, Papua New Guinea'. Unpublished PhD thesis, The Australian National University, Canberra.

Lilley, I. 2017. 'Melanesian maritime middlemen and pre-colonial glocalisation'. In *Routledge handbook of archaeology and globalisation*, edited by T Hodos, 335–353. London: Routledge.

Maahs, AM. 1949. 'A village of saucepans'. *Walkabout* 15 (6):37–40.

Malafouris, L. 2008. 'At the potter's wheel: An argument for material agency'. In *Material agency: Towards a non-anthropocentric approach*, edited by C Knappett and L Malafouris, 19–36. New York: Springer. doi.org/10.1007/978-0-387-74711-8_2.

Malafouris, L. 2010. 'Metaplasticity and the human becoming: Principles of neuroarchaeology'. *Journal of Anthropological Sciences* 88 (4):49–72.

Malinowski, B. 1922. *Argonauts of the Western Pacific: An account of native enterprise and adventure in the archipelagos of Melanesian New Guinea*. London: Routledge. doi.org/10.4324/9781315014463.

Mauss, M. 1934. 'Les techniques du corps'. *Journal de Psychologie* 32 (3–4):271–293.

May, P and M Tuckson. 2000. *The traditional pottery of Papua New Guinea*. 2nd edn. Honolulu: University of Hawai'i Press.

Mayor, A. 2005. 'Traditions céramiques et histoire du peuplement dans la Boucle du Niger (Mali) au temps des empires précoloniaux'. Unpublished PhD thesis, University of Geneva, Geneva.

Mennis, MR. 1980a. 'The first lalong canoe built for forty years, Bilbil village, Madang province'. *Oral History* 8 (1).

Mennis, MR. 1980b. 'Oral testimonies from Coastal Madang: Part 1'. *Oral History* 8 (10).

Mennis, MR. 2006. *A potted history of Madang: Traditional culture and change on the North Coast of New Guinea*. Aspley: Lalong Enterprises.

Mennis, MR. 2011. *Mariners of Madang and Austronesian canoes of Astrolabe Bay, Papua New Guinea*. Brisbane: Aboriginal and Torres Strait Islander Studies Unit, University of Queensland.

Mennis, MR. 2014. *Sailing for survival: A comparative report of the trading systems and trading canoes of the Bel People in the Madang area and of the Motu people in the Port Moresby area of Papua New Guinea*. Dunedin: Department of Anthropology and Archaeology, University of Otago.

Miklouho-Maclay, N. 1975. *Mikloucho-Maclay: New Guinea diaries, 1871–1883*. Translated by CL Sentinella. Madang, Papua New Guinea: Kristen Press.

Minar, CJ and PL Crown. 2001. 'Learning and craft production: An introduction'. *Journal of Anthropological Research* 57 (4):369–380. doi.org/10.1086/jar.57.4.3631351.

Pétrequin, AM and P Pétrequin. 1999. 'La poterie en Nouvelle-Guinée: Savoir-faire et transmission des techniques'. *Journal de la Société des Océanistes* 108 (1):71–101. doi.org/10.3406/jso.1999.2080.

Pétrequin, AM and P Pétrequin. 2006. *Objets de pouvoir en Nouvelle-Guinée*. Paris: Éditions de la Réunion des Musées Nationaux.

Ross, M. 1988. *Proto-Oceanic and the Austronesian languages of Western Melanesia*. Canberra: Pacific Linguistics.

Roux, V and MA Courty. 2005. 'Identifying social entities at a macro-regional level: Chalcolithic ceramics of South Levant as a case study'. In *Pottery making processes: Reconstruction and interpretation,* edited by D Bosquet, A Livingstone-Smith and R Martineau, 201–214. Actes du XIVéme Congrés de l'UISPP. Université de Liége, Belgique, 2–8 Septembre 2001. BAR International Series 1349. Oxford: Archaeopress.

Sahlins, MD. 1974. *Stone age economics.* Piscataway, New Jersey: Transaction Publishers.

Sassaman, KE and W Rudolphi. 2001. 'Communities of practice in the early pottery traditions of the American Southeast'. *Journal of Anthropological Research* 57 (4):407–425. doi.org/10.1086/jar.57.4.3631353.

Schechter, EM. 2011. 'Historic and modern pottery in the Aitape area'. In *Exploring prehistory on the Sepik Coast of Papua New Guinea*, edited by J Terrell and EM Schechter, 159–173. Fieldiana 42. Chicago: Field Museum of Natural History. doi.org/10.3158/0071-4739-42.1.159.

Sellet, F. 1993. 'Chaîne opératoire: The concept and its applications'. *Lithic technology* 18 (1–2):106–112. doi.org/10.1080/01977261.1993.11720900c.

Sillar, B and MS Tite. 2000. 'The challenge of "technological choices" for materials science approaches in archaeology'. *Archaeometry* 42 (1):2–20. doi.org/10.1111/j.1475-4754.2000.tb00863.x.

Smith, J. 1967. 'The potter of Yabob'. *Australian Territories* 7 (1–3):9–13.

Spriggs, M. 2008. 'Ethnographic parallels and the denial of history'. *World Archaeology* 40 (4):538–552. doi.org/10.1080/00438240802453161.

Stark, MT. 1998. 'Technical choices and social boundaries in material culture patterning: An introduction'. In *The archaeology of social boundaries,* edited by M Stark, 1–11. Washington, DC: Smithsonian Institution Press.

Suwa, JI. 2005. 'The abandonment of Yabob Island 1942–1975 and the memory of cultural continuity'. In *Refereed papers from the 1st International Small Island Cultures Conference: Held at Kagoshima University Centre for the Pacific Islands, February 7th–10th 2005, and organised as the inaugural conference of SICRI (the Small Island Cultures Research Initiative),* edited by M Evans, 108–116. Sydney: Small Island Cultures Research Initiative, Macquarie University.

Szabó, KA. 2004. 'Technique and practice: Shell-working in the western Pacific and Island Southeast Asia'. Unpublished PhD thesis, The Australian National University, Canberra.

Terrell, JE. 2011. 'Wooden platters and bowls in the ethnographic collections'. In *Exploring prehistory on the Sepik Coast of Papua New Guinea*, edited by J Terrell and EM Schechter, 175–195. Fieldiana 42. Chicago: Field Museum of Natural History. doi.org/10.3158/0071-4739-42.1.175.

Torrence, R, P Swadling, N Kononenko, W Ambrose, P Rath and MD Glascock. 2009. 'Mid-Holocene social interaction in Melanesia: New evidence from hammer-dressed obsidian stemmed tools'. *Asian Perspectives* 48 (1):119–148. doi.org/10.1353/asi.0.0014.

Tuckson, M. 1966. 'Pottery in New Guinea'. *Pottery in Australia* 5 (1):9–16.

Wellner, G, L Botin and K Otrel-Cass. 2015. 'Techno-anthropology: Guest editors' introduction'. *Techné: Research in philosophy and technology* 19 (2):117–124. doi.org/10.5840/techne20157630.

Werner, E. 1911. *Kaiser-Wilhelms-Land.* Freiburg im Breisgau: Herder.

14

A Melanesian view of archaeology in Vanuatu

Edson Willie

Archaeology in Vanuatu is generally considered a 'no go' field of study, as it ventures into areas which a typical ni-Vanuatu is taught at a very early age are restricted and forbidden to members of the community. A lot of archaeological areas of study such as human remains, old or abandoned villages, and sacred and spiritual sites are areas that are associated with spirits of our ancestors; disturbing these areas, or even entering the compound, could lead to unforeseen disease or the death of a relative as a warning—or even your own death. A recent archaeological survey carried out on Nalolo Bay, east Maewo (Sand et al. 2016), saw a cancellation of a visit to a sacred site as the local guides were fearful that something might happen, especially to the locals, as they knew the area was *tabu*. Venturing into the area might be seen by the spirits as an act of war and they would retaliate and punish us, but more of the punishment would befall the locals as they knew the place was *tabu* and still went.

Consequently, it is quite difficult to begin working as an archaeologist when growing up in a traditional cultural environment. However, through education and training, one can progressively understand the scope and aims of archaeology and end up comprehending the reasoning behind having to venture into such forbidden areas. As a result, being an archaeologist and a ni-Vanuatu has allowed me to attune the custom beliefs and practices of local communities with archaeological practices. Seeing the two sides of the same coin brings a sense of security and peace to the community, which then becomes a fertile ground for harmonious working relationships with archaeologists. This in turn motivates the parties involved to adhere to sound work ethics, leading to a much safer and respectful working environment.

Kastom in Vanuatu

Vanuatu is a small island nation that is deeply rooted in cultural traditions and beliefs. Daily lives of communities revolve around sacred rituals and *kastom* ceremonies that guide the activities that occur within local communities. Each individual, whether male or female, has a traditional obligation to ensure the continuation of custom and culture within societies. Such obligations include activities that are associated with different gender and age groups: young boys' initiation into manhood, ranking systems and girls' initiation into womanhood, up to the time a person dies.

The traditional practices that have been going on for over hundreds of years and over a lot of generations were not completely suppressed by the missionaries. Whilst some customs were modified by them—for example, on Futuna Island the planting of kava was considered by Christianity as forbidden and was abandoned—in most areas, such as south Vanuatu, Christianity was integrated into the local religious practices. For example, Christianity was widely accepted into communities after missionaries who were given sacred/taboo lands to settle did not get sick or die, proving their belief in a much stronger deity (Flexner 2016).

All in all, custom beliefs, practices and values are very important in Vanuatu. At first glance, this emphasis on tradition can pose an opposition to archaeological work. Being an archaeologist and a ni-Vanuatu has allowed me to identify the cultural aspects of local communities that can clash with archaeology when the objectives are not properly explained.

Respect is paramount, especially in Vanuatu where cultural beliefs, as mentioned before, are quite dominant. Respect is instilled into the young at a very early age by the elders. They are taught about the importance of traditions and customary laws, and a sense of responsibility is inculcated in them as they grow up and get involved in activities such as gardening, hunting or getting married. Because archaeologists often have to venture into, some would say disturb, culturally restricted areas in order to understand the past, they can appear in opposition to certain traditions and in consequence the field of archaeology can be frowned upon by the local population. In some cases, people can be afraid that their oral traditions related to migration or origins of clans or tribes could be discredited or contradicted by archaeological work.

Another classic example is the work done by archaeologists on human remains, which are usually associated with spirits and avoided altogether. 'Bone diggers' is the name given to the field of archaeology by the indigenous population as the field is relatively new and archaeologists are associated with human remains. The fear of disturbing human remains is something that is instilled at a very early age by customary stories that are told around the fire by elders and peers. Human remains are considered sacred, and it is said that disturbing them can lead to unforeseen illnesses that could also lead to death. This has caused limitations and restriction for archaeological research in certain areas where skeletal remains are quite taboo and are feared and/ or revered. In 2013, archaeological excavations on a mission site (Watt mission) on Kwamera, south Tanna, revealed skeletal remains beneath the foundation of the mission house. Further excavation of the burial to expose the skeletal remains was done in 2014 (Flexner and Willie 2015). A lot of curious bystanders came to witness as the remains were slowly being uncovered, a majority of whom were wary but soon became interested as the dig slowly began to uncover the rest of the remains. Although they were interested, they still maintained their beliefs and ordered that the remains were not to remain uncovered overnight for fear of upsetting the spirits which would result in illness, even death.

Indigenous perspective

Overcoming one's cultural beliefs and fears is a major achievement for a local archaeologist. Archaeologists who grow up with traditional customs and beliefs benefit from having a privileged perspective, as they grasp both archaeological and traditional aspects of a situation. Archaeology allows one who can relate to these restrictions to actually see and understand the benefits of carrying out research into sacred aspects of culture, and how research can be transmitted back to the communities concerned in layman's terms for them to also understand and appreciate the research that is taking place. By identifying these beliefs and traditions, one is able to see that archaeology does not interfere with customs and oral histories but rather that its findings often allows for their stories to be confirmed or extended further back in time, often to a period earlier than oral traditions.

In 2016, an archaeological survey was carried out on Maewo Island. The project was a collaboration between the Vanuatu Cultural Centre (VCC) and the Institute of Archaeology of New Caledonia and the Pacific (Sand et al. 2016). Maewo Island, as with most island communities in Vanuatu, holds very strong beliefs in their customs, traditions and oral histories. The news that a group of people had come to research their history was met with curiosity, even though some were opposed to the idea. The local population was very sceptical of what research was going to be carried out. The team had to define and explain the field of archaeology and also give assurance that sacred areas would not be disturbed and the purpose of the survey was to help them better understand their history and would in no way rewrite their oral traditions.

Fieldwork

The VCC's network of fieldworkers (commonly referred to as *filwokas)* has also helped greatly with archaeological research across Vanuatu. They contribute to awareness of the field of archaeology and its significance to the cultural heritage of societies, the island and the country as a whole. Archaeological training, funded by The Australian National University (Bedford et al. 2011; Bolton 1999) from 1997 to 1999 and the Sasakawa Pacific Island Nation Funds (Bedford and Regenvanu 2003) from 2001 to 2003, has also helped greatly in empowering the *filwokas* with knowledge, which they take back to their home islands, therefore allowing archaeological research to take place within the communities.

The VCC's *filwokas* work closely with researchers, the vast majority of whom come from outside of Vanuatu. *Filwokas* play a key role in communicating what is being done and how it will benefit the community they belong to. The fact that *filwokas* are part of the communities where research is undertaken facilitates gaining the trust of the community when arguing that the work will not pose any risk or threat to the cultural beliefs and that the research will be greatly beneficial to their cultural heritage.

Archaeologists follow traditional ways of life while on fieldwork in communities, which greatly helps to establish quality working relationships. Employing locals to work on the project is also a practice that has many advantages. Not only do the people hired learn about the significance of archaeology and about the history of their community, they also gain a bit of money in the process. Observing customs and traditions is also part of the working relationship between archaeologists and the communities: these include *kastom* ceremonies, feasts, funerary rites and marriages, as well as attending church on Saturdays or Sundays. Overall, this creates a pleasant environment which reduces the risk of people opposing archaeological excavations.

The Forestry and Protected Areas Management Project saw a holistic approach taken to conservation. The project considered the biological, social/cultural, economic and environmental aspects of conservation within an area. In dealing with cultural aspects of the area, cultural surveys were the main area of interest and therefore cultural traditions/ceremonies were observed before commencement of work. One of the areas selected for the conservation project was Lake Letas, Gaua Island, which is a lake formed in the crater of an old volcano, forming a semicircle around a current existing one (Mount Garett). A *nangarie* plant had to be planted at what is believed to be the entrance of the lake to appease the spirit looking after the lake so that this was a friendly visit and was not a threat to the area (Willie 2016).

Conclusions

As a local archaeologist who grew up with traditional customs and beliefs, I think the field of archaeology provides an in-depth understanding of the teachings and oral history which has been passed down over generations, which makes archaeological research really fascinating. Archaeology gives reasoning to traditional practices such as the irrigation systems on Aneityum (Spriggs 1981), which were left and used as we see them, and could also be revitalised in the present.

Although archaeology is a relatively new concept to the indigenous population of Vanuatu, recognition of the importance of this field and its contribution to the country's cultural heritage is slowly gaining momentum. The discovery of the Lapita cemetery at Teouma in 2004 and other findings from subsequent research projects have helped to shed light on the origins of the first settlers of Vanuatu and on the Pacific's history in general. Being a ni-Vanuatu archaeologist has helped me flesh out the stories that are told over the fire across the archipelago regarding our origins and our heritage.

References

Bedford, S and R Regenvanu. 2003. *Summary report for the Vanuatu government on distance education in the South West Pacific: Cultural Heritage training 2001–2003: Archaeology training program on Urivpiv and Wala Islands, Malakula, 2001*. The Sasakawa Pacific Island Nations Fund.

Bedford, S, M Spriggs, R Regenvanu and S Yona. 2011. 'Olfala histri we i stap andanit long graon. Archaeological training workshops in Vanuatu: A profile, the benefits, spin-offs, and extraordinary discoveries'. In *Working together in Vanuatu: Research histories, collaborations, projects and reflections*, edited by J Taylor and N Thieberger, 191–213. Canberra: ANU Press. doi.org/10.22459/WTV.10.2011.22.

Bolton, L (ed.). 1999. *Fieldwork, fieldworkers: Developments in Vanuatu research*. Sydney. University of Sydney.

Flexner, JL. 2016. *An archaeology of early Christianity in Vanuatu: Kastom and religious change on Tanna and Erromango, 1839–1920*. Terra Australis 44. Canberra: ANU Press. doi.org/10.22459/TA44.12.2016.

Flexner, JL and E Willie. 2015. 'Under the mission steps: An 800 year-old human burial from south Tanna, Vanuatu'. *Journal of Pacific Archaeology* 6 (2):49–55.

Sand, C, J Bolé, E Willie and A Tilly. 2016. *Rapport archaeologique sur la mission au Sud-Maevo (Vanuatu)*. Noumea: Institute of Archaeology of New Caledonia and the Pacific.

Spriggs, M. 1981. 'Vegetable kingdom: Taro irrigation and Pacific prehistory'. Unpublished PhD thesis, The Australian National University, Canberra.

Willie, E. 2016. 'Forestry and Protected Areas Management Project: Cultural survey of Lake Letes, Gaua Island'. Unpublished report. Port Vila: Vanuatu Cultural Centre.

Contributors

David Baret, Institute of Archaeology of New Caledonia and the Pacific, Nouméa, New Caledonia

Tim Bayliss-Smith, Department of Geography, University of Cambridge CB2 3EN, and St John's College, UK

Stuart Bedford, Department of Archaeology and Natural History, School of Culture, History and Language, The Australian National University, Canberra, Australia; Max Planck Institute for the Science of Human History, Jena, Germany

Jacques Bolé, Institute of Archaeology of New Caledonia and the Pacific, Nouméa, New Caledonia

Tim Denham, School of Archaeology and Anthropology, The Australian National University, Canberra, Australia

Stephanie Domergue, Institute of Archaeology of New Caledonia and the Pacific, Nouméa, New Caledonia

James Flexner, Department of Archaeology, University of Sydney, Australia

Dylan Gaffney, Department of Archaeology, University of Cambridge, UK

Mark Horrocks, Microfossil Research, Inc., Auckland, New Zealand

Mathieu Leclerc, Department of Archaeology and Natural History, School of Culture, History and Language, The Australian National University, Canberra, Australia

Stephen Manebosa, Solomon Islands National Museum, Honiara, Solomon Islands

Annette Oertle, Department of Archaeology, University of Sydney

André-John Ouetcho, Institute of Archaeology of New Caledonia and the Pacific, Nouméa, New Caledonia

Matthew Prebble, Department of Archaeology and Natural History, School of Culture, History and Language, The Australian National University, Canberra, Australia

Christophe Sand, Institute of Archaeology of New Caledonia and the Pacific, Nouméa, New Caledonia

Peter Sheppard, Department of Anthropology, University of Auckland, New Zealand

Matthew Spriggs, School of Archaeology and Anthropology, The Australian National University, Canberra, Australia

Katherine Szabó, Max Planck Institute for the Science of Human History, Jena, Germany

Karine Taché, Department of Anthropology, Queens College, City University of New York, USA

Tim Thomas, Archaeology Programme, School of Social Sciences, University of Otago, Dunedin, New Zealand

Frédérique Valentin, CNRS, UMR 7041, Nanterre, France

Jean-Marie Wadrawane, Institute of Archaeology of New Caledonia and the Pacific, Nouméa, New Caledonia

Edson Willie, Vanuatu Cultural Centre, Port-Vila, Vanuatu

www.ingramcontent.com/pod-product-compliance
Lightning Source LLC
Chambersburg PA
CBHW061219270326
41926CB00032B/4780